DISCONTINUOUS INNOVATION

Learning to Manage the Unexpected

Series on Technology Management*

Series Editor: J. Tidd (University of Sussex, UK)   ISSN 0219-9823

Published

Vol. 16 Perspectives on User Innovation
edited by S. Flowers & F. Henwood (*University of Brighton, UK*)

Vol. 17 Managing Process Innovation: From Idea Generation to Implementation
by T. Lager (*Grenoble Ecole de Management, France*)

Vol. 18 Perspectives on Supplier Innovation: Theories, Concepts and Empirical
Insights on Open Innovation and the Integration of Suppliers
edited by A. Brem (*University of Erlangen-Nuremberg, Germany*) &
J. Tidd (*University of Sussex, UK*)

Vol. 19 From Knowledge Management to Strategic Competence: Assessing
Technological, Market and Organisational Innovation (3rd Edition)
edited by J. Tidd (*University of Sussex, UK*)

Vol. 20 Bazaar of Opportunities for New Business Development: Bridging Networked
Innovation, Intellectual Property and Business
by J. Paasi (*VTT Technical Research Centre of Finland, Finland*),
K. Valkokari (*VTT Technical Research Centre of Finland, Finland*),
T. Rantala (*VTT Technical Research Centre of Finland, Finland*),
S. Nystén-Haarala (*University of Eastern Finland, Finland*),
N. Lee (*University of Eastern Finland, Finland*) & L. Huhtilainen
(*University of Eastern Finland, Finland*)

Vol. 21 Workbook for Opening Innovation: Bridging Networked Business, Intellectual
Property and Contracting
by J. Paasi (*VTT Technical Research Centre of Finland, Finland*),
K. Valkokari (*VTT Technical Research Centre of Finland, Finland*),
H. Hytönen (*VTT Technical Research Centre of Finland, Finland*),
L. Huhtilainen (*University of Eastern Finland, Finland*) &
S. Nystén-Haarala (*University of Eastern Finland, Finland*)

Vol. 22 Discontinuous Innovation: Learning to Manage the Unexpected
by P. Augsdörfer (*Technische Hochschule Ingolstadt, Germany*),
J. Bessant (*University of Exeter, UK*),
K. Möslein (*Universität Erlangen-Nürnberg, Germany*),
B. von Stamm (*Innovation Leadership Forum, UK*) &
F. Piller (*RWTH Aachen University, Germany*)

*The complete list of the published volumes in the series can be found at
http://www.worldscientific.com/series/stm

SERIES ON TECHNOLOGY MANAGEMENT – VOL. 22

DISCONTINUOUS INNOVATION

Learning to Manage the Unexpected

Peter Augsdörfer
Technische Hochschule Ingolstadt, Germany

John Bessant
University of Exeter, UK

Kathrin Möslein
Universität Erlangen-Nürnberg, Germany

Bettina von Stamm
Innovation Leadership Forum, UK

Frank Piller
RWTH Aachen University, Germany

Imperial College Press

ICP

Published by

Imperial College Press
57 Shelton Street
Covent Garden
London WC2H 9HE

Distributed by

World Scientific Publishing Co. Pte. Ltd.
5 Toh Tuck Link, Singapore 596224
USA office: 27 Warren Street, Suite 401-402, Hackensack, NJ 07601
UK office: 57 Shelton Street, Covent Garden, London WC2H 9HE

British Library Cataloguing-in-Publication Data
A catalogue record for this book is available from the British Library.

Series on Technology Management — Vol. 22
DISCONTINUOUS INNOVATION
Learning to Manage the Unexpected

Copyright © 2013 by Imperial College Press

ISBN 978-1-84816-780-3

Printed in Singapore

Introduction

Innovation matters – and in today's turbulent and uncertain world it is pretty clear that any organization which fails to change what they offer, or the ways they create and deliver that offering, will find it difficult to survive. That's always been the case, and it has led to a great deal of research about how to organize and manage the process of innovation. Learning and embedding the patterns of behaviour which help organizations repeat their success and deliver a steady stream of innovations in products, services and processes is only half of the story.

One of the paradoxes of innovative life is that successful innovators can get into trouble. It was this observation which led Clayton Christensen to explore how 'smart' organizations find themselves in difficulty and led to his influential book, *The Innovator's Dilemma*, which introduced the concept of disruptive innovation. His key observation was that sometimes doing the 'right' things to manage innovation successfully could be dangerous, as that form of innovation may be suited to a particular environment. If some aspect of that environment changes, such as a new market emerging or the appearance of a new technology, innovation may require a different approach. For example, a good prescription for successful innovation management is to work closely with your customers, listening to their needs and engaging in a dialogue which generates a steady stream of innovations linked to those needs. But if a brand new market emerges it is likely to have very different needs – and these may be poorly defined and fuzzy since the whole market is still developing. If the organization wants to engage with this new market it will need to develop different ways of exploring the market. They can use previously unused or even new channels to determine user needs and, as a result, they can then innovate to meet those needs. Using old innovation methods which worked with the existing market could actually turn out to be precisely the wrong innovative behaviour for the new market!

Together with a number of other writers we have been interested in trying to understand what happens when established and successful innovative players find themselves confronted with situations in which the game rules change, causing discontinuous innovation. What new approaches do they need, and how do they experiment with them?

Shifts along the technological frontier, emergence of new markets, and big changes to the regulatory environment don't happen every day, but when they do they have a nasty habit of upsetting the apple cart. The triggers of such change vary but in each case they all have the same effect. The old rules of the game no longer apply – and it is often here that agile new entrants are able to enter, and even dominate, the new market. Established players are trapped by their existing approaches, which they often find very difficult to alter, and they are also uncomfortable exploring new directions. Even if they do look in unexpected places, their 'immune systems' are likely to reject any new ideas because they fail to fit the existing business.

In 2005, an international network of researchers (in cooperation with a variety of public and private sector organizations) decided to study the challenges posed by discontinuous innovation as a shared learning process. The metaphor of a laboratory was central to this – a lab is a place where experiments are designed and carried out and where the experiences are reviewed and shared, slowly building towards a theory which might have more a general application. So, the Innovation Labs were established, first in the UK and then (with support from various bodies including the Advanced Institute of Management Research in the UK, the Dr. Theo and Friedl Schoeller Foundation and the Peter Pribilla Foundation in Germany) in a variety of other countries. At the moment, the Innovation Lab operates in 15 countries – mainly in Europe but also in Australia. Our aim is to identify and explore ways to deal with the challenge of discontinuity, and we have deliberately looked at edge and not at mainstream issues.

Our research reveals a number of principles around which study and education of these issues can take place, based on the experience of organizations experimenting in this way. We have structured this according to a simple process model of innovation which sees the innovation process as involving three core stages: searching for triggers; selecting from those ideas; and implementing the ideas.

This process is subject to a number of key influences and we focus on three: the overarching presence (or absence) of a clear innovation strategy; the enabling conditions of an organization designed to support innovation activities of individuals; and the development of pro-active linkages with a wide variety of partners.

Fig. 1. The challenge and how we approached it.

Finally, we consider the extent to which the organization is able to reflect on how it organizes and manages the innovation activity – and whether there is the capability to adapt and change the core operating mechanisms to keep pace with a shifting environment. Figure 1 shows the model in diagrammatic form.

The first five years of our project focused on the key questions of searching for, selecting and implementing discontinuous innovation. Our original questionnaire and some of the results can be found in the Appendix. In national workshops and at our international conferences, innovation managers and academics met, and still regularly meet, to share relevant experiences and scientific approaches. This book is about taking stock of what we have learned so far. It contains essays and cases dealing with different aspects of discontinuous innovation, following the search, select and implement phases of the innovation process model. We have also provided a wide range of resources developed during the programme and at the end of the book you can find some of these, together with an extensive bibliography.

We are still learning and the current Innovation Lab workshops are looking at the wider environment of discontinuous innovation, which includes aspects such as strategy, learning and networks. And, most importantly, companies have directed us towards a stronger focus on sustainable innovation issues. In this sense, we welcome feedback and invite both practitioners and academics to join our efforts in digging ever deeper into the subject of discontinuous innovation.

Before we move to the detailed findings, it is worth positioning discontinuous innovation and the Innovation Laboratory approach in a little more detail, and that is the focus of the next two chapters. In Chapter 1, John Bessant looks at the Innovation Labs, how and why they were established, how they worked, and some of the lessons learned. Chapter 2 (written by Peter Augsdörfer, Kathrin Möslein and Andreas Richter) presents a detailed literature review, which tries to explore definitions and debates around discontinuous innovation, drawing on over 100 articles and books.

Acknowledgements

During the life of the Innovation Labs we have been supported by a wide range of sponsors and we would like to acknowledge their help and facilitation here.

The Advanced Institute of Management (AIM) Research was founded in October 2002 as a multi-council initiative of the UK's Economic and Social Research Council (ESRC) and Engineering and Physical Sciences Research Council (EPSRC) – with activities at over 180 institutions in the UK and overseas. For details see www.aimresearch.org. Its sister organization, AIM Practice, offers practical tools and techniques for managers and consultants. Find out more at www.aimpractice.com.

The Dr. Theo and Friedl Schoeller Foundation has been supporting research and teaching in the field of economics since 2002. The establishment of the Dr. Theo and Friedl Schoeller Research Center for Business and Society at the University of Erlangen-Nuremberg strengthens the involvement in this specific area. The Dr. Theo and Friedl Schoeller Foundation was started in 1988 by Theo Schoeller in order to represent and preserve Theo's and Friedl's lifework in conjunction with the Schoeller Family Foundation. For details see www.schoeller-research.org.

The Peter Pribilla Foundation was established in July 2005 under the patronage of the Technische Universität München. The foundation supports collaborative research and academic teaching in the fields of innovation and leadership, in accordance with the spirit of Peter Pribilla's distinguished career. In a world holding too much varied information, the ambition of the foundation is to enhance personal contacts between business people and academics for the purpose of creating mutual understanding. The foundation also supports publications that highlight promising new ideas in the context of innovation and leadership. For details see www.pribilla-stiftung.de.

Contents

Chapter 1

Learning in the Discontinuous Innovation Laboratory

John Bessant
University of Exeter Business School, UK

Research has consistently highlighted a set of themes which underpin an emergent good practice model for product and process innovation (Nelson and Winter, 1982; Pavitt, 2002; Tidd *et al.*, 2005). Whilst this recipe needs adapting and configuring to suit specific contingencies, it can be argued that the core challenge has become one of *implementation* – getting individual enterprises to adopt and absorb such good practice. But the limitation of this good practice model is that it relates to what might be termed steady-state innovation – essentially innovative activity in product and process terms which is about 'doing what we do, but better'.

So, for example, in product development the prescription is for close links throughout the process with users (getting them to act as innovators where possible), early and cross-functional involvement of key players inside and across the extended enterprise, concurrent working, effective project management (with particular emphasis on the team dynamics) and appropriate project structures and staged risk management via some version of the stage-gate model.

The prescription is not a good guide when elements of discontinuity come into the equation. Such discontinuous challenges arise from shifts along technological, market, political and other frontiers and require new or at least significantly adapted approaches to their effective management (Tushman and O'Reilly, 1996; Day and Schoemaker, 2000; Leifer *et al.*, 2000). And, whilst we have some important clues from these and other studies, there is still a need to understand the particular contexts in which such approaches might help and the configuration of new practices within them.

The challenges centre on building routines – shared patterns of behaviour which become reinforced and embedded, eventually forming 'the way we do things around here'. Adapting and changing routines to cope with shifting environments is at the heart of dynamic capability, and in the context of discontinuous innovation (DI) the kinds of issues raised include:

- How to pick up weak signals about discontinuity
- How to interpret the signals and generate an appropriate response
- How to avoid the 'not invented here' and other defensive responses
- How to assess risks associated with weak signals about potentially discontinuous change
- How to allocate resources to high-risk ventures
- How to manage projects so that there is fast failure and rapid learning
- How to manage discontinuous innovation across systems and networks – for example with diverse suppliers
- How to enable links between new ventures based on discontinuous change and the rest of the organization (ambidextrous capability).

One approach to dealing with this challenge involves putting together a network of firms acting as a co-laboratory for articulating key research issues around DI, sharing experiences and developing and implementing experiments to come up with new routines for dealing with it. Here, learning support comes through interaction and mutual support within a facilitated framework – it offers an example of a community of practice. The potential benefits of such shared learning include:

- Challenge and structured critical reflection from different perspectives
- Different perspectives can bring in new concepts (or old concepts which are new to the learner)
- Shared experimentation can reduce perceived and actual costs and risks in trying new things
- Sharing experiences can provide support and open new lines of inquiry or exploration

- Shared learning helps explicate systems principles, seeing the patterns – 'separating the wood from the trees'
- Shared learning provides an environment for surfacing assumptions and exploring mental models outside of the normal experience of individual organizations – helps prevent the 'not invented here' and other effects.

These approaches can be mapped onto a basic model of the learning process. Figure 1 shows the well-known experiential learning cycle originally put forward by David Kolb (Kolb and Fry, 1975). It views learning as involving a cycle of experiment, experience, reflection and concept development.

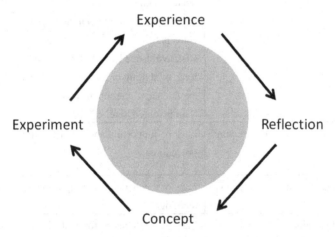

Fig. 1. Experiential learning cycle (Kolb and Frey, 1975).

Where an individual or firm enters is not important (although there is evidence for different preferred styles of learning associated with particular entry points). What does matter is that the cycle is completed – incomplete cycles do not enable learning.

Table 1 summarizes some of the key blocks to effective organizational learning, mapped onto Kolb's learning cycle (Kolb and Fry, 1975).

Table 1. Key blocks to learning.

Learning block	Underlying problem
Lack of entry to the learning cycle	Perceived stimulus for change is too weak Firm is isolated or insulated from stimulus Stimulus is misinterpreted, underrated or denied
Incomplete learning cycle	Motivation to learn is present but process of learning is flawed. Emphasis given to some aspects – e.g. experimentation – but not to all stages and to sequence
Weak links in the cycle	Reflection process is unstructured or unchallenging Lack of access to or awareness of relevant new concepts Risk avoidance leads to lack of experimentation Lack of sharing or exchange of relevant experiences – parochial search for new ideas 'Not invented here' effect
Lack of learning skills or structure	Lack of supporting and enabling structures and procedures
Knowledge remains in tacit form	Lack of mechanisms for capturing and codifying learning
Repeated learning	Lack of mechanisms for capturing and codifying learning leads to repetition of learning content
Learning is infrequent, sporadic and not sustained	Mechanisms for enabling learning are not embedded or absent

Arguably, shared learning can contribute to dealing with some of these issues. It allows for both challenge and support, providing a framework in which elaboration and experimentation are enabled and through which individual and collective knowledge is built. In the management context it underpins what has become known as action learning, in which individuals help enable learning amongst their peers through a process of challenge, reflection, shared experimentation, etc. (McGill and Warner Weil, 1989). Revans (1983) suggested the idea of comrades in adversity, which refers to working together to tackle complex and open-ended problems (also see Pedler *et al.*, 1991). There is growing interest in such approaches, for example the importance of individual-based networks and communities of practice in creating and carrying learning (Wenger, 1999; Brown and Duguid, 2000; Bogenrieder and Nooteboom, 2004). The underlying arguments relate to learning processes as 'intrinsically social and collective phenomena' (Teece *et al.*, 1994), which provide mechanisms that allow shared experimentation, interpretation and codification, and which scaffold knowledge creation in practice (Cook and Brown, 1999).

Learning Networks around Discontinuous Innovation

In the context of DI, the Innovation Lab initiative was started in 2005 in three countries: the UK, Germany and Denmark. The Innovation Lab had a number of operating mechanisms; at the centre was a regular series of experience-sharing workshops (held at four-month intervals) at which participating firms were encouraged to report on their experiences (both positive and negative). The academic partners captured and synthesized this experience and fed it back via presentations and workshop activities during the meetings. The meetings reflected areas where existing innovation management routines had proved inadequate for dealing with DI challenges. Importantly, they brought together members of large and smaller companies from different sectors to work on common strategic and operational issues surrounding DI. Their experiences were documented by researchers from the academic institutions and augmented through case studies of member firms. In selecting cases, the research team requested that the firms identify innovations that they deemed discontinuous in nature.

This model proved successful in terms of maintaining participation, extending membership, developing useful tools and resources and moving the research agenda forward. One consequence was the decision to try to extend the model to other countries, essentially mirroring the overall operating structures of regular workshops interspersed with case study work with participating companies. Labs were subsequently organized in a variety of other countries and currently there are 16 in operation.

With the accumulating experience of so many players it became clear that extending the interaction to an international level would be useful and in 2006 the inaugural annual conference was held in London. This provided the opportunity for participants from Labs in different countries to exchange ideas and laid the foundation for a wider network. One consequence has been increasing traffic between the Labs so that, for example, a meeting in London might be attended by participants from Denmark, Germany and Ireland. There was also increasing company-to-company engagement; for example, after a presentation of the Philips experience in London an invitation was extended to present the work at the headquarters of a major Danish company.

The network continues to thrive and now involves around 300 companies and public sector institutions together with around 35 academic research teams. Full details can be found at our website, www.innovation-lab.org.

References

Bogenrieder, I. and Nooteboom, B. (2004). Learning groups: What types are they? A theoretical analysis and an empirical study in a consultancy firm. *Organization Studies*, 2(1), 40–57.

Brown, J. and Duguid, P. (2000). *The Social Life of Information*. Harvard Business School Press, Boston, MA.

Cook, S. and Brown, J. (1999). Bridging epistemologies: The generative dance between organizational knowledge and organizational knowing. *Organization Science*, 10(4), 381–400.

Day, G. and Schoemaker, P. (2000). *Wharton on Managing Emerging Technologies*. Wiley, New York.

Kolb, D. and Fry, R. (1975). 'Towards a theory of applied experiential learning', in Cooper, C. (ed.), *Theories of Group Processes*. John Wiley and Sons, Chichester.

Leifer, R., McDermott, C., O'Connor, G.C, Peters, L., Rice, M. and Veryzer, R. (2000). *Radical Innovation*. Harvard Business School Press, Boston, MA.

McGill, I. and Warner Weil, S. (1989). *Making Sense of Experiential Learning*. Open University Press, London.

Nelson, R. and Winter, S. (1982). *An Evolutionary Theory of Economic Change*. Harvard University Press, Cambridge, MA.

Pavitt, K. (2002). Innovating routines in the business firm: What corporate tasks should they be accomplishing? *Industrial and Corporate Change*, 11(1), 117–133.

Pedler, M., Boydell, T., *et al.* (1991). *The Learning Company: A Strategy for Sustainable Development*. McGraw-Hill, Maidenhead.

Revans, R. (1980). *Action Learning*. Blond and Briggs, London.

Teece, D. and Pisano, G. (1994). The dynamic capabilities of firms: An introduction. *Industrial and Corporate Change*, 3(3), 537–555.

Tidd, J., Bessant, J. and Pavitt, K. (2005). *Managing Innovation: Integrating Technological, Market and Organizational Change, 3rd Edition*. John Wiley and Sons, Chichester.

Tushman, M. and O'Reilly, C. (1996). Ambidextrous organizations: Managing evolutionary and revolutionary change. *California Management Review*, 38(4), 8–30.

Wenger, E. (1999). *Communities of Practice: Learning, Meaning, and Identity*. Cambridge University Press, Cambridge.

Chapter 2

Radical, Discontinuous and Disruptive Innovation – What's the Difference?

Peter Augsdörfer
HAW Ingolstadt, Germany, and Grenoble Ecole de Management, France
Kathrin Möslein
Universität Erlangen-Nürnberg and HHL – Leipzig Graduate School of Management, Germany
Andreas Richter
University of Newcastle, UK

Introduction

Technological innovations are often analysed in terms of dichotomies: radical and incremental (Knight, 1940; Freeman, 1994), discontinuous and continuous (Bessant, 2005), disruptive and sustaining (Christensen, 1997), competence-destroying and competence-enhancing (Tushman and Anderson, 1986). This classification of types of innovation is used to distinguish between new and existing innovations or the big and small dimensions of an innovation. It is simple and at first sight seems easy to understand. But if you look closer, there is no clear delineation. What is radical for one firm might not be radical for another (Freeman, 1994). It depends very much on the 'question being asked and the perspective in which innovative activity is being considered' (Audretsch and Aldrige, 2008). The problem gets even trickier among the concepts which seem to have the same or a similar significant degree of newness: 'architectural', 'breakthrough', 'really new innovations', 'radical', 'discontinuous', 'disruptive' and so on. The technology and innovation management (TIM) literature uses these terms at times differently and at others synonymously. The disagreement among researchers is nicely illustrated by Garcia and Calantone (2002) with the electric typewriter example, which is described as incremental with radical componential change (Rothwell and Gardiner, 1988), moderate (Kleinschmidt and Cooper,

1991) and revolutionary (Abernathy and Clark, 1985). This report looks at the definition of the three terms 'radical', 'discontinuous' and 'disruptive'. It tries to capture the similarities, differences and ambiguities. Do they all have the same meaning or has the scientific community refined each separate concept? This question constitutes the research question of this report.

Literature Review

There is widespread uncertainty among the practitioners and academics of the TIM community about the right use of the terms. The literature has recognized the inconsistency of definitions and this research is not the first attempt to tackle the confusion. Five papers exploring the issue in more detail deserve explicit mention: Garcia and Calantone (2002), Phillips and Nokes (2003), Dahlin and Behrens (2005), Audretsch and Aldrige (2008) and Wassenaar (2009).

Garcia and Calantone (2002) focus on the newness factor of product development:

> Product innovativeness is a measure of the potential discontinuity a product (process or service) can generate in the marketing and/or technological process. From a macro perspective, 'innovativeness' is the capacity of a new innovation to create a paradigm shift in the science and technology and/or market structure in an industry. From a micro perspective, 'innovativeness' is the capacity of a new innovation to influence the firm's existing marketing resources, technological resources, skills, knowledge, capabilities, or strategy.

In their typology of different degrees of newness, radical innovation causes discontinuity in the world. They add the term 'really new' to bridge the gap between radical and incremental.

Phillips and Nokes (2003) focus on the understanding of technological discontinuous innovation. They subscribe to Linton's (2002) definition that 'disruptive technologies are discontinuous, but discontinuous technologies are not necessarily disruptive'. As Bower and Christensen (1995) explain, this is 'because disruptive technologies are not radically new technologically but offer superior performance along dimensions that customers value'.

Dahlin and Behrens (2005) do not elaborate much on the confusion and ambiguity of innovation terminology and typology. For them, 'radical', 'disruptive' and 'discontinuous' are similar terms. They focus on the definitional problems between incremental and radical innovation. Their research is based on the case of the tennis racket industry and analyses the patent data inherent in an innovation and its citation patterns.

Audretsch and Aldrige (2008) review the radical innovation literature and provide a table of definitions given by different authors for radical versus incremental innovation. They focus on the advantages and disadvantages of the different methods to identify the radicalness of innovations. Unfortunately, their paper lacks any reference to the difference between the three concepts which this report addresses.

Wassenaar (2009) also outlines the inconsistencies of what is written in the discontinuous innovation literature while also delimiting it from other innovation terms. She explicitly presents different linkages between (i) discontinuous innovation as an 'umbrella term', (ii) disruption leading to discontinuous innovation and (iii) linkages between discontinuous and 'other non-continuous innovations'.

Although the aforementioned papers provide an impressive number of definitions and new scales of what is new, none of them has specifically explored the difference between the three notions of 'radical', 'disruptive' and 'discontinuous' innovation. All papers try to redefine the terms, but focus mainly on the different degrees of novelty of innovations. The decisive element is either the newness factor (Garcia and Calantone, 2002; Phillips and Nokes, 2003; Wassenaar, 2009), the technical element (Dahlin and Behrens, 2005) or output (Audretsch and Aldrige, 2008).

The objective of this report is not to add another definition to the existing ones. Instead the focus is simply to show that there is uncertainty about the definition of the three terms 'radical', 'disruptive' and 'discontinuous'. In a simple comparison, some similarities and differences over time are elaborated. This brings some clarity to the picture.

Methodology

The research design for this report is a simple one. Literature was checked for definitions of the three terms. Subsequently an attempt was made to distil the main characteristics of the terms based on the findings. This provided a definition for each term and showed what they have in common and where they are distinct from each other.

The literature review for this research encompasses the past 50 years since 1960, but mainly the past two decades (from 1989 to 2009). The search logic for the scanning of the papers is based on VHB-Jourqual 2's recommendations. Established by the German Economic Association for Business Administration (Verband der Hochschullehrer für Betriebswirtschaft e.V.), VHB-Jourqual 2 is a ranking of international business administration journals. Its recommendations for technology and innovation management literature formed the basis for this research. Based on the EBSCO Business Source Complete ScienceDirect and SwetsWise databases, a systematic search was performed for publications dealing with the subject of newness in technological innovation over the past 20 years. The following keywords were used for the search across publication title and paper content: 'innovation', 'radical innovation', 'discontinuous innovation', 'disruptive innovation', 'disruption', 'discontinuity', 'technology', 'revolution and breakthroughs', 'change', 'innovativeness' and 'paradigm shift'. Moreover, any references in the first-round literature likely to elicit more information on the key terms were pursued further. That is why, for example, Schumpeter's books on innovation, reports on case-related studies or research and newspaper material are also included in this research. In total, 35 articles could be identified using the term 'radical innovation', 24 using 'discontinuous innovation' and 14 using 'disruptive innovation'. A list of all papers can be found in Table 1.

Key attributes given for the definitions of the three terms were collected and grouped. This can best be illustrated with an example. Dahlin and Behrens' paper (2005) gave the following attributes for a radical innovation: 'dissimilarity from prior/current inventions ... we use the label radical technological change when a radical invention has been successful in converting an industry'. It was grouped under the headings 'departure from existing' and finally 'change industry'.

Although the research method is a simple comparison, it suffers from some shortcomings. This is for three main reasons. First, the definitions of the terms were not stable across papers or over time. This made it difficult to pinpoint exactly the continuity of the definition of a term. Henderson and Clark (1990), for example, employ the terms 'radical innovation' and 'architectural and modular innovations' in one of their models. Here, 'radical innovation' is used with a slightly different meaning compared to previous mentions by other authors in the 1990s.

Second, articles were chosen without taking into account the journals' reputation or importance. One approach would have been to give more weight to journals with a higher ranking when searching for a definition, but this was deliberately ignored in order to keep the research design simple.

Third, authors who had published more extensively, always using the same definition, had a bigger impact on our search for a definition as there were more papers with the same definition for one term. The study may have provided a slightly different result had we based it on authors rather than articles.

Findings

The result of this research reveals, as expected, a plethora of definitions. The next three paragraphs collate the definitions for each term.

A significant number of authors refer to Schumpeter as one of the pioneers in research on innovation and particularly on radical innovation (see Augsdörfer, 2005). He coined the term 'basic innovation', which was used by many authors in subsequent years (Schumpeter, 1912); (see e.g. Barr and Knight, 1968; von Hippel, 1976; or Mensch, 1978, 1985). The academic community has since enriched Schumpeter's definition, but interestingly, the term 'basic innovation' has more or less disappeared from the literature today. It has been replaced by the three concepts of 'radical innovation', 'discontinuous innovation' and 'disruptive innovation'.

Table 1. A history of innovation terms.

Innovation Term	No.	Authors
Creation of something new/Creative destruction	5	Schumpeter (1912, 1934, 1939, 1942, 1954)
Basic Innovation	6	Siemon (1951); Barr & Knight (1968); von Hippel (1988); Mensch (1978, 1985); Brown (1991)
Radical Innovation	35	Knight (1967); Knight & Wind (1968); Dosi (1982); Ettlie (1983); Ettlie et al. (1984); Dewar & Dutton (1986); Henderson & Clark (1990); Pavitt (1990, 1991); Brown (1991); Henderson (1993); Mezias & Glynn (1993); Freeman (1994); Utterback (1994); Ehrnberg (1995); Utterback (1996); Lambe (1997); Tripsas (1997); Dowd & Walsh (1998); Tripsas & Gavetti (2000); Godoe (2000); Leifer et al. (2000); O'Connor & Veryzer (2001); Garcia & Calantone (2002); Hamel (2002); O'Connor & McDermott (2004); Dahlin & Behrens (2005); Hall & Martin (2005); Garud & Munir (2006); Leifer et al (2006); Markides (2006); Germunden et al. (2007); Herrmann (2007); Leifl (2007); Salomo et al (2007)
Disruptive Innovation	14	Mensch (1985); Bower & Christensen (1995); Christensen (1997, 2000, 2002, 2006); Walsh & Kirchhoff (2000); Linton & Walsh (2001); Kassicieh et al (2002); Linton (2002); Martinich (2002); Christensen & Raynor (2003); Adner & Zemsky (2005); Markides (2006)
Revolutionary Innovation	2	Abernathy & Clark (1985); Mezias & Glynn (1993)

Table 1 (continued). A history of innovation terms.

Term	Count	References
Discontinuous Innovation	24	Tushman & Anderson (1986); Abernathy & Utterback (1988); Pavitt (1990); McDermott (1998); McDermott & Handfield (1996); Utterback (1996); Dewd & Walsh (1998); O'Connor (1998); Rice et al. (2000); Veryzer (1998); Walsh & Kirchhoff (2000); Linton & Walsh (2001); Linton (2002); De Tienne & Koberg (2002); Kassicieh et al. (2002); Martinich (2002); Rothaermel (2002); Magnusson et al. (2003); Mascher & Richman (2004); O'Connor & McDermott (2004); Bessant et al. (2005); Utterback & Acee (2005); Phillips et al. (2006); Birkinshaw et al. (2007);
Fundamental Innovation	2	Dewar & Dutton (1986); Howard (1991)
Breakthrough Innovation	4	Ayres (1988); Rice et al. (1998); Mascitelli (2000); O'Connor & McDermott (2004); Salomo et al. (2007)
Architectural and Modular Innovation	3	Henderson & Clark (1990); Teece et al. (1997); Magnusson et al (2003)
Frame-Breaking Innovation	1	Mezias & Glynn (1993)
High Order Innovation	1	Herbig (1994)
Rule-Busting Innovation	1	Hamel (2002)
Really New Innovation	1	Garcia & Calantone (2002)
Step Out Innovation	1	O'Connor & McDermott (2004)
Horizon 3 Innovation	1	O'Connor & McDermott (2004)
Game Changing Innovation	1	O'Connor & McDermott (2004)
New to the World Innovation	1	O'Connor & McDermott (2004)

One of the first writers to refer to 'radical research' was Knight (1940). However, the term 'radical innovation' seems to have been used for the first time in 1963 by Schön. A number of definitions are presented in Table 2. Both 'disruptive innovation' (Abernathy and Clark, 1985) and 'discontinuous innovation' (Tushman and Anderson, 1986) appeared in the mid-1980s. In 1997 Christensen successfully redefined the term 'disruptive innovation' (Christensen, 1997). The definitions can be found in Tables 3 and 4.

Some authors use both 'radical innovation' and 'discontinuous innovation' without differentiating between them (e.g. Utterback, 1996; Dowd and Walsh, 1998). Or they state that radical innovation results in technological discontinuities (e.g. Garcia and Calantone, 2002). Although some authors make use of the term 'disruption' to refer to that caused by radical or discontinuous innovation, they don't subsequently call it 'disruptive innovation'. The late 1990s and the first half of the last decade again saw a further increase in new terms, such as 'game changing' and 'new to the world' (O'Connor *et al.*, 2004). They are used synonymously for radical or discontinuous innovation, but not for disruptive innovation. This leaves room for speculation about how radical innovations may be classified, named or bifurcated in the future.

Key Characteristics of Radical Innovation

In general, authors are not very specific about their definition of radical innovation. Many of them apparently switch freely between the terms 'radical innovation' and 'discontinuous innovation'. One has the impression that the choice of term depends entirely on the preference of the author. A synopsis of definitions can be found in Table 2.

Table 2. Definitions of 'radical innovation'.

Author	Definitions
Knight (1967)	'First, "performance radicalness" describes a measure of the increase … in the ability to perform a required task…', and '… is defined as the amount of change in output that results from the one innovation when compared to a second one. (A large change in output = an innovation high in performance radicalness.)' 'Second, "structural radicalness" defines a measure of the extent to which the structural arrangement differs from existing ones.'
Knight and Wind (1968)	'… faced with the trade-off between high uncertainty (low predictability) with the possibility of high payoffs on the one hand, and low uncertainty (high predictability) with the possibility of lost opportunities on the other hand.' '… radical and high profit changes are often nonprogrammed.'
Ettlie et al. *(1984)*	'… the innovation incorporates technology that is a clear, risky departure from existing practice.' '… the magnitude or cost of change required by the organization is sufficient to warrant the designation of a rare and radical … innovation.'
Dewar and Dutton (1986)	'… innovations vary in the degree of newness to an adopting unit.' 'Radical innovations are fundamental changes that represent revolutionary changes in technology. … They represent clear departures from existing practice.' 'The major difference captured by the labels radical and incremental is the degree of novel technological process content embodied in the innovation and hence, the degree of new knowledge embedded in the innovation.' '… radical innovations … incorporate a large degree of new knowledge …'
Henderson and Clark (1990)	'The distinction between radical and incremental innovation … is fundamentally incomplete. … and potentially misleading.' 'Radical innovation … is based on a different set of engineering and scientific principles and often opens up whole new markets and applications.' '… two further types of innovation: innovation that changes only the core design concepts of a technology (modular innovation) and innovation that changes only the relationships between them (architectural innovation).' 'Radical and incremental innovation are extreme points along both dimensions. Radical innovation establishes a new dominant design and, hence, a new set of core design concepts embodied in components that are linked together in a new architecture.'
Pavitt (1990)	'radical technological change' with 'technological discontinuities … which imply a radical increase in the rate of technical change and a marked shift in its associated skills and required organizational forms.'
Brown (1991)	'… fundamental innovations … the building blocks of the … revolution…'

citing Robert Howard from PARC	
Pavitt (1991)	'... a major source of entirely new ranges of products, and consequently of new product divisions.'
Mezias and Glynn (1993)	'Nonroutine, significant and discontinuous ... process of innovation' '... radical innovation ... produce fundamental changes in the activities of an organization and represent clear departures from existing practices ...' '... represents discontinuous or "frame-breaking" change that involves change in the underlying technology so that existing organizational skills and competence are rendered obsolete.'
Freeman (1994)	'An attempt has been made to rank innovations on a five point scale from "systemic" to "major", "minor", "incremental" and "unrecorded" (Freeman, 1971); Abernathy and Clark (1985) used four categories but the vast majority of authors make a simple two-fold distinction between "radical" (or "major") innovations and "incremental" (or "minor") (e.g. Stobaugh, 1988) ...' 'Mensch (1975) defines radical innovation as one that needs a new factory and/or market for its exploitation and this is similar to Utterback's (1979) definition of major or radical innovations. Freeman and Perez (1988) added to this the suggestion that, logically, radical innovations would need a new column and a new row in a complete input-output table.'
Ehrnberg (1995)	'[Technological discontinuities] ... large technological changes often have disruptive effects on the structure of an industry.'
Lambe and Spekman (1997)	'... a major change in the technology base for a mature industry ...'
Tripsas and Gavetti (2000)	'... a step function improvement in price/performance relative to other products in the market.'
Godoe (2000)	'... radical innovations are variously attributed to haphazard scientific breakthroughs, chance, serendipity, etc.' '... radical innovations may inaugurate the emergence of new technological paradigms, initiating developmental patterns ...' 'Earlier, a radical innovation was defined as a novel category, species or class of technological device(s), system or process/solution which represents a discontinuity compared to predecessors, if such exist.'
Leifer et al. (2000)	'... with the potential to produce one or more of the following: an entirely new set of performance features; improvements in known performance features of five times or greater; or a significant (30% or greater) reduction in cost ...' 'A radical innovation is a product, process, or service with either unprecedented performance features or familiar features that offer

	significant improvements in performance or cost that transform existing markets or create new ones.'
O'Connor and Veryzer (2001)	'... a product that creates a new line of business – new for both the business and the marketplace. Operationally, the project must be viewed within its firm to have the potential for fivefold to 10-fold improvements in performance or at least a 30% reduction in cost.'
Garcia and Calantone (2002)	'... radical innovation introductions result in discontinuities on both a macro and micro level.' They define it from a macro perspective: '... create[s] a paradigm shift in the science and technology and/or market structure in an industry.' And further a micro perspective: '... capacity of an innovation to influence the firm's existing market resources, technological resources, skills, knowledge, capabilities, or strategy.' 'Radical innovations ... create a demand ... This [new demand] cultivates new industries with new competitors, firms, distribution channels, and new marketing activities.' And as such 'Radical new technology acts as the catalyst for the emergence of new markets and/or new industries.'
Hamel (2002)	'Radical, nonlinear innovation is the only way to escape the ruthless hypercompetition ...' 'Nonlinear innovation requires a company to escape the shackles of precedent and imagine entirely novel solutions to customer needs and dramatically more cost-effective ways to meet those needs.' '... radical, rule-busting innovation ... is innovation that has the power to change customer expectations, alter industry economics and redefine the basis for competitive advantage.' '... successful, radical innovation alters the shape of an important improvement curve.'
O'Connor and McDermott (2004)	'Radical, breakthrough, discontinuous, step out, horizon 3, game changing innovation ... create new to the world offerings and, concomitantly, whole new lines of business for companies.'
Dahlin and Behrens (2005)	'... a radical invention is something novel ... it has distinctive features missing in previously observed inventions.' '... a key radical invention should influence future invention; that is, affect future technical content.'
Hall and Martin (2005)	'... radical technological innovations (often initiating new industries) that are controversial and potentially disruptive to secondary stakeholders.'
Garud and Munir (2006)	'... increasing frequency with which radical innovations are disrupting the functioning of existing technological systems.' 'Radical innovation is manifest by changes not only to the components of a technological system but also in the ways components interact with one another.'

Lettl et al. (2006)	'… radical innovation involves new products or services with a high degree of innovativeness. … An innovation is radical in the market dimension if it satisfies unmet needs for the first time, resulting in a quantum leap in customer value. … Existing knowledge often becomes obsolete. The innovation often relies on completely new technological principles, new architectures, or new materials.' 'The innovation can be called radical in the technological dimension if knowledge about the product architecture or its components differs significantly from existing knowledge.'
Gemünden et al. (2007) *Herrmann* et al. (2007)	'The innovation is radical for the market if the innovation satisfies former unsatisfied needs for the first time. There is a quantum leap in customer benefits. A completely new market may be created … The new product may require considerable changes in customer behavior as well as substantial financial investments from the customer.' 'The innovation can be called radical in the technological dimension if the knowledge about the product architecture or its components significantly differs from existing knowledge. Existing knowledge may become obsolete to some degree. The innovation often relies on completely new technological principles, new architectures or new materials.'
Lettl (2007)	'Products of a completely new kind have the potential to seriously change the balance of power in existing markets or even create new markets.' '… the discontinuities associated with radical innovations…' '… we define radical product innovations as those innovations which are characterized by a discontinuity along both dimensions on a macro-level [technology and market].' '… new products that incorporate substantially different technology from existing products and [can] fulfil customer needs either significantly better than existing products, or address different types of needs which could not be fulfilled at all with existing products.' '[radical] innovations typically incorporate completely new and highly complex technologies, shift market structures, and require user learning as they often induce significant behavior changes on side of the users.'
Salomo et al. *(2007)*	'Radical or breakthrough innovations transform the relationship between customers and suppliers, restructure marketplace economics, displace current products and create entirely new product categories.' '… radical innovations are characterized by a very high degree of innovativeness.'

Few authors give precise numerical definitions as to what qualifies as radical innovation. O'Connor and Veryzer (2001) use factors of performance improvement (e.g. fivefold/tenfold) and Rice *et al.* (1998) use percentages of cost reduction (e.g. 30%). More frequent are descriptive definitions. Authors use expressions which often include 'leaps, steps and non-linearity'. Several authors mention the following: a large technological change (9), new products/businesses/markets/ industries (8), a change in industry/market structures (7), a non-programmed/linear/routine (5), a departure from existing practice (5), a high degree of new knowledge (5), high price/performance improvement (4), paradigm shift/new principles (3), disruptive effects on industry (3), a satisfaction of needs for the first time (2), a quantum leap in customer value/benefit (2), a significant change in output (2), new to the world (1), modular and architectural (1), a new dominant design/core design concepts (1), affects future technical content/inventions (1). A synopsis of the characteristics can be seen in Table 3.

Disruptive Innovation

Although most authors assign certain disruptive effects to radical or discontinuous innovations, relatively few writers concentrate exclusively on the notion of 'disruptive innovation'. This is because the term is strongly associated with Christensen's model (1997). A synopsis of the definitions can be found in Table 3.

Table 3. Definitions of 'disruptive innovation'.

Author	Definitions
Abernathy and Clark (1985)	'technologies that change the industry-wide product/technology factors.' '... are based on a different technology base than current practice, thereby destroying the value of existing technical competencies ...'
Walsh and Kirchhoff (2000) citing Abernathy and Utterback (1988)	'... those that underlie discontinuous innovations that create entirely new technology-product-market paradigms that create new to the world markets that may be opaque to customers.'
Walsh and Kirchhoff (2000) citing Moore (1991)	'... they generate discontinuous innovations that require users/adopters to significantly change their behavior in order to use the innovation ...'

McKee (1992) (as interpreted by Kassicieh et al. (2002))	'Disruption: the gap between substitutable technological learning curves on cost or performance basis ...'
Walsh and Kirchhoff (2000) citing Bower and Christensen (1995)	'Disruptive technologies may not be radically new from a technological point of view but have superior performance trajectories along critical dimensions that customers value. Disruptive technologies typically emerge from a combination of information drawn from a mix of technical disciplines. As such, disruptive technologies are exogenous, i.e. external to the mainstream (sustaining) technologies that dominate a particular industry or firm.'
Christensen (1997)	'A technology, product or process that creeps up from below an existing business and threatens to displace it. Typically the disrupter offers lower performance and less functionality at a much lower price. The product or process is good enough for a meaningful number of customers – indeed, some don't need the older version's higher functionality and welcome the disruption's simplicity. And gradually, the new product or process improves to the point where it displaces the incumbent.'
Walsh and Kirchhoff (2000)	Two classes of technology: '(1) disruptive, radical, emergent or step-function technologies; and (2) sustaining, evolutionary, incremental or "nuts and bolts" technologies.'
Kassicieh et al. (2002)	'Disruptive innovations are scientific discoveries that break through the usual product/technological capabilities and provide a basis for a new competitive paradigm ...' 'Disruptive technologies have been referred to as inflection point, earthquake, game-breaking, whirlwind, typhoon or emergent technologies ... No longer the domain of entrepreneurial firms, disruptive technologies change the current product-technology paradigms. These paradigms are replaced by new manufacturing bases with new technological capabilities or by new technologies with a new manufacturing base for products and industries that do not yet exist. They initiate the development of new firm-based competencies and are the wellspring of future sustaining technologies.'
Adner and Zemsky (2005)	'A disruptive technology offers a novel mix of attributes compared to the established technology according to the needs of customers in the primary (mainstream) market segment. ... initially purchased by consumers in a secondary (niche) market ... but its perceived quality in the primary segment remains inferior to that of the established technology.' '... the new technology is able to enter the primary segment because the established technology is "oversupplying" customer needs.'
Utterback and Acee (2005)	'Disruptive technology ... is a powerful means for enlarging and broadening markets and providing new functionality.' And '... it may displace established products.'

	'a new technology having lower cost and performance measured by traditional criteria, but having higher ancillary performance.' '… enter and expand emerging niches, improving with time and ultimately attacking (from below) established products in their traditional markets.' 'Christensen ignores other discontinuous pattern of change, which may be of equal or greater importance.' (See also Utterback, 1996; Acee, 2001.) '… we present an alternative scenario in which a higher performing and higher priced innovation is introduced … and later moves to the mass market.'
Georgantzas and Katsamakas (2007)	'A disrupter firm offers new choices in the form of stripped down functionality at a lower price, for example, a "less for less" offering.'

Discontinuous Innovation

Exclusively descriptive definitions have been used by authors for discontinuous technological innovations. A synopsis of the definitions can be found in Table 4.

Table 4. Definitions of 'discontinuous innovation'.

Author	Definitions
Tushman and Anderson (1986)	'… demonstrate that technology evolves through periods of incremental change punctuated by technological breakthroughs (discontinuities) that either enhance or destroy the competence of firms in an industry.' 'These major technological shifts can be classified as competence-destroying or competence-enhancing because they destroy or enhance the competence of existing firms in an industry.' 'Technological change is a bit-by-bit, cumulative process until it is punctuated by a major advance.' 'Major technological innovations represent technical advance so significant that no increase in scale, efficiency, or design can make older technologies competitive with the new technology.'
Herbig (1994)	'…"high order innovations" that create new industries, products or markets …'
McDermott and Handfield (1996) and McDermott (1996)	'… they are typically longer in duration, and often deal with uncertain and evolving technologies which are being created for markets which may not yet perceive a need for the product. In addition, because of this high degree of uncertainty, market analysis becomes fuzzier and traditional financial measures fall short in their ability to capture the potential of these products in a meaningful way. Discontinuous

	innovation may also utilize process technologies which are revolutionary, and often unstable. Traditional process control technologies (design of experiments, SPC) may not be easily applicable in these situations.'
Utterback (1996)	'... evolutionary periods ... are often interrupted by a new cycle of creativity and discontinuous change. By discontinuous change or radical innovation, I mean change that sweeps away much of a firm's existing investment in technical skills and knowledge, designs, production technique, plant and equipment.'
Dowd and Walsh (1998)	'... often a discontinuous or radical innovation represents the destruction of traditional core competencies for the sake of new core competencies. These new competencies may not have existed at all, or may have existed only in other marketplaces.'
O'Connor (1998)	'We define discontinuous innovation as the creation of a new line of business – new for both the firm and the market place. By "new" to the firm and marketplace we mean a product or process either with unprecedented performance features or with already familiar features that offer potential for fivefold to tenfold improvements in performance or cost.'
Rice et al. *(1998)*	'... the discontinuous innovation project has the potential to produce a "game changer"; i.e. to have the potential, (1) for a 5–10-times improvement in performance compared to existing products; (2) to create the basis for a 30–50-percent reduction in cost; or (3) to have new-to-the-world performance features.'
Veryzer (1998)	'Discontinuous innovation refers to radically new products that involve dramatic leaps in terms of customer familiarity and use. Frequently these types of products involve the development or application of significant new technologies ...'
Mascitelli (2000)	'... typically refers to products that involve significant new technologies and are aimed at a market that is unfamiliar with the product class ...'
Rice et al. *(2000)*	'... transforms the relationship between customers and suppliers, restructures marketplace economies, displaces current products, often creates entirely new product categories, and provides a platform for the long-term growth sought by corporate leaders.'
Linton et al. *(2001) and Linton (2002)*	'... involves shifting from one technological learning curve to a more attractive technological learning curve, thereby obtaining a substantial gain in one or more performance metrics.' '... disruptive technologies are discontinuous, but discontinuous technologies are not necessarily disruptive.'
DeTienne and Koberg (2002)	'... major products/services and technological developments based on significant innovation. Some innovations change the entire order of things, making obsolete the old ways. Discontinuous innovations permit entire industries and markets to emerge, transform, or disappear. They are often described as technological breakthroughs that help companies rewrite industry rules or create entire new industries. Discontinuous

	innovations are analogous to Kuhn's "paradigm shifts"; they permit entire industries and markets to emerge, transform, or disappear, providing a firm a significant competitive advantage.' '… major changes or innovations in basic products or services or programs offered or markets served, or the creation of major product/service programs leading to new or expansion of current markets …'
Kassicieh et al. *(2002)*	'Discontinuous innovations are products/processes/services that provide order of magnitude improvements in the value received by the customer.' 'Discontinuous innovations have been called radical, architectural, generational and revolutionary among many others. They provide step-function improvements to current product market paradigms or produce the physical and service products that initiate new industries or markets that define a new and differing product platform from which incremental innovations are generated …'
Martinich (2002)	'… disruptive or discontinuous innovations include technologies that fundamentally change the way humans perform some activity.'
Rothaermel (2002)	'… destroys the incumbents' upstream, technology-orientated value chain activities. If the incumbent has valuable downstream assets that are needed to commercialize the new technology, i.e. complementary assets, and the new entrants are unable to integrate forward because of lack of capital and/or difficulty in building the appropriate downstream assets, then extensive inter-firm cooperation between incumbents and new entrants may ensue. Such inter-firm cooperation is motivated by a search for mutually complementary assets. It generally occurs in an industry where a few dominant incumbents control access to the market while many new entrants provide the technology.'
Magnusson et al. *(2003)*	'… discontinuous innovation refers to the development or application of new technologies, concepts or ideas. … Thus discontinuous innovation involves capabilities that do not exist in current products and cannot be achieved through extensions based on existing technologies.' 'In the case of architectural innovation, the discontinuity relates to the establishment of completely new interfaces between components. … In the case of modular innovation, the discontinuity relates to the introduction of new component technologies …' 'Radical innovation involves both the introduction of new component technologies (modular innovation) and the formation of new linkages (architectural innovation).'
Macher and Richman (2004)	'… discontinuous innovation as either radical or architectural …' 'Radical innovation requires knowledge that is usually based on engineering and scientific principles that are unfamiliar with incumbent firms. While such innovation opens up new markets, it also requires new and different … skills …'

	'Architectural innovation is the way in which the components of a product offering are linked together. … architectural innovation reconfigures established "systems" in new and (potentially) novel ways and … destroys … existing architectural knowledge.' '… discontinuities that trigger periods of technological and competitive ferment.'
Bessant et al. *(2005)*	'… dislocation happens because of the emergence of a completely new technology which offers a new or significantly different/improved functionality.'
Phillips et al. *(2006)*	'Discontinuous Innovation requires "doing things differently" and is "inherently messy", fraught with uncertainty and unfamiliarity.' 'Discontinuous Innovations do not follow conventional pathways, and the application of existing routines, procedures, skills and knowledge may not be appropriate.' 'DI differs from the so called "step change" as it results in not simply doing the same but to much higher levels of achievement, but in doing something entirely different.'
Birkinshaw et al. *(2007)*	'… new technologies, products or business models that represent a dramatic departure from the current state of the art in the industry.' '… development of an entirely new technology …'

Multidimensional and Other Types of Innovation of a More Important Magnitude of Novelty

Some scholars introduce the notion of basic innovation to characterize an innovation with a higher degree of novelty. Although this concept is not a subject of this research, it very much resembles one of the three terms we are looking at in this research. Table 5 shows a synopsis of the definitions.

Table 5. Definitions of 'basic innovation'.

Author	Definitions
Barr and Knight (1968)	'… basic structural changes or minor design and component improvements. Basic structural innovations change the entire mode of operation and performance …' '… we have a continuous form of technological change if the number of identifiable major structural changes is zero … we get measurable [discontinuous] jumps in performance with basic structural innovations.'
Mensch (1978)	'By basic innovations I mean social and technological innovations that create completely new social benefits, new lines of service or industrial products in the public sector or in the private business … which …

	necessitate the creation of new "markets", many new jobs, and profitable investment possibilities.'
Mensch (1985)	'… new technology developed in another subindustry is transferred into a seemingly mature, steady-state market where it quickly moves buyers, shifts market shares, and transforms market structures.'

Similarly this is true for the multidimensional Henderson and Clark (1990) model. The authors distinguish between incremental, modular, architectural and radical innovation. Their model is not simply a black-and-white model of magnitude, unfamiliarity and performance leaps. Both architectural and modular innovation types can be innovations of a higher magnitude. It depends on the degree of newness of the product components (modular) or the complexity of the architectural compositions (architectural). In the end, their model serves as an extension to the classical dichotomy model. It also shows that the same term can have different meanings. Henderson and Clark (1990), for example, employ the terms 'radical innovation' and 'architectural and modular innovations' in one of their models. Here, they use 'radical innovation' in a slightly different way from other authors in the 1990s. Referring to Henderson and Clark's model of architectural and modular innovations, the argument that innovation takes place on different levels and sub-levels culminating in a new technology is specified in more detail by Magnusson *et al.* (2003). Each single 'level-innovation' is a radical one or represents a discontinuity, whereas the top-level product might be a 'bigger innovation', or not (Magnusson *et al.*, 2003).

Another author, Mensch (1985), states that 'some innovations are complex because they involve very new technology or a dramatic change in user systems'. Moreover, complexity can also arise due to the mix of the following dimensions: product, process and service. His model corresponds to a triangle with the legs representing each dimension. For Mensch, the most radical innovations involve all three dimensions and can be expected to be located close to the centre of the triangle.

Results of Analysis of Definition Differences

The definitions of all three concepts included descriptions of the following: future technical content/inventions, change in industry/market structures, competence-destroying, customer/market unfamiliarity, departure from existing practice, dislocation, displacement of established products, disruptive effects on industry, high degree of new knowledge, high price/performance improvement, initially lower performance/ functionality/price, large technological change, modular and architectural, new dominant design/core design concepts, new products/ businesses/markets/industries, new to the world, non-existent capabilities/ something entirely different, paradigm shift/new principles, quantum leap in customer value/benefit, satisfies needs for the first time, satisfies not yet perceived needs, significant change in output, superior trajectory/learning curve gap, non-programmed/linear/routine.

As shown in Fig. 1, there are strong similarities between the attributes of all three innovation terms. Some attributes only intersect between two of the terms, whereas some seem to be significant for just one type of innovation. The most frequently cited attributes for all three are large technological change, new products/markets/industries, change in market structures, high uncertainty, high degree of new knowledge, departure from existing practice, high price/performance shifts and paradigm shifts.

'Radical innovation' was characterized as follows: significant change in output, affects future technical content, a quantum leap in customer benefit, satisfies needs for the first time. The following terms were reserved exclusively for discontinuous innovation: technological punctuation/shift/breakthrough, satisfies not yet perceived needs, entirely different/dislocation. And finally, only disruptive innovation was characterized by the following notions: initially lower performance/ functionality/price, displaces established products, disrupts incumbents. No intersection could be identified applying only to radical and disruptive innovation. The following terms could be found in the context of both definitions of 'radical' and 'discontinuous' innovation: new to the world, modular and architectural, disruptive effects on industry. At the intersection between 'discontinuous' and 'disruptive' innovation, the following descriptions are found: sometimes entirely different, sometimes competence destroying. The attributes of all the papers and articles analysed can be seen in Fig. 1. In order to see differences over the past 20 years (publication period for the majority of the papers), the attributes have been looked at in three different periods, starting with period 1 before 1990 (Fig. 2), period 2 from 1990 to 1999 (Fig. 3) and period 3 after 2000 (Fig. 4).

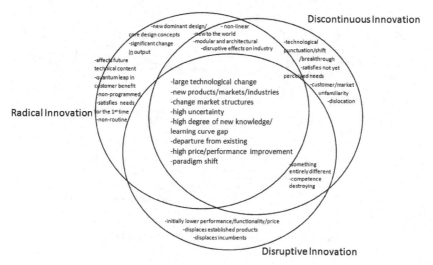

Fig. 1. Attribute intersection (all years).

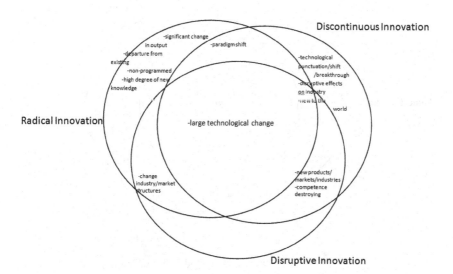

Fig. 2. Attribute intersection period 1 (before 1990).

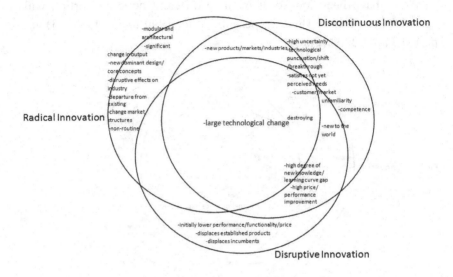

Fig. 3. Attribute intersection period 2 (1990–1999).

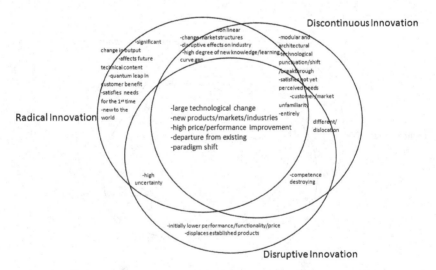

Fig. 4. Attribute intersection period 3 (from 2000).

Figures 2 through 4 refer to defined time periods. As can be seen, before 1990 there was no specific definition for 'disruptive innovation'; it overlapped with the other two terms, meaning it was used with a similar definition to these terms. It was only with the publication of Christensen's seminal book in 1997, when he defined the term 'disruptive innovation', that the definition began to take on a specific meaning (Christensen, 1997). 'Disruptive innovation' now had a distinct definition with discrete characteristics: initially lower performance/functionality/price. The definitions of the two other terms, 'radical innovation' and 'discontinuous innovation', did not change over the same period.

It seems that Christensen has 'occupied' the notion of 'disruptive innovation', giving it a very distinct meaning; more importantly, the academic community has clearly recognized this (e.g. Adner and Zemsky, 2005; Tidd *et al.*, 2005; Georgantzas and Katsamakas, 2007). When writing about disruptive innovation now, it is important for authors to note whether they are referring to the pre- or post-Christensen period (e.g. Abernathy and Clark, 1985; Mensch, 1985). Interestingly, in early papers Christensen did not use the term 'disruptive innovation'. He used 'radical innovation', meaning innovations 'which disrupted established trajectories of technological progress' (Rosenbloom and Christensen, 1994; Christensen and Rosenbloom, 1995).

Conclusions

This research has led to two important findings. First, analysis of the literature to a certain extent confirms the initial supposition that there is no clear definition of what is 'radical innovation' and what is 'discontinuous innovation'. The core elements of both concepts are too congruent to indicate a clear difference. By and large, both are used as synonyms. Interestingly though, in recent years, a number of new notions and refined concepts for each term have appeared. The term 'disruptive innovation' has branched off from the notion of radical innovation due to an effective definition provided by Christensen (1997). Despite this, some authors still seem to refer to a pre-Christensen definition. This is easy to see in the literature as authors referring to Christensen make distinct reference to him.

Second, the research clearly shows that selection of the terms pertaining to innovations of a larger magnitude seems to be an evolutionary process. The definitions of the three terms have undergone a gradual change over time. Very clearly, the notion of disruptive innovation has branched off and grown its own 'species'. While it was once used as a synonym in the public domain, Christensen has managed to give it a distinct definition. With the increasing complexity of the definitions, in the future it is likely that the other two notions will also branch off. The evolutionary process intrinsically excludes a single definition and shows very nicely that academia is dynamic and very much alive.

References

Abernathy, W.J. and Clark, K.B. (1985). Innovation: Mapping the winds of creative destruction. *Research Policy*, 14, 3–22.

Abernathy, W.J. and Utterback, J.M. (1988). 'Innovation over Time and in Historical Context', in Tushman, M.L. and Moore, W.L. (eds), *Readings in the Management of Innovation*. Ballinger, Cambridge, MA, pp. 25–36.

Acee, H.J. (2001). *Disruptive Technologies: An Extended View*. SM Thesis, Management of Technology, Massachusetts Institute of Technology.

Adner, R. and Zemsky, P. (2005). Disruptive technologies and the emergence of competition. *The Rand Journal of Economics*, 36(2), 229–254.

Audretsch, D. and Aldridge, T. (2008). Review of radical innovation in small and large firms. *Journal of Entrepreneurship Education*, 6(4), 241–254.

Augsdörfer, P. (2005). Bootlegging and path dependency. *Research Policy*, 34, 1–11.

Ayres, R.U. (1988). Barriers and breakthroughs: An 'expanding frontiers' model of the technology-industry life cycle. *Technovation*, 7, 87–115.

Barr, J.L. and Knight, K.E. (1968). Technological change and learning in the computer industry. *Management Science*, 14(11), 661–681.

Bessant, J. (2005). Enabling continuous and discontinuous innovations: Some reflections from a private sector perspective. *Public Money and Management,* 25(1), 35–42.

Bessant, J., Lamming, R., Noke, H. and Phillips, W. (2005). Managing innovation beyond the steady state. *Technovation,* 25, 1366–1376.

Birkinshaw, J., Bessant, J. and Delbridge, R. (2007). Finding, forming and performing: Creating networks for discontinuous innovation. *California Management Review,* 49(3), 67–84.

Bower, J.L. and Christensen, C.M. (1995). Disruptive technologies: Catching the wave. *Harvard Business Review,* January/February, 43–53.

Brown, J.S. (1991). Research that reinvents the corporation. *Harvard Business Review,* January/February, 102–111.

Christensen, C.M. (1997). *The Innovator's Dilemma: When New Technologies Cause Great Firms to Fail.* Harvard Business School Press, Boston, MA.

Christensen, C.M., Johnson, M.W. and Rigby, D.K. (2002). Foundations for growth: How to identify and build disruptive new business. *Sloan Management Review,* 433, 22–31.

Christensen, C.M. and Raynor, M.E. (2003). *The Innovator's Solution: Creating and Sustaining Successful Growth.* Harvard Business School Press, Boston, MA.

Christensen, C.M. and Rosenbloom, R.S. (1995). Explaining the attacker's advantage: Technological paradigms, organizational dynamics, and the value network. *Research Policy,* 24, 233–257.

Dahlin, K.B. and Behrens, D.M. (2005). When is an invention really radical? Defining and measuring technological readiness. *Research Policy,* 34, 717–737.

DeTienne, D.R. and Koberg, C.S. (2002). The impact of environmental and organizational factors on discontinuous innovation within high-technology industries. *IEEE Transactions on Engineering Management,* 494, 352–364.

Dewar, R.D. and Dutton, J.E. (1986). The adoption of radical and incremental innovations: An empirical analysis. *Management Science,* 32, 1422–1433.

Dosi, G. (1982). Technological paradigms and technological trajectories. *Research Policy,* 11, 147–162.

Dowd, M.K. and Walsh, S.T. (1998). Managing choice in a disruptive technology. *IEEE Transactions,* 49(4), 442–445.

Ehrnberg, E. (1995). On the definition and measurement of technological discontinuities. *Technovation,* 15(7), 437–452.

Ettlie, J.E. (1983). Organizational policy and innovation among suppliers to the food processing sector. *Academy of Management Journal*, 26(1), 27–44.

Ettlie, J.E., Bridges, W.P. and O'Keefe, R.D. (1984). Organizational strategy and structural differences for radical vs. incremental innovation. *Management Science*, 30, 682–695.

Freeman, C. (1971). The role of small firms in innovation in the UK since 1945. *Bolton Committee Research Report 6*, HMSO, London.

Freeman, C. (1994). The economics of technical change. *Cambridge Journal of Economics*, 18, 463–514.

Freeman, C. and Perez, C. (1988). 'Structural crises of adjustment: Business cycles and investment', in Dosi, G., Freeman, C., Nelson, R., Silverberg, G. and Soete, L. (eds), *Technical Change and Economic Theory*. London, Pinter, pp. 38–66.

Garcia, R. and Calantone, R. (2002). A critical look at technological innovation typology and innovativeness terminology: A literature review. *Journal of Product Innovation Management*, 19, 110–132.

Garud, R. and Munir, K. (2006). Socio-technical dynamics underlying radical innovation: The case of Polaroid's SX-70 camera. *Cambridge Judge Business School Working Paper Series*, 5.

Gemünden, H.G., Salomo, S. and Hölzle, K. (2007). Role models for radical innovations in times of open innovation. *Creativity and Innovation Management*, 16(4), 408–421.

Georgantzas, N.C. and Katsamakas, E. (2007). Disruptive innovation strategy effects on hard-disk maker population: A system dynamics study. *Information Resources Management Journal*, 20(2), 90–107.

Godoe, H. (2000). Innovation regimes, R&D and radical innovations in telecommunications. *Research Policy*, 29, 1033–1046.

Hall, J.K. and Martin, M.J.C. (2005). Disruptive technologies, stakeholders and the innovation value-added chain: A framework for evaluating radical technology development. *R&D Management*, 35(3), 273–284.

Hamel, G. (2002). *Leading the revolution: How to Thrive in Turbulent Times by Making Innovation a Way of Life*. Harvard Business Press, Boston, MA.

Henderson, R.M. (1993). Underinvestment and incompetence as responses to radical innovation: Evidence from the photolithographic alignment equipment industry. *RAND Journal of Economics*, 24(2), 248–270.

Henderson, R.M. and Clark, K.B. (1990). Architectural innovation: The reconfiguration of existing product technologies and the failure of existing firms. *Administrative Science Quarterly*, 35, 9–30.

Herbig, P.A. (1994). *The Innovation Matrix: Culture and Structure Prerequisites to Innovation.* Quorum Books, Westport, CT.

Herrmann, A., Gassmann, O. and Eisert, U. (2007). An empirical study of the antecedents for radical product innovations and capabilities for transformation. *Journal of Engineering and Technology Management*, 24, 92–120.

Kassicieh, S.K., Walsh, S.T., Cummings, J.C., McWhorter, P.J., Romig, A.D. and Williams, W.D. (2002). Factors differentiating the commercialization of disruptive and sustaining technologies. *IEEE Transactions on Engineering Management*, 494, 375–387.

Kleinschmidt, E.J. and Cooper, R.G. (1991). The impact of product innovativeness on performance. *Journal of Product Innovation Management*, 8, 240–251.

Knight, F.H. (1940). *Risk, Uncertainty and Profit, Reprint, 5th Impression.* London School of Economics and Political Science, London.

Knight, K.E. (1967). A descriptive model of the intra-firm innovation process. *Journal of Business*, 40(4), 478–496.

Knight, K.E. and Wind, Y. (1968). Innovation in marketing: An organizational behavior perspective. *California Management Review*, Fall, 67–78.

Lambe, C.J. and Spekman, R.E. (1997). Alliances and external technology acquisition and discontinuous technological change. *Journal of Product Innovation Management*, 14, 102–116.

Leifer, R., McDermott, C., Peters, L., O'Connor, G.C, Rice, M. and Veryzer, R. (2000). *Radical Innovation: How Mature Companies Can Outsmart Upstarts.* Harvard Business School Press, Boston, MA.

Leifer, R., O'Connor, G.C. and Rice, M. (2001). Implementing radical innovation in mature firms: The role of hubs. *Academy of Management Executive*, 15(3), 102–113.

Lettl, C. (2007). User involvement competence for radical innovation. *Journal of Engineering and Technology Management*, 24, 53–75.

Lettl, C., Herstatt, C. and Gemuenden, H.G. (2006). Users' contributions to radical innovation: Evidence from four cases in the field of medical equipment technology. *R&D Management*, 36(3), 251–272.

Linton, J.D. (2002). Forecasting the market diffusion of disruptive and discontinuous innovation. *IEEE Transactions on Engineering Management*, 494, 365–374.

Linton, J.D., Walsh, S., Lombana, C. and Romig, A. (2001). 'Line of sight: A process for transferring science from the laboratory to the market place', in Khalil, T.M., Lefebvre, L.A. and Mason, R.M. (eds), *Management of Technology: The Key to Prosperity in the Third Millennium*. Pergamon, New York, pp. 335–342.

Macher, J.T. and Richman, B.D. (2004). Organizational responses to discontinuous innovation: A case study approach. *International Journal of Innovation Management*, 8(1), 87–114.

Magnusson, T., Lindström, G. and Berggren, C. (2003). Architectural or modular innovation? Managing discontinuous product development in response to challenging environmental performance targets. *International Journal of Innovation Management*, 7(1), 1–26.

Markides, C. (2006). Disruptive innovation: In need of better theory. *Journal of Product Innovation Management*, 23, 19–25.

Martinich, L. (2002). Managing innovation, standards and organizational capabilities. *IEEE Transactions on Engineering Management*, 494, 58–63.

Mascitelli, R. (2000). From experience: Harnessing tacit knowledge to achieve breakthrough innovation. *Journal of Product Innovation Management*, 17, 179–193.

McDermott, C. (1996). Creating a virtual enterprise in manufacturing to manage the risk in discontinuous innovation. *IEMC*, 518, 366–369.

McDermott, C. and Handfield, R. (1996). Does the Parallel Approach Make Sense in the Development of Discontinuous Innovations? *IEMC*, 96, 370–374.

McKee, D. (1992). An organizational learning approach to product innovation. *Journal of Product Innovation Management*, 9, 232–245.

Mensch, G. (1978). 1984: A new push of basic innovations? *Research Policy*, 7, 108–122.

Mensch, G. (1985). PERSPECTIVE: Get ready for innovation by invasion. *Journal of Product Innovation Management*, 4, 259–265.

Mezias, S.J. and Glynn, M.A. (1993). The three faces of corporate renewal: Institution, revolution and evolution. *Strategic Management Journal*, 14, 77–101.

O'Connor, G.C. (1998). Market learning and radical innovation: A cross case comparison of eight radical innovation projects. *Journal of Product Innovation Management*, 15, 151–166.

O'Connor, G.C. and McDermott, C.M. (2004). The human side of radical innovation. *Journal of Engineering and Technology Management*, 21, 11–30.

O'Connor, G.C. and Veryzer, R.W. (2001). The nature of market visioning for technology-based radical innovation. *Journal of Product Innovation Management*, 18, 231–246.

Pavitt, K. (1990). What We Know about the Strategic Management of Technology. *California Management Review*, 32(3), 17–26

Pavitt, K. (1991). Key characteristics of the large innovating firm. *British Journal of Management*, 2, 41–50.

Phillips, W., Lamming, R., Bessant, J. and Noke, H. (2006). Discontinuous innovation and supply relationships: Strategic dalliances. *R&D Management*, 36(4), 451–461.

Phillips, W. and Nokes, H. (2003). Unpublished Literature Review for the DIF Project.

Rice, M.P., Leifer, R. and O'Connor, G.C. (2000). Managing the transition of a discontinuous innovation project to operational status. *IEEE Transactions on Engineering Management*, 586–590.

Rice, M.P., O'Connor, G.C., Peters, L.S. and Monroe, J.G. (1998). Managing discontinuous innovation. *Research Technology Management*, 41(3), 52–58.

Rosenbloom, R. and Christensen, C. (1994). Technological discontinuities, organizational capabilities, and strategic commitments. *Industrial and Corporate Change*, 3(3), 655–685.

Rothaermel, F.T. (2002). Technological discontinuities and interfirm cooperation: What determines a start-up's attractiveness as alliance partner? *IEEE Transactions on Engineering Management*, 49(4), 388–397.

Rothwell, A., Freeman, C., Horlesey, A., Jervis, V.T.P., Robertson, A.B. and Townsend, J. (1974). SAPPHO updated – project SAPPHO phase II. *Research Policy*, 3, 258–291.

Rothwell, R. and Gardiner, P. (1988). Reinnovation and robust designs: Producer and user benefits. *Journal of Marketing Management*, 3(3), 372–387.

Salomo, S., Gemünden, H.G. and Leifer, R. (2007). Research on corporate radical innovation systems – A dynamic capabilities perspective: An introduction. *Journal of Engineering and Technology Management*, 24, 1–10.

Schön, D.A. (1963). Champions for radical new innovations. *Harvard Business Review*, March/April, 77–86.

Schumpeter, J.A. (1912 and 2006). *Theorie der wirtschaftlichen Entwicklung, Nachdruck der 1. Auflage*. Duncker & Humbold, Berlin.

Schumpeter, J.A. (1934). *The Theory of Economic Development*. Harvard University Press, Cambridge, MA.

Schumpeter, J.A. (1939). *Business Cycles: A Theoretical, Historical, and Statistical Analysis of the Capitalist Process*. McGraw-Hill Book Company, New York.

Schumpeter, J.A. (1942). *Capitalism, Socialism and Democracy*. Harper & Brothers, New York.

Schumpeter, J.A. (1994). *History of Economic Analysis*. Oxford University Press, Oxford.

Stobaugh, R. (1988). *Innovation and Competition: The Global Management of Petrochemical Products*. Harvard Business School Press, Boston, MA.

Teece, D.J., Pisano, G. and Shuen, A. (1997). Dynamic capabilities and strategic management. *Strategic Management Journal*, 18(7), 509–533.

Tidd, J., Bessant, J. and Pavitt, K. (2005). *Managing Innovation: Integrating Technological, Market and Organizational Change, 3rd Edition*. John Wiley & Sons, West Sussex.

Tripsas, M. (1997). Unraveling the Process of Creative Destruction: Complementary Assets and Incumbent Survival in the Typesetter Industry. *Strategic Management Journal*, 18 (Summer Special Issue), 119–142

Tripsas, M. and Gavetti, G. (2000). Capabilities, cognition, and inertia: Evidence from digital imaging. *Strategic Management Journal*, 21, 1147–1161.

Tushman, M.L. and Anderson, P. (1986). Technological discontinuities and organizational environment. *Administrative Science Quarterly*, 31, 439–465.

Utterback, J.M. (1979). 'The dynamics of product and process innovation in industry', in Hill, C. and Utterback, J.M. (eds), *Technological Innovation for a Dynamic Economy*. Pergamon Press, Oxford, pp. 40–65.

Utterback, J.M. (1996). *Mastering the Dynamics of Innovation*. Harvard Business School Press, Boston, MA.

Utterback, J.M. and Acee, H.J. (2005). Disruptive technologies: An expanded view. *International Journal of Innovation Management*, 9(1), 1–17.

Veryzer, J.R.W. (1998). Discontinuous innovation and the new product development process. *Journal of Product Innovation Management*, 15, 304–321.

von Hippel, E. (1976). The dominant role of users in the scientific instrument innovation process. *Research Policy*, 5, 212–239.

Walsh, S. and Kirchhoff, B. (2000). Disruptive technologies: Innovators' problems and entrepreneurs' opportunity. *IEEE Transactions on Engineering Management*, 494, 319–324.

Wassenaar, C. (2009). *'Discontinous innovation?!' A systematic literature review about discontinuous innovation.* Bachelor's assignment, University of Twente, Enschede.

Part I

Chapter 3

Looking Beyond the Lamp-Post

John Bessant
University of Exeter Business School, UK
Kathrin Möslein
Universität Erlangen-Nürnberg and HHL – Leipzig Graduate School of Management, Germany
Bettina von Stamm
Innovation Leadership Forum, UK

Introduction

Searching is a key part of the innovation process. Whether you're a new entrant looking for a loophole to break into a market or an established player trying to renew and extend your range, innovation depends on how good you are at finding things out. Triggers for innovation come from all directions – customers, competitors, tech labs, governments, and even those wacky Archimedes moments in the bathtub. The challenge is making sure you pick up on them – and continue to do so to provide a steady stream of ideas to fuel the innovation process. And whilst economists may argue about the relative importance of pulls or pushes, the 'Monday morning' question confronting managers is *how?* How do you set up effective intelligence networks, how do you scan the horizon, how do you ensure you have adequate antennae in place to pick up the innovation trigger signals?

It's an old problem and poses a tricky choice. No-one has infinite resources, so you can't cover all the bases, can't look everywhere. So how do you spread the net widely enough to trawl for interesting fish whilst also ensuring you catch enough to keep your customers fed? The key issue is one of balance – you can find plenty of fish if you search in well-established fishing grounds but you'll only catch what everyone else can. You also need to make the occasional expedition into uncharted waters to find something others won't.

This exploit/explore dilemma has been around for a long time and we have not only a good understanding of the theory but plenty of charts and prospecting tools to help us organize for both kinds of expedition (Benner and Tushman, 2003). That doesn't mean the task is without its problems – by their nature the two kinds of search are very different and set up tensions across the organization. Searching isn't the same as finding and there's always some element of risk involved, some degree of betting the scarce resources of the business in order to carry it out. Arguing the case for one or the other leads to boardroom battles and spreads out across the organization, for example in the operations vs. research split where the one thinks the organization would be a lot better off without the other. Resolving these tensions requires a degree of ambidexterity – the ability to balance both styles under the same organizational roof – and things don't always go smoothly (Birkinshaw and Gibson, 2004).

Looking with Different Eyes: The Framing Problem

But there's another search challenge which goes beyond managing the exploit/explore dilemma. For as long as the search takes place within an accepted frame of reference – a way of looking at the world – then there's a good chance these tensions can be resolved. But these frames – dominant logic, business model, industry trajectory, etc. – are just that: frames. They are ways of making sense of a massively complex world – and whilst they help us deal with what psychologist Jerome Bruner famously called the 'blooming, buzzing confusion' (Bruner, 1983), they are simplifications. Nothing wrong with that – models are representations which help us make sense of things and act rather than stand bewildered and perplexed. A map isn't the territory but it gives us a simpler view of the world so we can work out how to travel around in it. But we shouldn't forget that such models are ways of looking at and interpreting the facts – not the facts themselves (Hodgkinson and Sparrow, 2002).

It's helpful to have a shared view of the world – but we need to remember that not everyone sees it in the same way. This is, of course, why business model innovation is so powerful: by looking through a different frame new things come to light as problems to be solved or opportunities to be exploited. Equally, old ones drop out of focus – they aren't as important in the new scheme of things. Thomas Kuhn in his famous studies of scientific progress talked about the 'paradigm shift' – the process whereby the world view held by the majority of scientists which they use to guide their research and theory-building is challenged and eventually replaced by a new way of looking at things. It isn't an easy or comfortable process – not for nothing did the title of Kuhn's book refer to scientific *revolutions* – but it does demonstrate the power of frames in shaping where and how we search (Kuhn, 1962).

Frames are hugely important in thinking about the search question because they define the space within which we look. We can concentrate our attention on exploiting knowledge which lies close at hand or explore the fringes of that space – in both cases creating innovations in products, services and processes. Searching can be both incremental – exploit – and radical, pushing the limits of our knowledge. Both strategies enable what Clayton Christensen calls 'sustaining' innovation and involve extensive and thorough search within the space defined by our frame of reference (Christensen *et al.*, 2007).

The trouble is that these innovation search skills may not be enough. Even smart firms with well-balanced mechanisms for dealing with exploit/explore can find themselves occasionally blind-sided by developments which take place right at the edge – or even off – their radar screens. Consider the music industry, a huge global network of artist and repertoire scouts, producers, marketing and promotional experts and a catalogue of established artistes – and how that world has been turned upside down by the Internet-driven revolution in creation and consumption.

And even if they do see the faint blip on the edge of the screen they may decide it's simply noise or clutter and not worth looking at. Their focus of attention is, quite rightly, on what they see as the core important things involved in their frame of reference. The view of Encyclopaedia Britannica and other knowledge providers was that their business was not the same as that being served by the new computer disk-based entrants such as Microsoft's Encarta. Yet the stepping stone that represented became a superhighway to a much wider readership using – and even creating – information resources such as Wikipedia, and leaving the original players stranded on a quiet by-road. In fact organizations have a well-developed repertoire of responses for rejecting the unfamiliar or strange – a kind of 'immune system' which stops them from committing time or energy to things which don't fit their frame.

Unfortunately these weak signals may spell out early warning of significant – and discontinuous – change in their industry. It might be a new market constituency emerging out of the needs of previously under-served or un-served markets – by definition new markets don't suddenly appear out of thin air, perfectly formed. They arise at the fringe amongst a bunch of people who want something none of the others do. For example, the early days of personal computing weren't characterized by queues of people outside the Apple store but by a few geeks sharing ideas and experiences around the weird and wonderful gadgets they had put together in their garages. Music and video downloading didn't start to happen because Sony's market research group saw opportunities for working with a non-existent market based on kids wanting to swap and share their favourite tunes. And low-cost airlines such as Southwest, Ryanair and EasyJet didn't set out with the aim of taking market share from British Airways or other flag carriers – they looked for markets which didn't exist, such as students and pensioners, and nurtured the business on the back of those. It was only when the parents of those students began to see the economic advantages of low-cost travel that the innovation became disruptive to the mainstream marketplace.

Or the tranquillity of the industry may be shattered by a new application using a technology emerging from outside the dominant industry space. The shattering of the cosy world of stock broking by the rise of online dealing is only a recent episode of a very long-running series of technology-fuelled transitions – the steamship usurping the sailing boat, the refrigerator displacing the ice harvesters or the typewriter revolutionizing the printing industry (Utterback, 1994).

Sometimes the trigger is in the context – the rules of the game – within which things happen. Just like the weather, these can change and sometimes do so rapidly – and when it suddenly starts to pour down with rain in the middle of a summer afternoon at an open-air concert, the guy who'd seen it coming and brought an umbrella (better yet, a spare umbrella!) is suddenly very popular. Enron may have ended its life in disgrace for financial shenanigans, but it began as a small gas pipeline supplier who saw early enough the big shifts coming in the utility industry as it deregulated – and developed a whole new game of utility trading in which it became the dominant player.

The result in each of these cases is the same – disruption. These weak signals may be the harbingers of a discontinuous shift in which the game changes – the old rules no longer apply, the carpet is pulled out from beneath the current players and the stage is set for a new scene which may involve new characters and leave behind the old. We know that under these circumstances the existing incumbents are often at a disadvantage relative to the new kids on the block.

It seems hard to believe that otherwise smart firms could miss something which – with hindsight – seems so obvious. How could they not get that the world was changing and do something about it? How does a smart firm such as Polaroid or Digital fail to spot the industry-changing tsunami until it has washed over them and left behind the wreckage of a formerly great firm? The answer isn't that these firms weren't looking – in fact they had committed extensive resources to the search process in technologies, markets and competitors. The problem wasn't even in *where* they were looking. The issue was instead in *how* they were doing it, as they were viewing the world through a particular frame and missing some key insights as a result (Tripsas and Gavetti, 2000). Reframing has major significance for innovation because the frame shapes where and how we look. We may simply not be looking in the right direction, or we may be looking with inadequate instruments – using a microscope to scan the stars. (How do you research and analyse markets that don't exist?) Or we look but with selective perception, which is to say, we see the things we want to see, even when we try to explore new territory. IBM's heartache in the early 1990s wasn't a case of being surprised by the shift to networked computing – they had research and even registered patents in the area. They could see it happening but chose to ignore its significance – a degree of selective perception which nearly broke the company and needed the arrival of a fresh pair of eyes in a new CEO to help them reframe the game as one of providing solutions, not pushing boxes.

Reconfiguring the Search System

The reframing problem is also difficult because it requires *rewiring* the knowledge systems used. As long as we stay within the frame the knowledge flows support a virtuous circle of *sustaining* innovation which grows the industry. Most of the time this involves incremental improvement – 'doing what we do but better' – but from time to time there may be larger jumps. Smart firms are often radical innovators, pushing the frontiers of knowledge through extensive exploration – but they are still working within their established frame.

This isn't a solo act – smart firms become adept at working closely with customers, suppliers and other players to help them run a successful innovation system in which regular and well-managed search leads to the kinds of innovation players will value. Building strong ties generates a healthy flow of innovation and everyone wins.

However, if the architecture changes – if there is a need to look through a different frame – then this set of assets becomes a liability. Knowledge needs to flow along different channels and between different points – we need to make new and different connections. For a newcomer firm that's not a problem – they lay down their knowledge networks from scratch and can begin to exploit the new opportunities offered by the emerging new model. The trouble is that for established players there is a natural tendency to reinforce the existing systems since those systems used to work so well for them. This strategy risks compounding the problem – the old networks can get in the way, overriding or clashing with the emerging new ones. Knowledge wires get tangled up and on occasion the result can cause short-circuits (Henderson and Clark, 1990).

For example, as Clayton Christensen points out, when the disk drive industry began to change with the emergence of new players, the response of the incumbent players wasn't to sit still and do nothing. The problem wasn't that they didn't listen to customers – they listened really well – but they were listening to the *wrong* customers. And all the organizational systems for reward and reinforcement supported the old wiring, which made the emergence of new connections very difficult. No wonder new entrants often make a better job of it when it comes to reframing and organizing search behaviour – they only have one set of wiring to develop and use, not the challenge of simultaneously disconnecting and rewiring (Christensen, 1997).

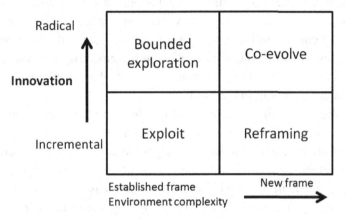

Fig. 1. A map of the innovation search space.

Figure 1 shows a map on which we can examine this innovation search challenge. The vertical axis refers to the familiar 'incremental/radical' dimension in innovation – how novel are the ideas we are going to deploy? On the other axis we've put 'complexity' – the number of elements in the environment which our organization puts into its frame *and* all their potential interactions. When we simplify our way of looking at the world to concentrate on a few elements then things are manageable – but as we increase the number of things we consider and as the ways in which they could interact increases, so things rapidly become unpredictable. As we move left to right so the number of different ways of seeing and framing the world grows.

Zone 1 is essentially the 'exploit' domain and presumes a stable and shared frame – 'business as usual' – within which adaptive and incremental development takes place. Search behaviour is all about refining and sharpening tools for technological and market research and deepening relationships with established key players. As the sector matures so the tools become ever more refined and subtle.

Responsibility for this kind of search lies with specialist departments responsible for market research, product (service) development, etc.

They build strong external networks with customers, suppliers and other relevant partners, and put considerable effort into managing these relationships. For example, Coloplast (a Danish medical devices firm, featured in Chapter 16 of this book) has built a considerable reputation for innovation by working closely with specialist nurses around the world who contribute ideas, test prototypes and generally form part of a very successful front end of innovation in the business. This valuable set of relationships is 'owned', managed and developed by a senior management team within the business.

At the same time, there are high levels of participation in the innovation process by others across the organization – because the search questions are clearly defined and widely understood, high involvement of non-specialists is possible. So procurement, sales and marketing can provide a valuable channel for feeding in ideas from outside whilst process innovation can be enabled by inviting suggestions from within the organization for incremental improvement – the *kaizen* model (Imai, 1987).

Zone 2 involves searching new territory, pushing the frontiers of what is known and then deploying different search techniques accordingly. This still takes place within the same basic frame – 'business model as usual'. R&D involves making a few big bets on the front edge of an established technological trajectory (for example semiconductor firms using Moore's law to target their activity and using patenting and other intellectual property (IP) strategies to mark out and stake claims on the new territory they find). Market research similarly aims to push the frontiers of understanding the customer via empathic design, latent needs analysis, etc.

Carrying out this kind of search is the province of specialists, often located in separate dedicated facilities. They mobilize external networks of other specialists – for example R&D groups link with university, public and commercial laboratories and co-ordinate joint ventures around particular areas of deep technology exploration. In a similar fashion market research includes a rich network of external professional agencies working on providing sophisticated business intelligence around a focused frontier. The highly specialized nature of the work makes it difficult for others in the organization to participate – and indeed this gap between worlds can often lead to tensions between the operating and the exploring units and the boardroom battles between these two camps as resources are often tense.

These first two zones represent familiar territory in search behaviour. They take place within a way of seeing the world which shapes perceptions of what is relevant and important – the 'box' that organizations occasionally talk about wanting to get out of. Nevertheless, this frame is not the only way of looking at the world – and zone 3 is associated with *reframing*. It involves searching a space where alternative architectures are generated, exploring different permutations and combinations of elements in the environment. This process is risky and often results in failure but can also lead to the emergence of new and powerful alternative models. Significantly this often happens by working with elements in the environment not embraced by established business models – for example, working with extreme users or fringe markets.

Developing the low-cost airline industry involved rethinking many of the elements – turnaround times at airports, modified plane designs, different Internet-based booking and pricing models, etc. – and addressing markets such as students and pensioners who had not been major elements in the traditional business model. Much of the growth in mobile telephony is coming from emerging markets which have very different cost structures and usage patterns (including fractional ownership) – but which are leading major players such as Vodafone and Nokia to rethink their models and learn new approaches. Importantly, such experimentation at the edge may identify alternative models which then migrate back to the mainstream – what John Seely Brown calls 'innovation blowback' (Seely Brown, 2004).

Consider developments in India where the giant Tata Corporation is building the 1-Lakh car (the Tata Nano) – essentially trying to bring automobiles to the masses at an affordable price. One way of framing this is to see it as offering 'cheap and cheerful' models to suit an undiscriminating market. But another is to see the Tata Nano as a 21st-century version of the Model T, and the extensive work which Tata is putting into developing an entirely new system – a network of suppliers, service agents, driving schools, insurance companies, etc. – as creating a new model which may pose significant threats to the mainstream auto industry. Of course this bold plan may founder on the rising costs of fuel and raw materials – but if they can make it work at a price tag of $3,000 and learn from the vast markets this opens up, then they could do what the low-cost airlines have done for air transportation.

This may involve extensive learning across sectors, looking for analogies – essentially broad search rather than frontier search. Since it also tries to include new or previously excluded elements there is also strong focus on market and user information – it is here that understanding different user needs can help reframe alternative models.

Zone 4 is where new-to-the-world innovation takes place. It's the 'edge of chaos' – a complex environment where innovation emerges as the result of complex interactions between many independent elements. Processes of amplification and feedback reinforce what begin as small shifts in direction and only gradually define a trajectory. It's the pattern in the innovation life cycle before a dominant design emerges and sets the standard – what is often called the fluid or ferment state. All sorts of things are possible because they're bubbling away in a soup of possibilities – the challenge is finding which one will actually amount to something.

Search strategies here are difficult since it is, by definition, impossible to predict what is going to be important or where the initial emergence will start and around which feedback and amplification will happen. Under such conditions the strategy breaks down into three core principles:

- Be in there
- Be in there early
- Be in there influentially (i.e. in a position to be part of the feedback and amplification mechanisms).

The difficulty is that you don't have any clear idea at the outset about where 'there' happens to be – the best you can do is to position yourself in the space where things might happen, for example where different stakeholders converge. Think, for example, about the looming healthcare challenge around chronic diseases such as diabetes. An ageing population and rising childhood obesity are deemed to represent a time bomb which will create an unsustainable load on healthcare systems. There will be new solutions – innovations – to deal with the challenge, but at this stage it is impossible to predict what they will be since they are going to emerge out of the interplay of some very powerful stakeholders with very different perspectives. Something will come out of the co-evolution of healthcare funders, insurance companies, pharmaceutical and medical devices companies, patient associations, carers and the patients themselves. Faced with this challenge, the smart strategy would be to try to position the organization at the centre of the debate and thus be able to pick up early on possible trends and begin to influence the debate and the emergent innovation trajectory. Innovation search here is less about following a clear lead than placing a number of 'probe and learn' bets.

Working in this zone has formed part of the innovation strategy of Danish pharmaceutical company Novo Nordisk. In 2003 they helped set up the Oxford Health Alliance (OxHA), an independent non-governmental organisation (NGO), whose aim is to prevent the epidemic of chronic disease and whose mission is 'to raise awareness among influencers and educate critical decision-makers so that the pressing case for preventative measures can advance, and we can begin to combat chronic disease' (Oxford Health Alliance, 2010).

Novo Nordisk CEO Lars Rebien Sørensen doesn't underestimate the mindset change this represents:

> in moving from intervention to prevention – that's challenging the business model where the pharmaceuticals industry is deriving its revenues! … We believe that we can contribute to solving some major global health challenges – mainly diabetes – and at the same time create business opportunities for our company.

It was a view echoed at the launch by Lise Kingo (Executive VP of Novo-Nordisk): 'We are not heading for a paradigm shift; we're already in the middle of one in terms of how we treat chronic diseases'.

Professor Stig Pramming, Executive Chairman of OxHA, sees it as a laboratory, a place where different kinds of exploration can happen with and amongst key stakeholders from diverse backgrounds. A key underlying theme is reframing from pharmaceutical treatment to prevention through diet, exercise and lifestyle changes. This course of action carries with it major challenges for the company and even an element of thinking outside the box; after all, the pharmaceutical industry is oriented towards disease! It is a long-term project where the concept of emergence becomes central – innovation is going to be the product of a process of co-evolution. However, as Mads Øvlisen, Chairman of Novo Nordisk, put it: 'unless we get out there, get our foot in the water – unless we dare to take some risks, we're never going to get anywhere!' A summary of the challenges posed by the four zones is given in Table 1.

Table 1. Summary of the challenges posed by the four zones.

Zone	Search challenges	Tools and methods	Enabling structures
1: 'Business as usual' – innovation but under steady-state conditions, little disturbance around core business model	Exploit – extend in incremental fashion boundaries of technology and market. Refine and improve. Close links/strong ties with key players	'Good practice' entailing new product/service development. Close to customer. Technology platforms and systematic exploitation tools	Formal and mainstream structures. High involvement across organization. Established roles and functions (including production, purchasing, etc.).
2: 'Business model as usual' – bounded exploration within this frame	Explore – push frontiers of technology and market via advanced techniques. Close links with key strategic knowledge sources	Advanced tools in R&D and market research. Increasing open innovation approaches to amplify strategic knowledge search resources	Formal investment in specialized search functions – R&D, market research, etc.

3: Alternative frame – taking in new/ different elements in the environment. Variety matching, alternative architectures	Reframe – explore alternative options, introduce new elements. Experimentation and open-ended search. Breadth and periphery important	Alternative futures. Weak signal detection. User-led innovation. Extreme and fringe users. Prototyping – probe and learn. Creativity techniques. Bootlegging, etc.	Peripheral/*ad hoc*. Challenging – 'licensed fools'. CV units. Internal entrepreneurs, scouts futures groups, brokers, boundary spanning and consulting agencies
4: Radical – new-to-the-world – possibilities. New architecture around as yet unknown and established elements	Emerge – need to co-evolve with stakeholders. Be in there. Be in there early. Be in there actively	Complexity theory – feedback and amplification, probe and learn, prototyping and use of boundary objects	Far from mainstream. 'Licensed dreamers.' Outside agents and facilitators

Four Challenges in Innovation Search

So how do organizations search the different zones on the chart? Since each zone represents a different kind of challenge they are going to need to use different methods and tools – and whilst the toolbox is well stocked for zones 1 and 2, the same can't be said for zones 3 and 4. Here, there is a need to try new approaches, develop new and parallel structures and evolve new roles, tools and techniques.

Smart firms get this – they know the risk of local search and of bounded exploration – they recognize that you can't afford to live in your box and need periodic and systematic excursions outside. They have learned how to resolve the explore/exploit tensions within their frames but see a need to move outside – to develop parallel mechanisms which can help them handle the search problem on the right-hand side of the table. The question is how?

It's not simply a matter of setting up a special scouting group, or even hiring consultants more familiar with the new space or model. Extending the search repertoire means dealing with four major challenges.

The 'lamp-post' problem

A powerful metaphor for the problem is the story of the drunk looking desperately for his keys under the lamp-post outside the bar. When asked why he's looking there instead of where he actually dropped them he explains that it's easier to search under the lamp-post because it's lighter there! Smart firms know how to search close to their own lamp-posts – they have a deep understanding of the technologies, markets, competitors and customers within which they normally operate. But the problem of disruption is that the signals which give early warning of this aren't going to emerge in that space, they'll emerge somewhere out in the darkness instead. And there are 360 degrees of dark space to look in – not even the best-resourced firm can afford to cover all that territory. So how do they handle the challenge of exploring the deep, dark areas?

The 'messenger' problem

Faced with the 'lamp-post' challenge firms find different ways of sending out search parties into the dark space to try to pick up weak signals about potential innovation challenges. What happens though when the scouts come back with a message that's way outside the normal? Firms can often exhibit signs of what psychologists call cognitive dissonance – they have a view of what the world is like and when something comes along challenging these views they are very good at doing things to the message to make it fit their view rather than change their minds. They reinterpret the information, they discount its importance ('It's not our business/not a business/not invented here', etc.) and they reshape their view of the world to accommodate the new information without changing their underlying view. In other words, they see the world the way they want to see it – and on occasion this selective perception may require shooting the messenger to get rid of anything which reminds them of the irritating fact that it doesn't really fit their world view. So part of the search challenge is how to get ideas heard and then consequently how to repress the 'immune system', which might be best done with some kind of temporary 'immune-suppressant'.

The 'rewiring' problem

Innovation is a multi-player game and involves building and managing networks – customers, suppliers, brokers and intermediaries, even at times collaborators who are also competitors. Getting these networks to perform effectively is a time-consuming learning process in which different knowledge sets are wired up to the system – and when it works it can deliver a steady stream of innovation of the sustaining variety. But when the challenge is to search in new places and develop a new frame, these connections aren't much help and may even get in the way. The challenge here is to build new networks to make the new frame work – and this involves finding, forming and getting them to perform.

Finding refers essentially to the breadth of search that is conducted. How easy is it to identify the right individuals or organizations with which to interact? By definition this process involves new players and may require considerable effort to locate the right participants. It is hindered by a combination of geographical, technological and institutional barriers (Birkinshaw *et al.*, 2007).

Forming refers to the attitude of prospective partners towards your firm. How keen are they likely to be to work with you? Do you expect them to work hard to build the relationship themselves, or do you expect them to resist your overtures because of their different perspectives?

Performing is about making such relationships work to deliver value. Do the anticipated synergies actually emerge and what needs to be done to ensure this happens? How can you be sure there is a win–win situation for all players and what new operating frameworks will you need to ensure this happens?

The 'balancing' problem

Dealing with different zones sets up tensions across the organization because the ways of searching involve different approaches. Their use – and the structures which enable them – pose challenges for the organization and raise potential conflicts. In particular the approaches which deal with the right-hand side of Fig. 1 – the reframing zones – are often carried out at the fringe or in licensed groups where different rules are seen to apply. Internal entrepreneurship and bootlegging is about encouraging the breaking of rules, whilst corporate venturing often has a philosophy of: 'short life, but a happy one'!

Part of the difficulty of carrying through this role is the relative fragility of the resource commitment – open-ended search is not perceived as core and is threatened with sudden switches when the business environment changes. There is also a challenge around skills and experience – the complex mix of entrepreneurial and search skills makes finding people for the role challenging – and in many cases has been dealt with by outsourcing the activity. In high-velocity and turbulent sectors such as mobile and media there is a significant service sector providing open-ended search – trend spotting, cool hunting, etc., in this fashion. But even when outsourced the organization still needs some form of gateway structure to allow the information to flow back into the decision and resource allocation process.

Expanding the search toolkit

Whilst there is a well-established set of structures and tools for dealing with the left-hand side of our model, the routines for handling zones 3 and 4 are far less developed. Here, the task is less about exploration in depth but rather in *breadth*, developing peripheral vision in order to see new elements in the environment. These techniques are much more about open-ended and open-minded search. They extend the space in which organizations search and allow the possibility of 'bumping into' new elements which may be relevant or could be configured. They are about *generation* of new ideas and options rather than in-depth analysis, and they require a degree of suspension of disbelief on the part of the agent carrying them out – a tolerance for ambiguity about the organization's dominant logic.

So what additional search processes are firms experimenting with as they try to cover the edge of their radar screens? Our work with Innovation Labs across Europe suggests 12 core themes, which are being tried out in different forms, and these are summarized in Table 2.

Table 2. Search strategies for discontinuous innovation.

Search strategy	Mode of operation
Sending out scouts	Dispatch idea hunters to track down new innovation triggers
Exploring multiple futures	Use futures techniques to explore alternative possible futures and develop innovation options from that
Using the Web	Harness the power of the Web, through online communities and virtual worlds, for example, to detect new trends
Working with active users	Team up with product and service users to see the ways in which they change and develop existing offerings
Deep diving	Study what people actually do, rather than what they say they do
Probing and learning	Use prototyping as mechanism to explore emergent phenomena and act as boundary object to bring key stakeholders into the innovation process
Mobilizing the mainstream	Bring mainstream participants into the product and service development process
Corporate venturing	Create and deploy venture units with the mandate to find and exploit radical ideas
Corporate entrepreneurship and intrapreneuring	Stimulate and nurture the entrepreneurial talent inside the organization
Using brokers and bridges	Cast the idea net far and wide and connect with other industries
Deliberate diversity	Create diverse teams and a diverse workforce
Idea generators	Use creativity tools to stimulate new search directions

Sending out scouts

A good place to start the search process is with dedicated scouts – sending out people (full- or part-time) whose role is to search actively for new ideas to trigger the innovation process (in German they are called *Ideenjaeger* – idea hunters – a term which captures the concept well). They could be searching for technological triggers, emerging markets or trends, competitor behaviour, etc., but what they have in common is a remit to seek things out, often in unexpected places. Search is not restricted to the organization's particular industry; in looking for new ways of seeing, the fringes of an industry or even currently entirely unrelated fields can be of interest. For example, German company Arvato works in the high-velocity world of mobile content – messaging, games, entertainment and beyond – which can be delivered on a mobile phone or handheld device. To keep abreast of this they depend on a network of 'cool hunters' working in online communities and in highly segmented youth markets to pick up and test early concepts. But traditional players can also make use of scouts – for example, Swedish paper giant SCA have extensive scouting operations in emerging markets such as India and Africa where weak signals about potential new product or market configurations can be fed back into their innovation process.

Building alternative futures

Another way of handling the search challenge is to imagine alternative futures, especially those which do not necessarily follow the current trajectory. Increasingly firms are moving from straightforward trend extrapolation and into complex scenarios – more like writing science fiction film scripts and employing a team of writers to help them do so. Only in this case the team of writers is drawn from widely different worlds and the 'film' is a rich representation of another future world into which firms – and often their partners and collaborators – can climb to explore threats and opportunities and find triggers for innovation. Increasingly organizations and even sector agencies are building such scenarios and using them as the tent within which shared exploration of future possibilities can take place – for example, Bord Bia is an Irish government agency which configures and co-ordinates such scenario work on behalf of the increasingly sophisticated and global set of food industry players such as Kerry and Glanbia. Companies such as Novo Nordisk not only develop internal futures models (such as their Diabetes 2020 programme) but also use multi-agency forums – such as OxHA – to create, debate and explore futures with chronic disease. These ventures demonstrate a strong sense of corporate social responsibility but they also help provide early warning signals about core markets.

Using the Web

Popular folklore suggests that Reuters began life through getting information back to London most quickly about the outcome of the Battle of Waterloo. These days early warning systems are more advanced and can take advantage of the huge power of the Internet. But the very availability of information sets up its own problem – with some two billion people now connected the challenge becomes one of finding what is relevant. Whilst big strides have been made in search technology – from mass market players such as Google and Yahoo through to specialist knowledge search and management firms such as Autonomy – there is still plenty of scope for creative use of the Web as a way of extending and exploring search space. This strategy seeks to use the power of the Internet to access and explore different developments – connecting to multiple sources of information and operating various forms of Web-enabled marketplace.

In its simplest form the Web is a passive information resource to be searched – an additional space into which the firm might send its scouts. Increasingly there are professional organizations who offer focused search capabilities to help with this hunting – for example, in trying to pick up on emerging 'cool' trends among particular market segments. High-velocity environments such as mobile telecoms, gaming and entertainment depend on picking up early warning signals and often make extensive use of these search approaches across the Web.

This rich information source aspect can quickly be amplified in its potential if it is seen as a two-way or multi-way information marketplace. One of the first companies to take advantage of this was Eli Lilly who set up www.innocentive.com as a match-making tool, connecting those with scientific problems with those able to offer solutions. There are now multiple sites offering a brokering service, linking needs and means and essentially creating a global marketplace for ideas – in the process providing a rich source of early warning signals. BMW, the German automaker, has established its Virtual Innovation Agency as one mechanism to amplify the range and reach of signals about possible new innovation pathways – essentially inviting submissions from companies and individuals via the Web. Another German firm, Webasto, which specializes in roofing systems for carmakers such as BMW, Audi, Porsche and VW, is using the Web as a tool to explore end-user design ideas and create early warnings about new product directions.

Working with active – and extreme – users

User-led innovation isn't a new concept but has become a powerful tool in helping firms explore new ways of framing and of linking into fuzzy and emergent trends before they become mainstream developments. As Eric von Hippel (1986) has shown across a variety of sectors, the ideas and insights of lead users can provide the starting point for very new directions and create new markets, products and services.

The challenge lies in developing ways of working with this principle. Lead users may be key players, but how can we find them? One of the clues is that active users are often at the fringes of the mainstream – in diffusion theory they are not even early adopters but rather active innovators. They are tolerant of failure, prepared to accept that things can go wrong although through mistakes they can get to something better – hence the growing interest in participating in perpetual beta testing and development of software and other online products.

Several firms are combining the power of the Web with user-led approaches – for example, the British Broadcasting Corporation (BBC) is using the Web to help deal with the discontinuous challenges of the new digital media environment. They are trying to engage a rich variety of players in this emerging space via a series of open innovation experiments. One example of this is the now retired BBC Backstage programme. It was an attempt to do with new media development what the open source community did with software development. The model was deceptively simple – developers were invited to make free use of various elements of the BBC's site (such as live news feeds, weather, TV listings, etc.) to integrate and shape innovative applications. The strap line to this was 'use our stuff to build your stuff' – and when the site was launched in May 2005 it attracted the interest of hundreds of software developers up until its closure in 2010. Ben Metcalf, one of the programme's founders, summed up the approach:

> Top line, we are looking to be seen promoting innovation and creativity on the Internet ... if someone is doing something really innovative, we would like to ... see if some of that value can be incorporated into the BBC's core propositions. (Tidd and Bessant, 2011.)

A similar model is being deployed by the UK's Ordnance Survey – a 300-year-old public service agency responsible for cartography but now trying to reposition itself as a commercial provider of geographical information services. In the process it is partnering up with a wide range of firms such as Nokia, Philips and Garmin but it is also opening up its website to invite users to suggest ways forward for joint developments.

Danish toymaker Lego has also developed extensive links with user communities following its success with an open innovation approach with the Mindstorms product. For example, in the area of model trains, they recognized the power of user communities as designers and developers; a group of ten lead users came up with a total of 76 new designs for products which Lego is now able to sell. Its Lego Factory website offers users the chance to design their own projects and Lego will then work out the necessary bricks and components to produce the project together with the relevant building instructions. In this way it is increasingly tapping into a much richer population of designers/ developers.

Deep diving

Most market research has become adept at hearing the voice of the customer via interviews, focus groups, panels, etc. But sometimes what people say and what they actually do is different. And how would you uncover the needs they don't know they have? As Henry Ford once said, 'If I had asked people what they wanted they would have told me: fast horses.' In recent years there has been an upsurge in the use of techniques to get closer to what people need/want in the context in which they operate. 'Deep diving' is one of many terms used to describe the approach – 'empathic design' and 'ethnographic methods' are others (Kelley *et al.*, 2001). This approach has been behind work by the UK's National Health Service Institute for Innovation and Improvement aimed at improving the patient experience – a key driver in the challenging conditions of public health provision in the UK. Their work, watched closely by many other health agencies, includes working closely with patients in developing experience-based design, understanding care and treatment needs and leading to radical service innovation. Approaches of this kind become powerful because they can highlight early indicators of under-served or un-served markets and give clues to new directions and frames for innovation. Looking at behaviour in radically different contexts can generate templates which can translate back to the mainstream – for example, the development of mobile banking via cell phone in countries such as the Philippines and Kenya has provided powerful insights for companies such as Nokia and Vodafone.

Probing and learning

If we don't know what's out there in our innovation space, a useful approach is to send out probes – to carry out controlled experiments whose purpose is not to prove a point but rather to enable learning. Understanding what doesn't work or isn't relevant can be just as helpful when the task is mapping uncharted space. Probe and learn approaches also offer a way of identifying and getting involved with key stakeholders in a process of co-evolution. This is the underlying rationale behind the widespread use of prototyping in developing new products and services – the difference is the context to which this is applied. When trying to get a handle on a fuzzy and emergent future, such boundary objects become powerful ways of focusing attention and giving momentum to emerging innovation.

For example, British Telecom (BT), the telecommunications provider, has been deploying this strategy in the development of an innovative approach to help the elderly live longer at home. BT has a legal responsibility to provide services for all members of society. They have used the connections in this stakeholder network to make an early move into understanding and then creating services for the significantly growing number of ageing people. (It is predicted that by 2026 30% of the UK population will be more than 60 years old (Bessant and Tidd, 2011, p. 60).) The pilot innovation is based on placing sensors in the home to monitor movement and the use of power and water – if something goes wrong it triggers an alarm. It has already begun to generate significant revenues for BT but has also opened up the possibility of relieving pressure on the National Health Service. Estimates suggest savings of around £700 million per year if the service was fully deployed. Most significant, the initial project can be seen as a stepping stone, a transitional object to help BT learn about what will be a huge and very different market in the future.

In another case a successful business strategy for the UK do-it-yourself retailer B&Q has evolved through real-time learning from partnerships between individual stores and local disability organizations. Following pioneering experiments in having stores entirely staffed by older people, B&Q wants to ensure that disabled people are able to access goods and services easily. In the UK alone there are eight million disabled people; it is estimated that the 'disabled pound' could be worth £30 billion in total. However, B&Q also sees this initiative as a way to improve wider customer care competencies: 'if we can get it right for disabled people we can get it right for most people'.

An important aspect of probe and learn strategies is that they represent planned experiments to explore alternative hypotheses – for example, looking for opportunities in the segments of the market they are not active or strong in. It's clear that the centre of gravity as far as economic growth is concerned is moving towards the new economic players in emerging markets such as India and Latin America – and behind them lies the potential of other markets, such as Africa. Developing new products and services to serve the needs of this 'next billion' or seeking 'the fortune at the bottom of the pyramid' is not simply about translating what currently works into a new market context. Instead it is about picking up on – or even setting – new trends which may lead to very different frames and innovation trajectories. For existing mainstream players – such as Unilever, Procter & Gamble (P&G) or SCA – the radically different context of emerging markets provides a powerful laboratory for radically different development paths.

Novo Nordisk is also using this approach to help understand and explore radically different market conditions and business models around diabetes care. For example, its National Diabetes Programmes operate in around 40 countries and represent not only good corporate responsibility practice but also a valuable innovation learning opportunity. The core underlying principle is one of developing and testing generic prototype plans which can then be customized for a variety of other countries. For example, Tanzania was an early pilot. It was initially difficult to convince authorities to take chronic diseases such as diabetes into account since they had no budget for them and were already fighting hard with infectious diseases. With little likelihood of new investment Novo Nordisk began working with local diabetes associations to establish demonstration projects. It set up clinics in hospitals and villages, trained staff and provided relevant equipment and materials. This gave visibility to the possibilities in a chronic disease management approach – for example, before the programme someone with diabetes might have had to travel 200 km to the major hospital in Dar-es-Salaam, whereas now they can be dealt with locally. The value to the national health system is significant in terms of savings on the costs of treating complications such as blindness and amputations, and the expensive consequences of poor and delayed treatment. As a result the Ministry of Health is able to deal with diabetes *management* without the need for new investment in hospital capacity or recruitment of new doctors and nurses. Novo Nordisk is essentially a facilitator here – but in the process is very much centrally involved in an emerging and shifting healthcare *system*. Perhaps more significant is the understanding it develops in the process for how a radically different business model suited to chronic healthcare at low cost might be developed – a challenge which it may confront in coming years in its current mainstream markets in Europe.

Mobilizing the mainstream

An inevitable problem in extending search activity beyond the 'lamp-post' zone is that there aren't enough resources to cover everything. One approach is to add specialized capacity targeted at a particular area, but another is to make better use of existing capacity – to engage players in the organization more actively in the innovation task. For example, it could refocus the core tasks of groups such as procurement, sales or finance staff to pick up peripheral information about trends in the wider world.

The growing cult of open innovation recognizes the significant potential of what P&G call 'connect and develop' in beefing up the innovation process. But in order to succeed it requires ways of making connections to the rich variety of external sources – a bit like the human brain whose potential is only realized when synapses are connected and new patterns of thought are enabled. Reckitt Benckiser have developed a sophisticated early warning system to pick up weak signals about relevant new market trends by mobilizing a large number of its externally facing agents in purchasing, marketing and customer relations.

Corporate venturing

The frontier search problem isn't new – and one approach which has been widely used involves setting up special units with the remit – and more importantly the budget – to explore new diversification options. Loosely termed corporate venture (CV) units, they actually cover a spectrum ranging from simple venture capital funds (for internally and externally generated ideas) through to active search and implementation teams, acquisition and spin-out specialists, etc.

The purpose of corporate venturing is to provide some ring-fenced funds to invest in new directions for the business. Such models vary from being tightly controlled (by the parent organization) to being fully autonomous. Although a popular option, the experience of many firms is that CVs are not always successful; indeed, many fail. As one commentator put it, 'Most CVs have a short life – but a happy one!' Part of the problem is that expectations are often very high but it isn't always easy to spot the significant new directions in which to invest – precisely our DI search problem. What's beginning to emerge is a maturing of models for CV activity which separates out the mainstream entrepreneurial activity from the wilder leap stuff – and provides structures and funding (and organizational patience/tolerance!) across the spectrum. For example, Unilever has not one but three vehicles for their CV activity, whilst Nokia has a similar stable of different CV horses for different courses. Nokia Ventures Organization is focused on corporate venturing activities that include identifying and developing new businesses, or as they put it, 'the renewal of Nokia'. Nokia Venture Partners invests exclusively in mobile and Internet protocol (IP) related start-up businesses. They have a very interesting third group called Innovent that directly supports and nurtures nascent innovators with the hope of growing future opportunities for Nokia.

Other organizations – such as BT with its Wakaba programme and Unipart with its Green Shoots programme – try to provide an internal incubator which links to internal sources of capital to provide vehicles for identifying and progressing radical ideas.

Corporate venturing/intrapreneuring

The other side of setting up a unit with the responsibility for external entrepreneurial activity is to find ways of mobilizing internal entrepreneurship – intrapreneuring. The classic example has been 3M, which gives its scientists 15% of working time to spend on projects of their own choosing and has a set of mechanisms to take bright ideas forward, including various internal development grants and an increasingly difficult venture funding process. More recently attention has been focused on Google, whose policy of allowing its engineers 20% playtime has led to a stream of innovations including Google Mail and Google Earth.

Intrapreneurs offer both a source of new ideas *and* an implementation pathway to make sure those ideas get taken forward. Many intrapreneurship programmes stress the importance of informal networking, bootlegging and other mechanisms to take ideas forward below the radar screen of formal corporate systems (Augsdörfer, 1996).

For example, BMW recognizes the value of what they call 'U-boat' projects which run along below the surface of formal management approval but which can provide ways around the company's immune system. The 3 Series estate car came into being not because of a formal product plan but as a consequence of the efforts of internal bootleggers working below the radar screen. Their nocturnal experimentation included welding together a prototype made from whatever bits they could scavenge – including the chassis of an old VW saloon!

In another variation on this theme Danish enzyme company Novozymes has a strategy of deliberately seeking out experienced entrepreneurs and recruiting them into the company. The idea is that such characters not only provide challenging new perspectives but also make internal waves – as one manager put it, they create a little grit to stimulate the oyster to produce pearls.

Brokers and bridges

Innovation often happens not at the frontier of knowledge but at the boundary between one knowledge set and another. The scope for transferring ideas from one sector to another is huge – and a powerful source of discontinuous innovation. Henry Ford's revolutionary ideas which formed the basis for mass production came from a deliberately recruited team of engineers from diverse industries – meat packaging, grain storage, sewing machine, bicycle construction and even brewing – who shared their ideas and insights to come up with a completely new approach (Hargadon, 2003). Based on the assumption that 'the future is already here, it's just unevenly distributed', many firms are experimenting with ways of making extended connections – 'bridging small worlds'.

It's important to recognize that building links isn't simply a matter of finding new information – it's about making connections, rewiring the firm's knowledge networks. This is placing emphasis on the skills and activities of individuals and groups who can act as brokers or bridges in the process. Sometimes these lie outside the firm – and not every organization can afford the army of technology entrepreneurs which firms such as P&G can muster. Consequently there is considerable growth in business services specializing in different forms of broking – for example Innovation Exchange specializes in confidential company-to-company IP broking whilst other agencies such as the UK's NESTA are working in conjunction with major firms such as P&G to provide a focus for open innovation and connection.

Not all brokerage involves external third parties – there is a long tradition of internal gatekeeping which firms are recognizing and trying to tap into. Many – such as Danish pump-maker Grundfos – are trying to mobilize knowledge across different parts of the company via physical and intranet-linked communities of practice. UK engineering services company Arup has done extensive work on mapping its social networks inside and outside the business to better exploit the connectivity. They have a map of the Arup 'brain' which indicates where connections are made and could be made and who could engineer such links.

Deliberate diversity

'Get close to your customers' or 'Build productive partnerships with your suppliers' are typical and valuable recipes for successful innovation. But under discontinuous conditions there is a risk that 'the ties that bind become the ties that blind', meaning, close, long-term links build and sustain a particular world view which makes reframing difficult. So one strategy for search outside the steady-state zone is to seek out 'odd' partners with whom you wouldn't normally expect to work, but who might bring a fresh way of looking. Instead of emphasizing strategic alliances the idea is short-term 'strategic dalliances'. At the limit there is considerable scope for learning across sectors and out of industry – for example, the UK's NHS Institute for Innovation and Improvement has been facilitating learning events across sectors. In one session they brought the pit stop crew from Ferrari's Formula 1 motor racing team into the Great Ormond Street children's hospital to explore different ways of thinking about fast changeover of patients in the operating theatre and other operating theatre practices!

This idea of deliberately seeking diversity extends to individual recruitment – organizations are realizing the potential value of hiring in very different perspectives to spice up their knowledge mix. Firms whose living depends on being able to generate innovations do this routinely – for example specialist innovation agencies such as ?What If! and IDEO deliberately hire people from backgrounds as diverse as medicine, engineering, anthropology and physics in order to create a team capable of coming up with groundbreaking new ideas.

Idea generators

Last – but by no means least – is the strategy of using creativity tools and techniques to increase the flow of radical ideas. A long tradition of research has shown that organizations can 'get out of the box' and develop new insights and ideas using such tools. This can be done internally – for example UK instrumentation firm Cerulean makes regular use of creativity training to explore radical options for their product range. Or it can make use of external agencies whose role is to provide stimulus and catalyse new thinking. One increasingly interesting option is to recruit representatives from very different sectors to participate in creative sessions – for example the charity Macmillan Cancer Relief recently ran workshops with partners including Royal Mail. NESTA – the UK's National Endowment for Science, technology and the Arts – has been working with Oracle on a pioneering programme, Open Alchemy, which involves facilitated workshops exploring the frontier of current development and beyond, and drawing in participants from widely different sectors, including the BBC, Arup, Rolls-Royce, BP and Virgin Atlantic.

Conclusions

The challenge of discontinuous innovation means that firms have to be able to extend their search space – otherwise they risk being blind-sided by developments going on just out of eyeshot. As George Day and Paul Schoemaker put it, they need to develop peripheral vision (Day and Schoemaker, 2006). But this is easier said than done – not least because searching in new places is costly in resources – our 'lamp-post' problem

– and risky in nature – you may spend a long time looking but not find anything.

The problem isn't one of incremental vs. radical innovation – firms can be very sophisticated in their approaches to managing the explore/exploit question within their existing frames and still be surprised by new developments. A new model which creates new rules for the game doesn't always have to involve radical breakthroughs at the technological frontier but instead can just be a new combination of what is already there. The key requirement is being able to see in new ways – to reframe.

Setting up new approaches to search in unexpected places and try on new frames through which to look at the world brings with it a new set of tensions to manage. Not only is there a need to balance the competing views about committing resources to exploit or explore, but there's also a second dimension associated with existing and new frames. It's hard enough developing ambidextrous capability but when you are being pulled in four directions it gets really tricky! Not surprisingly, many of the agents we spoke with in our DI Lab commented on the relative fragility of their position, of working at the fringes of their organizations.

Of course, developing effective search approaches is part of the solution to the discontinuous innovation challenge – but it is not the whole story. Firms still have to deal with the problem of how they react to incoming signals which may point them in radically different directions and require very different strategies to deal with them.

References

Augsdörfer, P. (1996). *Forbidden Fruit*. Avebury, Aldershot.

Benner, M.J. and Tushman, M.L. (2003). Exploitation, exploration, and process management: The productivity dilemma revisited. *Academy of Management. The Academy of Management Review*, 28(2), 238–256.

Bessant, J. and Tidd, J. (2011). *Innovation and Entrepreneurship, Second Edition*. Wiley and Sons, Chichester.

Birkinshaw, J., Bessant, J. and Delbridge, R. (2007). Finding, forming, and performing: Creating networks for discontinuous innovation. *California Management Review*, 49(3), 67–83.

Birkinshaw, J. and Gibson, C. (2004). Building ambidexterity into an organization. *MIT Sloan Management Review*, 45(4), 47–55.

Bruner, J.S. (1983). *Child's Talk: Learning to Use Language*. Oxford University Press, Oxford.

Christensen, C. (1997). *The Innovator's Dilemma*. Harvard Business School Press, Cambridge, MA.

Christensen, C., Anthony, S. and Roth, E. (2007). *Seeing What's Next*. Harvard Business School Press, Boston, MA.

Day, G.S., Schoemaker, P.J.H. (2006). *Peripheral Vision: Detecting the Weak Signals that Will Make Or Break Your Company*. Harvard Business School Press, Cambridge, MA.

Hargadon, A. (2003). *How Breakthroughs Happen*. Harvard Business School Press, Boston, MA.

Henderson, R. and Clark, K. (1990). Architectural innovation: The reconfiguration of existing product technologies and the failure of established firms. *Administrative Science Quarterly*, 35, 9–30.

Hodgkinson, G. and Sparrow, P. (2002). *The Competent Organization*. Open University Press, Buckingham.

Imai, K. (1987). *Kaizen*. Random House, New York.

Kelley, T., Littman, J. and Peters, T. (2001). *The Art of Innovation: Lessons in Creativity from IDEO, America's Leading Design Firm*. Currency, New York.

Kuhn, T. (1962). *The Structure of Scientific Revolutions*. University of Chicago Press, Chicago.

Oxford Health Alliance (2010). *About Us*.

http://www.oxha.org/about-us/. [Accessed 15 April 2013.]

Seely Brown, J. (2004). Minding and mining the periphery. *Long Range Planning*, 37, 143–151.

Tidd, J. and Bessant, J. (2011). *Managing for Innovation, 4th Edition*. Wiley and Sons, Chichester.

Tripsas, M. and Gavetti, G. (2000). Capabilities, cognition and inertia: Evidence from digital imaging. *Strategic Management Journal*, 2, 1147–1161.

Utterback, J. (1994). *Mastering the Dynamics of Innovation*. Harvard Business School Press, Boston, MA.

von Hippel, E. (1986). Lead users: A source of novel product concepts. *Management Science*, 32(7), 791–805.

Chapter 4

Ambidexterity in the Search Phase of the Innovation Process

Silvia Cantarello, Roberto Filippini, Anna Nosella
University of Padova, Italy

Introduction

Searching for and identifying ideas and knowledge is the starting point of almost all innovation processes (Van den Bosch *et al.*, 2006; Crawford and Di Benedetto, 2003; Backman *et al.*, 2007); in this phase firms are constantly seeking new ideas and knowledge, concerning both the market and technological domains. In particular, they search for knowledge that deepens and improves their existing core knowledge and simultaneously broadens their knowledge base by identifying new possibilities (Argyris and Schön, 1978; March, 1991; Leonard-Barton, 1995). The tension between improving the existing (exploitation) and facing the not previously experienced (exploration) seems to characterize this phase. Managing this tension is fundamental as, on the one hand, an organization that engages excessively in improving existing knowledge undergoes problems such as organizational inertia, competency traps and the conversion of core capabilities into core rigidities (Leonard-Barton, 1992), and on the other hand, engaging too much in the search for completely new and unfamiliar knowledge could lead to many undeveloped ideas and neglecting to improve and adapt existing routines (March, 1991). In other words, firms have to manage the tension between exploitation activities that correspond to the search for familiar, mature, current or proximate knowledge – local search – and exploration activities that correspond to the search for unfamiliar, distant and remote knowledge – distant search. Here, ambidexterity comes into play: ambidextrous firms are those firms that are able to deal with the exploration and exploitation tension (Tushman and O'Reilly, 1996), showing the capability to generate both local and distant knowledge at the same time.

The aim of this work is to study ambidexterity capability in the search phase of the innovation process; in particular we want to look at the differences in terms of search practices between firms that show ambidexterity capability in the search phase of the innovation process and firms that do not show such a capability. In other words our interest is focused on analysing the practices put in place by a sample of Italian firms to search for new knowledge (both local and distant) and to examine if there is some heterogeneity in the use of these practices between ambidextrous and non-ambidextrous firms. To this purpose, a survey has been carried out to collect data from a sample of medium-high- and high-tech Italian firms.

Conceptual Framework

Search practices

Search practices carried out in the first phase of the innovation process aim at both broadening and deepening the company's knowledge base. A variety of search practices has been suggested in the literature (Hargadon and Sutton, 2000; Thomke and von Hippel, 2002; Chesbrough, 2003; Flynn *et al.*, 2003) for generating knowledge that could be used to feed radical and incremental innovations. An extensive literature review reveals that, although the list of practices is not identical across different studies, a similar set of practices for the creation of local and distant knowledge seems to be recommended by most of them. In the following, we separately analyse the practices suggested by the literature for the generation of distant and local knowledge, because these present some area of discrepancies due to the different aims pursued.

Search practices for distant knowledge

If we consider the practices that are commonly used to generate distant knowledge, five cited search practices emerge.

Learning about markets for radical innovation

These practices refer to a set of mechanisms put in place to explore new markets by a firm's specialized functions and dedicated groups of people and by involving users as sources of innovative ideas. Customers are, in fact, viewed as active players in the innovation process whose ideas can provide the starting point for new directions and help create new markets, products and services. This involvement can occur through market research, interviews or by involving lead users (Thomke and von Hippel, 2002).

Connecting internal employees

These practices refer to the set of organizational mechanisms put in place to favour the gathering and dissemination of knowledge in the organization, making it accessible to everyone; thanks to these practices, individuals with different backgrounds and skills are linked together in order to leverage their knowledge and experiences and to learn to view new perspectives (Hargadon and Sutton, 2000; Kelley, 2005).

Openness to external sources

This groups together practices such as attending conferences and events which not only allow the firm to keep up to date with the developments in a particular field of expertise but also provide a useful opportunity to exchange ideas, establish relationships with external stakeholders and encourage various functions to systematically collect ideas and opinions from outside sources such as universities and research centres (Chesbrough, 2003; Linder *et al.*, 2003; Tenenhouse, 2004; Swink, 2006).

ICT for managing the creation of new radical ideas

This set of practices is related to the use of ICT systems in capturing and collecting ideas both inside and outside the organization: company-wide centralized idea management systems to which all employees can submit ideas for evaluation and receive quick feedback, and forums, blogs, wikis, etc., where external participants can submit their ideas or suggest solutions for problems posted by R&D (Chesbrough, 2003; George *et al.*, 2005).

Internal context for supporting radical innovation

These practices include various ways of mobilizing high-involvement innovation across the organization (Gibson and Birkinshaw, 2004; Phillips *et al.*, 2006). They encompass the development of a culture that sustains innovation and communication throughout the organization, supporting within the firm the importance of innovation for their long-term survival. Creating such a culture is not simple and requires a set of mechanisms to put forward bright ideas, including having a dedicated support unit to assist teams involved in innovative activities and the creation of an entrepreneurial environment that sustains, using strong incentive schemes, those employees who put forward innovative ideas (Hargadon and Sutton, 2000; McLaughlin *et al.*, 2008).

Search practices for local knowledge

As outlined by the literature, some of the practices described above can be adopted by firms with the purpose of supporting not only the generation of distant knowledge but also of local knowledge; for this reason, we explicitly distinguish in our questionnaire between search practices that could be used towards the generation of either local knowledge or distant knowledge

The search practices for local knowledge that have been considered in this study are as follows.

Learning about markets for incremental innovation

Some of the practices that are included in this dimension are similar to those used for searching for new knowledge. In particular, practices such as a closer connection with final customers (Leonard-Barton, 2002;

Ulwick, 2002) in order to obtain regular feedback on their demands, as well as the use of conventional market research tools (such as focus groups, interviews and online surveys) are included. We do not include the practices related to searching for completely new markets.

Connecting internal employees

These practices are similar to those identified for distant knowledge generation. They refer to a set of organizational practices through which individuals with different backgrounds and skills are linked together and exchange their knowledge and experience, and so favour the improvement of the firm's existing knowledge base (Hargadon and Sutton, 2000; George *et al.*, 2005).

Openness to external sources

This dimension includes the same practices considered for radical innovation, even if the purpose is to generate local knowledge. Consequently, participation in conferences and events, as well as efforts made to open up to different external sources, has the target of stimulating the broadening of the company's core knowledge.

ICT for managing the creation of incremental ideas

This set of practices involves systems for capturing and collecting ideas both inside and outside the organization. Some of the key features of such a system include having a central system in which employees can submit their ideas, or forums, blogs, wikis, etc., where external participants can offer their ideas (Van Dijk and Van den Ende, 2002; Flynn *et al.*, 2003).

In the set of practices used to foster the creation of local knowledge we have not examined the internal environment, because characteristics such as a risk-taking culture, communication of the importance of radical innovation and mindset diversity are considered by the literature to be important building blocks that favour the development of distant knowledge.

Ambidexterity capability

Ambidexterity is defined as 'the ability of a complex and adaptive system to manage and attain conflicting activities by achieving high levels of both at the same time' (Gupta *et al.*, 2006). In the context of the search phase of the innovation process, ambidexterity is a capability of those firms that excel in generating completely new knowledge, broadening their knowledge base and identifying new possibilities, and simultaneously improving their existing core knowledge.

To measure ambidexterity we follow prior studies (Gibson and Birkinshaw, 2004; He and Wong, 2004); the authors propose distinct measures for capturing, on the one hand, the extent to which firms depart from existing knowledge and, on the other hand, the extent to which firms build on and improve existing knowledge. We have therefore identified two already tested scales suitable for our purpose for measuring ambidexterity: exploration competence and exploitation competence.

In order to reach our objective, which is to verify if there are differences in search practices between firms that present ambidexterity capability and firms that do not present this capability, we test a null hypothesis (H_0) against an alternative hypothesis (H_1).

The null hypothesis can be described as 'the boring case', i.e. nothing has changed: 'There is no difference in the search dimensions between firms that present ambidexterity and firms that do not present such a capability'.

The alternative hypothesis is effectively saying the opposite of the null hypothesis – for example, for the previous case the alternative hypothesis would be: 'There is a difference in the search dimensions between firms that present ambidexterity and firms that do not present such a capability'.

Methodology

In order to reach our objective, we use data collected from Italian medium-high- and high-tech companies through a survey questionnaire.[a] Of the 500 surveys mailed between November 2009 and March 2010, 104 responses have been received, resulting in a response rate of 22.4%. Of the responses, 16 questionnaires have been discarded due to incomplete information, resulting in an effective response rate of 17.6% (88 usable questionnaires).

The questionnaire is structured into three separate parts:

- Section 1: The first part of the survey gathers demographic data from the respondent companies such as the company name, company size, market position, industry, R&D expenses, etc.
- Section 2: The second part collects information relating to the use of a number of practices for search, identified thanks both to the case studies developed within the Innovation Lab and a review of the literature.
- Section 3: The third part includes some previously validated scales that allow us to measure if a firm has developed ambidexterity capability or not.

---

[a] To this purpose, medium-high- and high-tech companies were selected from Italian database AIDA (2009) according to the international OECD science classification. The target population frame thus consisted of Italian companies with more than 50 employees and covering the specific two-digit ATECO (2007) codes 20, 21, 25, 26, 27, 28, 29, 30 and 32. An online questionnaire was created and mailed to the respondents (who normally was the chief of R&D, or, if not present, the company's CEO) through www.surveymonkey.com. To avoid the low response rate associated with this tool, the questionnaire was accompanied by a cover letter that gave evidence of the advantages associated with filling in the questionnaire. A series of follow-ups were also planned in order to solicit respondents. Data collection was conducted in collaboration with a team of researchers at the University of Pisa.

The second part of the questionnaire represents the core of the survey and is based on a framework that assesses comprehensively a firm's level of experience with a number of search practices that echo, in part, the contents of the questionnaire developed by the Innovation Lab founded by Prof. John Bessant, albeit with some modifications and expansion. We therefore modify the Innovation Lab questionnaire in order to cover both these dimensions: local search and distant search. Twenty-three search practices are included in the questionnaire. For each practice the respondents are asked to indicate, on a 1–5 Likert scale (1 = strongly disagree; 5 = strongly agree), the extent to which their firm makes use of such a practice in order: (1) to improve the existing knowledge base and/or (2) to generate completely new knowledge. So, apart from some practices which are directed specifically at the generation of local or distant knowledge, for the majority of practices two questions are posed: one concerning the use of the practice in order to generate local knowledge and the other concerning the use of the practice in order to generate distant knowledge.

In order to analyse the differences in terms of search practices between firms that show ambidexterity capability in the search phase of the innovation process and firms that do not show such a capability, we first carry out exploratory factor analysis on the search practices and confirmatory factor analysis on the ambidexterity capability, and then we perform cluster analysis and the Mann–Whitney U test to verify our hypothesis.

Searching for local and distant knowledge and ideas: Results of exploratory factor analysis

In total, 23 practices that describe the search capability are considered in our study. We reduce the items to a smaller number of underlying dimensions (factors) to carry out exploratory factor analysis. More precisely, two exploratory factor analyses are conducted: one for the practices that have the purpose of generating distant knowledge and ideas (distant knowledge) and the other for the practices that have the purpose of generating improved knowledge (local search).

Six factors, representing the sub-dimensions of searching for distant knowledge, emerge from exploratory factor analysis. Reliability is tested using the internal consistency method that is estimated using Cronbach's alpha (Cronbach, 1951; Nunnally, 1978); for all the factors the coefficients are over 0.70, which is considered adequate (Table 1).

Four out of the five factors outlined earlier are confirmed by the exploratory factor analysis, while the dimension 'Learning about new markets for radical innovation' is split into two main factors: 'Listening to the customer (D)' and 'Market sentinels (D)'. The former, which has heavy loadings with two items, mainly relates to the involvement of users as sources of innovative ideas. Customers are viewed as active players in the innovation process whose ideas can provide the starting point for new directions and help create new markets, products and services. This involvement can occur through conventional market research, interviews or by involving the lead users as active players in the innovation process. The practices included in this factor are therefore centred on customers' ideas and insights that can provide the starting point for new directions and help create new markets, products and services. The latter ('Market sentinels (D)') concerns the exploration of new markets by specialized functions and dedicated groups of people whose role is to actively search for new ideas and knowledge to trigger the innovation process. The four items relate to the practices that organizations use when trying to open up new markets. These practices include sending out 'idea hunters' whose role is to actively search for new ideas and having a dedicated group of people that explores new ways to apply existing technology to new industries and new customers.

Table 1. Dimensions of distant knowledge search.

	Item loading					
	1	2	3	4	5	6
Listening to the customer (D) (Sig. = 0.01%)						
We make use of focus groups, interviews, on-line surveys and brainstorming in order to gather market ideas	−0.028	**0.818**	−0.070	0.257	−0.179	−0.213
We actively involve lead users	0.002	**0.784**	0.254	−0.225	0.065	0.147
Market sentinels (D) (α = 0.826)						
Our organization sets up teams to actively search out new ideas that will take our business in new strategic directions	0.126	−0.063	**−0.749**	0.075	−0.129	0.251
We have a dedicated group of people that explores new ways to apply our existing technology to new industries and new customers	0.120	0.146	**−0.666**	0.029	0.268	−0.076
We have people officially charged with scouting for new ideas, finding new sources of potential radical ideas and looking for trends and developments that might have implications for the organization's future	−0.192	0.136	**−0.601**	0.142	0.208	0.236

When we have a very new and different technology, we search for multiple applications and conduct several market experiments to discover promising markets	0.303	−0.037	**−0.555**	0.080	0.067	0.044
Connecting internal employees (D) (α = 0.847)						
Our organization has organizational practices that allow bringing together people with different knowledge sets, backgrounds or functions	**0.653**	0.184	−0.216	0.218	0.073	−0.071
Our organization deliberately encourages diversity in terms of mindset and thinking	**0.626**	0.073	−0.082	0.097	−0.130	0.381
In our organization, innovation teams are encouraged to expand their resource network by tapping into the knowledge of any employee in our firm	**0.570**	0.120	−0.009	0.043	0.185	0.300
In our organization, we have 'network ambassadors' who can help innovation teams connect with other people company-wide when knowledge or insight is needed	**0.537**	0.183	−0.066	0.177	0.328	−0.055

Openness to external sources (D) (Sig. = 0.01%)					
Our organization mobilizes its mainstream resources to systematically collect information, ideas and opinions from external sources	0.265	−0.035	0.140	−0.022	**0.751**	−0.064
We actively encourage people to go to events/conferences/ courses, etc.	−0.198	0.050	−0.262	0.225	**0.672**	0.077

ICT for managing the creation of new radical ideas (D) ($\alpha = 0.671$)					
We use an open innovation system in which technology-related challenges are posted online by our R&D staff so that a community of registered scientists anywhere in the world can propose their solutions	0.049	−0.001	−0.202	**0.748**	−0.083	−0.039
We have a website (blog, wiki, corporate social network) where outsiders can submit their suggestions and ideas for markets, products and/or services	0.013	0.010	0.252	**0.738**	0.114	0.144

We have one company-wide centralized idea management system in place to which all employees can submit ideas for evaluation and receive quick feedback	0.062	−0.049	0.021	**0.576**	0.236	0.242

Internal context for supporting radical innovation (D) ($\alpha = 0.782$)

We encourage people to come forward with ideas, even if they have only a vague idea of the potential market applications of the idea	0.081	−0.002	−0.071	0.190	−0.080	**0.764**
Radical innovation is clearly communicated throughout our organization as necessary for the long-term survival of our organization	0.019	0.106	−0.020	0.066	0.302	**0.665**
Our organization supports those employees that have innovative ideas by giving them the opportunity to manage such ideas into dedicated units	0.302	0.047	−0.077	0.109	0.019	**0.528**
Our top management works to develop an innovation culture within the organization	−0.047	0.230	−0.214	0.028	0.433	0.462

We have implemented an open and collaborative research environment with other companies	0.443	0.146	−0.149	−0.041	0.356	0.121
We frequently use prototypes as means of learning and refining an idea	0.124	0.454	−0.195	−0.094	0.150	0.164

As far as the local search is concerned, results of exploratory factor analysis show the presence of four underlying dimensions (Table 2). In particular the two dimensions outlined earlier ('Connecting internal employees' and 'ICT for managing the creation of incremental ideas') are confirmed by exploratory factor analysis, while the dimension 'Learning about markets' is split into two sub-factors: 'Listening to the customer (L)' and 'Insight into the customer (L)'. The former, which is in line with the similar factor identified for distant search, concerns practices through which the actual users take part in the innovation process by conveying their ideas and insights on existing products. This occurs through a closer connection with final customers in order to obtain regular feedback on their demands and the involvement of lead users in the innovation process. In this case such practices are aimed at generating useful proposals for the improvement of the existing offer. The latter is made up of one single item that concerns the technique of getting closer to what people need and want in the context they operate in. Rather than asking consumers and customers what they might like, researchers observe the everyday life of real people, capturing the experiences of people as and when they occur. This leads to the creation of new insights and a deeper understanding of how existing products and services are actually used. Finally, the practices related to 'Openness to external sources' are not confirmed by our analysis.

Table 2. Dimensions of local knowledge search.

	Item loading			
	1	2	3	4
Listening to the customer (L) (Sig. = 0.05%)				
We make an effort to connect to our final customers in order to obtain regular feedback on their demands	−0.098	**0.769**	0.099	0.244
We actively involve lead users	0.151	**0.659**	−0.111	−0.272
Insight into the customer (L)				
Our organization looks deeply into how people actually use our products	−0.212	0.248	**0.829**	0.093
Connecting internal employees (L) (α = 0.799)				
In our organization, innovation teams are encouraged to expand their resource network by tapping into the knowledge of any employee in our firm	**0.840**	0.089	0.071	0.062
In our organization, we have 'network ambassadors' who can help innovation teams connect with other people company-wide when knowledge or insight is needed	**0.799**	−0.043	−0.105	0.199

Our organization has organizational practices that allow bringing together people with different knowledge sets, backgrounds or functions	**0.792**	0.208	0.047	0.049

ICT for managing the creation of incremental ideas (L) (Sig. = 0.01%)

We have a website (blog, wiki, corporate social network) where outsiders can submit their suggestions and ideas for markets, products and/or services	−0.056	0.000	0.396	**0.734**
We have one company-wide centralized idea management system in place to which all employees can submit ideas for evaluation and receive quick feedback	0.418	−0.014	−0.192	**0.721**
We actively encourage people to go to events/conferences/courses, etc.	0.522	−0.316	0.471	0.044
We frequently use prototypes as means of learning and refining an idea	0.439	0.396	0.135	−0.164

Our organization mobilizes its mainstream resources to systematically collect information, ideas and opinions from external sources	0.424	−0.212	0.502	−0.227
We make use of focus groups, interviews, online surveys and brainstorming in order to gather market ideas	0.099	0.495	0.119	−0.158

Ambidexterity capability: Results of confirmatory factor analysis

The measurement of ambidexterity capability (in particular the constructs exploration competence and exploitation competence) has been already validated in the literature; so confirmatory factor analysis is carried out on our data and the results are shown in Table 3.

Table 3. Confirmatory factor analysis.

Construct	Operational measures of construct	Item loading	
	Over the last three years, to what extent has your firm:		
Exploration competence	Acquired manufacturing technologies and skills entirely new to the firm?	**0.798**	0.062
	Learned product development skills and processes entirely new to the industry?	**0.726**	0.410
	Acquired entirely new managerial and organizational skills that are important for innovation (such as forecasting technological and customer trends; identifying emerging markets and technologies)?	**0.747**	0.307
	Strengthened innovation skills in areas where it had no prior experience?	**0.819**	0.217

Exploitation competence	Enhanced skills in exploiting mature technologies that improve the productivity of current innovation operations?	0.237	**0.658**
	Enhanced competencies in searching for solutions to customer problems that are near to existing solutions rather than completely new solutions?	0.055	**0.783**
	Upgraded skills in product development processes in which the firm already possesses significant experience?	0.251	**0.751**
	Strengthened knowledge and skills on mature technologies?	0.309	**0.708**

Following prior studies that consider exploration competence and exploitation competence as orthogonal (Gibson and Birkinshaw, 2004; He and Wong, 2004), in order to develop a measure for ambidexterity capability in the search phase, we compute the multiplicative interaction between exploration competence and exploitation competence.

What are the differences between ambidextrous and non-ambidextrous firms in the search phase?

In order to reach the aim of our paper, which is to understand whether there are some differences in search practice between ambidextrous and non-ambidextrous firms, we cluster the firms on the basis of their ambidexterity capability in the search phase and perform the Mann–Whitney U test on the search dimensions (both local and distant) identified.

In order to identify firms that have developed ambidexterity capability in the search phase, the constructs of exploitation competence and exploration competence are used as taxons in a hierarchical cluster analysis. Two clusters are identified, with 54 firms (61%) making up Cluster 1 and 34 firms (39%) making up Cluster 2. The firms falling into Cluster 1 show low or medium levels of exploration and exploitation competences and ambidexterity while the firms that fall into Cluster 2 present significantly higher (p values < 0.001) mean scores on exploration and exploitation competences and ambidexterity (Table 4 and Fig. 1). Cluster 2 hence contains firms that have developed ambidexterity capability in the search phase of the innovation process.

Table 4. Cluster analysis results: Comparison of exploration competence, exploitation competence and ambidexterity means by cluster.

	Cluster 1 (N = 54) mean value	Cluster 2 (N = 34) mean value	Mann–Whitney U test	Wilcoxon W	Z	Asymp. sig. (two-tailed)
Exploration competence	2.5309	3.7721	6.000	1491.000	−7.864	0.000
Exploitation competence	3.0262	3.6618	375.500	1860.500	−4.688	0.000
Ambidexterity	7.7874	13.8327	9.000	1494.000	−7.795	0.000

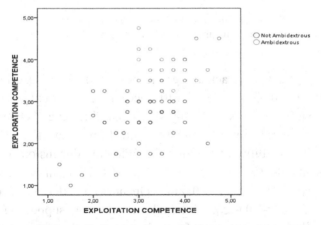

Fig. 1. Cluster analysis results (bold circles signify the presence of more than one firm).

We then investigate the variation of the search dimensions, previously identified with exploratory factor analysis, between the two clusters. The results in Fig. 2, whose rays correspond with the ten search dimensions identified with exploratory factor analysis, show that the

Discontinuous Innovation

ambidextrous group (Cluster 2) exhibits the highest mean value for all the search dimensions (both distant and local search dimensions).

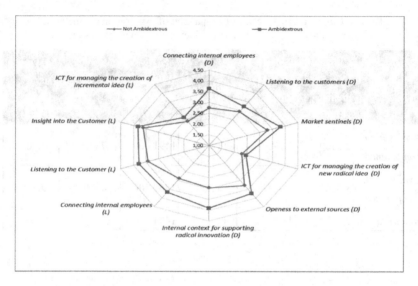

Fig. 2. Differences in search dimensions between the two clusters
(ambidextrous and non-ambidextrous).

Table 5 presents the actual significance value of the test. From this data, at the $\alpha = 0.05$ level of significance, there is enough evidence to conclude that there is a statistically significant difference between firms that present ambidexterity capability and firms that do not present ambidexterity capability concerning the following dimensions of search: 'Market sentinels (D)' ($U = 635$, $p = 0.015$), 'Connecting internal employees (D)' ($U = 426$, $p = 0.000$), 'Openness to external sources (D)' ($U = 658.5$, $p = 0.023$), 'Internal context for supporting radical innovation (D)' ($U = 380$, $p = 0.000$), 'Listening to the customers (L)' ($U = 689$, $p = 0.045$) and 'Connecting internal employees (L)' ($U = 526.5$, $p = 0.001$). It can be further concluded that the ambidextrous firms are characterized by statistically significant higher values of these search dimensions than the non-ambidextrous firms.

Table 5. Mann–Whitney U test output.

Null hypothesis	Mann–Whitney U test	Wilcoxon W	Z	Asymp. sig. (two-tailed)
The distribution of 'Listening to the customer (D)' is the same across the two clusters	744.500	2229.500	−1.510	0.131
The distribution of 'Market sentinels (D)' is the same across the two clusters	635.000	2120.000	−2.437	0.015
The distribution of 'Connecting internal employees (D)' is the same across the two clusters	426.000	1911.000	−4.234	0.000
The distribution of 'Openness to external sources (D)' is the same across the two clusters	658.500	2143.500	−2.268	0.023
The distribution of 'ICT for managing the creation of incremental ideas (D)' is the same across the two clusters	781.500	2266.500	−1.178	0.239
The distribution of 'Internal context for supporting radical innovation (D)' is the same across the two clusters	380.000	1865.000	−4.649	0.000
The distribution of 'Listening to the customer (L)' is the same across the two clusters	689.000	2174.000	−2.002	0.045
The distribution of 'Insight into the customer (L)' is the same across the two clusters	759.500	2244.500	−1.485	0.138

The distribution of 'Connecting internal employees (L)' is the same across the two clusters	526.500	2011.500	−3.380	0.001
The distribution of 'ICT for managing the creation of incremental ideas (L)' is the same across the two clusters	788.000	2273.000	−1.128	0.259

Discussion and Conclusions

The aim of this study is to explore the relationship between practices put in place by firms in order to generate local and distant knowledge and ambidexterity capability. The objective is in fact to assess if any difference exists between firms that have ambidexterity capability and firms that do not present such a capability in the search phase, when taking into consideration a number of practices for conducting the search for knowledge and ideas.

According to our results, the ambidextrous firms are characterized by greater internal connections between employees pertaining to different functions: inter-functional integration and bringing together people with different knowledge sets, backgrounds or functions are in fact widely used practices. Such practices, which are useful both for the generation of local and distant knowledge, involve sharing information among members, collaborative decision-making and agreement focusing all employees' activities on common goals. Unsurprisingly ambidextrous firms are characterized by a higher value of the 'Connecting internal employees' dimension. Having an internal network allows the organization to better overcome conflicts, disagreements and uncoordinated action by creating a common set of values and shared meanings that provide a common identity, even if employees are called on to perform different and opposite tasks and even if they pursue different business strategies. This is in line with the works of Westerman *et al.* (2006) and Siggelkow and Rivkin (2006) which maintain that in order to capture the benefits of local and distant search, the organization should provide the targeted integration necessary to leverage both activities and capture the benefits of both, by fostering a better understanding of organizational values and objectives through an improved transmission of knowledge and experience.

Firms that have developed ambidexterity capability in the search phase additionally appear to have built an open environment by creating not only strong connections among employees, but also with external participants for the purpose of continuously looking outside their normal knowledge zones and keeping up to date with developments in their particular field of expertise. According to Chesbrough (2003), external networking is one of the big management challenges of the 21st century. The different functions of the ambidextrous firms are in fact strongly encouraged to collect ideas and opinions from outside sources in a systematic way and to build intensely on inter-organizational knowledge transactions to extend their internal knowledge base. Organizational boundaries are porous and firms strongly interact with different groups and individuals in their environment (universities, research labs, customers, exhibitions, venture capital firms, etc.) in the search for interesting ideas and knowledge. Our result is in line with the results of Herzog and Leker (2010) who stress the importance of openness to external sources for building ambidexterity, for the reason that adopting an open perspective fosters the generation of distant knowledge, thus ensuring a high level of exploration.

According to Smith and Tushman (2005), realizing ambidexterity brings with it a further set of challenges for senior managers who have to clearly communicate the importance of engaging in the experimentation with the new and not previously experienced, and to provide support to employees with new ideas by encouraging them to put such ideas forward. In the absence of an explicit strategy that justifies this experimentation, the default option is to focus on short-term profitability, usually by eliminating variance and costs. Our result is perfectly in line with these considerations: ambidextrous firms in fact show significantly higher values for 'Internal context for supporting radical innovation (D)' than non-ambidextrous firms. Ambidextrous firms have managers who succeed in creating a culture of innovation characterized by a high degree of autonomy, risk-taking and tolerance of mistakes. A culture that promotes innovation is one that allows the most creative employees to manifest their creativity.

As regards the 'Market sentinels' dimension, ambidextrous firms invest more deeply in specialized search functions in order to have a dedicated group of people whose role is to search actively for new ideas and knowledge to trigger the innovation process. They could be searching for technological triggers, emerging markets or trends, or competitor behaviour. They are officially charged with searching out new ideas that will take the business into new strategic directions. Clearly, focusing actions helps to maximize the different benefits of contrasting poles, maintaining multiple competencies within the organization (Scarbrough *et al.*, 2004; Gilbert, 2005), since it allows complex activities to be split up into small, more elementary tasks. In fact, specialized people clearly know what their jobs are and how they should do their work. This is in accordance with the organizational literature that analyses the differentiation process in depth, highlighting its benefits for organizations.

Finally, ambidextrous firms appear to be engaged in closer relationships with their customers. The exploratory factor analyses have underlined three factors that describe how firms can interface with customers. These factors are 'Listening to the customer' in order to generate local and distant knowledge, and 'Insight into the customer'. These dimensions are quite different: while the first two factors ('Listening to the customer (D)' and 'Listening to the customer (L)') view customers as active players in the innovation process whose ideas can, on the one hand, provide the starting point for new directions and help create new markets, products and services and, on the other hand, suggest improvements to the existing offer, the 'Insight into the customer' dimension refers to a deep observation of the everyday life of real people, capturing the experiences of people as and when they occur in order to gain a deeper understanding of how existing products and services are actually used. The results of the Mann–Whitney U test support the hypothesis that a statistically significant difference exists only for the dimension 'Listening to the customer (L)', aimed at generating local knowledge, while no statistically significant difference exists between ambidextrous and non-ambidextrous firms when considering the 'Listening to the customer (D)' dimension, aimed at generating distant knowledge, and the 'Insight into the customer (L)' dimension. At first we were surprised by these results. However, we have to consider that our sample is made up of B2B, B2C and simultaneously B2B and B2C firms. It could therefore be interesting to split the sample according to the business approach used and to compare ambidextrous and non-ambidextrous firms within each sub-group. Table 6 shows the mean values of the different dimensions for ambidextrous and non-ambidextrous firms within the three groups. It is interesting to notice that, while B2B firms present similar values for these dimensions for ambidextrous and non-ambidextrous firms, for B2C firms and firms that adopt both B2B and B2C approaches, the difference in these practices between ambidextrous and non-ambidextrous firms is much more pronounced.

Table 6. Mean values of the different dimensions for ambidextrous and non-ambidextrous firms within B2B, B2C and both B2B and B2C groups.

	B2B		B2C		B2B and B2C	
	Non-ambidextrous	Ambidextrous	Non-ambidextrous	Ambidextrous	Non-ambidextrous	Ambidextrous
Listening to the customer (D)	3.01	3.05	3.08	3.95	2.36	3.00
Listening to the customer (L)	3.44	3.50	3.46	4.40	3.21	3.58
Insight into the customer (L)	3.62	3.63	3.85	4.20	3.14	3.83

We have therefore conducted a Mann–Whitney U test within each group. The results of this test are presented in Tables 7, 8 and 9. The data clearly indicate that significant differences between ambidextrous and non-ambidextrous firms affect only the group of companies adopting a B2C approach. Ambidextrous B2C firms view customers as active players in the innovation process and not just as passive consumers, whose contribution is considered to be extremely important not only in providing the starting point for new business directions (i.e. to generate distant knowledge) but also in improving the existing offer (i.e. to generate local knowledge). Through these techniques, ambidextrous firms succeed in getting closer to what people need and want within the context in which they operate.

Table 7. Test statistics for B2B group.

Null hypothesis	Mann–Whitney U test	Wilcoxon W	Z	Asymp. sig. (two-tailed)
The distribution of 'Listening to the customer (D)' is the same across the two clusters	279.000	450.000	−0.528	0.597
The distribution of 'Listening to the customer (L)' is the same across the two clusters	282.500	877.500	−0.460	0.646
The distribution of 'Insight into the customer (L)' is the same across the two clusters	290.500	885.500	−0.320	0.749

Table 8. Test statistics for B2C group.

Null hypothesis	Mann–Whitney U test	Wilcoxon W	Z	Asymp. sig. (two-tailed)
The distribution of 'Listening to the customer (D)' is the same across the two clusters	23.000	114.000	−2.667	0.008**
The distribution of 'Listening to the customer (L)' is the same across the two clusters	19.000	110.000	−2.931	0.003**
The distribution of 'Insight into the customer (L)' is the same across the two clusters	51.000	142.000	−0.994	0.410

Table 9. Test statistics for B2B and B2C group.

Null hypothesis	Mann–Whitney U test	Wilcoxon W	Z	Asymp. sig. (two-tailed)
The distribution of 'Listening to the customer (D)' is the same across the two clusters	10.500	38.500	−1.534	0.125
The distribution of 'Listening to the customer (L)' is the same across the two clusters	16.500	44.500	−0.671	0.502
The distribution of 'Insight into the customer (L)' is the same across the two clusters	12.000	40.000	−1.493	0.135

To conclude, the survey's results show that ambidextrous firms face the search activities with a dual mindset, characterized by a both/and approach, where tensions for local and distant knowledge are simultaneously solved: in fact ambidextrous firms in our sample put in place different practices directed at both renewing their existent core knowledge and finding completely new knowledge. In this way, valuing each side of the tensions as well as the synergies between opposite poles, they are able to generate exploration and exploitation competences. Reaching this objective means that top management should have a paradoxical mindset. Starting from our results, managers can in fact find a useful guide for formulating the appropriate strategies that foster the generation of both local and distant knowledge.

References

Argyris, C. and Schön, D. (1978). *Organisational Learning: A Theory of Action Perspective.* Addison Wesley, Reading, MA.
Backman, M., Börjesson, S. and Setterberg, S. (2007). Managing concepts in the fuzzy front end: Exploring the context for different kind of concepts at Volvo Cars. *R&D Management*, 37(1), 17–28.

Chesbrough, H. (2003). *Open Innovation: The New Imperative for Creating and Profiting from Technology.* Harvard Business School Press, Boston, MA.

Crawford, C.M. and Di Benedetto, C.A. (2003). *New Products Management.* Irwin Publishers, Homewood, IL.

Cronbach, L.J. (1951). Coefficient alpha and the internal structure of tests. *Psychometrika*, 16, 297–334.

Flynn, M., Dooley, L., O'Sullivan, D. and Cormican, K. (2003). Idea management for organisational innovation. *International Journal of Innovation Management*, 7(4), 417–442.

George, M.L., Works, J. and Watson-Hemphill, K. (2005). *Fast Innovation: Achieving Superior Differentiation, Speed to Market, and Increased Profitability.* McGraw-Hill, New York.

Gibson, C.B. and Birkinshaw, J. (2004). The antecedents, consequences, and mediating role of organizational ambidexterity. *Academy of Management Journal*, 47(2), 209–226.

Gilbert, C. (2005). Unbundling the structure of inertia: Resource versus routine rigidity. *Academy of Management Journal*, 48, 741–763.

Gupta, A.K., Smith, K.G. and Shalley, C.E. (2006). The interplay between exploration and exploitation. *Academy of Management Journal*, 49(4), 693–706.

Hargadon, A. and Sutton, R.I. (2000). Building an innovation factory. *Harvard Business Review*, 78(3), 157–166.

He, Z.L. and Wong, P.K. (2004). Exploration vs. exploitation: An empirical test of the ambidexterity hypothesis. *Organization Science*, 15(4), 481–494.

Herzog, P. and Leker, J. (2010). Open and closed innovation: Different cultures for different strategies. *International Journal of Technology Management*, 52(3/4), 322–343.

Kelley, T. (2005). The 10 faces of innovation. *Fast Company*, 99, 74–77.

Leonard-Barton, D. (1992). Core capabilities and core rigidities: A paradox in managing new product development. *Strategic Management Journal*, 13, 111–125.

Leonard-Barton, D. (1995). *Wellsprings of Knowledge: Building and Sustaining the Sources of Innovation.* Harvard Business School Press, Boston, MA.

Leonard-Barton, D. (2002). *Hewlett-Packard: Singapore (D).* Harvard Business School Cases, Boston, MA.

Linder, J.C., Jarvenpaa, S. and Davenport, T.H. (2003). Toward an innovation sourcing strategy. *MIT Sloan Management Review*, 44(4), 43–49.

March, J. (1991). Exploration and exploitation in organizational learning. *Organization Science*, 2(1), 71–87.

McLaughlin, P., Bessant, J. and Smart, P. (2008). Developing an organisation culture to facilitate radical innovation. *International Journal of Technology Management*, 44(3–4), 298–323.

Nunnally, J.C. (1978). *Psychometric Theory*. McGraw-Hill, New York.

Phillips, W., Lamming, R., Bessant, J. and Noke, H. (2006). Discontinuous innovation and supply relationships: Strategic dalliances. *R&D Management*, 36(4), 451–461.

Scarbrough, H., Swan, J., Laurent, S., Bresnen, M., Edelman, L. and Newell, S. (2004). Project-based learning and the role of learning boundaries. *Organization Studies*, 25(9), 1579–1600.

Siggelkow, N. and Rivkin, J. (2006). When exploration backfires: Unintended consequences of organizational search. *Academy of Management Journal*, 49, 779–796.

Smith, W.K. and Tushman, M.L. (2005). Managing strategic contradictions: A top management model for managing innovation streams. *Organization Science*, 16(5), 522–536.

Swink, M. (2006). Building collaborative innovation capability. *Research Technology Management*, 49(2), 37–47.

Tenenhouse, D. (2004). Intel's open collaborative model of industry-university research. *Research Technology Management*, 47(4), 19–26.

Thomke, S. and von Hippel, E. (2002). Customer as innovators: A new way to create value. *Harvard Business Review*, 80(4), 74–81.

Tushman, M.L. and O'Reilly, C. (1996). Ambidextrous organizations: Managing evolutionary and revolutionary change. *California Management Review*, 38, 8–30.

Ulwick, A.W. (2002). Turn customer input into innovation. *Harvard Business Review*, 80(1), 91–97.

Van den Bosch, B., Saatcioglu, A. and Fay, S. (2006). Idea management: A systemic view. *Journal of Management Studies*, 43(2), 259–288.

Van Dijk, C. and Van den Ende, J. (2002). Suggestion system: Transferring employee creativity into practicable ideas. *R&D Management*, 32(5), 387–395.

Westerman, G., Iansiti, M. and McFarlan, W. (2006). Organization design and effectiveness over the innovation life cycle. *Organization Science*, 17(2), 230–238.

Chapter 5

Unpacking Exploratory Innovation: Search Practices, Organizational Context and Performance

Antonella Martini and Davide Aloini
University of Pisa, Italy

This chapter explores how Italian firms face the radical innovation process under discontinuous conditions. More specifically, it empirically investigates (1) the search phase of the innovation process, in terms of search practice profiles and (2) how organizational context, search practices and exploratory outcomes (performance) are related. The analysis, based on the Italian Discontinuous Innovation (DI) Lab research, is drawn from a survey of 500 medium-high- and high-tech Italian firms.

Introduction

Innovation can be defined as a process with three consecutive phases: search, select and implement (Bessant *et al.*, 2005). The success of every innovative action is rooted in the very early phase of the process where firms look both internally and externally for new ideas to renew themselves. Most of the innovation literature is focused on steady-state conditions, where firms are dealing with 'doing what we do but better'; discontinuous conditions, i.e. 'doing things differently', is less researched (Bessant, 2008). At the same time, the old exploration/ exploitation question is challenged by the scope of changes in environmental elements and by the level of interactivity amongst them. This means that the incidence of discontinuities is likely to rise.

In other words: to survive firms must satisfy, at the same time, the requirements of today's customers (in terms of functionality, price, time, quality, place and service) and the needs of tomorrow's customers, in a context that cannot be expected to have the same characteristics as in the past. While the first requirements develop along a defined pathway, i.e. existing trajectories, and produce incremental as well as radical innovation, the aforementioned needs also result in small, i.e. incremental, or large, i.e. radical, innovation but refer to new trajectories, i.e. new directions. Therefore, it can be argued that the exploit/explore binary divide refers to search activity direction: same direction, i.e. along a defined pathway, or different direction, i.e. beyond the envelope, out of the box. In both cases the actions taken may result in small or large steps forward in terms of incremental and radical innovation.

The real challenge for firms is therefore to develop and manage these situations with their consequent tensions and under the same organizational root. This leads to the ambidexterity issue, demanding opportune conditions – or antecedents.

Based on an extensive survey carried out in Italy, this chapter unpacks the innovation process search phase under discontinuous conditions (exploratory search). The framework to unpack it as well as the relations between search practices, organizational context and innovation performance are here analysed.

Literature background

We can review the literature on the search topic according to two main dimensions: *where* to search and *how* to search. Contributions on the first dimension (*where*) refer to the choice of knowledge boundary (internal and external), knowledge domain (market and technology), knowledge proximity (local and distant) and search intensity and scope (depth and breadth). The literature on the second dimension (*how*) investigates the organizational practices used for searching, managerial approaches, organizational solutions and technological tools.

Where *to search: The dimensions*

Contributions on the boundaries dimension consider whether an organization is drawing on internal or external knowledge sources. External sources for innovation are customers, suppliers, competitors and research centres: for the first two sources of knowledge the impulse is market-driven, while in the others it is technology-driven. Other sources are conferences, trade, fairs and press. Internal sources are individuals who can act in boundary-spanning roles, or as champions, scouts, idea generators and gatekeepers. Here, issues such as knowledge management, idea generation and incentives have great impact. Recent literature has pointed out the importance of openness for search (Chesbrough, 2003) and refers to external knowledge identification as a search strategy (Laursen and Salter, 2006).

When dealing with discontinuous innovation the problem is not the lack or presence of search but the overall *direction* of search. This direction can be constrained as bounded exploration if a firm continues to direct its efforts along a defined pathway to extend the boundaries of a known business frame, or it can be unconstrained by the old rules of the game towards a reframing of different elements in the environment or even towards an open space where a completely new game can emerge. It is the binary divide of local search and distant search (Lavie and Rosenkopf, 2006). Linked with this latter classification, it is the distinction between deep and broad search, which refer respectively to the search extensiveness within a given knowledge area and to the search scope (no. of external sources).

How *to search: The practices*

According to the early front-end literature, activities can be broken up into two broad categories: the first is about the process of idea generation while the second is related to idea management and knowledge management.

Idea generation refers to the identification and analysis of opportunities by environmental scanning, seeding ideas and application exploration.

Idea management is the process of capturing, storing and organizing ideas, while knowledge management is a process which is transversal to both categories.

The how-to-search dimension refers to organizational practices used for idea generation and management activities (KM included). It is possible to identify in the literature a number of recurrent themes within these interlinked categories. These are summarized in Table 1, with their main references.

Table 1. Search domain.

DIMENSION	MEASUREMENT FOCUS	MAIN REFERENCES
Idea generation		
Learning about markets	Practices such as lead users, experimentation, unconventional tools	Thomke (2001); O'Connor (1998); O'Connor and Veryzer (2001); Tidd *et al.* (2005); Christensen *et al.* (2005); von Hippel and Katz (2002); Heinerth (2006); Kim and Mauborgne (2005)
Openness to external sources	Practices that enable the search breadth	Chesbrough (2003a,b); Chesbrough (2004); Gassmann (2006); West and Gallagher (2006)
Idea management & knowledge management		
Managing idea generation	A system for capturing ideas to look both inside and outside the firm, idea hunters, dedicated teams	Leifer *et al.* (2000); Flynn *et al.* (2003); Andriopoulos and Gotsi (2005); Hargadon and Sutton (2000)
Network management system	Practices related to internal organization	Hargadon and Sutton (2000); Kelley *et al.* (2010); O'Connor and Veryzer (2001); O'Connor and McDermott (2004)

The streams which emerged from the early front-end literature review and referred to the three categories of idea generation, idea management and knowledge management are:

- *Learning from the market*: comprised of sub-factors related to lead users, experimentation, scouting for new ideas and deep diving.

- *Idea generation management:* related to the company-wide system for submitting ideas, corporate intrapreneurship and management support for people to come forward with ideas.

- A *network management system for idea generation*: comprises sub-factors related to bringing people together with different knowledge sets and network ambassadors to help teams connect with other people company-wide.

- *Openness to external sources*: related to the practices which ensure insights from the outside.

The above search domain has been populated with specific search practices derived from the literature and integrated with practices empirically drawn from the 80 cases developed by the DI Lab, and discussed with industry experts in focus groups. In total, we collected 28 search practices. These 28 search practices have been classified into the four areas reported earlier, which depict the search domain and labelled '(DI) Search Practices' (Martini *et al.*, 2011; Aloini and Martini, 2012).

All the 12 search strategies (each of them captures more than one practice) identified by Bessant and von Stamm (2008) can be brought back to the four areas (Table 2) (see also Chapter 3).

In addition, the literature also indicates the role played by incentives, firm culture, entrepreneurial environment and by the ability to focus on both the present and the future, balancing adaptability and alignment, i.e. ambidexterity (Gibson and Birkinshaw, 2004; Jansen *et al.*, 2006). All these factors have a considerable impact on search practices as they determine whether or not a favourable environment for fostering search practices is created.

Table 2. Search practice streams and search strategies.

	MARKET LEARNING	**IDEA GENERATION MANAGEMENT**	**NETWORK MANAGEMENT**	**OPENNESS TO EXTERNAL SOURCES**
		DI SEARCH DIMENSIONS		
12 DI SEARCH STRATEGIES	[1] Sending out Scouts *Dispatch idea hunters to track down new innovation triggers* [4] Working with Active Users *Team up with knowledgeable product and service users to see the ways in which they change and develop existing offerings* [5] Deep Diving *In consumer research, study what people actually do, rather than what they say they do* [6] Probe and Learn *early prototyping to explore quickly* [2] Exploring Multiple Futures *Use futures techniques to explore alternative possible futures; and develop innovation options from that*	[9] Corporate Entre/Intra *Stimulate and nurture the entrepreneurial talent inside the organization* [7] Mobilize the Main stream *Bring mainstream participants into the product and service development process* [2] Exploring Multiple Futures *Stimulate innovation by periodically commissioning teams to generate ideas around major platforms or themes* [12] Idea Generators *Operate some form of creative idea generation to support DI*	[10] Use Brokers and Bridges *Build cross-sector, cross-disciplinary and geographically dispersed linkages* [11] Deliberate Diversity *Create diverse teams to help challenge assumptions*	[3] Using the Web *Harness the power of the web, through online communities, and virtual worlds, for example, to detect new trends* [7] Mobilize the Main stream *System or procedures in place that ensure insights from outside facing people are being collected systematically*

Research framework and methodology

Figure 1 illustrates the framework used to unpack exploratory innovation. It is composed of three boxes: organizational context, search practices and outcomes.

Organizational context refers to specific management approaches and organizational structures which contribute to create a proper environment for the innovation process. The specific items used to analyse such a context have been previously validated in the literature (see boxes 3 and 4 below). Bessant *et al.* (2005) identified two organizational archetypes to manage respectively steady-state and discontinuous innovation. Although they are ideal types, their comparison brings about the need for very different ways to deal with innovation. It appears necessary on one hand to have a systematic search within known or knowable environments, and on the other to have a much more open and agile approach to manage emergent and unknown fields. As said before, the challenge for firms is to manage both archetypes – and their consequent tensions – under the same organizational root. This is how the ambidexterity issue arises, demanding appropriate conditions or antecedents.

The organizational context box contains items which are referred to in the literature as 'antecedents' for ambidexterity: the combination of these items contributes to the creation of a proper organizational environment with its impact on the innovation process search phase.

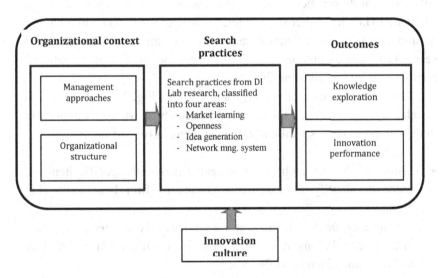

Fig. 1. Research framework.

The second box deals with search practices, and it contains practices empirically derived from the DI Lab research.

The last box involves the outcomes, i.e. the performance as a result of the exploration process, in terms of both knowledge exploration and exploratory innovation. While the first mainly reflects the results of the innovation process, i.e. the engendered procedural knowledge or skills, the exploratory innovation construct is an operative measure of both market and technological results which firms gained through the innovation process.

The rationale of the framework posits that the organizational context has an impact on search practices, which in turn have an impact on outcomes. The relationship between the constructs was tested by the authors in a number of previous works. Evidence from a structural equation modelling test showed that the search practices box has a significant impact on outcomes (Aloini and Martini, 2013). Moreover, authors found empirical evidence that the organizational context (and innovation culture) has a direct impact on both the search practices and outcomes boxes (Aloini and Martini, 2011, 2012).

In addition, mediation tests highlight the strong two-way link between search practices and organizational context. They reinforce each other (i.e. the higher the former, the higher the latter) while having an impact on innovation performance. At the same time, the impact of search practices on outcomes is amplified by the level of organizational context (Aloini and Martini, 2012).

These results consolidate the framework in Fig. 1 and allow us to develop a way to unpack the search practices box, which we report on in this chapter. More specifically, this happens in two different steps:

- *Inside the boxes*: each box has been filled with specific items in order to identify homogeneous groups of firm behaviours (i.e. clusters).
- *Throughout the boxes*: the search practices box has been unpacked in terms of relationship between organizational context on one side and outcome clusters on the other.

Finally, we also analysed the influence of control variables, such as innovation culture and firm size, on the three main boxes.

The box constructs were operationalized by scales which are all well consolidated in the literature (see next section for further details), and for the search practices construct, we mainly adopted the DI Lab research practices.

Methodology

Survey data were first subjected to cluster analysis. Successively they were classified using descriptive statistics, based on the score obtained by firms when measuring the items they had in each of the three main boxes. The survey design is summarized in Box 1.

Box 1. Survey design.

A cross-sectional survey was used for data collection and a structured questionnaire was developed to measure the theoretical constructs on a five-point Likert scale. The target sample consisted of medium-high- and high-tech Italian companies selected according to the international OECD science classification. Five hundred firms were randomly selected from all the (2009) AIDA companies with more than 50 employees.

HIGH-TECH	Aerospace
	Computers, office machinery
	Electronics-communications
	Pharmaceuticals
MEDIUM-HIGH TECH	Scientific instruments
	Motor vehicles
	Electrical machinery
	Chemicals
	Other transport equipment
	Non-electrical machinery

The data collection process was carried out using www.surveymonkey.com. Respondents were typically the vice presidents or directors of R&D departments, or the CEOs of participating firms. In an effort to increase the response rate, all the target firms were first contacted by phone so as to present the initiative to them. After that, an email with a cover letter and a Monster account was sent to all participants. A phone call and an email were then used as reminders two weeks later. Finally, 102 responses were received, resulting in a response rate of about 20%. Fifteen responses were discarded due to incomplete information, resulting in an effective response rate of 17.5%.

Inside the boxes: Characterizing the clusters

The first step of our research requires a preliminary cluster analysis in order to characterize each of the boxes. In other words, clusters of firm behaviours were identified for each box.

Search practices box

The 28 search practices identified on page 115 of this chapter are reported in Box 2.

Groups of firms were identified by cluster analysis according to different uses of search practices. Clusters do not differ in the type of practices implemented by the firms; on the contrary, they highlight three patterns of firm behaviour which only differ in the intensity adopted when implementing search practices (Fig. 2):

- *Low intensity*: Firms in this first cluster (23%) are beginners. They make little use of practices in all the four groups (NET, OPEN, MKT, MNG). As a consequence, their potential for improvement in this direction is the highest.
- *Medium intensity*: These firms (56%) implement search practices in a systematic and conscious way. Compared to the low-intensity group these firms benefit more from existing practices and also implement new ones.
- *High intensity*: These firms are search practice lead users. Their knowledge and tools for DI search are on the cutting edge.

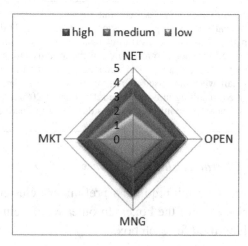

Fig. 2. Search practices: The profiles.

Box 2. Search practices.

Learning about market (MKT)

MKT-1. We make use of conventional market research methods such as focus groups, interviews or telephone surveys, online surveys, brainstorming

MKT-2. We form relations with lead users (users of a particular product/service who can suggest changes or improvements to existing products that are able to anticipate the still untapped needs of the market)

MKT-3. We establish relationships with end customers (customers of customers in the B2B case) and get regular feedback on their needs

MKT-4. We analyse the use of products and services in various real-life situations

MKT-5. Often, prototypes and pilot tests are used as tools for learning and refining, to test new ideas

MKT-6. We explore the future, using tools and techniques such as scenario analysis, exploration of trends and other forecasting techniques

MKT-7. We use scenarios to help understand and influence our organization's future

MKT-8. We currently have someone (full- or part-time) officially charged with scouting for new ideas outside the organization and looking for trends and developments that might have implications for our organization's future

MKT-9. We have a dedicated group of people (e.g. from marketing, sales, R&D) that explores new ways to apply our existing technology to new industries and new customers

MKT-10. When we have a very new and different technology, we search for multiple applications and conduct several market experiments to discover promising markets

MKT-11. We appeal to organizations/companies engaged in the search for innovative ideas

Managing radical idea generation (MNG)

MNG-1. The company has teams dedicated to research and implementation of strategically relevant ideas for new business

MNG-2. We encourage people to come forward with ideas, even if they have only a vague idea of the potential market applications for the idea

MNG-3. Our organization supports corporate entrepreneurship as part of our discontinuous innovation efforts

MNG-4. There is a centralized system for managing ideas, available throughout the enterprise, where each employee can submit ideas and receive feedback

MNG-5. There is a financing system designed to support radical innovation projects

MNG-6. In R&D budgets are sufficient resources dedicated to exploring new technologies that could potentially lead the company beyond its existing products and markets

---

Network management system for idea generation (NET)

NET-1. We consciously hire people who are different to encourage diversity within our organization

NET-2. In the firm there are organizational practices that enable the integration of skills, backgrounds or other features to support innovation

NET-3. In our organization, we encourage radical innovation teams to expand their resource network by tapping into the knowledge of any employee in our firm

NET-4. In our organization, we have 'network ambassadors' who can help radical innovation teams connect with other people company-wide when new knowledge or insight is needed

Openness to external sources (OPEN)

OPEN-1. We have a website where outsiders can submit their suggestions and ideas for new markets, products and/or services

OPEN-2. There are brokers, which establish relationships outside the enterprise, to transfer knowledge

OPEN-3. The different functions in the organization are encouraged to systematically collect ideas and opinions from outside sources

OPEN-4. There is a website (e.g. blog, wiki, corporate social network) where suggestions and ideas about markets, products and/or services can be submitted

OPEN-5. We encourage people to attend events/conferences/workshops that help to increase knowledge and experience

OPEN-6. We use an open innovation system in which technology-related challenges are posted online by our R&D staff so that a community of registered scientists anywhere in the world can propose their solutions

OPEN-7. The research environment is open to collaborations with universities, research centres and specialized agencies

OPEN-8. The company, along with long-term strategic alliances and consolidation, develops short-term technology partnerships with other companies

Organizational context box

Regarding the organizational antecedents, the literature has focused on three broad approaches enabling ambidexterity within an organization: (1) structural solutions that allow two activities to be carried out in different organizational units; (2) contextual solutions that allow two activities to be pursued within the same unit; (3) leadership-based solutions that make the top management team responsible for reconciling and responding to the tensions between the two activities. In this chapter, the first two approaches have been considered: organizational structure and management approaches, which refer to the organizational context box.

According to the classification from Birkinshaw and Gibson (2007) (see Box 3), companies were clustered using the percentile method with a cut-off point of 3.75 in relation to both their level of social support and to the level of performance management. After that, the two clustering dimensions were crossed and four sub-groups were defined (Fig. 3).

In what follows we report a brief description of the four groups' features according to the Birkinshaw and Gibson framework.

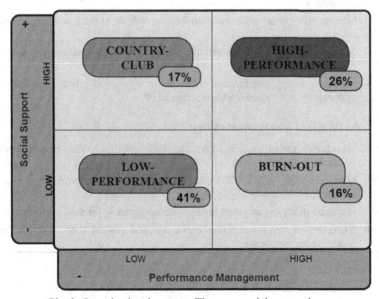

Fig. 3. Organizational context: The managerial approaches.

- *High-performance context*: this context drives people to deliver high-quality results and at the same time provides long-term social support and security.
- *Low-performance context*: in this context there is little concern for performance, there is lack of trust and support among the employees.
- *Country-club context*: in this context no-one works hard so mediocre performance is tolerated. At the same time there is a strong sense of support and trust among people. Many government departments, universities and state-owned companies experience this kind of context, as well as a high number of commercial organizations.
- *Burn-out context*: this context emphasizes the performance management dimension while the social support one is often neglected.

Box 3. Organizational context: The managerial approaches.

Social support context *(Birkinshaw and Gibson, 2007)*
CNTX-2. Managers in my organization devote considerable effort to developing subordinates
CNTX-3. Managers in my organization push decisions down to the lowest appropriate level
CNTX-4. Managers in my organization have access to the information they need to make good decisions
CULT-3. Managers in my organization treat failure in a good effort as a learning opportunity, not something to be ashamed of
Performance management context *(Birkinshaw and Gibson, 2007)*
CNTX-5. Managers in my organization issue creative challenges to their people instead of narrowly defining tasks
CNTX-6. Managers in my organization use business goals and performance measures to run their businesses
CNTX-7. Managers in my organization hold people accountable for their performance
CNTX-8. Managers in my organization encourage and reward hard work through incentive compensation

We also tested the role of the organizational structure (see Box 4) inside the organizational context box. Results show that differences among groups are small but significant (Fig. 4).

Box 4. Organizational context: The structure.

Organization structure (CNTX) *(Jansen et al., 2009)*
CNTX-9.   Innovation and production activities are structurally separated within our organization
CNTX-10. Our organization has separate units to enhance innovation and flexibility
CNTX-11. We have units that are either focused on the short term or the long term

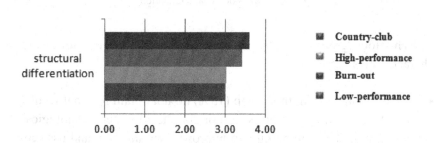

Fig. 4. Organizational context: The effect of organizational structure.

Outcomes box

Companies were first clustered according to both their innovation performance (low and high) and knowledge exploration (high and low) level (see also Box 5 for details on the items). After that, the two clustering dimensions were crossed to define four sub-groups corresponding to four combinations of innovation and knowledge exploration as reported in the matrix (Fig. 5).

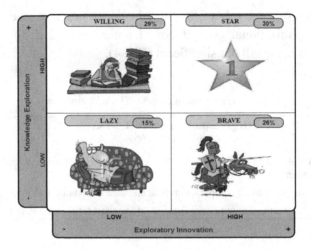

Fig. 5. Outcomes box characterization.

The four groups can be addressed according to the following characteristics:

- *Lazy*: Companies in this group (15%) do not obtain relevant results for their knowledge and skills nor for their market/technological innovation. They do nothing to improve their situation and use few practices often in a counterproductive manner.
- *Brave*: These companies (26%) are characterized by a low level of knowledge exploration but they are able to take advantage of their knowledge by efficiently implementing combined practices. As a result, exploratory innovation is usually high.
- *Star*: These firms (30%) are efficient and effective in implementing both exploratory innovation and knowledge exploration.
- *Willing*: Companies in this group (29%) usually obtain high performance in their level of knowledge but obtain very few market/technological results (exploratory innovation side). They have good intentions but they do not get results.

Box 5. Outcomes box.

Knowledge exploration (KW_EXR)
(Zahra et al., 2000; Atuahene-Gima, 2005)
KW_EXR-1. Acquired manufacturing technologies and skills entirely new to the firm
KW_EXR-2. Learned product development skills and processes (such as product design, prototyping new products, timing of new product introductions and customizing products for local markets) entirely new to the industry
KW_EXR-3. Acquired entirely new managerial and organizational skills that are important for innovation (such as forecasting technological and customer trends; identifying emerging markets and technologies; coordinating and integrating R&D, marketing, manufacturing, and other functions; managing the product development process
KW_EXR-4. Strengthened innovation skills in areas where it had no prior experience
Exploratory innovation (INN_EXR)
(He and Wong, 2004; Lubatkin et al., 2006)
INN_EXR-1. Introduction of new generations of products
INN_EXR-2. Extension of product range
INN_EXR-3. Opening up new markets
INN_EXR-4. Entering new technological fields

The Role of the Innovation Culture

As far as innovation culture is concerned (see Box 6), we used descriptive statistics to investigate its role as a control variable. In particular, we pointed out how innovation culture may change in relation to both organizational context (Fig. 6) and search profiles (Fig. 7) and, finally, in relation to the outcomes (Fig. 8).

Box 6. Innovation culture.

Innovation culture (CULT)
(Francis et al., 2003; Martins and Terblanche, 2003; Gibson and Birkinshaw, 2004; Birkinshaw and Gibson, 2007)
CULT-1. The top management works to develop an innovation culture
CULT-2. The importance of radical innovation for survival in the long term is clearly communicated throughout the organization
CULT-3. Failures and mistakes are accepted as they are considered a necessary part of the learning process

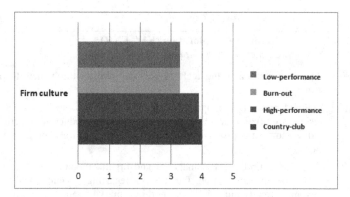

Fig. 6. Organizational context and innovation culture.

As for the organizational context, empirical evidence shows that firms with a high degree of social support (high-performance and country-club) are characterized by a higher score in innovation culture than firms in the other two clusters (low-performance and burn-out).

When investigating the relation between innovation culture and firm search profiles (Fig. 7), it is interesting to observe that advanced firms have a higher inclination to innovation culture than others. The variable level progressively increases in the clusters from low towards high firms.

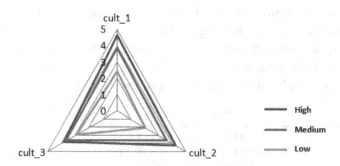

Fig. 7. Search profiles and innovation culture.

Finally, concerning the outcomes in terms of innovation performance, we investigated the innovation culture distribution on the Star, Brave, Willing and Lazy clusters (Fig. 8). As Fig. 8 shows, the Star and Brave clusters are quite aligned with respect to innovation culture which globally presents high scores.

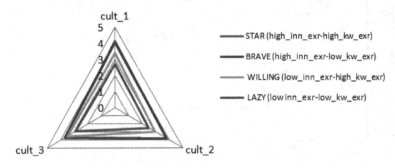

Fig. 8. Outcomes box and innovation culture.

The other two groups of firms, Willing and Lazy, show lower values of innovation culture and follow the first two respectively in this order. Evidence suggests that a pattern attached to the relation between cultural context and performance is likely to merge.

Unpacking Exploratory Innovation: Throughout the Boxes

This analysis investigates potential links between the organizational context, search practices and outcomes. When approaching innovation performance, it is possible to describe firm behaviours in terms of the adopted search profiles and organizational context that characterize a specific cluster of firms.

The matrix in Fig. 9 highlights the most common search profile for each outcome cluster.

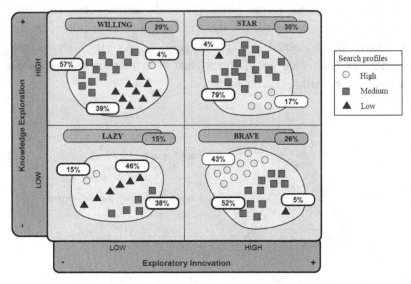

Fig. 9. Unpacking search profiles within the outcomes box.

Star and Brave firm groups are mainly characterized by medium-high search profiles while Willing and Lazy are catarcterized by medium-low search profiles.

The same analysis was performed with respect to the organizational context (Fig. 10).

In this case, firms from different contexts are present in each of the groups. However, the Star cluster is characterized by the highest percentage of firms in a high-performance context. Country-club context firms are mainly placed in the groups Star and Brave, while the majority of low-performance context firms are gathered in the Lazy and Willing groups. This distribution leads us to suppose that an inadequate organizational context can represent a strong barrier to high exploratory performance.

In order to deeply explore each quadrant in Fig. 10, we finally considered the use of each search practice, grouped in the four areas (MKT, OPEN, MNG, NET). Figures 11, 12, 13 and 14 assemble the details.

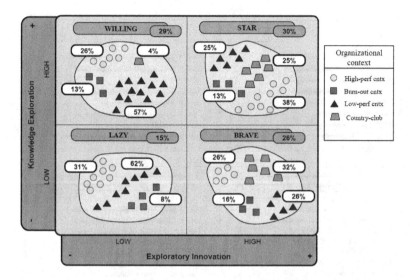

Fig. 10. Unpacking search profiles within the organizational context.

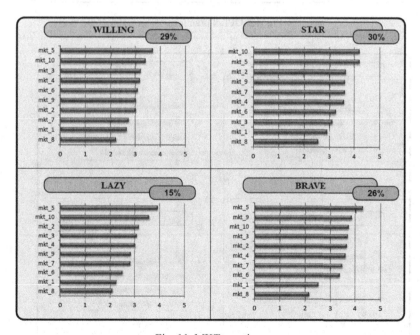

Fig. 11. MKT practices.

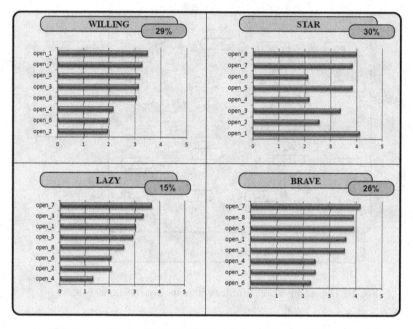

Fig. 12. OPEN practices.

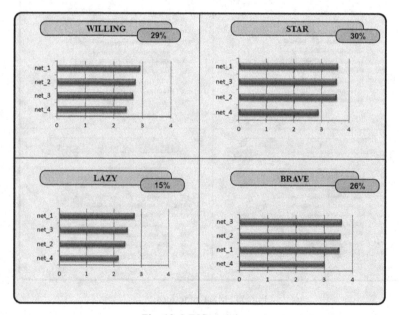

Fig. 13. MNG practices.

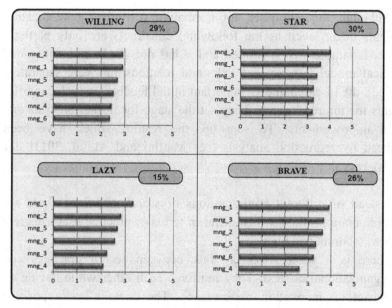

Fig. 14. NET practices.

On the evidence of the last analysis we can conclude that firms with a high level of innovation performance have higher usage of search practices than others. In fact, although similar firm behaviours seem to emerge in terms of choosing how to combine the different practices, the usage intensity is higher in the Star and Brave groups than in the other two.

Conclusion

This chapter reports some research findings of the Italian DI Lab survey. It proposes a framework to unpack exploratory search, and reports the analysis of the relationship between search practices, organizational context – in terms of a firm's structure and management approaches – and exploration outcomes – in terms of knowledge and innovation performance. Control items, such as innovation culture and firm size, have also been taken into account.

Although this study is not normative (different generalization problems occur, such as the following: constructs are only partially validated, sample size is limited and it has not allowed an integrated statistical model test, so that links and relationships were separately verified), the research allows important initial feedback which can offer insights for future research. They set the stage for further analysis and model improvements. To sum up, the results, which have been validated by regression analysis (see Martini and Aloini, 2011b for details), reveal:

- Instead of different configurations of search practices, there are three main profiles, which differ in terms of practice usage degree: low, medium and high.
- There is a strong two-way link between search practices and organizational context. They reinforce each other while having an impact on innovation performance. The context has a positive influence on the search, so that the higher the former, the higher the latter, while they also have a positive influence on the outcomes. At the same time, the impact of search practices on innovation performance is amplified by the level of the organizational context.
- Innovation culture has a strong role in the innovation performance process as it amplifies the impact of both the search practices and organizational context.

The last considerations bring forward the ambidexterity concept. The items used to operationalize the organizational context (Boxes 3 and 4) are considered antecedents for ambidexterity. It is demonstrated (Gibson and Birkinshaw, 2004) that high levels of these dimensions are associated with ambidexterity. We can now add that organizational context is also an enabler for search practice effectiveness.

The relevance of the ambidexterity theme is evident if we consider that the incumbent challenge for firms is to develop parallel innovation routines to deal with both steady-state and discontinuous contexts. The results suggest the following hypothesis, which will require future empirical tests: high organizational context values have a positive impact on organizational ambidexterity and subsequently on firm performance.

References

Andriopoulos, C. and Gotsi, M. (2005). The virtues of 'blue sky' projects: How lunar design taps into the power of imagination. *Creativity and Innovation Management*, 14(3), 316–324.

Aloini, D. and Martini, A. (2011). How firms deal with radical innovation under discontinuity: Search practices, innovation context and performance. *Proc. XXII ISPIM Conference.*

Aloini, D. and Martini, A. (2012). 'Disruptive technologies, innovation and global redesign: Emerging implications', in Ekekwe, N. and Islam, N. (eds), *How Firms Deal with Discontinuous Innovation: An Empirical Analysis.* IGI Global, Hershey, PA.

Aloini, D. and Martini, A. (2013). Exploring the exploratory search for innovation: A structural equation modelling test for practices and performance. *International Journal of Tech Management,* 61(1), 23–46.

Atuahene-Gima, K. (2005). Resolving the capability-rigidity paradox in new product innovation. *Journal of Marketing*, 69, 61–83.

Bessant, J. (2008). Dealing with discontinuous innovation: The European experience. *International Journal of Tech Management*, 42, 35–50.

Bessant, J., Lamming, R., Noke, H. and Phillips, W. (2005). Managing innovation beyond the steady state. *Technovation*, 25, 1366–1376.

Bessant, J. and von Stamm, B. (2008). Twelve search strategies that could save your organisation. *AIM Research Report.*

Birkinshaw, J. and Gibson, C.B. (2007). The ambidextrous organization. *AIM Research Report.*

Chesbrough, H. (2003). *Open Innovation: The New Imperative for Creating and Profiting from Technology.* Harvard Business School Press, Boston, MA.

Chesbrough, H. (2003a). A better way to innovate. *Harvard Business Review*, July, 12–13.

Chesbrough, H. (2003b). The era of open innovation. *MIT Sloan Management Review*, Spring, 35–41.

Chesbrough, H. (2004). Managing open innovation: Chess and poker. *Research Technology Management*, 47(1), 23–26.

Christensen, C., Cook, S. and Hall, T. (2005). Marketing malpractice: The cause and the cure. *Harvard Business Review*, December, 74–83.

Flynn, M., Dooley, L., O'Sullivian, D. and Cormican, K. (2003). Idea management for organizational innovation. *International Journal of Innovation Management*, 7(4), 417–442.

Gassmann, O. (2006). Opening up the innovation process: Towards an agenda. *R&D Management*, 36(3), 223–228

Gibson, C.B. and Birkinshaw, J. (2004). The antecedents, consequences, and mediating role of organizational ambidexterity. *Academy of Management Journal*, 47, 209–226.

Hardagon, A. and Sutton, R.I. (2000). Building and innovation factory. *Harvard Business Review*, 78, May–June, 157–166.

He, Z.L. and Wong, P.K. (2004). Exploration vs. exploitation: An empirical test of the ambidexterity hypothesis. *Organization Science*, 15, 481–94.

Hienerth, C., 2006. The commercialization of user innovations: The development of the rodeo kayak industry. *R&D Management*, 36(3), 273–294.

Jansen, J., Tempelaar, M., Van den Bosch, F.A. and Volberda, H.W. (2009). Structural differentiation and ambidexterity: The mediating role of the integration mechanisms. *Organization Science*, 4, 797–811.

Jansen, J., Van den Bosch, F.A.J. and Volberda, H.W. (2006). Exploratory innovation, exploitive innovation and performance: Effects of organizational antecedents and environmental moderators. *Management Science*, 52, 1661–1674.

Kelley, D.J., Peters, L. and O'Connor, G.C. (2010). Leveraging the organizational network for radical innovation: Three broker models. *Academy of Management Review*, 24(3), 221–235.

Kim, W.C. and Mauborgne, R. (2005). *Blue Ocean Strategy: How to Create Uncontested Market Space and Make the Competition Irrelevant*. Harvard Business School Press, Boston, MA.

Laursen, K. and Salter, A. (2006). Open for innovation: The role of openness in explaining innovative performance among UK manufacturing firms. *Strategic Management Journal*, 27(2), 131–150.

Lavie, D. and Rosenkopf, L. (2006). Balancing exploration and exploitation in alliance formation. *Academy of Management Journal*, 49(4), 797–818.

Leifer, R., McDermott, C.M., O'Connor, G.C., Peters, L.S., Rice, M.P. and Veryzer, R.W. (2000). *Radical Innovation: How Mature Companies Can Outsmart Upstarts*. Harvard Business School Press, Boston, MA.

Lubatkin, M.H., Simsek, Z., Ling, Y. and Veiga J.F. (2006). Ambidexterity and performance in small- to medium-sized firms: The pivotal role of TMT behavioral integration. *Journal of Management*, 32, 1–17.

O'Connor, G.C. (1998). Market learning and radical innovation: A cross case comparison of eight radical innovation projects. *Journal of Product Innovation Management*, 15(2), 151–166.

O'Connor, G.C. and McDermott, C.M. (2004). The human side of radical innovation. *Journal of Engineering and Technology Management*, 21, pp. 11–30.

O'Connor, G.C. and Veryzer, R.W. (2001). The nature of market visioning for technology-based radical innovation. *Journal of Product Innovation Management*, 18, 231–246.

Thomke, S.H. (2001). *Enlightened Experimentation: The New Imperative for Innovation*, Harvard Business School Press, Boston, MA.

Tidd, J., Bessant, J. and Pavitt, K. (2005). *Managing Innovation – Integrating Technological Market and Organizational Change*, 3rd Ed. John Wiley and Sons, Chichester.

von Hippel, E. and Katz, R. (2002). Shifting innovation to users via toolkits. *Management Science*, 48(7), 821–833.

West, J. and Gallagher, S. (2006). Challenges of open innovation: The paradox of firm investment in open-source software. *R&D Management*, 36(3), 319–331.

Zahra, S.A., Ireland, R.D. and Hitt, M.A. (2000). International expansion by new venture firms: International diversity, mode of market entry, technological learning, and firm performance. *Academy of Management Journal*, 43(5), 925–950.

Chapter 6

Organizing Discontinuous Innovation at Established SMEs

Desie Lenferink and Dries Faems
University of Twente, Netherlands

Introduction

The world is moving at a fast pace, requiring firms to respond to short product life cycles and frequently changing customer demand. To remain competitive in the long term, firms should not only focus on developing continuous innovations, i.e. doing something better, but should also focus on developing discontinuous innovations, i.e. doing something different (McDermott and Handfield, 1996; Bessant *et al.*, 2004; Tidd *et al.*, 2005). However, managing discontinuous innovation is not a straightforward task. In particular, it is argued that the organizational structures, cultures, processes and mechanisms that foster continuous innovation are detrimental in the context of discontinuous innovation (Christensen and Overdorf, 2000; DeTienne and Koberg, 2002; Bessant *et al.*, 2004; Reid and de Brentani, 2004). Scholars have therefore started examining how firms can effectively manage discontinuous innovation, focusing on the organizational structures (Christensen and Overdorf, 2000), processes (Veryzer, 1998; Tidd *et al.*, 2005) and mechanisms (Bessant and von Stamm, 2007; Gertsen *et al.*, 2007; Bessant, 2008) by which firms can increase the likelihood of successful discontinuous innovation.

   Although these previous studies have made important contributions to our understanding of discontinuous innovation in large, established firms, they largely ignored the setting of small- and medium-sized enterprises (SMEs). Nevertheless, SMEs often comprise an important part of national economies. In the Netherlands, for instance, 99.7% of all firms are SMEs (MKB Servicedesk, 2009). Moreover, small enterprises and established firms represent 'entirely different species', exhibiting distinct mindsets, organizational cultures, resource profiles, agendas and desired outcomes (Prashantham and Birkinshaw, 2008, pp. 9–10). As a result, we might expect that (i) the challenges that SMEs experience in discontinuous innovation processes and (ii) the solutions they apply to address these challenges are substantially different from established firms. The purpose of this study is therefore to explore the discontinuous innovation process at SME firms.

To accomplish this research objective, we conducted case study research at three established SMEs in the Netherlands. We decided to focus on *established* SMEs (i.e. SMEs that are older than five years) because existing SME research on innovation tends to focus on young, start-up firms, implicitly assuming that older SMEs are much less focused on innovation. For each case we conducted at least two interviews and analysed a wide variety of documents.

Our findings suggest that established SMEs do not pre-structure their search for discontinuous ideas, but rather embark upon opportunities as they emerge. Concerning the selection of discontinuous ideas, we observed an informal selection stage-gate process, in which selection decisions are made sequentially throughout the discontinuous innovation process, creating an emergent selection environment. We also observed that, throughout the whole discontinuous innovation process, established SMEs experienced a lack of resources and capabilities necessary to accomplish the necessary steps. At the same time, we observed that these established SMEs relied heavily on collaboration with external partners to compensate for this liability of smallness.

We contribute to the emerging discontinuous innovation literature by providing in-depth insights into how established SMEs manage the discontinuous innovation processes. In addition, we show that discontinuous innovation research should not only examine the formal structures, processes and mechanisms that allow discontinuous innovation to be fostered, but should also consider the more informal actions, decisions and strategies that might give rise to discontinuous innovations. Regarding existing SME research, we contribute by showing that not only high-tech start-ups but also established SMEs can be successful in discontinuous innovation. In addition, we provide managers of established SMEs with a number of guidelines to effectively and efficiently organize for discontinuous innovation.

Managing Discontinuous Innovation: State of the Art

In this section, we first define the concept of discontinuous innovation, explain its importance and illuminate the challenges of developing discontinuous innovation. Subsequently, we summarize the organizational structures and processes that existing research has identified as viable solutions to manage discontinuous innovations. Finally, we emphasize the need for studying discontinuous innovation in the setting of SMEs.

Discontinuous innovations

Innovations can be of a continuous or a discontinuous nature. Continuous innovations are concerned with 'doing something better', hence slightly improving the product or service (Tidd *et al.*, 2005). Discontinuous innovations, on the other hand, are about 'doing something different' (Tidd *et al.*, 2005). Discontinuous innovations can be triggered or caused by a wide variety of sources, such as the emergence of new markets, new technologies or shifts in regulatory regimes and unthinkable events (Bessant and Tidd, 2007). Discontinuous innovations have the ability to change the rules of the game by creating new lines of business and by questioning the steady state of the firm (Christensen and Overdorf, 2000; O'Connor and Veryzer, 2001; DeTienne and Koberg, 2002).

The discontinuous innovation literature provides several reasons for the importance of developing discontinuous innovations. First of all, given that discontinuous innovations can change or create entirely new markets (Christensen and Overdorf, 2000), it is important for firms to engage in the development of discontinuous innovation, to help capture and retain market shares in the new or changed market and increase profitability. Second, but related to the latter, discontinuous innovations can be considered a powerful tool to achieve competitive advantage and to secure a strategic position (Tidd *et al.*, 2005). The drawback is that it does not guarantee success, but it may take firms 'out of the "zero sum" game that characterizes many industry battlegrounds' (Bessant *et al.*, 2004).

Although developing discontinuous innovations is important for firms in order to survive and remain profitable in today's fast-moving world, scholars have also indicated that developing discontinuous innovations is far from easy and that it brings along a number of challenges. First of all, the discontinuous innovation process is complex, messy, takes longer than the continuous innovation process and is unpredictable in nature, due to organizational, resource, technical and market uncertainties (Rice *et al.*, 2002). Second, discontinuous innovations may be opaque to customers and may require dramatic behavioural changes by the market (McDermott and O'Connor, 2002). Third, existing core capabilities can become core rigidities in the face of discontinuous change (Barton, 1992). The older the firm, the stronger and more persistent its dominant logic is likely to be, which strengthens the firm's corporate immune system. Fourth, many organizations fail to recognize the value of the discontinuous innovations and do not respond in a timely matter, thus decreasing the survival and success of discontinuous innovation projects (Rice *et al.*, 2002).

Organizing for discontinuous innovations

Existing research on discontinuous innovation provides several guidelines to address the main challenges in developing discontinuous innovations. These methods include: (i) adjusting the organizational structure, (ii) changing the development process and (iii) implementing specific mechanisms to enable the development of discontinuous innovations.

One of the challenges that firms are faced with in terms of discontinuous innovations is to break away from their corporate immune system or their core rigidities. Firms should be able to explore beyond their core business to allow for the development of discontinuous innovations. Some scholars therefore advise firms to create a new organizational structure, spin out an independent organization or acquire another organization (Birkinshaw and Gibson, 2004; Christensen, 1997; Christensen and Overdorf, 2000; O'Reilly and Tushman, 2008). The aim of setting up a separate organizational structure is to create the necessary space to experiment with and react upon discontinuous changes, without disrupting the core activities of the firm.

The discontinuous innovation process is fundamentally different from the traditional new product development (NPD) processes as it is inherently messy, with far less structure and formalization (Mascitelli, 2000). Given that the development of discontinuous innovations is quite uncertain, scholars emphasize the importance of trial and error learning (Lynn *et al.*, 1996; DeTienne and Koberg, 2002). Some scholars (Veryzer, 1998; Tidd *et al.*, 2005) have tried to map the discontinuous innovation process by presenting a model with a series of events leading to the commercialization of discontinuous innovations. Both Veryzer (1998) and Tidd *et al.* (2005) identify specific sequential stages in their discontinuous innovation model, which are depicted as discrete events in the model. Although the number of stages varies per model, each model is meant to guide managers during the discontinuous innovation process from idea emergence to commercialization. The discontinuous innovation model by Tidd *et al.* (2005), for instance, identifies only three stages, namely, the search for a discontinuous idea, the selection of the idea and the implementation (development and commercialization) of the idea.

The international Innovation Lab has used the model of Tidd *et al.* (2005) to conduct research on the applicability of specific mechanisms for each stage of the discontinuous innovation process. Examples of the formal mechanisms proposed for the search stage are: (i) sending out scouts, (ii) corporate venturing and (iii) using brokers and bridges (Bessant, 2008). Examples of formal mechanisms proposed for the selection stage are: (i) internal idea-markets, (ii) presentation rounds and (iii) external ventures with different selection criteria (Bessant *et al.*, 2010).

Firm type and discontinuous innovation ability

Although existing discontinuous innovation research has provided valuable insights into the importance, challenges and managerial practices for discontinuous innovations, it has mainly focused on large established firms, ignoring discontinuous innovations within SMEs. Nevertheless, we expect that large established firms and SMEs have different advantages and disadvantages when considering their ability to develop discontinuous innovations (see Table 1).

Table 1. Firm type and innovation ability.

Firm type	Advantages	Disadvantages
SMEs	• Less bureaucratic • Flexible communication and shorter decision-making lines • Adaptive to the environment and receptive to change • Stronger commitment, due to frequent ownership stake	• Fewer resources and greater chance of experiencing a competency gap • Less access to complementary assets • Weaker marketing skills and social legitimacy for large launch of the innovation
Large established firms	• R&D budget, larger resource base to develop and launch technological capabilities • Bargaining power (with suppliers, distributors, regulatory agencies) • Greater environmental control	• More bureaucratic, due to standardized authority, routines and formulized procedures • Less flexible and stronger inertia • Internal resistance (R&D employees, shareholders) • Lower managerial commitment

One of the main advantages of large established firms is that they generally have more resources available and more financial means to invest in R&D. In other words, they have the ability to 'finance large research and development staff, leading to economies of scale in R&D' and an enhanced ability 'to exploit unforeseen innovation given their diversified product lines' (Debackere, 1997, p. 6). Given the size of large established firms, they have the advantage of having greater environmental control and bargaining power, which may increase the likelihood of successfully launching discontinuous innovations.

The main advantage of SMEs is that they are more flexible and nimble. As a result, they are less hampered by organizational inertia and have greater capacity to react quickly to internal and external pressures. Within SMEs, managers are often less isolated by organizational hierarchy and play a greater role in the innovation process (Lefebvre and Lefebvre, 1992). Employees in SMEs often have a significant ownership stake, which creates strong incentives to successfully develop discontinuous innovations (Christensen and Overdorf, 2000). These incentives positively influence R&D activities, which are often based on the creativity of the owner or key employees (Lefebvre and Lefebvre, 1992), carried out without a formal budget and often take place outside working hours (Bougrain and Haudeville, 2002, p. 744). As a result, one may state that the informal atmosphere within SMEs facilitates discontinuous innovation (Alvarez and Barney, 2001).

Both firm types also have distinct disadvantages in relation to their ability to develop discontinuous innovations. Although large established firms commonly have sufficient resources to develop discontinuous innovations, they generally commit these resources to lower-risk projects, which are of a continuous nature (Leifer *et al.*, 2000). There are several reasons for this choice. First, large established firms are often restricted when it comes to pursuing discontinuous opportunities due to internal or external resistance (Christensen, 1997). A second reason is that repeated success in the established markets may negatively influence the ability and desire of large established firms to move into new areas. A third reason is that as firms grow larger, the more organizational structure and formalized R&D activities are implemented, which may hamper the necessary creativity and decision-making speed for generating discontinuous innovations.

The main disadvantage of SMEs in respect to the development of discontinuous innovations is the lack of resources, which may lead to a competency gap. A competency gap means that the firm does not have the resources and competencies available to develop the innovation.

Among these competencies may be the explicit technological know-how or the marketing skills required to launch a truly discontinuous innovation. Regarding the launch of a discontinuous innovation, SMEs often lack the social legitimacy to introduce the discontinuous innovation into the market.

Overall, we can conclude that large established firms and SMEs have a different culture, mindset and structure, triggering different advantages and disadvantages in terms of developing discontinuous innovations. As a result, we can expect that SMEs experience different challenges and require different strategies when developing discontinuous innovations. An in-depth exploration of how SME firms manage discontinuous innovation developments therefore seems to be necessary. In the next section, we explain the methodology that we applied to accomplish this research objective.

Methodology

Research design and setting

We relied on a multiple-case study design (Yin, 2003) to explore the management of discontinuous innovation at SMEs. In the end, we managed to get access to three established SMEs in the Netherlands that were engaged in high-potential discontinuous innovation projects (see Table 2). The term 'high-potential' refers to the fact that the discontinuous innovations were nominated for a regional or national innovation award. To ensure that the focus is on discontinuous innovations, we used the criteria of Rice *et al.* (2002, p. 332), who state that an innovation must fulfil either of the following criteria in order to be discontinuous: 'new to the world performance features (or a fundamentally new product or service), five- to ten-fold (or greater) improvement in performance features, or 30% to 50% reduction in costs'.

Table 2. Overview of key information.

Established SME	Foot	Cool	Machine
Core business	Development and production of orthoses	Development of climate control systems	Development, construction and maintenance of production lines
Year established	1994	1965	2000
Number of employees	10	15	28
Discontinuous innovation	Orthosis	Climate control system	RF production line
Why discontinuous?			
New-to-the-world performance features (fundamentally new product/service)	Movement with an orthosis for club-foot correction is new to the world	Provides houses and office buildings with 80 to 90% with heat and cold using open air	It is a fundamentally new product; radiofrequency has not been applied in production lines of this type before
Five- to ten-fold (or greater) improvement in performance features	The orthosis allows movement, largely improving the performance	No CO_2 emission, no gas consumption and no radiators are required and the system can be managed online	The heating time will be reduced from 4–6 hours to 4–6 minutes
30 to 50% (or greater) reduction in costs	NA	Reduces energy costs by 40%	More (sausages) can be heated in less time. Less resources are needed, e.g. the skin of intestines
Period of innovation process from idea emergence to launch	April 2007– February 2008	(Idea emerged 2001) 2003 – May 2008	June 2004 – (anticipated) June 2009
Number of interviews	2 interviews with the owner, 1 interview with core employee	2 interviews with the owner	2 interviews with the owner
Number of documents	No documents available	Publicly available information about discontinuous innovation	Internal reports on the innovation process, subsidy request forms, printouts of e-mail correspondence, marketing reports

The study is focused on established (at least five years old) SMEs, i.e. firms that employ fewer than 250 people. The decision to focus on established SMEs was inspired by the existing discontinuous innovation literature, which is mainly focused on (i) large established firms or (ii) one specific group of SMEs, namely start-ups. Established SMEs differ from start-ups in terms of age and differ from large established firms in terms of size.

Start-ups are often referred to as the driving force behind discontinuous ideas and innovations (Sorensen and Stuart, 2000; Kassicieh and Walsh, 2002). Start-ups are said to be more capable of pursuing emerging growth markets as their values and cost structures allow them to focus on niche markets. Because established SMEs are older than start-ups, they might experience more rigidity and ossification of communication patterns (Sorensen and Stuart, 2000), making it more difficult to anticipate discontinuous innovations. Furthermore, in comparison to start-ups, established SMEs are more linked to their existing consumer base (Kaufmann and Tödtling, 2002). In comparison to large, established firms, established SMEs are smaller and may suffer the liability of smallness.

In sum, it seems that in terms of age and size, established SMEs are disadvantaged in their ability to innovate and may have great difficulty developing discontinuous innovations. Therefore, we expected that studying established SMEs, which at least have shown the potential to be able to come up with discontinuous innovation, might provide valuable insights into how this kind of firm can address the different innovation challenges.

Data collection and analysis

Data on the four cases were collected retrospectively between September 2008 and January 2009. Such retrospective data collection allows for focused data gathering and the recognition of overall patterns in the process (Leonard-Barton, 1990; Van de Ven, 2007). Nevertheless the disadvantage is that there is the 'danger of unconsciously accepting respondent bias' (Leonard-Barton, 1990, p. 253) and the researcher may have the 'tendency to filter out events that do not fit or that render the story less coherent' (Van de Ven, 2007, p. 208). To address such biases, data triangulation was applied, using two sources of evidence, namely interviews and documents.

Data collection and analysis was divided into three stages. In the first stage, we conducted unstructured interviews with key persons (either the idea initiator, innovation manager or the owner of the established SME) involved in the discontinuous innovation process and analysed documents (e.g. internal reports on the innovation process, e-mail correspondence, marketing reports). All the interviews for this study were conducted face to face in the native language of the interviewee. The interviews took approximately one hour and were all transcribed verbatim. Using the information retrieved from the interviews and documents, the discontinuous innovation process of the established SMEs was mapped in chronological order.

In the second stage, semi-structured interviews were conducted with the same key persons. The interviews were structured based on the discontinuous innovation process as mapped in the first stage. Based on these interviews, we wrote case study reports for each individual case, illuminating the history of the discontinuous innovation project.

In the third stage, the case study reports were sent back to the interviewees to give them the opportunity to provide additional comments or notes and check for validity. The case study reports were adjusted according to the comments and within-case analysis was conducted, identifying the problems and challenges experienced by the established SMEs and the mechanisms applied to address the problems and challenges. Once the within-case analyses were finished, cross-case analysis was performed to enhance generalizability. The cross-case analysis allowed for a deeper understanding and explanation (Miles and Huberman, 1994) of the discontinuous innovation process at the established SMEs.

Findings

In this section, we present, for each case, the discontinuous innovation process in chronological order, making an explicit distinction between (i) the emergence of the idea, (ii) the development of the discontinuous innovation and (iii) its commercialization.

Orthosis for club-foot deformity at Foot

Idea emergence

The idea to develop a new orthosis for correcting club-foot did not originate from Foot, but from an orthotist. The orthotist knew about an existing orthosis for correcting club-foot deformity and the related disadvantages. As a result he contacted the owner of Foot, with the question of improving the existing orthosis. Foot discovered that the existing orthosis was at least a hundred-years old and Foot believed that a better orthosis could be developed.

In April 2007 the owner and an employee (who had a combined function as designer and IT systems manager) spent one afternoon brainstorming about the specific problems children with club-foot deformity experience and how the deformity can be corrected with the fewest negative side effects. The owner referred to this brainstorm session as 'before-the-box thinking' because existing solutions were not taken into account. The brainstorming process was started by solely taking the problem into account. The output was a general structure of the design, but still in very abstract terms. At this stage of the project, no external parties were involved to avoid disruption of the creative process. The owner of Foot said:

> We did not want the third parties to be present in the initial design process. Our experience told us that all the existing things had to be neglected to start fresh and look at a problem from a different angle, thus to be more creative... If in this stage we would have involved an external partner such as a hospital, they would soon state that certain things are not allowed or not possible, or that they would not want it.

Development

After brainstorming about the potential solution, the first concept design was constructed, involving intensive interaction between the two project members (i.e. owner and employee of Foot). In June 2007, the second concept design was constructed and discussed. The first stages ran quite smoothly and good results were achieved in a limited amount of time. At the same time, the owner of Foot agreed that the overall process could have been structured better:

> The process went quite fast, but it could have been structured better and more time could have been saved. The process lacked a specific structure, because in a relatively small company such as Foot daily business plays a strong role.

Managing daily business and innovating at the time same was one of the major challenges. Daily business demanded a lot of time in terms of technical and non-technical problems which had to be solved. Foot did not appoint an employee to the project on a full-time basis. The employee involved as previously mentioned was not only a designer, but also the IT systems manager. To financially support the innovation process, Foot solicited for a subsidy, which compensated for part of the hours spent on R&D.

The first prototype was constructed in November 2007. Once constructed, it went through several feasibility tests, such as balance tests, and subsequently the prototype was tested on patients. These latter tests triggered some unanticipated results. One of the major challenges was the need to anticipate how the prototype would function as children make a lot of unexpected movements. An additional challenge was estimating how long patient testing would take until the deficiencies were discovered and solved.

In February 2008 the first batch of 0-series orthoses were produced, which were supplied to the partner hospital in March 2008. To produce the 0-series, the employees of Foot became involved. Foot was capable of developing the first prototypes, but did not have sufficient capabilities to produce all the parts of the 0-series for patients themselves. Foot therefore ordered parts from external suppliers and assembled the parts themselves. Ordering the parts from external suppliers required patience.

The Dutch economy was doing well and the owner had to pull strings to receive the parts within eight weeks, instead of 13 weeks, or even more. In addition, the owner stressed that an additional consequence of having to wait so long is that you tend to continue developing the innovation and learn new aspects, meaning that you change your mind. As a result, new parts had to be ordered, which again took a long time. Foot deliberately ordered its parts from Dutch suppliers, because the established SME knew from past experience that developing innovations requires frequent alterations for which new parts are needed. If these changes had to be communicated abroad in a different language, the supply might not only take longer, but the quality might have been insufficient.

Commercialization

Foot is positive about the cooperation with the hospital, which even resulted in one of the orthopaedic surgeons dedicating his PhD research to the orthosis. Foot is convinced that the research will positively influence the market launch and further development of the orthosis. Foot is also positive about the cooperation with the orthotist, who provided valuable input, but left the final decisions to Foot. In general, the cooperation with third parties positively influenced the progress of the innovation process.

When we collected our data, the first orthoses had been supplied to the hospital partner and had proved to work well. The objective therefore became to expand the supply of the orthosis to other hospitals and orthotists. From experience Foot learned that when a product functions well at one location, new deficiencies may be discovered at another location. In order to launch a well-functioning product and to establish brand equity, Foot deliberately opted for a slow market entry strategy.

One of the difficult facets of introducing a new product in the treatment market is that orthopaedic surgeons are used to a particular treatment and the associated product. The orthopaedic surgeons need to be convinced of the new product, which is difficult in the initial stages and needs to be done by providing evidence. Potential market estimations are difficult to make. The number of children suffering from club-foot deformity can be estimated, but the choice of the orthopaedic surgeon to adhere to the new product is questionable. In October 2008, Foot also solicited for an international patent because the main competitors of Foot are located in Germany, England and the United States.

Climate control systems at Cool

Idea emergence

In the nineties, market developments were taking place concerning heating based on aquifer systems. These systems heat buildings using groundwater, stored in the earth, underneath the house. As global warming takes place and the earth becomes warmer, one may expect thermic pollution to occur in the earth as more warm water will be sent back into the earth. The owner of Cool doubted this system and feared that the government would set taxes to prevent thermic pollution. Moreover, he noticed that, whereas many firms develop and produce parts of a heating system, they do not really change the energy systems. He said: 'It is like pimping up a car, you can put new headlights in, but the rest will stay the same'.

The owner of Cool believed that a new system could be developed by taking an integrative approach. The system should be environmentally friendly, but not taxable by the government. He therefore decided to merge his knowledge about cooling installations, air and process technology, to find a proper combination for a new system. As a result, he decided to develop a system that enables both warming and cooling by using air. Eventually the idea of developing a system using air as a source for heating emerged in 2001, but due to time constraints caused by daily business the idea was only pursued in 2003. The decision to pursue the idea was mainly driven by the owner's conviction in the idea.

Development

For developing the system, the owner of Cool decided not to opt for a subsidy because of the administrative burden and the need to document product specifications. At the same time, he faced difficulties receiving a bank loan for his innovative work: 'There are not many banks, most think the same and allow little playground. Banks are authorities where you can pick up a bag of money, but not when you are pursuing radical ideas'. He therefore decided to take the risk and fund the development by means of cash flows from his daily business.

In 2003 the innovation process was started, which entailed developing the technology specifications of the heat pump and developing a management system to allow for process management via the Internet. Developing an integrative system is a challenging task and was referred to by the owner as working on a puzzle: 'You start working on a puzzle piece and you need to search for all the right puzzle pieces in a puzzle consisting of over a thousand pieces'.

According to the owner, simultaneously managing both the innovation process and the daily business was a very challenging task, requiring a great deal of commitment and trust in the idea to continue the innovation process. During the further development of the innovation, two more employees with technical backgrounds became involved in the process, but still only on a part-time basis.

At the end of 2004, the first prototype was finished, proving that the idea was technologically feasible. Energy systems require labels, stating that the system adheres to the market standards. However, due to the discontinuous nature of the innovation, there was no measurement standard for the system. As a result, the firm decided to consult a research institute with the question of developing a procedure with which the innovation could receive a similar label. This process was started at the end of 2005 and in 2006 the label was received.

In 2006, Cool started consumer testing, which involved placing the innovation in newly built consumer houses and monitoring the functioning of the innovation under the given conditions. Consumer testing was started on a small scale, enabling sufficient attention to be given to the consumers. Consumer testing was continued until 2008 and the results were positive. Cool was very satisfied with the comments received during the testing period: 'During consumer testing you receive more focus and sharper knowledge about the product, how to present it in brochures and how to guide system installers'.

In 2006 further developments on the system involved architectonic research on how the system functions in different buildings. In 2007 the first monitoring results were received and were sent to a governmental organization stimulating innovative activities. Given the positive monitoring results, the governmental organization decided to grant subsidies to consumers purchasing the energy system.

Commercialization

Cool decided to set up a separate firm for the commercialization of the discontinuous innovation. The new firm is a joint venture, of which the owner of Cool owns 51% and another party 49%. The other party is a large established firm, providing several advantages, such as greater capital wealth and the social legitimacy of an external partner, due to which a larger market can be supplied. To enable larger production, production lines were set up abroad.

The joint venture hired an employee to manage the marketing of the innovation and the owner of Cool remained responsible for the technical aspects of the innovation. In total, the development of the innovation took five years. One of the major problems experienced during these years related to the investment costs. There were times during the development process when the owner of Cool experienced setbacks and feared bankruptcy, making not losing one's temper and continuing the discontinuous innovation process a great challenge.

RF production line at Machine

Idea emergence

In 2004, the owner of Machine was invited to join a meeting at one of the largest meat producers in the Netherlands. During this visit, he realized that the production of sausages was a very time-consuming process. At the same time, he was convinced that the process could be improved and he swiftly made a sketch of an altered production process. He said:

This is how the first step towards the innovation was made. I made a sketch on a piece of paper, which disappeared in the cupboard of the director of this meat company. After half a year I was called again to talk about the sketch made on that piece of paper. This is how the process took off.

The food sector is quite a side-step from what Machine used to do and one may question how the owner generated the idea of a production line for sausages. When asked this question, he answered:

I think it has to do with the person. When walking somewhere, I always tend to think about how things came into existence, how they were made and how they can be improved. It is a trait you ought to have.

To receive feedback on the feasibility of the idea, the owner of Machine contacted a researcher at a Dutch university with whom he had spoken before.

Development

As suggested by people from the Dutch university, the owner divided the innovation process into six stages. In April 2005 the first stage of the discontinuous innovation process, 'proof of principle of electromagnetic heating', was started. This stage entailed the theoretical testing of radiofrequency (RF) technology. The meat-producing company was involved from this point onwards, providing information on the production of sausages and their preferences. The feasibility study was conducted by the Dutch university. The results of this feasibility study were positive, providing the necessary enthusiasm to continue the innovation process and to solicit for a subsidy, but not in an ordinary fashion. The owner of Machine said:

I like short lines and I like being straightforward. I therefore went to the ministry myself and asked for a subsidy. My appearance did amaze them, but anyway, I did receive entrance due to my contacts at the Dutch university.

In the second stage, theory was transformed into practice by developing a small-scale pilot machine and by carrying out tests. This stage included the same participants as in the previous stage. This stage was successfully completed and the next step should have been the development of a large-scale pilot, but the owner of Machine decided to skip this stage in order to save costs and time.

The third stage was concerned with the development and testing of a large-scale 0-series production. From this stage onwards, the innovation process became more formalized both in terms of activities and organizational structure. To build a solid large-scale 0-series, more diverse activities had to be performed for which involvement of third parties was necessary. The owner of Machine therefore hired two employees with food knowledge to work on the innovation. The employees were put to work at a different location:

> The developments took place externally. We rented a building for a year. I decided to keep the developments behind closed doors. In this way, nobody would walk in and see what we were doing. Even the suppliers were not allowed in until the innovation was legally protected.

The activities really started to take off at this point. The owner of Machine therefore decided to create a separate firm for the development and commercialization of the RF production line.

Stage four involved the further development and construction of the 0-series. Because of the novelty of the innovation, several adjustments were necessary. The owner of Machine said: 'This technology has never been applied in a similar way. Everything is new, we started something, we calculated it, but in practice you need to redefine it, manage and adjust it'.

Commercialization

To reach commercialization of the production line, two more stages had to be completed: stage five, which is related to the production of the machine (production line), and stage six in which the machine will be (further produced and) sold. At the time of our data collection, the owner of Machine was busy planning the transition to stages five and six. Although he was still convinced about the huge market potential for the innovation, he also saw some challenges in successfully launching the product: 'Currently the biggest problem is to launch the production line on the market, because the money provided by the subsidy has been used for the development of the innovation. We are now considering cooperating with external investors'.

Given that Machine had a lack of financial resources and social legitimacy it was considering cooperating with external investors to enable commercialization beyond the Netherlands. A further challenge, due to the discontinuity of the innovation, was to gain customer trust in the RF technology. After all, customers have to get accustomed to 'radiated food', a facet at which consumers may look critically. To prepare for this challenge, Machine Food Systems outsourced market research.

Comparative Analysis and Discussion

In this section, we compare the discontinuous innovation processes across the three cases. The discontinuous innovation processes will be compared in terms of idea emergence, development and the commercialization of the discontinuous innovation.

Idea emergence

Discontinuous ideas can be triggered by a variety of sources, such as new technology or new political rules (Bessant and Tidd, 2007). Large established firms are often said to suffer from inertia and therefore do not respond in a timely manner to such triggers. In comparison, start-ups are said to be much more responsive to them.

Our findings indicate that the observed established SMEs were able to react to environmental triggers in a timely manner. However, they did not structure the search for discontinuous ideas. The SMEs did not intentionally scan the environment for discontinuous ideas, but rather ran into the ideas or were approached with ideas or problems. The latter is opposed to Bessant and Tidd (2007) who argue that established firms need to search and scan their external and internal environment to pick up signals about potential innovations.

In each case, the most important mechanism, enabling the established SMEs to recognize the discontinuous idea, was the entrepreneurial mindset of the owner. Besides this entrepreneurial ability, two additional mechanisms were applied. One of the mechanisms was probing and learning, which is concerned with prototyping quickly rather than spending a lot of time on planning (Bessant and von Stamm, 2007) and the other mechanism is before-the-box thinking, which relates to brainstorming about possible solutions to a problem without taking existing solutions into account.

Development

After the idea emerged, the established SME had to make the decision whether to pursue it or not. Whereas the selection of discontinuous ideas is often depicted as a separate stage in the discontinuous innovation process (Veryzer, 1998; Tidd *et al.*, 2005) , our findings indicate that the established SMEs create an emergent selection environment, in which they continuously monitor process, using different evaluation tools over time. At the initial stages of the development process, selection mechanisms are mainly based on subjective judgement. Later on, feasibility tests are conducted to justify the decision to continue the development process and build external legitimacy. The fact that the established SMEs are able to select and pursue discontinuous innovations indicates that they are not largely hampered by their age, which is often said to increase organizational rigidity and ossification of communication patterns (Sorensen and Stuart, 2000).

In all observed cases, the established SMEs faced a lack of financial resources to fund the development process. Most of the established SMEs addressed this challenge by applying for a subsidy. An additional challenge was to overcome the competency gap, which refers to a situation in which a firm lacks one or more competencies to develop the innovation (Leifer *et al.*, 2000). To address this latter challenge, the established SMEs preferred to cooperate with universities or research institutes as they possess valuable knowledge and are less threatening than large established firms. In addition, all established SMEs outsourced to a wide variety of third parties to further close-up the competency gap.

In all cases, interviewees emphasized that the development of the discontinuous innovation was a messy process with huge uncertainty. In order to gradually decrease the uncertainty, the observed established SMEs heavily relied on prototyping. These prototypes were not only evaluated within the firm, but were also discussed with important stakeholders (i.e. end customers and external partners).

Machine was the only established SME that decided to develop the discontinuous innovation behind closed doors at a different location to avoid unintended knowledge outflows. After the necessary intellectual property was acquired, the discontinuous innovation project was disclosed. Not only Machine but also Foot invested in applying for patents to protect their discontinuous innovation. Cool, however, deliberately chose not to opt for a patent as it did not want to disclose the technical specifications of the discontinuous innovation.

Commercialization

All interviewees explicitly referred to the commercialization of the discontinuous innovation as a huge additional step that required substantial investments. Although they had great ambitions and wanted to launch the innovation on an international scale, they lacked the financial resources and social legitimacy to independently commercialize the innovation. Cool therefore decided to create a joint venture with an external investor for the launch of their discontinuous innovation. In a similar vein, Machine was looking for investors to fund the commercialization stage of its development trajectory. At the same time, Foot closely collaborated with hospitals and orthotists to improve their visibility and legitimacy.

The established SMEs also faced the challenge of accurately predicting the size of their potential markets. Getting in touch with end customers (i.e. patient testing in the case of Foot, implementing the first climate control systems in consumer houses in the case of Cool) was seen as the only viable strategy to get better insights into the potential market response.

Conclusion

In this chapter, we have conducted an in-depth exploration of discontinuous innovation at established SMEs. This study complements existing discontinuous innovation literature by focusing on discontinuous innovation within small firms. At the same time, our study deviates from previous SME research by focusing on established SMEs instead of high-tech start-ups. Our findings show that the owners of these established SMEs had the necessary entrepreneurial spirit to identify and embrace discontinuous opportunities. Instead of relying on a wide variety of formal mechanisms to manage the discontinuous innovation processes, they relied on informal approaches to identify, select and implement their innovation. They also heavily relied on an open innovation approach (Chesbrough, 2003) to fill up competency gaps that emerged during the process. At the same time, they were very careful in selecting external partners in order to avoid opportunistic abuse of the collaboration by the external partner. In Table 3, we provide a number of specific recommendations that can help managers in optimizing their discontinuous innovation processes.

Table 3. Managerial advice for established SMEs.

Throughout the whole process	• Collaborate with external partners to get access to necessary complementary competencies. Universities and other knowledge institutes can be a valuable and safe source of in-depth knowledge • Entrepreneurial mindset is a must, which includes courage, conviction and the ability to recognize a means-end framework • Be patient, allow for uncertainty and be aware of long development times • Find a healthy balance between daily business and the discontinuous innovation process

Idea emergence stage	• Combine out-of-the-box thinking and before-the-box thinking to identify truly discontinuous ideas • Allow for an informal selection stage-gate process, which will decrease uncertainty throughout the discontinuous innovation process
Development stage	• Search for additional financial resources. Applying for subsidies might be a viable strategy in this respect • Implement a clear and structured process and meeting schedule (framework) to allow for clear milestones and discussion on various facets of the process, even though the process may require going back and forth • Depending on the innovation, involvement of the end consumers in the innovation process can be very valuable in terms of product experience, preferences and consumer reactions
Commercialization stage	• When aiming for international commercialization, anticipate the need for additional (financial) resources, social legitimacy and capabilities

We hope that our findings might help managers to successfully complete the challenging adventure of realizing discontinuous innovation. At the same time, we encourage future research on discontinuous innovation in alternative organizational settings in order to increase our knowledge on how different kinds of firms manage and respond to discontinuous innovation.

References

Alvarez, S.H.and Barney, J.B. (2001). How entrepreneurial firms can benefit from alliances with large partners. *Academy of Management Executives*, 15(1), 139–148.

Barton, L.D. (1992). Core capabilities and core rigidities: A paradox in managing new product development. *Strategic Management Journal*, 13, 111–125.

Bessant, J. (2008). Dealing with discontinuous innovation: The European experience. *International Journal of Technology Management*, 42(1), 36–50.

Bessant, J., Birkinshaw, J. and Delbridge, R. (2004). Innovation as unusual. *Business Strategy Review*, 15(3), 32–35.

Bessant, J. and Tidd, J. (2007). *Innovation and Entrepreneurship*. John Wiley & Sons, West Sussex.

Bessant, J. and von Stamm, B. (2007). Beyond the lamp-post: Innovation search strategies for discontinuous conditions. Working paper.

Bessant, J., von Stamm, B., Moeslein, K.M. and Neyer, A. (2010). Backing outsiders: Selection strategies for discontinuous innovation. *R&D Management*, 40, 345–356.

Birkinshaw, J. and Gibson, C. (2004). Building ambidexterity into an organization. *MIT Sloan Management Review*, 45, 47–55.

Bougrain, F. and Haudeville, B. (2002). Innovation, collaboration and SMEs internal research capacities. *Research Policy*, 31(5), 735–747.

Chesbrough, H. (2003). The era of open innovation. *MIT Sloan Management Review*, 44(3), 35–41

Christensen, C.M. (1997). *The Innovator's Dilemma: When New Technologies Cause Great Firms to Fail*. Harvard Business School Press, Boston, MA.

Christensen, C.M. and Overdorf, M. (2000). Meeting the challenge of disruptive change. *Harvard Business Review*, 78(2), 66–76.

Debackere, K., (1997). *Topics in the Management of Technology and Innovation: A Synopsis of Major Findings*. Bedrijfseconomische Verhandeling, Leuven: Department of Applied Economics, K.U. Leuven.

DeTienne, D.R. and Koberg, C.S. (2002). The Impact of environmental and organizational factors on discontinuous innovation within high-technology industries. *IEEE Transactions on Engineering Management*, 49(4), 352–364.

Gertsen, F., Sloan, T., Chapman, R. and Kyvsgaard, P. (2007). A trilogy on discontinuous innovation. Part 1: Search. *Proceedings of 21st ANZAM Conference, Sydney*.

Kassicieh, S.K. and Walsh, S.T. (2002). Factors differentiating the commercialization of disruptive and sustaining technologies. *IEEE Transactions on Engineering Management*, 49(4), 375–387.

Kaufmann, A. and Tödtling, F. (2002). How effective is innovation support for SMEs? An analysis of the region of Upper Austria. *Technovation*, 2, 147–159.

Lefebvre, L.A. and Lefebvre, E. (1992). Competitive positioning and innovative efforts in SMEs. *Small Business Economics*, 5, 297–305.

Leifer, R., McDermott, C.M., O'Connor, G.C., Peters, L.S., Rice, M.P. and Veryzer, R.W. (2000). *Radical Innovation. How Mature Companies Can Outsmart Upstarts.* Harvard Business School Press, Boston, MA.

Leonard-Barton, D. (1990). A dual methodology for case studies: Synergistic use of a longitudinal single site with replicated multiple studies. *Organization Science*, 1(3), 248–266.

Lynn, G.S., Morone, J.G. and Paulson, A.S. (1996). Marketing and discontinuous innovation: The probe and learn process. *California Management Review*, 38, 7–38.

Mascitelli, R. (2000). From experience: Harnessing tacit knowledge to achieve breakthrough innovation. *Product Innovation Management*, 17, 179–193.

McDermott, C. and Handfield, R. (1996). Does the parallel approach make sense in the development of discontinuous innovations? *International Engineering and Technology Management Conference.*

McDermott, C. and O'Connor, G.C. (2002). Managing radical innovation: An overview of emergent strategy issues. *Journal of Product Innovation Management*, 19(6), 424–438.

Miles, M.B. and Huberman, A.M. (1994). *An Expanded Sourcebook. Qualitative Data Analysis.* Sage Publications, Thousand Oaks, CA.

MKB Servicedesk (2009). Informatie over MKB in Nederland. Cijfers en organisaties bij het midden- en kleinbedrijf. Available at: http://www.mkbservicedesk.nl/569/informatie-over-mkb-nederland.htm. [Accessed 4 March 2009.]

O'Connor, G.C. and Veryzer. J.R.W. (2001) The nature of market visioning for technology-based radical innovation. *Journal of Product Innovation Management*, 18, 231–246

O'Reilly, C.A. and Tushman, M.L. (2008). Ambidexterity as a dynamic capability: Resolving the innovator's dilemma. *Research in Organizational Behavior*, 28, 185–206.

Prashantham, S. and Birkinshaw, J. (2008). Dancing with gorillas: How small companies can partner effectively with MNCs. *California Management Review*, 51(1), 6–23.

Reid, S.E. and de Brentani, U. (2004). The fuzzy front end of new product development for discontinuous innovations: A theoretical model. *Journal of Product Innovation Management*, 21(3), 170–184.

Rice, M.P., Leifer, R. and O'Connor, G.C. (2002). Commercializing discontinuous innovations: Bridging the gap from discontinuous innovation project to operations. *IEEE Transactions on Engineering Management*, 49(4), 330–340.

Sorensen, J.B. and Stuart, T.E. (2000). Aging, obsolescence and organizational innovation. *Administrative Science Quarterly*, 45, 81–112.

Tidd, J., Bessant, J. and Pavitt, K. (2005). *Managing Innovation. Integrating Technological, Market and Organizational Change.* John Wiley and Sons, Chichester.

Van de Ven, A.H. (2007). *Engaged Scholarship. A Guide for Organizational and Social Research.* Oxford University Press, Oxford.

Veryzer, R.W. (1998). Discontinuous innovation and the new product development process. *Journal of Product Innovation Management*, 15(4), 304–321.

Yin, R.K. (2003). *Case Study Research. Design and Methods, Vol. 5. 3rd edition.* Sage Publications, Thousand Oaks, CA.

Chapter 7

Discontinuous Innovation Search for SMEs and Large Organisations

John Nicholas and Ann Ledwith
University of Limerick, Ireland

Introduction

Companies of all sizes require both exploration and exploitation search activities for long-term success and survival (Eisenhardt and Martin, 2000; Benner and Tushman, 2002; Feinberg and Gupta, 2004; March, 2006). Creating an appropriate balance between these two different kinds of activity represents a route to success for most companies (Benner and Tushman, 2003; He and Wong, 2004). Given their different natures, these two search activities require very different enabling mechanisms and routines (von Stamm, 2008).

Small companies are often credited as being the most likely source of innovation (Schumpeter, 1934). Certain studies point to the fact that small- and medium-sized enterprises (SMEs) are better at innovation than large companies (Rothwell, 1978). Wakasugi and Koyata (1997) found that while the number of new products developed and the number of patent applications increased in accordance with firm size, there was no evidence of economies of scale in relation to new product development (NPD) activities, suggesting that small firms can be as efficient in their product development activities as large firms. Typically, established small companies are likely to follow a 'defender strategy' (Brouthers *et al.*, 1998; Aragón-Sánchez and Sánchez-Marín, 2005), meaning that they focus only on their existing products and markets with no thought to exploration of new territory. Engaging in this type of behaviour is inherently dangerous, particularly for small companies. Niche markets, once the preserve of SMEs, are often aggressively targeted by larger organisations. If a company does not engage in innovative activity, they carry the risk of becoming over-dependent on their existing customers. Soderquist *et al.* (1997) found smaller companies often have little choice but to foster closer links with a very few key customers due to a lack of resources and increased market sector competition. This customer dependency results in a company being very vulnerable to market changes (Raymond and St-Pierre, 2004). Engaging in innovative activity reduces this dependency and exposes companies to new untapped markets. Accordingly, excellence in the search phase of discontinuous innovation is of key importance to discontinuous innovation success.

Importance of and Danger Posed by Discontinuous Innovation

Discontinuous innovation is crucial to the growth of firms and industries. Successful innovations can propel small companies into a position of industry dominance and can result in the failure of those incumbents that do not recognise the potential of very new technologies (Chandy and Tellis, 2000; Srinivasan *et al.*, 2002; Utterback, 1996). Empirical studies (Koberg *et al.*, 2003) have demonstrated that established and successful organisations manage incremental innovation well but are less able to develop and manage radical and discontinuous innovation. The risks and barriers that incumbent firms face when attempting to deal with radical innovation are well documented (Christensen, 1997; Leifer *et al.*, 2001). The ability to remain a market leader through radical change requires the constant acquisition of new knowledge (Drucker, 1991; Grant, 1996); first to drive radical innovation within the company and second as a detection tool to evaluate the potentialities of additional new knowledge from external sources. The problem with discontinuous innovation is that it presents challenges which, for most firms, do not fit the existing schema and require a reframing – something which existing incumbents find hard to do (Christensen, 1997). Established companies can become locked into the behaviours and systems that have worked successfully in the past (Bate, 1994) but ones that may not be capable of dealing with future challenges.

Studies have shown that the continual introduction of new-to-market innovations is a route to survival and growth for large and small firms (Cooper, 1993; Storey, 1994). Storey (1994) found that many small companies have no ambition to grow and expand. The added risk in attempting to develop new products outweighs the possible growth benefits, and therefore companies are content with their existing products and customers. Mosey *et al.* (2002) demonstrated that the small companies with aggressive growth ambitions who repeatedly introduced innovative new products that opened up new market niches were also the best-performing companies. A continual incremental improvement strategy is the major driving force behind any improvement effort; however, radical innovations should be used to jump-start critical products, services and processes intermittently (Terziovski *et al.*, 2002). If a company is looking for growth levels that are significantly larger than the growth of the industry, then it must take discontinuous or radical innovation seriously (Bessant *et al.*, 2004).

Searching for Discontinuous Innovations

Small companies vs. large companies

The fuzzy front end or the front end of innovation represents the activities which take place before an idea or concept enters a formal, well-structured NPD process. The fuzzy front end includes all activities from original opportunity identification and analysis up to the concept selection and early development stage (Koen *et al.*, 2001). These early stages are the root of success for firms involved with discontinuous new product innovation (Reid and de Brentani, 2004). The search for new ideas to create a stream of potential new products is an important step in the innovation process which is relatively low in cost compared to the cost of actually implementing any one idea (Urban and Hauser, 1993). A large body of research has been completed on best practices in NPD and innovation, though it is worth noting that the majority of this research focuses on the best practices of larger organisations (Griffin, 1997; Leifer *et al.*, 2000; Cooper *et al.*, 2002a; Cooper *et al.*, 2002b;

McDermott and O'Connor, 2002; Adams-Bigelow, 2004). The applicability of this research to SMEs may be questioned due to inherent differences in the management and structure of SMEs. Best practices for radical innovation search might not vary with company size given that the search for new ideas is relatively low in cost compared to implementing the ideas, effectively negating the greatest barrier facing smaller companies – resources.

How and where to search?

Searching for radical new product ideas is different from searching for incremental ideas (Bessant *et al.,* 2005). Success in radical innovation requires the capability to scan for signals about potential change and to move into new areas and cannibalise current markets (Tidd and Bessant, 2009). Some practices that have the potential to increase a company's search capacity are briefly summarised in the following literature review.

The companies with the best innovation performance tend to have frequent interaction and close relationships with customers and with other businesses (Ahmed, 1997). Market orientation is key for companies (Narver and Slater, 1990; Langerak *et al.*, 2004). Market-orientated firms succeed by staying close to their customers, understanding, predicting and solving their needs. Lead users, those who experience needs ahead of the average consumer, are particularly important as a source of ideas for radical or discontinuous innovation (von Hippel, 1986). The role of lead users in exploiting products in ways that had not been considered by manufacturers – frequently by modifying or adapting products in innovative ways – has been the topic of extensive research (Herstatt and von Hippel, 1992; Lilien *et al.,* 2002; Franke and Shah, 2003; Jeppesen and Molin, 2003). Lilien *et al.* (2002) found that projects which utilised lead users resulted in higher novelty and typically addressed more original and newer customer needs, and also had significantly higher forecasted sales than other projects. Bessant and von Stamm (2007) discuss how important lead users become within the discontinuous innovation context because the challenge is often to find the things which no-one has yet noticed and create markets which currently do not exist.

There has been a shift from a closed innovation model to a more open innovation model (Chesbrough, 2003) in recent times with companies involving external organisations in the knowledge creation and capture activities. Formal links with other stakeholders in the innovation process have been identified as a predictor of innovation success (Griffin and Hauser, 1996). Guan *et al.* (2005) found that collaboration with universities and research institutes resulted in the development of more novel technologies. Barczak *et al.* (2009) demonstrated the importance of collaboration for radical innovation and reported that more than 50% of radical projects involved collaboration with partner organisations.

Employees are commonly recognised as a key source of new product ideas (Rothwell, 1994; Leiponen, 2005; Mohnen and Roller, 2005). In 3M, a company renowned for its innovation, emphasis is placed on recruiting innovative people (Gundling and Porras, 2000). Bessant and von Stamm (2007) highlight the importance of using employees as scouts to trigger the innovation process. Hiring creative people will promote the continuous challenging of the status quo and experimentation necessary for radical innovation (Leonard-Barton, 1992; Bessant and von Stamm 2007) while people with risk-taking propensity, personal drive and out-of-the-box thinking are more likely to be involved in radical projects (Leifer *et al.*, 2001).

Innovation, though it cannot be planned, rarely happens by accident. Innovation requires work and commitment and to be successful it must be embraced by the entire organisation (Rothwell, 1992). Mobilising the entire workforce and utilising their potential leads to increased search capacity (Bessant and von Stamm, 2007). Treating innovation as a company-wide task ensures that it is given high priority throughout the organisation (Ahmed, 1997). Hickman and Raia (2002) argue that innovation thrives on disorder, imagination and ambiguity while Tang (1998) suggests that 'innovation thrives on challenge'. People are the source of creativity, but innovation is influenced by organisation and attitude rather than solitary genius (Hargadon and Sutton, 2000). However, individual creativity leads to group creativity, which in turn leads to innovative new products (Woodman *et al.*, 1993; Kanter, 2000).

From the AIM report on radical search (Bessant and von Stamm, 2007) and other literature, a list of search practices that potentially were positive predictors of radical innovation success were identified (Table 1). It is important to stress that these practices are not presented as an exhaustive list of all possible practices that companies, small and large, can implement in the search for discontinuous ideas and knowledge. It is possible that there are other practices or different nuances of practices that are not covered in this list. However, this list is intended as a starting point to stimulate discussion and is open to refinement. These practices went on to form the basis of a survey subsequently distributed to a selection of companies in Ireland.

Table 1. Discontinuous innovation search practices.

Practice	Shorthand
Our organisation sets up teams to actively search out and implement new ideas that will take our business in new directions	Create active teams
When we have a very new and different technology, we search for multiple applications and conduct several market experiments to discover promising markets	Seek multiple applications
We have people (part-time or full-time) officially charged with scouting for new ideas, finding new sources of potential radical ideas and looking for trends and developments that might have implications for the organisation's future	Employ scouts
We have a website where outsiders can submit their suggestions and ideas for new markets, products and/or services	Suggestion website
We use an open innovation system in which technology-related challenges are posted online by our R&D staff so that a community of registered scientists anywhere in the world can propose their solutions	Open innovation system
Our organisation is able to identify and collaborate with its lead users	Work with lead users
We make an effort to connect to our customers' consumers (end users) and obtain regular feedback on their demands, as we recognise that they drive what our customers need	Connect with end consumers
We currently have systems or procedures in place that ensure insights from mainstream staff that have the opportunity to gather information from external sources are being collected systematically	Mobile mainstream staff

We actively encourage people to go to events/conferences/ courses that are outside their current realms of experience	Activity diversity
In our organisation, we have one company-wide centralised idea management system in place where all employees can submit ideas for evaluation and receive quick feedback	Idea management system
In our organisation, we encourage radical innovation teams to expand their resource network by tapping into the knowledge of any employee in our firm	Connect people internally
Our organisation operates some form of brokering/bridge-building that involves bringing together people from different knowledge sets, backgrounds or functions in order to support discontinuous innovation	Broker knowledge sets

Methodology

A survey was developed using the search practices described in Table 1. The survey was administered to a sample of 580 Irish firms in 2009. Firms were broad-based across several high-tech industries, including medical devices, software development, pharmaceuticals and electronics. The data collection process was supported by the use of Survey Monkey. Respondents were typically the vice president or director of the R&D department or the CEO. Out of the 580 contacted, 107 companies completed the survey. The data was analysed with SPSS using various 'cuts' on the data including large companies, SMEs, non-innovator companies (zero radical innovation in previous five years) and serial innovators (two or more radical innovations in previous five years). Following the survey, focus groups were held with practitioners to establish what barriers small companies face when attempting to engage in the practices described in the survey instrument.

Results

Table 2 shows the usage of each of the practices in SMEs vs. large companies and serial innovators vs. non-innovators. Scores shown are mean scores on a usage scale of 1–5.

Table 2. Usage of search practices; SME vs. large companies, serial innovator vs. non-innovator companies.

Practice	Small	Large	Small vs. Large	Serial inno-vator	Non-inno-vator	nno-vator vs. non-innovator
Create active teams	2.93	3.83	−2.789***	4.22	3.05	−3.197****
Seek multiple applications	3.16	3.66	−1.682*	4.00	3.02	−3.283****
Employ scouts	2.98	3.80	−2.086**	4.00	3.02	−1.942**
Suggestion website	1.76	2.22	−2.537**	2.29	1.90	−0.466
Open innovation system	1.60	2.00	−2.445**	2.07	1.56	−1.506
Engage lead users	3.53	3.85	−0.941	4.00	3.49	−2.733***
Connect with end consumers	3.49	4.33	−3.303****	4.16	3.79	−1.647*
Mobile mainstream staff	2.69	2.89	−1.101	3.40	2.50	−2.112**
Activity diversity	3.12	3.21	−0.248	3.63	3.00	−1.050
Idea management system	2.70	2.48	−0.033	2.94	2.51	−1.204
Connect people internally	2.79	3.18	−1.637	3.39	2.71	−2.065**
Broker knowledge sets	2.90	3.36	−1.769*	3.65	2.90	−2.360**
**** $p > 0.001$, *** $p > 0.01$, ** $p > 0.05$, * $p > 0.1$						

Table 3 shows the correlations between company size, market position and involvement in radical innovation. Company size was measured in terms of employee head count. Market position was measured on a scale from non-viable to dominant.

Table 3. Correlations between company size, market position, radical innovation involvement and industry sector.

	Company size	Market position	No. of radical innovations
Company size	1	−0.452**	−0.481**
Market position		1	0.210*
No. of radical innovations			1
** $p < 0.01$, * $p < 0.05$			

Table 4 shows the results from the innovation focus group sessions. Three clusters of barriers facing small companies when attempting to search for ideas for radical innovation were identified. These clusters can be summarised as culture-based, resource-based and knowledge-based barriers to innovation.

Table 4. Barriers to innovation for small non-dominant companies.

Cluster	Barrier
Cultural	• Fear of failure • Lack of management support • Existing risk-averse culture • Fear of sharing ideas (both internal, i.e. within NPD teams, and external, i.e. open innovation) • Radical innovation not required unless company is in trouble
Resource	• Too expensive • Time: too busy manufacturing, too busy fighting fires, etc. • Lack of qualified personnel, need for training • Lack of support systems for implementation
Knowledge	• Awareness of search strategies • Know-how regarding implementation of strategies, e.g. how to identify lead active users, where to send scouts, how to look at futures, etc.

Discussions and Implications

The sample represented a broad cross-section of high-tech companies in Ireland from industries including medical devices, software development, pharmaceuticals and electronics, with the medical devices sector representing 23% of the sample. The sample was balanced in terms of size, with 51.5% of the sample representing SMEs and the remaining 48.5% representing large organisations. The correlations between company size, involvement in radical innovation and perceived market position demonstrate a relationship between these three variables but no relationship with industry sector. Large companies are significantly more likely to be engaging in radical innovation than SMEs. Companies in a strong/dominant market position are also significantly more likely to be engaged in radical innovation than companies in favourable or viable positions. Finally, large companies are more likely to consider themselves 'strong' or 'dominant' within their industries.

The search practices were developed from the literature in addition to studying a combination of case studies, surveys and experience-sharing within a variety of incumbent firms highly involved in innovation. A comparison of the usage of the practices by the serial innovator companies with the usage of the practices by the non-innovator companies revealed that the serial innovators are more likely to use all of the practices than the non-innovators and use eight of the search practices significantly more than non-innovators. This high usage of the practices by the innovators is not an unexpected result but it does provide validation of the practices as being suitable for discontinuous innovation search. Practices such as creating active teams, seeking out multiple applications for existing technologies and employing scouts were the key practices employed by the serial innovators. These practices are proactive, encourage risk-taking and demonstrate that a company is open to change, which are characteristics the most innovative companies share (Johannessen *et al.*, 1999).

An examination of the small companies' usage in comparison to the large companies' usage of the search practices reveals that small companies are much more likely to use almost all of the practices less than large companies and use six of the practices significantly less than large companies. The key practices differing between the two groups were creating active teams, seeking out multiple applications for existing technologies and employing scouts; the practices shown to differentiate the serial innovators from the non-innovators. In addition to these practices, neglect of their end consumers was also a key difference. Typically, SMEs are very close to their existing customers (Soderquist *et al.*, 1997; Tidd and Bessant, 2009); however, the relationship with the end user clearly has a bearing on successful innovation.

There was no difference in the perceived importance of the strategies between the innovators and the non-innovators or between the small and large companies, so the question remains: why are so many of the small companies not using the strategies in their innovation efforts? What barriers exist to utilising these search strategies?

The focus groups identified several clusters of barriers facing companies wishing to search for ideas for radical innovation in Ireland. These clusters represent culture-based, resource-based and knowledge-based barriers to engaging in innovation. A lack of resources is commonly cited as a key barrier to innovation (Tidd and Bessant, 2009), in particular by smaller companies (Hadjimanolis, 1999). Resources are limited in all companies and as a result choices have to be made regarding their allocation and the prioritisation of individual projects. Limited and scarce resources do not have to represent a significant disadvantage for a company wishing to engage in innovation. As highlighted by Christensen's (1997) review of the disk drive industry, a market leader with a large amount of resources at its disposal does not always achieve continued success, particularly when faced with a shift in market needs. Often the more important issue is the management of the scarce resources. Searching for radical ideas need not necessarily be an expensive and resource-intensive endeavour. Strategies such as employing scouts, engaging lead users, seeking multiple market applications and connecting people internally can be implemented successfully in a cost-effective manner. The central theme of radical innovation search is the idea of 'doing things differently' and 'outside-of-the-box' search; thus companies should consider implementing the strategies in an alternative manner rather than focusing on high-cost implementation. Essentially the search strategies represent best practice for radical innovation search. However, this excellence in radical search cannot be directly transferred by copying instances of best practice from exemplar firms or training staff. Specific training is difficult for radical idea search as each project differs so much from the next. Thus a capability must be built up over time with systematic learning between projects. As companies and their employees gain experience and credibility by transferring their own technologies into new areas, they can then experiment with sourcing new technologies to meet emerging needs (Mosey, 2005).

Cultural barriers to innovation and change, as reported by the focus groups, are well documented in previous research (Ghobadian and Gallear, 1997; Hadjimanolis, 1999; de Brentani, 2001; Loewe and Dominiquini, 2006) and indeed strategies for overcoming these barriers to innovation have been proposed (Mascitelli, 2000; Lemon and Sahota, 2004; Alegre and Chiva, 2008; McLaughlin *et al.*, 2008). A lack of knowledge and awareness is identified as a major barrier to engaging in innovation by the respondents and the other two major barriers relating to resources and culture are linked to this knowledge issue. Companies appear to lack the knowledge of how to overcome cultural barriers and implement radical search strategies in a cost-effective manner.

The search strategies outlined in this chapter represent methods companies can use to increase their ability to search for ideas for radical or discontinuous innovations. This study has highlighted that there is a gap between the practices of firms who have a record of successfully introducing radical innovations and those which do not. The 12 search strategies presented were validated as being linked with successful radical innovation in our sample. A comparison of the use of these strategies within the serial innovator and non-innovator companies demonstrated that the innovators use all the strategies to a larger degree than the non-innovators. Small companies do not engage in discontinuous innovation to the same degree as large companies. SMEs utilise the discontinuous innovation search practices to a lesser degree than the large companies. If innovation managers want to develop discontinuous new products and prepare their company for inevitable discontinuous shifts that may occur, then they need to consider the search practices outlined in this research.

The identification of successful search practices offers a practical way for SMEs and large companies to measure their discontinuous innovation search capacity as the model focuses on dimensions and practices that are required for a company to be considered as competent in radical innovation search. Many markets are extremely competitive and companies when following their current trajectories often need to 'sprint' in order to keep pace with their competitors. If a company shifts their focus from their current trajectory and takes a few steps in an alternative direction and explores alternate spaces, then they may find the marketplace less crowded and more rewarding.

References

Adams-Bigelow, M. (2004). 'First results from the 2003 comparative performance assessment study (CPAS)', in Kahn, K.B. (ed.), *PDMA Handbook of New Product Development.* Wiley, Hoboken, NJ.

Ahmed, P. (1997). Benchmarking innovation best practice. *Benchmarking for Quality Management and Technology,* 5, 45–58.

Alegre, J. and Chiva, R. (2008). Assessing the impact of organizational learning capability on product innovation performance: An empirical test. *Technovation,* 28(6), 315–326.

Aragón-Sánchez, A. and Sánchez-Marín, G. (2005). Strategic orientation, management characteristics, and performance: A study of Spanish SMEs. *Journal of Small Business Management,* 43(3), 287–308.

Barczak, G., Griffin, A. and Kahn, K. (2009). Perspective: Trends and drivers of success in NPD practices: Results of the 2003 PDMA best practices study. *Journal of Product Innovation Management,* 26, 3–23.

Bate, P. (1994). *Strategies for Cultural Change.* Butterworth-Heinemann, Oxford.

Benner, M.J. and Tushman, M. (2002). Process management and technological innovation: A longitudinal study of the photography and paint industries. *Administrative Science Quarterly,* 47(4), 676–706.

Benner, M. and Tushman, M. (2003). Exploitation, exploration, and process management: The productivity dilemma revisited. *The Academy of Management Review*, 28(2), 238–256.

Bessant, J., Birkinshaw, J. and Delbridge, R. (2004). Theories of creation. *People Management*, 10(3), 28–31.

Bessant, J., Lamming, R., Noke, H. and Phillips, W. (2005). Managing innovation beyond the steady state. *Technovation*, 25(12), 1366–1376.

Bessant, J. and von Stamm, B. (2007). *Twelve Search Strategies that Could Save Your Organisation*. Advanced Institute of Management Research Executive Briefing, London.

Brouthers, K., Andriessen, F. and Nicolaes, I. (1998). Driving blind: Strategic decisionmaking in small companies. *Long Range Planning*, 31(1), 130–138.

Chandy, R.K. and Tellis, G.J. (2000). The incumbent's curse? Incumbency, size, and radical product innovation. *Journal of Marketing*, 64(3), 1–17.

Chesbrough, H. (2003). *Open Innovation: The New Imperative for Creating and Profiting from Technology*. Harvard Business School Press, Boston, MA.

Christensen, C. (1997). *The Innovator's Dilemma: When New Technologies Cause Great Firms to Fail*. Harvard Business School Press, Boston, MA.

Cooper, R.G. (1993). *Winning at New Products, 2nd Edition*. Perseus, Reading, MA.

Cooper, R.G., Edgett, S.J. and Kleinschmidt, E.J. (2002a). Optimizing the stage-gate process: What best-practice companies do I. *Research-Technology Management*, 45(5), 21–27.

Cooper, R.G., Edgett, S.J. and Kleinschmidt, E.J. (2002b). Optimizing the stage-gate process: What best-practice companies do II. *Research-Technology Management*, 45(6), 43–49.

de Brentani, U. (2001). Innovative versus incremental new business services: Different keys for achieving success. *Journal of Product Innovation Management*, 18(3), 169–187.

Drucker, P.F. (1991). The new productivity challenge. *Harvard Business Review*, 37(6), 69–76.

Eisenhardt, K. and Martin, J. (2000). Dynamic capabilities: What are they? *Strategic Management Journal*, 21(1), 1105–1121.

Feinberg, S.E. and Gupta, A.K. (2004). Knowledge spillovers and the assignment of R&D responsibilities to foreign subsidiaries. *Strategic Management Journal*, 25(8–9), 823–845.

Franke, N. and Shah, S. (2003). How communities support innovative activities: An exploration of assistance and sharing among end-users. *Research Policy*, 32(1), 157–178.

Ghobadian, A. and Gallear, D. (1997). TQM and organization size. *International Journal of Operations and Production Management*, 17, 121–163.

Grant, R.M. (1996). Toward a knowledge-based theory of the firm. *Strategic Management Journal*, 17, 109–122.

Griffin, A. (1997). PDMA research on new product development practices: Updating trends and benchmarking best practices. *Journal of Product Innovation Management*, 14(6), 429–458.

Griffin, A. and Hauser, J. (1996). Integrating R&D and marketing: A review and analysis of the literature. *Journal of Product Innovation Management*, 13(3), 191–215.

Guan, J., Yam, R. and Mok, C. (2005). Collaboration between industry and research institutes/universities on industrial innovation in Beijing, China. *Technology Analysis & Strategic Management*, 17(3), 339–353.

Gundling, E. and Porras, J. (2000). *The 3M Way to Innovation: Balancing People and Profit*. Kodansha International, Boston, MA.

Hadjimanolis, A. (1999). Barriers to innovation for SMEs in a small less developed country (Cyprus). *Technovation*, 19(9), 561–570.

Hargadon, A. and Sutton, R. (2000). Building an innovation factory. *Harvard Business Review*, 78(3), 157–166.

He, Z.L. and Wong, P.K. (2004). Exploration vs. exploitation: An empirical test of the ambidexterity hypothesis. *Organization Science*, 15, 481–494.

Herstatt, C. and von Hippel, E. (1992). From experience: Developing new product concepts via the lead user method: A case study. *Journal of Product Innovation Management*, 9(3), 213–221.

Hickman, C. and Raia, C. (2002). Incubating innovation. *Journal of Business Strategy*, 23(3), 14–18.

Jeppesen, L. and Molin, M. (2003). Consumers as co-developers: Learning and innovation outside the firm. *Technology Analysis & Strategic Management*, 15(3), 363–383.

Johannessen, J., Olsen, B. and Olaisen, J. (1999). Aspects of innovation theory based on knowledge-management. *International Journal of Information Management*, 19, 121–140.

Kanter, R. (2000). 'When a thousand flowers bloom: Structural, collective, and social conditions for innovation in organization', in

Swedburg, R. (ed.), *Entrepreneurship: The Social Science View.* Oxford University Press, Oxford.

Koberg, C., DeTienne, D. and Heppard, K. (2003). An empirical test of environmental, organizational, and process factors affecting incremental and radical innovation. *Journal of High Technology Management Research,* 14(1), 21–45.

Koen, P., Ajamian, G., Burkart, R., Clamen, A., Davidson, J., D'Amore, R., Elkins, C., Herald, K., Incorvia, M. and Johnson, A. (2001). Providing clarity and a common language to the 'fuzzy front end'. *Research-Technology Management,* 44(2), 46–55.

Langerak, F., Hultink, E.J. and Robben, H.S.J. (2004). The impact of market orientation, product advantage, and launch proficiency on new product performance and organizational performance. *Journal of Product Innovation Management,* 21(2), 79–94.

Leifer, R., McDermott, C.M., O'Connor, G.C., Peters, L.S., Rice, M. and Veryyzer, R.W. (2000). *Radical Innovation: How Mature Companies Can Outsmart Upstarts.* Harvard Business School Press, Boston, MA.

Leifer, R., O'Connor, G.C. and Rice, M. (2001). Implementing radical innovation in mature firms: The role of hubs. *The Academy of Management Executive,* 15(3), 102–113.

Leiponen, A. (2005). Skills and innovation. *International Journal of Industrial Organization,* 23(5–6), 303–323.

Lemon, M. and Sahota, P. (2004). Organizational culture as a knowledge repository for increased innovative capacity. *Technovation,* 24(6), 483–498.

Leonard-Barton, D. (1992). Core capabilities and core rigidities: A paradox in managing new product development. *Strategic Management Journal,* 13(S1), 111–125.

Lilien, G., Morrison, P., Searls, K., Sonnack, M. and von Hippel, E. (2002). Performance assessment of the lead user idea-generation process for new product development. *Management Science,* 48, 1042–1059.

Loewe, P. and Dominiquini, J. (2006). Overcoming the barriers to effective innovation. *Strategy & Leadership,* 34(1), 24–31.

March, J.G. (2006). Rationality, foolishness, and adaptive intelligence. *Strategic Management Journal,* 27(3), 201–214.

Mascitelli, R. (2000). From experience: Harnessing tacit knowledge to achieve breakthrough innovation. *Journal of Product Innovation Management,* 17(3), 179–193.

McDermott, C. and O'Connor, G.C. (2002). Managing radical innovation: An overview of emergent strategy issues. *Journal of Product Innovation Management*, 19, 424–438.

McLaughlin, P., Bessant, J. and Smart, P. (2008). Developing an organisation culture to facilitate radical innovation. *International Journal of Technology Management*, 44(3), 298–323.

Mohnen, P. and Roller, L.H. (2005). Complementarities in innovation policy. *European Economic Review*, 49(6), 1431–1450.

Mosey, S. (2005). Understanding new-to-market product development in SMEs. *International Journal of Operations & Production Management*, 25(2), 114–30.

Mosey, S., Clare, J. and Woodcock, D. (2002). Innovation decision making in British manufacturing SMEs. *Integrated Manufacturing Systems*, 13(3),176–184.

Narver, J.C. and Slater, S.F. (1990). The effect of a market orientation on business profitability. *Journal of Marketing*, 54, 20–35.

Raymond, L. and St-Pierre, J. (2004). Customer dependency in manufacturing SMEs: Implications for R&D and performance. *Journal of Small Business and Enterprise Development*, 11(1), 23–33.

Reid, S. and de Brentani, U. (2004). The fuzzy front end of new product development for discontinuous innovations: A theoretical model. *Journal of Product Innovation Management*, 21(3), 170–184.

Rothwell, R. (1978). Small and medium sized manufacturing firms and technological innovation. *Management Decision*, 16(6), 362–370.

Rothwell, R. (1992). Successful industrial innovation: Critical factors for the 1990s. *R&D Management*, 22(3), 221–240.

Rothwell, R. (1994). Towards the fifth-generation innovation process. *International Marketing Review*, 11(1), 7–31.

Schumpeter, J.A. (1934). *The Theory of Economic Development: An Inquiry into Profits, Capital, Credit, Interest, and the Business Cycle*. Harvard University Press, Cambridge, MA.

Soderquist, K., Chanaron, J. and Motwani, J. (1997). Managing innovation in French small and medium-sized enterprises: An empirical study. *Benchmarking for Quality Management and Technology*, 4, 1–8.

Srinivasan, R., Lilien, G.L. and Rangaswamy, A. (2002). Technological opportunism and radical technology adoption: An application to e-business. *Journal of Marketing*, 66(3), 47–60.

Storey, D.J. (1994). *Understanding the Small Business Sector*. Routledge, London.

Tang, H. (1998). An integrative model of innovation in organizations. *Technovation*, 18(5), 297–309.

Terziovski, M., Sohal, A. and Howell, A. (2002). Best practice in product innovation at Varian Australia. *Technovation*, 22(9), 561–569.

Tidd, J. and Bessant, J. (2009). *Managing Innovation: Integrating Technological, Market and Organizational Change, 4th Edition.* Wiley, Chichester.

Urban, G.L. and Hauser, J.R. (1993). *Design and Marketing of New Products, 2nd Edition.* Prentice-Hall, Englewood Cliffs, NJ.

Utterback, J. (1996). *Mastering the Dynamics of Innovation: How Companies Can Seize Opportunities in the Race of Technological Change.* Harvard Business School Press, Cambridge, MA.

von Hippel, E. (1986). Lead users: A source of novel product concepts. *Management Science*, 32(7), 791–805.

von Stamm, B. (2008). *Managing Innovation, Design and Creativity.* Wiley, Chichester.

Wakasugi, R. and Koyata, F. (1997). R&D, firm size and innovation outputs: Are Japanese firms efficient in product development? *Journal of Product Innovation Management*, 14(5), 383–392.

Woodman, R., Sawyer, J. and Griffin, R. (1993). Toward a theory of organizational creativity. *Academy of Management Review*, 18(2), 293–332.

Chapter 8

The BMW Group Co-Creation Lab: From Co-Creation Projects to Programmes

Michael Bartl, Gregor Jawecki, Volker Bilgram and Philipp Wiegandt HYVE, Germany

Introduction

Companies with superior R&D units have traditionally been technology-driven innovation leaders. Since the turn of the millennium, however, many of these companies have undergone a radical change in innovation strategy by opening up their innovation processes to external stakeholders (Chesbrough, 2003; von Hippel, 2005). Henry Chesbrough (2003, p. xxiv), who introduced the term 'open innovation', defines it as 'a paradigm that assumes that firms can and should use external ideas as well as internal ideas, and internal and external paths to market, as the firms look to advance their technology'. Meanwhile open innovation is a powerful movement in the business world and in academic research alike (Enkel *et al.*, 2009), touching a whole family of related concepts such as user innovation (von Hippel, 1988; Thomke and von Hippel, 2002; von Hippel, 2005), collaborative innovation (Sawhney *et al.*, 2005), crowdsourcing (Howe, 2006), mass customization (Pine, 1993; Piller and Walcher, 2003), wikinomics (Tapscott and Williams, 2006) and virtual customer integration (Dahan and Hauser, 2002) or co-creation. The latter was introduced first by Prahalad and Ramaswamy (2000) in their *Harvard Business Review* article, 'Co-Opting Customer Competence', followed by detailed books, *The Future of Competition* (Prahalad and Ramaswamy, 2004) and *The New Age of Innovation* (Prahalad and Krishnan, 2008).

All concepts have at least in common that they go beyond organizational boundaries and foster the collaborative exchange and integration of resources and know-how outside the company into the value chain. While the open innovation paradigm emphasizes the role of business models and IP rights as devices to capitalize on internal R&D spillovers as well as on external knowledge, the co-creation research stream emphasizes the importance of collaboration and co-creation with customers and end consumers. Author and management expert Prahalad states: 'The future of competition, however, lies in an altogether new approach of value creation, based on an individual-centered co-creation of value between consumers and companies' (Prahalad and Ramaswamy, 2004, p. 12).

This means that consumers are not only asked to contribute information according to their wants, needs and product requirements but are also invited to bring in their creativity and problem-solving skills. Users are asked to be actively involved in different tasks, e.g. to generate and evaluate new product ideas, to elaborate a detailed concept, to evaluate or challenge it, to discuss and improve optional solutions, to select or individualize the preferred virtual prototype or to test and experience new product features (Prahalad and Ramaswamy, 2004; Sawhney *et al.*, 2005). The application of cutting-edge Internet technology allows playgrounds and forums for collaboration to be created, interactive content creation and strongly facilitates the dissemination of co-creation.

In the following, a conceptual framework of how to organize and align co-creation activities for new product development (NPD) within a programmatic approach is introduced. In order to present insights into practice, the application of an ongoing co-creation programme is then presented along with an example from the German automotive industry.

Conceptual Framework Based on a Programmatic View of Co-Creation

Programmatic approaches are known from government leadership and intervention strategies dealing with a great variety of topics such as unemployment, environmental protection, integration policy, development aid and many more. The programmes are characterized by a defined degree of intentional planning and central leadership. Instead of concentrating upon the particulars of an individual case, aspects are addressed as a complex phenomenon where many players bear a responsibility. The assumption is that when diverse participants join their forces, the net effect will be bigger than the sum of the individual activities. Applying the programmatic view to a concept such as co-creation from a firm's perspective enables a more holistic view of how to facilitate and foster openness to drive innovation. A prominent example of a programmatic approach in the field of open innovation is the Connect and Develop programme initiated by Procter & Gamble (P&G). For P&G, the motivation to change the way it developed and commercialized products was the declining innovation success rates at the beginning of this century. P&G lost more than half of its market cap when the stock slid from $118 to $52 a share.

It was obvious that the traditional invent-it-ourselves model was not capable of sustaining high levels of top-line growth. The management's directive was that 50% of product innovation should involve significant collaboration with innovators outside the company in areas such as packaging, design, distribution, business models, trademark licensing, technology as well as new products and services. The model proved to be successful. By means of the Connect and Develop programme – along with improvements in other aspects of innovation strategy related to product costs, design and marketing – R&D productivity increased by nearly 60%. The innovation success rate more than doubled while the cost of innovation decreased. Five years after the company's stock collapse, P&G had doubled its share price and has a portfolio of 22 billion-dollar brands (Sakkab, 2002; Huston and Sakkab, 2006). The P&G case is still one of the rare examples of a programmatic open innovation approach integrated on a corporate level.

Based on the findings and many years of practical insights in the field of co-creation, the authors propose three major perspectives to ensure a programmatic view of the concept of co-creation: (1) Methods and Tools, (2) Process and (3) Organization and Culture (see Fig. 1).

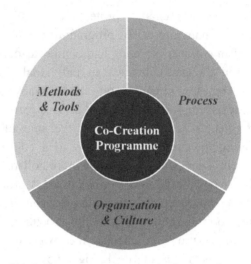

Fig. 1. Programmatic framework of co-creation.

Methods and Tools

Companies can choose from a whole landscape of methods and tools for collaborative innovation with users. Most of the developments and advancements of these techniques are driven by using the Web as a vast library of dialogue on products and brands as well as a network to identify and connect creative minds. Furthermore, Web-based techniques for co-creation allow users to fulfil defined innovation tasks by themselves, i.e. letting them translate their needs directly into ideas or first concepts with the help of interactive online tools.

In order to illustrate the broad spectrum of available approaches for collaborative innovation, in the following crowdsourcing, co-creation toolkits, the lead user method and netnography are introduced as modern tools and methods for co-creation in new product development.

Crowdsourcing

Crowdsourcing involves the act of taking tasks traditionally performed by companies and outsourcing them to an undefined, generally large group of people in the form of an open call (Howe, 2006; Kozinets *et al.*, 2008). The concept is closely related to social software or online collaboration platforms on which companies broadcast defined problems to potential solvers in the form of an open call for solutions (Lakhani, 2006; Piller and Walcher, 2006). The crowd, consisting of amateurs, volunteers working in their spare time, experts or small businesses which were initially unknown to the company, then creates possible solutions according to the problem stated. These solutions are submitted online and can be explored and evaluated by the crowd. The invested effort of the crowd is generally compensated, either monetarily, with prizes, with recognition or with intellectual satisfaction. The Netflix Prize (Fortune, 2009), Swarovski (Forrester Best Practices in User-Generated Content, 2009) or Innocentive (Lakhani, 2006) are only a small selection of a huge variety of examples and platforms driving the diffusion of the approach in the business world. Through crowdsourcing companies can tap a wider range of talent than might be present in its own organization. The users' significant investments of time, knowledge and creativity are usually incentivized by prizes as well as the exhibition of user ideas and coinciding publicity. However, the co-creation activity itself has also been found to be intrinsically rewarding (Csikszentmihalyi, 2002; Dahl and Moreau, 2007; Füller, 2010).

Co-creation toolkits

The aim of co-creation toolkits is to equip users with online applications which empower them to develop and transfer their creativity into solutions (von Hippel and Katz, 2002). Various co-creation modules such as configuration tools or drag-and-drop features constitute a playful experience, resulting in a high engagement of users and an enjoyable 'gamification' of innovation tasks (Bilgram *et al.*, 2011). For example, interactive development kits allow users to compose a product concept along certain feature dimensions, receiving instant feedback on their actions and decisions. Combined with research in the back end of the application users' preferences and needs can be observed and multiple attributes can be jointly measured. Online co-creation studies and labs can be either used on an individual basis, i.e. each user is integrated separately, or in a networked and collaborative structure adding a social dimension and allowing users to connect and communicate with one another. Integrated communication features such as online discussion forums allow for rich interaction on a user-to-user as well as on a user-to-company level and may be either moderated or free-flowing.

Lead user method

The lead user method was developed by Eric von Hippel (1986) and describes the systematic identification and collaboration with lead users in NPD. Lead users are far ahead of market trends relative to the majority of product users as they are familiar with future conditions and virtually 'live in the future' (Urban and von Hippel, 1988). They experience extreme needs not met by products that are currently on the market and thus are motivated to develop innovative solutions for their problems. Additionally, further characteristics have been found to correlate with 'lead userness', e.g. opinion leadership or product experience (Lüthje, 2004; Bilgram *et al.*, 2008; Schreier and Prügl, 2008). Various search methods such as screening (von Hippel *et al.*, 1999), pyramiding (von Hippel *et al.*, 2009) and signalling (Tietz *et al.*, 2006) have been developed to efficiently identify lead users with complementary skills and characteristics both online and offline. Lead users expect the outstanding high benefit of satisfying their very specific needs by solving individual problems through self-developed solutions and prototypes. Lead users frequently come from analogue fields of applications rather than the actual product innovation. Altogether, lead users are capable and motivated partners with whom to co-develop new products and services.

Netnography

Netnography is the linguistic blend of 'Internet' and 'ethnography' introduced by marketing professor Robert Kozinets (1998). Evolved from ethnographic research, the core idea of netnography is to gain unbiased, unobtrusive consumer insights through observing the conversation and social interaction of community members in an empathic way without intrusion and exertion of influence. There is little doubt that the Internet has changed the way consumers communicate. An increasing number of users actively gather together online and communicate on Web forums, blogs and various kinds of user-generated content platforms. They exchange personal experiences and opinions about products and their usage and talk about opportunities for solving product-related problems. Some of them even develop product modifications and innovations which they post online and share with other community members. This turns online communities into distinctive consumer tribes where highly involved consumers exchange existing needs, ideas, attitudes and perceptions regarding products and brands (Kozinets, 1998, 2002, 2006). They represent a powerful source of innovation (Füller *et al.*, 2006). As a methodological guideline for netnography, Bartl *et al.* (2009) introduced a systematic five-step approach which helps to identify relevant online sources, analyse and interpret user statements and transfer consumer insights into initial product solutions.

The different co-creation methods can be characterized by different degrees of openness. Whereas crowdsourcing is characterized by a high level of openness as the accessibility for users is generally unrestricted, i.e. via a Web portal open to the public, netnography represents an observational and therefore by nature a moderate approach of consumer integration. From an operational perspective successful co-creation projects call for hard skills, especially methodological and tool-related competencies, as well as soft skills such as in-depth experience in the social media landscape, sourcing suited co-creators and managing and maintaining communities of co-creators. However, the proficient realization of single co-creation projects is not a warranty for the overall success of co-creation. The right methods and tools have to be selected and combined depending on the phase of NPD and the specific innovation goals, which brings us to processes as second dimension of a programmatic co-creation view.

Process

One of the core questions of co-creation is at what stage in the NPD process the involvement of users should take place. An idealized innovation process represents how products move from opportunities and ideas, to concepts, to design and engineering, to testing and launch (Dahan and Hauser, 2002). The question as to when users should be involved is directly linked to the actual purpose of the co-creation task, e.g. generating ideas, evaluating and refining concepts, specifying product features or creating prototypes. Whereas the integration of customers in the latter stages such as testing and launch is common practice especially in market research, more and more modern techniques of co-creation and open innovation focus on the fuzzy front end of innovation as well as on the design and development itself. Netnography, for instance, allows the identification of new opportunities to innovate, crowdsourcing platforms help to unleash the creativity of the masses and toolkits enable thousands of users to create their preferred future products using virtual prototypes. The challenge for the innovating company is to assign development tasks which are congruent to the customers' skill level, meaning that the participant is challenged, but not more than she/he can manage. Originally emerging in marketing services literature and quality management literature, various customer roles in service delivery and quality management were identified (Lengnick-Hall, 1996). These roles mostly differ in their terminology and context, not in the attempt to offer a structured analysis of the phenomenon of customer involvement in value creation.

Within the field of NPD the authors distinguish three customer roles which are closely related to the necessary customer skills, attributes and characteristics to fulfil the transferred development task: (1) customers as a source of ideas, (2) customers as lead users and innovators and (3) customers as end users and representative buyers. These roles support a better understanding of co-creation. Nevertheless, it is important to keep in mind that the transition from user to innovator as well as from consumer to a virtual development team member is often fluent and strongly depends on the Internet-based methods used. Bringing in the process view of co-creation shows quite plainly that excellence in single co-creation projects is not a warranty for the overall success from a programmatic point of view. Particularly in the case of long-term development projects aiming at the generation of breakthrough innovations, it is necessary to select and orchestrate single co-creation projects conducive to the overall innovation goals. A co-creation process consists of alternating outbound and inbound exchanges of information to connect internal innovation activities and the input of users. Through this route, internal technological know-how can be merged with external knowledge and creativity. At one stage of the co-creation process, for example, it may be necessary to define a narrow solution space for users in order to meet certain technological or strategic requirements. On the contrary, at another stage the solution space may be left open to gain ideas off the well-known paths. Also, the input of users needs to be interpreted and, occasionally, slightly adapted or enriched before it is played back at the users for repeated evaluation and enhancement in a following co-creation project.

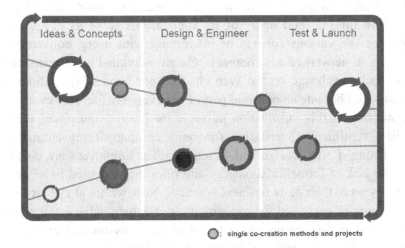

Fig. 2. Co-creation roadmap along the NPD process.

These sequences of inbound flows of creativity and knowledge from users and outbound flows of information from inside the company may be considered a co-creative ping-pong game (see Fig. 2).

Organization and Culture

The intention to implement co-creation activities along the NPD process definitely has major impacts on an organizational and cultural level such as an inherent change of the company's attitude from 'not invented here' to an enthusiasm for ideas and innovations which were 'proudly found elsewhere' (Bartl *et al.*, 2012). At this point it becomes obvious that additional issues, which are based on the fact that firms are often very persistent in sticking to 'the old way of doing things', must be addressed. 'Not invented here' syndrome manifests as an unwillingness to adopt an idea because it originates outside the company boundaries (Katz and Allen, 1982). Limited 'absorptive capacity' (Cohen and Levinthal, 1990; Vanhaverbeke *et al.*, 2007) means that the mechanisms for distributing information are missing so that this information can't be exploited. These issues are two major challenges which need to be tackled from an organizational perspective to ensure co-creation success. Hence, the key to co-innovation is to overcome resistance and promote the willingness to accept that not all the smart people work for your company. Rather, it is essential to work with smart people inside and outside the company.

The Internet and many of its applications serve as key tools to manage the various spheres of interacting with users, consumers or experts in networked environments. On an individual level, transactions and social exchange on the Web changed our habits, expectations and norms, and became an essential part of our everyday life. However, when immersing in this information universe for business purposes, there is still a sentiment of irritation for many company representatives in Marketing, R&D, Design and Research alike. Employees are confused by the lack of formal relationships and rules they are used to relying so heavily on in their daily business practices. Now we are at eye level with thousands of users and we can simply ask for help, advice and creative ideas to solve problems. As a result of this 'anytime communication mode' with consumers, well-known interface discussions between market and technology-driven departments (Gupta *et al.*, 1986; Souder, 1988) will gain momentum once more. It is not clearly defined yet who finally is in charge to involve the consumers in the value creation tasks. Should it be Marketing, R&D or Research, or is it feasible for any of these areas at the same time? To the authors' knowledge the ideal allocation of responsibilities and the role play to integrate users online in the different stages of NPD have not been empirically investigated in depth.

A further issue associated with a culture of Web-based co-creation is the setting up of incentive structures which take users into account who act outside the company and are not legally linked via contracts of employment. From a user's view, engaging in co-creation activities can be considered a function of intrinsic and extrinsic motivation. Consumers are intrinsically motivated if they value an activity for its own sake. They are extrinsically motivated if they focus on outcomes that are separable from the activity *per se*. Drawing on a rich body of motivation research, relevant motives are curiosity, self-efficacy, skill development, information seeking, intrinsic playful task, recognition, altruism and community support, making friends, personal need/dissatisfaction or compensation and monetary rewards (Csikszentmihalyi, 2002; Dahl and Moreau, 2007; Füller, 2010).

Research, as well as the experiences from numerous real business projects, shows that the intrinsic motivational dimension should be the focus to engage highly involved, interested and creative co-creation partners. Nevertheless, when more and more companies aim to co-create with users a sustained future motivational mix will consequentially include a balance of intrinsic and extrinsic incentives such as licensing models or other monetary compensations for successful user innovations. First, the willingness to acquire, assimilate and exploit knowledge from engaged people outside the company; second, a clear view about who should be in charge of the interaction; and third, incentive structures which are also valid outside the company form a new co-creation culture and organization to utilize the full potential of users' knowledge within NPD.

The BMW Group Co-Creation Lab

The BMW Group co-creation history

German automobile and motorcycle manufacturer BMW Group is a pioneer in co-creation and one of the most innovative companies not only in Germany but also worldwide. The company, with its three premium brands BMW, Mini and Rolls-Royce Motor Cars, was ranked among the top 20 most innovative companies by *Businessweek* magazine and named 'Best Innovator 2010' by A.T. Kearney and the business journal *WirtschaftsWoche*. For years the BMW Group has recognized that users represent a valuable source of knowledge and ideas. As the company states on its website: 'We are not only interested in our own research and development departments, but also in the creative minds outside the BMW Group'. For this reason the company also launched the Virtual Innovation Agency, a permanent platform which enables creative consumers and other external stakeholders to submit their ideas to the company. Remarkably, the platform was launched in 2001, two years before the seminal work on open innovation by Henry Chesbrough (2003) ushered innovation management into a new era. Today, on average 800 ideas are submitted via the website per year.

Besides this ongoing platform which is not focused on a special topic but rather on the 'mobile future' in general, the BMW Group also addressed users for specific innovation topics. In 2003, for instance, more than 1,000 users participated in the Customer Innovation Lab and used a virtual multimedia toolkit to co-develop and test 215 ideas for telematic and future driver assistance services. In 2006 the company elaborated concepts for the topic 'BMW on the Internet' together with lead users. One year later, online communities focusing on sustainable energies were analysed applying the netnography approach. A more recent project is the BMW Group's Interior Idea Contest which was conducted in 2010, focusing on new ideas for individualized car interiors (BMW Group, 2011). As part of this project, 1,188 participants contributed more than 760 ideas within eight weeks.

While all outlined projects have in common that they embraced users for innovation, they differ with regard to the phase of the innovation process in which they provided value. For instance, the netnography approach aimed to deliver insights into trends and first ideas in the fuzzy front end whereas the lead user workshop aimed to elaborate initial ideas into concepts. In contrast, other projects, such as the idea contest, asked users to become active co-creators of new products and services. Depending on the stage of the innovation process and the desired contribution, different user groups were targeted. The netnography covered any users discussing sustainability topics on the Internet, including non-car-related social media content. The topic 'BMW on the Internet' was addressed by lead users characterized by high innovativeness and trend leadership and the Customer Innovation Lab invited early adopters and pilot customers. Figure 3 shows an overview of different projects at BMW throughout the innovation process and the targeted users who were involved.

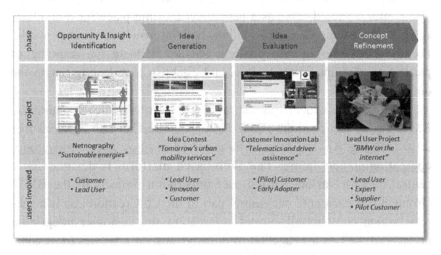

Fig. 3. Co-creation projects of the BMW Group in different phases of the innovation process and with different users.

The Co-Creation Lab as a central open innovation hub

Driven by the continuous aspiration to improve its innovation mechanisms, the BMW Group recognized that there was enormous potential arising from synergies of multiple co-creation encounters and a systematic management of users in particular. As the examples show, for each innovation project a different group of users with specific characteristics was required, consequently demanding a lot of effort and expertise in terms of search strategies and identification of individuals. The co-creation projects were often conducted by different teams within the organization and typically the identification of participants was redone from scratch for each new project. The relationships with participants were often nourished only during the time of a single project and either abated afterwards or continued unsystematically on a personal level.

As a consequence, the BMW Group decided to develop a central platform which unites all co-creation projects, independent of their topic, the stage of the innovation process and the specific group of participants. The platform should serve as a permanent meeting place for individuals eager to share their ideas and opinions on tomorrow's automotive world. For the BMW Group the platform should facilitate the sourcing of participants for upcoming projects and establish long-lasting ties to the outside world.

As a response to this vision, after six months of development the BMW Group launched the BMW Group Co-Creation Lab in September 2010 (see Fig. 4). The lab can be accessed at https://www.bmwgroup-cocreationlab.com/home. The Web-based platform is designed as a central hub for various virtual user integration projects of the BMW Group. For participants, the central part of the Co-Creation Lab is a sub-page which contains all current co-creation and customer integration projects as well as a collection of already finished activities (accessible under 'Projects'). The projects range from idea contests, user toolkits, virtual concept tests and co-creation studies to lead user workshops. For each project, members of the Co-Creation Lab can read a short summary including the topics addressed and the results that were gathered (as far as they can be revealed with regard to confidentiality). For all currently on-going projects, members can go directly to the specific project website.

Another part of the Co-Creation Lab is dedicated to the members themselves, who are referred to as 'co-creators' to underline their active contribution to innovation. In the development of the lab, one of the key decisions was that the platform should not primarily facilitate a dialogue between members outside of specific projects. In light of the BMW Group's social media sites (e.g. the Facebook fanpage) and the huge variety of independent social networking sites (e.g. automotive message boards), individuals were expected to be more attracted by an offer focused on innovation rather than on social exchange. However, to provide participants with a sense of who their fellow members are, a selection of user avatars as well as an overview of the car types they drive is shown on the website. With these rather basic functionalities a feeling of familiarity and community is conveyed even when the direct interaction outside of projects is not fostered (see Fig. 5).

As outlined earlier, the Co-Creation Lab is developed as an open platform. The decision to make the lab and projects accessible to the public was considered essential to attract a high number of participants and to live up to the self-stated goal of open innovation. Only when individuals actually want to participate in a specific project is registration needed. The registration process is more extensive than on other platforms, such as Facebook. The basic assumption is that in order to build up long-lasting relationships with users it is also key to know more details about them. Additional information such as the individual's field of interests, professional background or car model they own allows the BMW Group to invite participants to projects that match their particular backgrounds. Also, in the registration process the question regarding IP rights for contributions in the Co-Creation Lab and integrated projects is addressed.

Fig. 4. The BMW Group Co-Creation Lab (screenshot of entry page and projects overview).

The Co-Creation Lab was launched together with the BMW Group's latest idea contest on personalization of the car's interior. It was announced in an official press release, posted on the BMW Group Facebook fanpage, and communicated on other car-related websites via postings and banners. The response was impressive. Within 72 hours after the launch, more than 3,100 Facebook users had registered their 'Like'. As of mid-September more than 1,000 members were registered to the Co-Creation Lab. Members not only come from countries which are known as key players in the automotive industry, such as Germany and the United States, but also from emerging, less industrialized countries such as India, Romania, Malaysia and Egypt. In total, members from more than 80 different countries have registered on the platform within the first two weeks. Despite the limited content on projects that was available on the platform right after the launch, users spent approximately 10 minutes and viewed seven pages per visit on the platform.

Fig. 5. Visualizations of co-creators and community appeal.

Learning more about the co-creators

Unsurprisingly, the participants of the Co-Creation Lab are predominately male (97%). They are rather diversified in terms of profession and family status with a relatively high educational background (45% with university degrees). On average, the participants own 1.5 cars. Interestingly, only 54% of the participants drive one of the

BMW Group brands BMW or Mini. Figure 6 provides additional information with regard to the co-creators' characteristics.

The most important reason for members to participate in the lab is that they are fans of the BMW and Mini brands. Eighty-nine percent of all members state their attachment to the brand as the main reason to contribute. Other important reasons for participants are the interest in automotive technologies and developments, the hope that in the future one of their ideas may be realized on the market, and the desire to connect with the BMW Group innovation team. Only 41% state that they participate to get in touch with other car enthusiasts. This number supports the company's decision to focus the Co-Creation Lab on innovation projects rather than providing another platform for personal exchange. The motives stated by members also explain why the assignment of rights to the BMW Group is no impediment to their contribution. They are intrinsically motivated and strive for the co-creation experience rather than for monetary benefits.

As outlined earlier, one of the main drivers for the BMW Group to establish the Co-Creation Lab was to build a relationship with different user groups, such as lead users, early adopters or opinion leaders. An analysis of current users supports the idea that the lab unites individuals with different characteristics and skills. For instance, 60% state that they 'like to fix and improve things' and 57% consider themselves 'creative and original in their thinking and behavior'. Although these numbers are based on a self-assessment they indicate that a considerable number of participants have above-average creativity and motivation to improve products – two cardinal qualifications of the lead user theory. Another more objective indication that lead users can be found on the platform is that 39% of all participants have already built their own product solution based on an innovative idea. And 9% of all members have even already applied for a patent for one of their ideas. Although true lead userness is difficult to assess, these figures indicate that a remarkable share of members have lead user characteristics. Other data also show that a considerable number of early adopters and opinion leaders can be met on the platform.

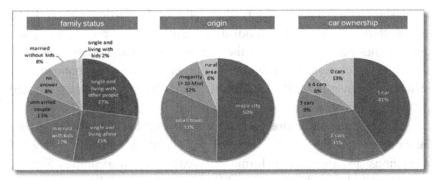

Fig. 6. Overview of co-creators (*N* = 432).

Benefits for co-creators and the BMW Group

The Co-Creation Lab offers several benefits for users, particularly in terms of a range of presented activities, convenience, public visibility and firm recognition. Members of the lab have a variety of possibilities: they can browse summaries of completed projects, directly access current co-creation projects, stay informed about upcoming activities or explore the profiles of other co-creators. The lab's IT infrastructure facilitates convenient participation, e.g. registered members have one central user name and password which allows them to access all projects instead of registering for each one separately (single sign-on). As the lab is the central hub for all co-creation activities, participants can be sure that they will be updated about all projects that are interesting for them via the website – one strong reason to visit the Co-Creation Lab repeatedly. Finally, users are no longer anonymous contributors as in many other temporary projects but are acknowledged as partners in co-creation. They are not only asked to participate in innovation projects initiated by the company but can also suggest additional topics on their own.

For the BMW Group, the Co-Creation Lab concentrates the co-creation expertise at one central location and allows long-lasting relationships with users to be established. Even if members may not be interested in every topic proposed, they remain connected to the lab and become active once an innovation task is announced that matches their interests. The IT infrastructure enables more to be learned about users, for instance in which projects they previously participated and the contributions they made. Innovation tasks from various company departments can be opened to the consumers in the Co-Creation Lab, allowing for economies of scale. At the same time, the abundance of different innovation tasks appeals to the diversity of users on the platform and ensures high engagement.

The modular structure of the website enables all projects to be integrated, ranging from surveys, co-creation toolkits, ideation workshops to application forms for lead user workshops. Finally, projects already conducted are archived in the form of short reports and over time constitute a 'co-creation history'. This does not only attract new users to the platform but can also be used by the BMW Group to communicate the continuous and fruitful consumer orientation more actively to the outside world.

Additional benefits arise on the level of projects which are embedded into the Co-Creation Lab. The lab stimulates a high quality of contributions, not only as a result of efficient and targeted sourcing of participants. Due to the evolving relationship, members will show a high commitment to the company and the innovation task. Also, the variety of users and projects may inspire their creativity and fuel their motivation. One example impressively showing the lab's impact is the idea contest on individualization of the car interior, which was launched together with the Co-Creation Lab as its first project. Within 2.5 weeks 500 members submitted more than 300 ideas and made 13,000 evaluations and 6,200 comments. The most active participants submitted more than 100 ideas by the end of the contest and made 2,000 evaluations (see Fig. 7). In total, when adding up all members' visits to the contest website, they spent more than 16 days on the platform. This equals an average of 50 minutes each participant spent on the website in the first 2.5 weeks after the launch. These numbers clearly exceed the response of other similar contests.

Fig. 7. BMW Group Interior Idea Contest: Submitted ideas and most active participants (http://interior-ideacontest.bmwgroup-cocreationlab.com/).

Discussion and Implications

The introduced programmatic approach implies the need to think of co-creation as a strategic programme rather than as a 'just in time' outsourcing of innovation tasks. A co-creation programme is characterized by a continuous collaborative relationship with users consisting of various interactions along the innovation process, including iterative internal and external cycles of acquiring and assimilating the users' value contributions. Eventually, a co-creation programme supports the idea of a continuously learning organization by expansion of its boundaries and should not be narrowed down to single project outcomes. It has been emphasized earlier that three major dimensions have to be taken into account: (1) developing a co-creation skill set allowing excellence to be attained in terms of methodologies, tools and experience; (2) continuous co-creation activities with alternating inbound and outbound flows between consumers and the company throughout the whole NPD process, starting from the fuzzy front end to the testing and launch of products; and (3) establishing organizational structures and routines not only to acquire external input but also to assimilate, digest and capitalize on the value co-creation within the company.

The introduced example of the BMW Group Co-Creation Lab shows a recent application of a programmatic approach in co-creation. It is designed to host several different methods and tools for co-creation as well as to constantly feed the whole process of NPD with consumer input. The project also shows the synergies that can be used in a permanent co-creation hub in contrast to single innovation projects. The continuous approach opens up a new dimension of co-creation beyond single co-innovation projects and creates a new understanding of shared value creation as a corporate strategy.

References

Bartl, M., Füller, J., Mühlbacher, H. and Ernst, H. (2012). A manager's perspective on virtual customer integration for new product development. *Journal for Product Innovation Management*, 29(6), 1031–1046.

Bartl, M., Hück, S. and Ruppert, S. (2009). Netnography for innovation. Creating insights with user communities. *Conference Proceedings ESOMAR Consumer Insights*, pp. 1–12.

Bilgram, V., Bartl, M. and Biel, S. (2011). Getting closer to the consumer: How Nivea co-creates new products. *Marketing Review St. Gallen*, 28, 34–40.

Bilgram, V., Brem, A. and Voigt, K.I. (2008). User-centric innovations in new product development: Systematic identification of lead users harnessing interactive and collaborative online-tools. *International Journal of Innovation Management*, 12(3), 419–458.

BMW Group. Interior Idea Contest. Available at: http://interior-ideacontest.bmwgroup-cocreationlab.com/. [Accessed 15 April 2011.]

Chesbrough, H. (2003). The era of open innovation. *MIT Sloan Management Review*, 44(3), 35–41.

Chesbrough, H.W. and Appleyard, M.M. (2007). Open innovation and strategy. *California Management Review*, 50(1), 57–76.

Cohen, W.M. and Levinthal, D.A. (1990). Absorptive capacity: A new perspective on learning and innovation. *Administrative Science Quarterly*, 35(1), 128–152.

Csikszentmihalyi, M. (2002). *Creativity: Flow and the Psychology of Discovery and Invention.* Harper Perennial, New York.

Dahan, E. and Hauser, J. (2002). The virtual customer. *Journal of Product Innovation Management*, 19(5), 332–353.

Dahl, D.W. and Moreau, C.P. (2007). Thinking inside the box: Why consumers enjoy constrained creative experiences. *Journal of Marketing Research*, 44(3), 357–369.

Enkel, E., Gassmann, O. and Chesbrough, H. (2009). Open R&D and open innovation: Exploring the phenomenon. *R&D Management*, 39(4), 311–316.

Fortune (2009). Box office boffo for brainiacs: The NetflixPrize. Available at: http://tech.fortune.cnn.com/2009/09/21/box-office-boffo-for-brainiacs-the-netflix-prize/. [Accessed 10 May 2011.]

Füller, J. (2010). Refining virtual co-creation from a consumer perspective. *California Management Review*, 52(2), 98–122.

Füller, J., Bartl, M., Ernst, H. and Mühlbacher, H. (2006). Community based innovation: How to integrate members of virtual communities into new product development. *Electronic Commerce Research*, 6(2), 57–73.

Gassmann, O., Enkel, E. and Chesbrough, H. (2009). The future of open innovation. *R&D Management*, 39(4), 311–316.

Gupta, A.K., Raj, S.P. and Wilemon, D. (1986). A model for studying R&D – Marketing interface in the product innovation process. *Journal of Marketing*, 50(2), 7–17.

Howe, J. (2006). The rise of crowdsourcing. Available at: www.wired.com/wired/archive/14.06/crowds.html. [Accessed 21 March 2012.]

Huston, L. and Sakkab, N. (2006). Connect and develop: Inside Procter & Gamble's new model for innovation. *Harvard Business Review*, 84(3), 58–66.

Katz, R. and Allen, T.J. (1982). Investigating the Not Invented Here (NIH) syndrome: A look at the performance, tenure and communication patterns of 50 R&D project groups. *R&D Management*, 12(1), 7–19.

Kozinets, R.V. (1998). On netnography: Initial reflections on consumer research investigations of cyberculture. *Advances in Consumer Research*, 25, 366–371.

Kozinets, R.V. (2002). The field behind the screen: Using netnography for marketing research in online communities. *Journal of Marketing Research*, 39(1), 61–72.

Kozinets, R.V. (2006). Click to connect: Netnography and tribal advertising. *Journal of Advertising Research*, 46(3), 279–288.

Kozinets, R.V., Hemetsberger, A. and Schau, H.J. (2008). The wisdom of consumer crowds: Collective innovation in the age of networked marketing. *Journal of Macromarketing*, 28(4), 339–354.

Lakhani, K.R. (2006). Broadcast search in problem solving: Attracting solutions from the periphery. *MIT Sloan Research Paper*, 6, 2450–2468.

Lengnick-Hall, C.A. (1996). Customer contributions to quality: A different view of the customer-oriented firm. *Academy of Management Review*, 21(3), 791–824.

Lüthje, C. (2004). Characteristics of innovating users in a consumer goods field: An empirical study of sport-related consumer products. *Technovation*, 24(9), 683–695.

Piller, F. and Walcher, D. (2006). Toolkits for idea competitions: A novel method to integrate users in new product development. *R&D Management*, 36(3), 307–318.

Pine, J. (1993). *Mass Customization*. Harvard Business School Press, Boston, MA.

Prahalad, C.K. and Krishnan, M.S. (2008). *The New Age of Innovation*. McGraw-Hill Professional, New York.

Prahalad, C.K. and Ramaswamy, V. (2000). Co-opting customer competence. *Harvard Business Review*, 78(1), 79–91.

Prahalad, C.K. and Ramaswamy, V. (2004). *The Future of Competition: Co-Creating Unique Value with Customers*. Harvard Business School Press, Boston, MA.

Sakkab, N. (2002). Connect & develop complements research & develop at P&G. *Research Technology Management*, 45, 38–45.

Sawhney, M., Verona, G. and Prandelli, E. (2005). Collaborating to create: The Internet as a platform for customer engagement in product innovation. *Journal of Interactive Marketing*, 19(4), 4–17.

Schreier, M. and Prügl, R. (2007). Extending lead user theory: Antecedents and consequences of consumers' lead userness. *Journal of Product Innovation Management*, 25(4), 331–346.

Souder, W.E. (1988). Managing relations between R&D and marketing in new product development projects. *Journal of Product Innovation Management*, 5, 6–19.

Tapscott, D. and Williams, A.D. (2006). *Wikinomics: How Mass Collaboration Changes Everything*. Atlantic Books, New York.

Tietz, R., Füller, J. and Herstatt, C. (2006). Signaling – an innovative approach to identify lead users in online communities. *International Mass Customization Meeting (IMCM06), Technical University Hamburg.*

Thomke, S. and von Hippel, E. (2002). Customers as Innovators. *Harvard Business Review*, 80 (4), 74–81

Urban, G.L. and von Hippel, E. (1988). Lead user analyses for the development of new industrial products. *Management Science*, 34(5), 569–582.

Vanhaverbeke, W., Van de Vrande, V. and Cloodt, M. (2007). Connecting absorptive capacity and open innovation. Available at: http://ssrn.com/abstract=1091265. [Accessed 21 March 2012.]

von Hippel, E. (1986). Lead users: A source of novel product concepts. *Management Science*, 32(7), 791–805.

von Hippel, E. (1988). *The Sources of Innovation*. Oxford University Press, New York.

von Hippel, E. (2005). *Democratizing Innovation*. MIT Press, Cambridge, MA.

von Hippel, E., Franke, N. and Prügl, R. (2009). Pyramiding: Efficient search for rare subjects. *Research Policy*, 38(9), 1397–1406.

von Hippel, E. and Katz, R. (2002). Shifting innovation to users via toolkits. *Management Science*, 48(7), 821–833.

von Hippel, E., Thomke, S. and Sonnack, M. (1999). Creating breakthroughs at 3M. *Harvard Business Review*, 77(5), 47–57.

Chapter 9

Strengthening the Role of the Users

Helle Vibeke and Stine Dahl Børglum
Ministry of Taxation, Denmark

Introduction

Taxes have always interested the citizens in Denmark, which is quite natural, since Parliament imposes taxes on almost everything, and Denmark has the second-highest tax rate in the world. Since 2006, the Danish Ministry of Taxation has strengthened the role of the users (citizens and companies) in the innovation process internally and cross-ministerially by forming an innovation unit, MindLab, with two other ministries. In 2009 the efforts were enhanced further by forming an internal unit for innovation and knowledge sharing. The staff of 17 is a heterogeneous group with an age span from 25 to 64 and with a wide range of formal training (e.g., economics, law, anthropology, sociology, engineering and communication). Amongst other things, discontinuous innovation is spurred by diversity in formal training, hence the heterogeneity among the staff. Inspiration from experts, users, trendsetters and other people with alternative perspectives is also an important prerequisite for discontinuous innovation. Therefore the tasks performed in this innovation unit are centred on the role of the users, and people from the surrounding society are consulted in the development of the tax system and the administrative processes.

Why Strengthen the Role of the Users?

The Ministry is facing a political demand for cost reduction and efficiency. This includes a staff reduction from the 15,000 employees in 1990 to 6,400 by 2014. In order to meet these demands and at the same time maintain a high standard in law production, as well as administration and services, the Ministry has strengthened the role of the users in their innovation process.

How is the role being strengthened?

The Ministry has defined three different user roles in the innovation process (Fig. 1).

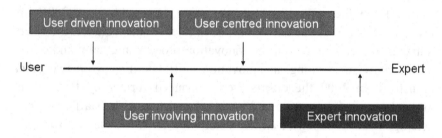

Fig. 1. Different user roles (The Danish Ministry of Taxation, 2007).

In the *user-centred* innovation process the users are studied – directly or indirectly – in order to learn about their routines, behaviour, attitudes and thoughts regarding the activity in focus. In the *user-involving* process the users are actively and systematically involved in developing new products, services or administration processes (e.g. IT solutions). *User-driven* innovation is innovation by users, where citizens or companies come up with innovative solutions that the Ministry can use directly, copy and refine.

The process of constantly and systematically learning about, from and with the users ensures that the problem solved is the right one, and that the solution developed is the best one. The iterative process consists of three main steps and is centred around the user (Fig. 2).

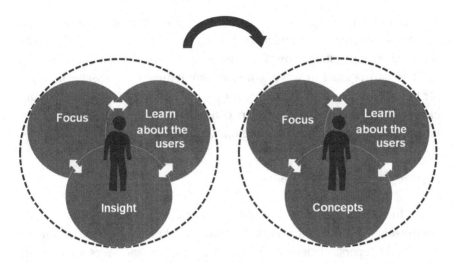

Fig. 2. The users in the innovation process (The Danish Ministry of Taxation, 2011).

Examples of the different user roles

Example 1: User-centred innovation

The Ministry has experienced a decrease in compliance among entrepreneurs. In order to discover the root of the problem, the entrepreneurs were interviewed and filmed while doing their accounting and VAT declarations. The routines were mapped in order to identify where in the process system failures or breaches in communication occurred. Both VAT and innovation experts participated in the mapping process, using their knowledge and ideas to improve the registration and administration process. One of the ideas stemming from this process was instructional videos on how to handle business registration and VAT accounting digitally.

Example 2: User-involving innovation

Upon sending out standardised letters, the Ministry often experiences several calls from confused citizens who do not know how to act or, even worse, who act wrongly. Citizens with very different backgrounds were invited to interpret a standardised letter artistically, in order for the Ministry to understand how the citizens perceive the letters. Then the citizens participated in a workshop reformulating the message in order for the Ministry to learn how they might communicate the message more clearly. This resulted not only in constructive ideas for rewriting the letters, but also in an idea for a digital solution.

Example 3: User-driven innovation

The Ministry is currently running a project to increase tax and VAT compliance of small companies by better bookkeeping, where lead users (e.g. bookkeepers, IT developers, accounting firms and users in analogue markets and foreign tax experts) are identified in ascertain their solutions and ideas on how to increase compliance.

Barriers and Progression

The Ministry sometimes faces barriers, such as lack of time and recognition of the value of user contribution, to the innovation process. In order to overcome this, courses on the innovation process and on methods of bringing the users actively and systematically into the innovation process are offered to its employees.

Does the Strengthened Role of the Users Enhance the Possibility of Discontinuous Innovation?

For centuries the Ministry has done well regarding continuous innovation – improving existing tax systems, inventing new taxes and improving the ways tax laws are enforced. However, globalisation, new technologies and the current demand for drastic reduction of costs and staff call for something else – they call for radical change, they call for discontinuous innovation. Strengthening the role of the users and actively searching for inspiration in the surrounding society are some of the actions taken by the Ministry in order to enable discontinuous innovation.

User-centred innovation helps the Ministry to pick up on future expectations and demands from citizens and companies. The more the Ministry is tuned in on the future needs of the users, the greater the possibilities for discontinuous innovation. Cases from MindLab show other important aspects that influence the chances of discontinuous innovation, e.g. how well the ministries are connected to the users, homogeneous or heterogeneous staff in the ministries and how the ministries approach innovation professionally.

The experience so far shows that *user-involving processes* do help the Ministry meet unexpected needs and demands, and thereby enhance the possibility for discontinuous innovation. Users often surprise the Ministry with their needs and demands and often new ideas emerge in the innovation process – ideas that neither the citizens nor civil servants have anticipated.

Since neither the Ministry nor other public organisations in Denmark have much experience with *user-driven innovation* yet, the contribution from this type of innovation remains to be seen. However, the positive experience from the private sector with lead users indicate increased capability to meet disruptions in demands and needs.

Long story short, strengthening the role of the users enhances the possibility to meet discontinuous shifts in the demands and needs of the citizens and in the circumstances for delivering public goods.

Part II

Netnography in the Food Industry: How the German Supplier for Flavors and Scents Symrise Made Use of Online Community Discussions as a Source of Innovation

Johann Füller and Julia Jonas
HYVE, Germany

Online Communities as a Source of Innovation

The Internet is growing and with it are the number of online communities and online community members. There is basically no topic that is not discussed in a forum or blog somewhere out there in the World Wide Web. In particular, those users that show high involvement in a product category meet in their community, their tribe, their 'hood', to talk about their shared interest. Members of online communities and forums discuss the products they love and hate, they exchange experiences and think about new developments and trends – together, they even try to find solutions for their unsolved problems and proudly present how they managed to solve a problem, sometimes with their self-made product modifications or ideas for new products. By doing so, these users contribute significantly to innovations as their discussions serve as a great source of information and knowledge for companies worldwide.

The Netnography Insights Method

Market researchers can learn a lot from the unfiltered, freely discussed opinions. One way to analyze relevant online conversations and social interactions of thousands of highly involved community members in a qualitative and empathic way is called netnography. Marketing professor Robert Kozinets established the term 'netnography' in 1998 (Kozinets,

1998, 2002, 2006; Bartl *et al.*, 2009). The word 'netnography' is a linguistic blend of two words, 'Internet' and 'ethnography'. It is a qualitative, interpretive research methodology that uses Internet-optimized ethnographic research techniques to study selected social context. Due to the immeasurable amount of potential online sources on the Internet, a systematic five-step approach (Fig. 1) enables the gathering of relevant online communities and discussions as well as in-depth analysis and aggregation of the derived insights.

1) Definition of Research Field

2) Identification and Selection of Online Communities and Sources

3) Community Observation and Software-aided Data Gathering

4) Qualitative in-depth Analysis, Interpretation and Aggregation of Consumer Insights

5) Insight Translation into Product and Service Solutions

Fig. 1. Process of Netnography Insights[©].

In this human resource–intensive research set-up, software primarily helps researchers at three points in the process: identifying relevant online sources, storing the text data of user statements and analyzing and interpreting the content. The main part of the study, however, is the researchers' empathic reading, structuring and condensing of the data. The results of a netnography project are aggregated consumer insights, based on a high number of single user posts analyzed by the researcher in depth. At the end of the process, product designers translate the derived consumer insights into initial product solutions as a last step, facilitating efforts to assimilate the consumer insights and integrate them into the innovation process.

To illustrate the application of the netnography method itself and the methodological steps of the research approach, the Netnography Insights project on perceptions and attitudes regarding healthy nutrition for Symrise, one of the leading suppliers of flavors and scents worldwide, serves as a typical showcase.

The Application of Netnography at Symrise: Understanding Consumers' Attitudes towards Healthy Nutrition

As a B2B supplier in the food industry, Symrise does not get directly in touch with the consumers of their products. For successful innovation, it is essential for Symrise to understand not only their customers, mainly international consumer goods brands, but also the final consumers of their products. Analyzing the voice of the end consumer fulfills different aims for Symrise: On the one hand, Symrise can develop innovations for their own products according to the research findings to be able to offer flavors and scents that reflect the consumers' expectations and current market trends. On the other hand, they can use the resulting consumer insights and derived concept boards for communication to their clients – for presenting new flavor and scent products, for consulting on food branding or for acquisition purposes.

The starting point for this project was influenced by the company's environment in two respects. First, nutritional guidelines and taxes on soft drinks were heavily discussed in the media, and second, research had found that consumers did not link light products to good taste. Symrise wanted to address both topics with a product called SymLife Sweet®, a sweetness enhancer, but at the time did not really know how to position the product. This is why Symrise decided to assign HYVE to conduct a Netnography Insights study to find out how customers really feel about healthy food, sweetness and saltiness.

The research questions that the researchers specified together with Symrise in the first step of the project, the research field, were:

- What are the main purchasing criteria for consumers when buying products such as candy and bakery, cereals, dairy products or ice cream?
- What are the consumers' perceptions of and attitudes towards 'healthy nutrition', 'taste', 'balanced lifestyle' and 'calorie intake'?
- How do consumers deal with the indication of ingredients, labeling and nutrition guidelines such as the traffic light system?
- What are intrinsic and extrinsic drivers for healthy and tasty nutrition?

Fig. 2. Community cloud.

The researchers took their first step into the topic field by systemizing topics, trends, markets and products in the form of a mindmap containing a classification and structured set of topics to be used as a starting point for defining search strategies and identifying adequate online sources.

In the second step, community identification and selection, communities and Internet sources with relevant information on the defined research area are collected and filtered according to research criteria such as the number of members, the frequency and length of communication, the value of content and the retention of topics. For Symrise's research questions, 249 identified online sources were identified, of which 16 English- and German-speaking online communities and blogs were selected. The final community selection included discussion boards on food and cooking such as chefkoch.de and cookinglight.com, health and nutrition sites such as healthboards.com and weightwatchers.de, as well as parent and children discussion boards such as meet-teens.de and elternfragen.net (Fig. 2).

In the third and fourth stages of the netnography approach, the selected online communities are observed by the researchers, who immerse themselves in the community and its social context. This is accomplished by extensively reading the already existing consumer dialogues, secondary data so to speak, with a focus on conversations which are recent, extensively replied to, referenced and frequently viewed by the community members. During the immersion process, the researchers become sensitive towards the attitudes and the communication mode of the community members. At this stage the researchers' knowledge on content analysis, qualitative data analysis and discourse analysis is incorporated as an iterative process of (1) noticing consumer statements, (2) collecting statements and (3) thinking about interesting consumer statements. The selected user discussions are read through carefully and patiently, analyzed with the help of qualitative data analysis software and coded by a vivid coding system. Within the selected 16 communities, 1,042 original user posts were analyzed, structured and clustered in three weeks of research work by assigning all relevant text passages to the categorized topics they address.

Subsequent to the detailed qualitative content analysis, the findings need to be interpreted by the team of researchers. The aim is to look for patterns and relationships within and across the collections of consumer statements to be able to make general discoveries about the research subject. Therefore the researchers compare and contrast the collected consumer records in order to discover similarities and differences, build typologies or find sequences. The analysis and interpretation process in this study result in six consumer insights reflecting the landscape of needs, motivations, desires, attitudes, experiences and problems on an aggregated level.

When Consciousness meets Temptation
Eating healthy is difficult, eating sweet
stuff makes you feel guilty. But taste
should never suffer from compromise.

Would your Ancestors know it?
Follow 2 rules. 1) Only buy food with
ingredients your ancestors would have
known. 2) The less ingredients on the
ingredients list, the better.

Fig. 3a. Summary of insights.

Cracking the Consumers' "Health-Code"
Cooking myself is the only way to control
what you eat. Balanced and home-made
food are the key to a healthy diet.

Blurred Senses
Convenience food is overflavored, too
intense , even child food is packed full
with sugar and additives. No wonder
that people have forgotten the natural
taste and got addicted.

Fig. 3b. Summary of insights

These consumer insights are shown in the final presentation as a key visual. They are illustrated by a number of representative consumer quotes and described in terms of detailed management summaries and business implications. Four of the six derived consumer insights in Symrise's netnography study on healthy food are shown in Fig. 3a and 3b.

According to Symrise, SymLife Sweet® makes it possible to offer natural products that are perceived as credible and natural as it enhances the natural sweet flavoring of food, enabling food producers to save on sugar and at the same time avoid the classification of products as 'diet products'. For Symrise, these consumer insights, being derived from unbiased consumer statements, show that SymLife Sweet® can address the needs of consumers regarding their wish for food without artificial sweeteners.

Transferring the insights into innovative product and service solutions in the fifth step of the netnography method is a crucial step which requires an integrated perspective that combines the analytical thinking of researchers with the creative thinking of designers, including their creativity tools and approaches for ideation and product prototyping. In this final step that builds upon the consumer insights, Symrise elaborated pictures of imaginative worlds and mood boards, as a foundation for the development of consumer brand products. These mood boards include visual and verbal story-telling to serve as a key element for the B2B communication of SymLife Sweet®. They also serve as input for creative innovation workshops, where consumer insights are translated into product, positioning and communication solutions for Symrise's customers. Of course Symrise used the generated input to create new products for themselves as well.

Summary

A key benefit of netnography is the possibility to access unfiltered, unbiased information from highly experienced and involved users. The huge number of conversations and the vivid online dialogue about products and brands enable marketing and innovation managers to obtain deep insights into consumers' everyday problems and their solutions. By listening to social media, Symrise manages to gain competitive advantages. In particular, the netnography approach enables Symrise to innovate in accordance with consumers' needs and to use the results of the research findings as a starting point for new product development with their business partners, which also strengthens their role as a preferred supplier.

References

Bartl, M., Hück, S. and Ruppert, S. (2009). Netnography research: Community insights in the cosmetics industry. *Conference Proceedings ESOMAR Consumer Insights*, pp. 1–12.

Kozinets, R.V. (1998). On netnography: Initial reflections on consumer research investigations of cyberculture. *Advances in Consumer Research*, 25, 366–371.

Kozinets, R.V. (2002). The field behind the screen: Using netnography for marketing research in online communities. *Journal of Marketing Research*, 39(1), 61–72.

Kozinets, R.V. (2006). Click to connect: Netnography and tribal advertising. *Journal of Advertising Research*, 46(3), 279–288.

Chapter 11

Selection Strategies for Discontinuous Innovation

John Bessant
University of Exeter Business School, UK
Kathrin Möslein
Universität Erlangen-Nürnberg and HHL – Leipzig Graduate School of Management,
Germany
Anne-Katrin Neyer
Universität Erlangen-Nürnberg, Germany
Frank Piller
RWTH Aachen, Germany
Bettina von Stamm
Innovation Leadership Forum, UK

Introduction

Triggers for innovation can be found all over the place. The world is full of interesting and challenging possibilities for change – the trouble is that even the wealthiest organization doesn't have deep enough pockets to do them all. Sooner or later it has to confront the issue of 'out of all the things we could do, which one should we to do?' This isn't easy – making decisions is about resource commitment and choosing to go in one direction closes off opportunities elsewhere. Organizations cannot afford to innovate at random – they need some kind of framework that articulates how they think innovation can help them survive and grow and they need to be able to allocate scarce resources to a portfolio of innovation projects based on this view.

But in a complex and uncertain world it is nonsense to think that we can make detailed plans ahead of the game and then follow them through in systematic fashion. Life – and certainly organizational life – isn't like that; as John Lennon famously said, 'Life is what happens when you're busy making other plans'! So our strategic framework for innovation should be flexible enough to help monitor and adapt projects over time as ideas move towards more concrete solutions – and rigid enough to justify continuation or termination as uncertainties and risky guesswork become replaced by actual knowledge.

The challenge of innovation decision-making is made more complex by the fact that it isn't a simple matter of selecting amongst clearly defined options. By its nature innovation is about the unknown, about possibilities and opportunities associated with doing something new and so the process involves dealing with *uncertainty*. The problem is that we don't know in advance if an innovation will work – will the technology actually do what we hope, will the market still be there and behave as we anticipated, will competitors move in a different and more successful direction, will the government change the rules of the game, and so on? All of these are uncertain variables which makes our act of decision-making a little like driving in the fog. The only way we can get more certainty is by starting the project and learning as we go along. So making the initial decision – and the subsequent ones about whether to keep going or cut our losses and move in a different direction – becomes a matter of calculating as best we can the risks associated with different options.

Decision-Making at the Edge

When the innovation decision is about incremental – 'do what we do but better' – innovation along a particular trajectory, there is relatively little difficulty. A business case with requisite information can be assembled, costs-benefits can be argued and the 'fit' with the current portfolio demonstrated. But as the options move towards the more radical end so the degree of resource commitment and risk rises and decision-making resembles more closely a matter of placing bets – and emotional and political influences become significant.

But under what can be called discontinuous conditions – triggered, for example, by the emergence of a radical new technology or the emergence of a new market, or a shift in the regulatory framework – established players often face a major challenge. Many of their internal rules for resource allocation are unhelpful and may actively militate against placing bets on the new options because they are far outside the firm's 'normal' framework.

Selection and Reframing

A key part of this challenge lies in the difficulties organizations face with reframing – viewing the world in different ways and changing the ways they make selection decisions as a result. Human beings cannot process all the rich and complex information coming at them and so they make use of a variety of simplifying frameworks – mental models – with which to make sense of the world. And the same is true for organizations – as collections of individuals they construct shared mental models through which the complex external world is experienced. Of necessity such models are simplifications – for example, business models which provide lenses through which to make sense of the environment and guide strategic behaviour.

The problem with discontinuous innovation (DI) is that it presents challenges which do not fit the existing model and require reframing – something which established players find hard to do. For example, they will often selectively perceive and interpret the new situation to match or fit their established world views. Since by definition discontinuous shifts usually begin as weak signals of major change, picked up on the edge of the radar screen, it is easy for the continuing interpretation of the signals in the old frame to persist for some time. By the time the disconnect between the two becomes apparent and the need for radical reframing is unavoidable, it is often too late. What start off as core competencies become core rigidities.

The case of Polaroid highlights the difficulty – an otherwise technologically successful company, which had opened up the market for instant photography and had enjoyed a strong reputation for over 40 years, suddenly found itself facing bankruptcy at the turn of the 21st century. The problem wasn't that they didn't see digital imaging coming – they were quite well up on the technology and even had patents in the area. But they were unable to reframe their business model to take advantage of the new conditions – with disastrous consequences.

Another problem is that established firms don't have weak or ineffective strategic resource allocation mechanisms for taking innovation decisions – they actually have systems which are too good! For as long as the decisions are taken within a framework – their 'box' – they are effective, but they break down when the challenge comes from outside that box.

Much of the difficulty in radical or discontinuous innovation selection arises from this framing problem. Innovation rarely involves dealing with a single technology or market but rather a bundle of knowledge which is brought together into a configuration. Successful innovation management requires that we can get hold of and use knowledge about *components* but also about how those can be put together – what we can call the *architecture* of an innovation. And the problem is that we are often unable to imagine alternative configurations, new and different architectures.

So, for example, the famous 'not invented here' rejection is easier to understand if we see it as a problem of what makes sense within a specific context – the firm has little knowledge or experience in the proposed area, the area is not its core business, it has no plans to enter that particular market, etc. Table 1 lists some examples of justifications which can be made to rationalize the rejection decision associated with radical innovation options.

Table 1. Examples of justifications for non-adoption of radical ideas.

Argument	Underlying perceptions from within the established mental model	Examples
'It's not our business'	Recognition of an interesting new business idea but rejection because it lies far from the core competence of the firm	Encyclopaedia Britannica – once a major player in the information game but failed to move with the technologies of multimedia CDs and later the Internet
'It's not a business'	Evaluation suggests the business plan is flawed along some key	Fred Smith came up with the idea of an overnight delivery service while he was a student at Yale. His business

	dimension – often underestimating potential for market development and growth	professor, the United States Postal Service, UPS, and almost every expert in the US said that such an idea would never work. Smith persevered in spite of this feedback and went on to found Federal Express In the world of IT even some of the great names can get it wrong: '640K ought to be enough for anybody.' (Bill Gates, Microsoft, 1981) 'There is no need for any individual to have a computer in their home.' (Ken Olson, President of DEC, 1977) 'I think there is a world market for maybe five computers.' (Thomas Watson, IBM, 1943)
'It's not big enough for us'	Emergent market size is too small to meet growth targets of large established firm	The problem faced by large and successful corporations is that if they are to grow they need something pretty big as the next new idea. For example, Procter & Gamble is a huge multi-billion-dollar business which needs to create a new business the size of a Starbucks every year if it is to meet its growth targets. This often means that interesting new ideas are dismissed not because they aren't interesting but because they are seen as simply not big enough to help meet these ambitious growth targets But niche and 'boutique' products (e.g. home computers, open source software), processes (e.g. mini-mill steel-making) and services (e.g. low-cost airlines, Web-based bookselling or online share trading) have a habit of starting life as tiny markets meeting the needs of some fringe customers but then migrating to the mainstream. And when they catch on it is often too late for the major players to be anything other than a 'fast second'

| *'Not invented here'* | Recognition of interesting idea with potential but reject it – often by finding flaws or mismatch to current internal trajectories | In 1937 Chester Carlson invented the process of making photocopies, called 'xerography' at that time, from the Greek words *xeros* for 'dry' and *graphos* for 'writing'. Almost every company Mr Carlson approached, including General Electric, IBM, Kodak, RCA and many more, along with the experts, said the idea had no merit. Their argument was essentially that people were unlikely to buy an expensive copy machine when carbon paper was so cheap, plentiful and convenient. Like so many entrepreneurs Carlson – with the help of the US Battelle Institute – went on to set up his own company – Xerox – to exploit the idea |
| *'Invented here'* | Recognition of interesting idea but rejection because internally generated version is perceived to be superior | In the 1950s the electronics giant RCA developed a prototype portable transistor-based radio using technologies which it had come to understand well. However, it saw little reason to promote such an apparently inferior technology and continued to develop and build its high-range devices. By contrast Sony used the new technologies to gain access to the emerging consumer market and to build a whole generation of portable consumer devices – and in the process acquired considerable technological experience which enabled them to enter and compete successfully in higher-value, more complex markets

In a similar fashion Siemens invented the fax machine but did not see a relevant market in which to deploy it, preferring to work with what they perceived as the more interesting 'seamless' technology of 'teletext' |

'We're not cannibals'	Recognition of potential for impact on current markets and reluctance to adopt potential competing idea	Part of the resistance to James Dyson's cyclone-based vacuum cleaner came from existing major players (such as Hoover) in the cleaner industry concerned about the impact on their markets for traditional bag-based cleaners. Earlier the shift from cross-ply to radial tyres posed problems for existing players because it challenged them to cannibalize their existing markets
'Nice idea but doesn't fit'	Recognition of interesting idea generated from within but whose application lies outside current business areas – often leads to inventions being shelved or put in a cupboard	Xerox ran a hugely influential research centre in Palo Alto California (PARC) which supported their own business – but also came up with a variety of technologies including the graphical user interface (basis of Windows and before that the Macintosh interface) and Ethernet which enabled networked computing and formed the basis of the Internet backbone. Yet it failed to exploit these hugely significant innovations because they were not perceived as core
'It ain't broke so why fix it?'	No perceived relative advantage in adopting new idea	Slow adoption of new techniques – once the new idea emerges major players are often slow to adopt. So newcomers are often able to seize what Richard Foster calls 'the attacker's advantage' – something which was clear in the emergence of the solid-state electronics industry where players such as Texas Instruments took over the lead from the established valve companies
'Great minds think alike'	'Groupthink' at strategic decision-making level – new idea lies outside the collective frame of reference	The Polaroid case involved extensive discussion at board level about the ways to play the emerging digital imaging game – but their response crystallized around the existing business model and 'groupthink' helped rationalize their approach as correct

'(Existing) customers won't/ don't want it'	New idea offers little to interest or attract current customers – essentially a different value proposition	Clayton Christensen's work on disk drives, steel mini-mills and mechanical excavators are all good examples of working with fringe markets and developing technologies and products which the mainstream market then migrates towards – in the process upstaging the established players. Disruptive innovation undoubtedly led to the shake-up in the airline industry with the shift towards low-cost, no-frills travel
'We've never done it before'	Perception that risks involved are too high along market and technical dimensions	Fast followers who were too slow – being cautious may place the firm too far behind on the learning curve. In the 1970s Xerox was the dominant player in photocopiers, having built the industry from its early days when it was founded on the radical technology pioneered by Chester Carlson and the Battelle Institute. But despite their prowess in the core technologies and continuing investment in maintaining an edge it found itself seriously threatened by a new generation of small copiers developed by new entrants including several Japanese players. Importantly these new products were finding application in new markets – smaller businesses and home offices. Despite the fact that Xerox had enormous experience in the industry and a deep understanding of the core technology it took them almost 8 years of mishaps and false starts to introduce a competitive product. In that time Xerox lost around half its market share and suffered severe financial problems

'We're doing OK as we are '	The success trap – lack of motivation or organizational slack to allow exploration outside of current lines	One of the big challenges to existing incumbents comes from their very success in using existing approaches. For example the major airlines in the 1990s were doing well on the back of strong business demand and did not consider the emerging low-cost carriers as any kind of threat – they were seen as targeting a different market and working with a different business model
'Let's set up a pilot'	Recognition of potential in new idea but limited and insufficient commitment to exploring and developing it – lukewarm support	A common pattern in radical innovation is that senior management are concerned enough to set up a small team to come up with ideas and plans for how to deal with it. However, the team may come up with suggestions that have serious implications for the organization, operationally as well as culturally – at which point senior management may get cold feet. In many cases this is the point where the plug is pulled on the innovation team

In many ways these responses represent an 'immune system' response which rejects the strange in order to preserve the health of the current body.

It is important to understand the problem of reframing since it provides some clues as to where and how alternative routines might be developed to support decision-making around selection under high uncertainty. Using 'rational' methods of the kind which work well for incremental innovation is likely to be ineffective because of the high uncertainty associated with this kind of innovation. Since there is a high degree of uncertainty it is difficult to assemble 'facts' to make a clear business case, whilst the inertia of the existing framework includes the capacity to make justifiable rejection arguments of the kind highlighted in Table 1. The problem is complicated by the potential for radical innovation options to conflict with mainstream projects (for example risking 'cannibalization' of existing and currently profitable markets) and the need to acquire resources different from those normally available to the firm.

Instead, some form of alternative approach may be needed to handle the early-stage thinking and exploring of opportunities outside the 'normal' decision-making channels but bring them back into the mainstream when the uncertainty level has been lowered. Resolving these tensions may require development of parallel structures or even setting up of satellite ventures and organizations outside the normal firm boundary.

Mapping the Selection Space

Every organization tries to balance its 'exploit' (do what we do better) innovation activities with those more open-ended 'explore' activities – doing something different. The trouble is that there are limits to what is 'acceptable' exploration – essentially organizations have comfort zones beyond which they are reluctant or unable to search. So their decision-making, even around radical options, is often constrained – this gives rise to the anxiety often expressed about the need for out-of-the-box thinking. Stage-gate and portfolio systems depend on using criteria which are 'bought into' by those bringing ideas – a perception that the resource allocation process is fair and appropriate even if the decisions go the wrong way. Under steady-state conditions these systems can and do work well and criteria are clearly established and perceived to be appropriate. But higher levels of uncertainty put pressure on the existing models – and one effect is that they reject ideas which don't fit – and over time build a self-censoring aspect. As one interviewee researching the way radical ideas were dealt with by his company's portfolio and stage-gate systems explained, 'Around here we no longer have a funnel, we have a tube!'

One way of looking at the innovation selection space is shown in Fig. 1, which we saw earlier in Chapter 3. The vertical axis refers to the familiar 'incremental/radical' dimension in innovation whilst the second relates to environmental complexity – the number of elements and their potential interactions. Rising complexity means that it becomes increasingly difficult to predict a particular state because of the increasing number of potential configurations of these elements. And it is here that problems of decision-making become significant because of the very high levels of uncertainty.

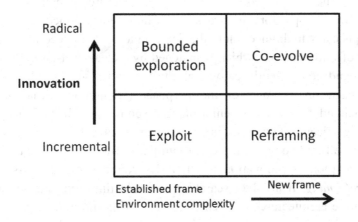

Fig. 1. Innovation selection space.

Zone 1 is essentially the 'exploit' domain in innovation literature. It presumes a stable and shared frame – business model/architecture – within which adaptive and incremental development takes place. Selection is associated with the steady state – portfolio methods, stage-gate reviews, clear resource allocation criteria, project management structures, etc. The structures involved in this selection activity are clearly defined with relevant participants, clear decision points, decision rules, criteria, etc.

Zone 2 involves selection which is a bit more adventurous but which still takes place within the same basic mental frame – 'business model as usual'. Whilst the bets may have longer odds, the decision-making is still carried out against an underlying strategic model and sense of core competencies. There may be debate and politicking about which choices to make but there is an underlying framework to define the arena in which this takes place. Often there is a sector-level trajectory – for example Moore's law shaping semiconductor, computer and related industry patterns.

The structures involved in such selection activity are, of necessity, focused at high-level – these are big bets – key strategic commitments rather than tactical investments. There are often tensions between the 'exploit' and the 'explore' views and the boardroom battles between these two camps for resources are often tense. Since exploratory concepts carry high uncertainty the decision to proceed becomes more of an act of faith than one which is matched by a clear, fact-based business case – and consequently emotional characteristics such as passion and enthusiasm on the part of the proposer ('champion' behaviour) or personal endorsement by a senior player ('sponsorship' behaviour) play a more significant role in persuading the decision-makers.

These first two zones represent familiar territory in the discussion of exploit/explore in innovation selection. By contrast zone 3 is associated with *reframing*. It involves searching and selecting from a space where alternative architectures are generated, exploring different permutations and combinations of elements in the environment. This process – essentially entrepreneurial – is risky and often results in failure but can also lead to the emergence of new and powerful alternative business models. Significantly this often happens by working with elements in the environment not embraced by established business models – and this poses problems for existing players. Why change an apparently successful formula with relatively clear information about innovation options and well-established routines for managing the process? There is a strong reinforcing inertia about such systems for search and selection – the value networks take on the character of closed systems which operate as virtuous circles and, for as long as they are perceived to create value through innovation, act as inhibitors to reframing.

As we mentioned in Chapter 3 the example of low-cost airlines involved developing a new way of framing the transportation business based on rethinking many of the elements – turnaround times at airports, different plane designs, different Internet-based booking and pricing models, etc. – and also working with different new elements – essentially addressing markets such as students and pensioners which had not been major elements in the traditional business model. Other examples where a reframing of the dominant model has taken place include hub and spoke logistics, digital imaging, digital music distribution and mobile telephony/computing. The critical point here is that such innovation does not necessarily involve pushing the technological frontier but rather working with new architectures – new ways for framing what is already there.

Selection under these conditions is difficult using approaches which work well for zones 1 and 2. Whilst the innovations themselves may not be radical, they require consideration through a different lens and the kinds of information (and their perceived significance) which are involved may be unfamiliar or hard to obtain. For example, in moving into new under-served markets the challenge is that traditional market research and analysis techniques may be inappropriate for markets which effectively do not yet exist. Many of the reasons advanced for rejecting innovation proposals outlined in Table 1 can be mapped onto difficulties in managing selection in zone 3 territory. For example, 'It's not our business' relates to the lack of perceived competence in the analysis of new and unfamiliar variables. 'Not invented here' relates to a similar lack of perceived experience, competence or involvement in a technological field and the inability to analyse and take rational decisions about it. 'It's not a business' relates to apparent market size which in initial stages may appear small and unlikely to serve the growth needs of established incumbents. But such markets could grow – the challenge is seeing an alternative trajectory to the current dominant logic of the established business model.

Here, the challenge is seeing a new possible pattern and absorbing and integrating new elements into it. This is hard to do because it requires reframing, but also because it challenges the existing system – something Machiavelli was aware of many centuries ago:

> It must be remembered that there is nothing more difficult to plan, more doubtful of success nor more dangerous to manage than the creation of a new system. For the initiator has the enmity of all who profit by the preservation of the old institution and merely lukewarm defenders in those who would gain by the new one. (Machiavelli, 1935)

Powerful social forces towards conforming come into play and we see plenty of ways in which the 'immune system' kicks in to reject the 'oddball' idea. Significantly, where there are examples of radical changes in mindset and subsequent strategic direction these often come about as a result of crisis – which has the effect of shattering the mindset – or with the arrival from outside of a new CEO with a different world view.

Zone 4 is where new-to-the-world innovation takes place – and represents the 'edge of chaos' complex environment where innovation emerges as a product of a process of co-evolution. It's not the product of a predefined trajectory so much as the result of complex interactions between independent elements. Processes of amplification and feedback reinforce what begin as small shifts in direction and gradually define a trajectory. All bets are potentially options – and high-variety experimentation takes place. Selection is a real problem since it is, by definition, impossible to predict what is going to be important or where the initial emergence will start and around which feedback and amplification will happen.

Once again this zone poses major challenges to an established set of selection routines – in this case they are equipped to deal with uncertainty but in the form of *known unknowns* whereas zone 4 is essentially the territory of *unknown unknowns*. Analytical tools and evidence-based decision-making – for example reviewing business cases – are inappropriate for judging plays in a game where the rules are unclear and even the board on which it is played has yet to be designed! An example here might be the ways in which the Internet will co-evolve and the products/services which will emerge as a result of a complex set of interactions amongst users. Or the ways in which chronic diseases such as diabetes will be managed in a future where the incidence is likely to increase, where the costs of treatment will rise faster than health budgets can cope and where many different stakeholders are involved – clinicians, drug companies, insurance companies, carers and patients themselves.

Table 2 summarizes the challenges posed across our selection space and highlights the need to experiment with new approaches for selection in zones 3 and 4.

Table 2. Selection challenges, tools and enabling structures.

Zone	Selection challenges	Tools and methods	Enabling structures
1: 'Business as usual' – innovation but under steady-state conditions, little disturbance around core business model	Decisions taken on the basis of exploiting existing and understood knowledge and deploying in known fields. Incremental innovation aimed at refining and improving. Requires building strong ties with key players in existing value network and working with them	'Good practice' entailing new product/service development. Portfolio methods and clear decision criteria, stage-gate reviews along clear and established pathways	Formal and mainstream structures – established stage-gate process with defined review meetings. High involvement across organization roles and functions in decision-making
2: 'Business model as usual' – bounded exploration within this frame	Exploration – pushing frontiers of technology and market via calculated risks – 'buying a look' at new options through strategic investments in further research. Involves risk-taking and high uncertainty	Advanced tools for risk assessment, e.g. R&D options and futures. Multiple portfolio methods and 'fuzzy front end' toolkit – bubble charts, etc. Criteria used are a mix of financial and non-financial. Judgmental methods allow for some influence of passion and enthusiasm – the 'Dragons' Den' effect	May form part of existing stage-gate and review system with extra attention being devoted to higher-risk projects at early stages. May also involve special meetings outside that frame – and decision-making will be at strategic (board) level rather than operational

3: Alternative frame – taking in new/different elements in environment	Reframing – exploring alternative options, introducing new elements. Challenge involves decision-making under uncertainty but not simply a problem of lack of information and the need to take risky bets to learn more. Here there is also the issue of unfamiliar frames of reference and the difficulty of letting go of a dominant logic. Cognitive dissonance means that incumbents have trouble 'forgetting' enough to see the environment through new eyes	May use variations of existing toolkit, e.g. portfolio methods, but extend the parameters, e.g. 'fuzzy front end', bubble charts, etc. Alternative futures and visioning tools. Constructed crisis. Prototyping – probe and learn. Creativity techniques. Use of internal and external entrepreneurs to decentralize development of early business case. Alternative funding models and decentralized authority for early-stage exploration	Unlikely to fit with established decision structures – stage-gate and portfolio – since these are designed around established business model frame. Needs parallel or alternative evaluation structures for at least the early stages
4: Radical – new-to-the-world – possibilities. New architecture around as yet unknown and established elements	Emergence – need to co-evolve with stakeholders. Be in there. Be in there early. Be in there actively	Complexity theory – feedback and amplification, probe and learn, prototyping and use of boundary objects	Far from mainstream. Satellite structures – skunk works or even outside the firm. 'Licensed dreamers'. Outside agents and facilitators

Tools to Help

Faced with the reframing and high uncertainty challenges of zones 3 and 4, how can organizations manage the selection process? We've seen that established methods such as stage gates, business cases, portfolio tools, etc., start to break down under these conditions – so what else can they use? Research and experience-sharing within the AIM Discontinuous Innovation Laboratory[a] suggests a number of promising lines for development, including:

- Building alternative visions
- Bridge-building to/from outside the box
- Probe and learn methods
- Using alternative evaluation and measurement criteria
- Mobilizing sponsorship and championship
- Using alternative decision-making pathways
- Deploying alternative funding structures
- Using alternative – dedicated/devolved/decentralized – implementation structures
- Mobilizing entrepreneurship inside and outside the firm.

We will discuss these briefly in the following section.

Building alternative futures

As we have seen, a core difficulty in selection for DI lies in the problem of reframing – of seeing the world through different lenses and allowing for the possibility of alternative arrangements. If nothing else firms ought to look at alternative models as an 'insurance policy' – to at least consider different approaches and attempt to assess their relevance and

---

[a] This is an experience-sharing network involving around 170 companies and 35 academic institutions across 12 countries. Its focus is on how firms can develop new capabilities to deal with the challenges of discontinuous innovation. More details can be found at the end of this report.

salience for their business strategies. One powerful set of tools to help with this lies in the area of futures studies, using tools such as forecasting, trend extrapolation and scenario building to create and explore alternative models of the future and the potential threats and opportunities which they contain. Arguably the benefit comes not so much from specific innovations which emerge from the process but from the flexibility in framing that develops. Working out in the 'futures gym' helps build a tolerance for ambiguity within the decision-making structures of the organization.

Increasingly futures tools are being deployed in frameworks which are designed to open up new innovation space – for example, the GameChanger programme has been widely used in organizations such as Shell and Whirlpool, whilst other companies such as BMW, Novozymes and Nokia make extensive use of similar approaches. They deploy a range of techniques including metaphors, storytelling and vision-building and increasingly do so in a cross-sectoral fashion, recognizing that the future may involve blurring of traditional market or demographic boundaries. For example, Siemens uses storytelling to create a setting in which discontinuous innovations are seen as visions and not as threats. To do so, they identify trends of the future (such as mega cities) and use these as the basis for storytelling about the importance of selecting discontinuous ideas to deal with the future challenges that go hand in hand with these trends.

In Ireland, Bord Bia – the national agency for the food industry – has been running a programme exploring alternative futures for the many food companies in the country. Through a process of shared construction and exploration of rich alternative pictures of the future it becomes possible not only to spot potential threats and opportunities but also to build valuable new alliances and gain commitment and support for radical new ventures.

An important variant on this is the use of what is termed 'constructed crisis' – deliberately exploring radical and challenging futures to create a sense of unease – a 'burning platform' from which new directions forward can be developed. Sometimes strong leadership is critical to carrying the company forward into new territory. When Intel was facing strong competition from Far Eastern producers in the memory chip market, board-level discussion focused on the need to 'think the unthinkable', i.e. get out of memory production (the business on which Intel had grown up), and to contemplate moving into other product niches. They trace their subsequent success to the point where they found themselves 'entering the void' and creating a new vision for the business. Intel now has a process called 'constructive confrontation', which essentially encourages a degree of dissent. The company has learned to value the critical insights which come from those closest to the action rather than assume senior managers have the right answers every time.

In some cases the company may make use of what could be termed 'licensed fools' – in the Shakespearean sense, to describe a character who is allowed to challenge the king and his courtiers. Because he is outside their system and has nothing to lose the fool can tell it like it is, or present radically different views to the collective wisdom of the ruling group. Many firms make use of consultants in this fashion, actively seeking their provocation and challenge.

Prototyping as a way of building bridges in the selection process

The big advantage of incremental innovation is that it is easy to make decisions about because it represents 'doing what we do better'. We already know what is there and so we can assess the proposed change against that – there is a high degree of certainty and judgements can be made based on concrete data. But radical innovation is essentially a 'leap into the unknown' – and part of the problem is that we don't have anything against which to compare it. We are short on facts and have to rely on imagination and guesswork. Not surprisingly there is often a tendency to play it safe – especially if the imagined picture of the innovation looks like nothing we have ever seen before.

When confronted by innovation trigger signals outside the 'normal' frame, organizations face the classic entrepreneur's challenge. It is possible to see something new but in order to take that forward, to make the idea a reality, the entrepreneur needs to mobilize resources and to do this he/she needs to convince others of the potential. The process involves building bridges in the minds of potential supporters between the current state of affairs and what might be. It is here that boundary objects become important – things which can act as stepping stones between the two. Prototyping offers a way of creating such stepping stones towards that new option – and importantly stepping stones which allow both building up of better understanding and also shaping the idea whilst it is still in its formative stages. Matthias Gold, senior manager of Egozentrik, a German start-up company that designs hybrid bikes, reports that they developed around 40 prototypes over a five-year period to collect information about the unknown territory of hybrid bikes and to learn from the feedback gained.

There are many different ways of prototyping, including physical models, simulation, etc., and these span both manufactured products and service concepts. The process can also involve the use of consultants who act in a bridging fashion, helping to reduce the risk by outsourcing the exploration to them. By employing consultants such as IDEO or ?What If!, organizations can conduct a safe experiment and then use their involvement with an external agency to develop and work with the emerging prototype.

An important role for prototyping is in highly complex environments (zone 4) where there is no clear direction and where processes of co-evolution are involved. Under such conditions we know that tools such as feedback and amplification around key points – 'attractor basins', in the jargon of complexity theory – are important. Arguably, prototypes provide the boundary objects to enable this to happen – the speck of impurity around which a new crystal can begin to form. For example, in the UK the NHS has been working with a team from the Design Council on prototypes for radical new approaches to diabetes care – recognizing that this huge and growing problem will require very different approaches to its management in the future (see www.designcouncil.info/RED/health for more information).

Probe and learn

Part of the problem of making selection decisions about radical innovation ideas is the scale of uncertainty. It's easy enough to decide which path to take when the options on offer are clearly visible, straight lines leading towards a pot of gold which conveniently is in the line of sight and not too far away. It's quite another thing when the paths are little more than vague tracks in the mud, disappearing rapidly into a deep fog which shrouds any sense of direction after the first few steps. Not surprisingly most organizations err on the side of caution and stick to the relative certainty of the first set of options.

One way of dealing with the uncertainty problem is to use probe and learn approaches – essentially making small steps into the fog and shining a torch (or swirling a fan) to illuminate enough of the pathway to see where it might lead next. Closely related to boundary objects, the idea here is to help move from outside the box to a new place outside the comfort zone by a series of planned experiments. These serve two functions – they provide new information about what does (and doesn't) work and so help build the case for selection along the 'rational' axis of Fig. 1. But they also represent ways of mapping 'unsafe' territory and reducing the emotional anxiety. In this sense they are investments in what Robert Cooper calls 'buying a look' – and they help assemble the beginnings of a case for further support and exploration (Cooper, 2001).

Research on prototyping as a communication and integration tool (Neyer and Doll, 2008) shows that the work on the prototypes helped entrepreneurial teams create an understanding of the feasibility of their idea and select the best idea out of the hundreds of possible ideas they came up with. This reduced uncertainty and fostered the teams' engagement in the idea.

Such investments in 'buying a look' may fail – progress on the pathway may end up confirming that this is not a good road to travel. But they may also help point in new and exciting directions – and in the process justify the investment. What the probe and learn approach does in the context of selection decision-making is to stage the risk into smaller steps – rather than forcing a once-for-all commitment. It's got a lot in common with taking options in the stock market – and indeed many organizations are using options approaches as an input to their R&D strategy.

Probe and learn approaches have always been used within the traditional R&D or market research portfolio to push the frontiers and allow a little blue-sky thinking. But increasingly, smart organizations are deploying such approaches as a deliberate strategy to explore and take options on uncertain but interesting future directions. There are plenty of methods to choose from but they all share the characteristic of being deliberate experiments in the unknown. Prototyping here becomes less a means of confirming and shaping an idea which has already been established than a planned experiment to test a hypothesis – and failure of the experiment is worth as much as success in terms of learning about directions not to travel in. Collecting data from extreme environments and fringe users is relevant less for its ability to test and understand early adoption patterns in established markets than for getting early warning about possible weak signals for change – and learning how to work under these very different conditions.

Examples of probe and learn include work done by Nokia in exploring different uses of mobile phones in radically different contexts such as Kenya or the Philippines, where the technology is being used in surprising ways such as providing an alternative banking system for those on low incomes. In the UK Vodafone has been exploring how its technology might provide new healthcare services to diabetes sufferers. Danish pharmaceutical firm Novo Nordisk has made extensive use of its national diabetes programmes in different regions of the world to build up its understanding of the alternative ways in which diabetes care and management might be framed and delivered in the future. BBC Backstage, as we saw in Chapter 3, was another example. They used an open source approach in which developers are invited to make free use of various elements of the BBC's site (such as live news feeds, weather, TV listings, etc.) to integrate and shape innovative applications.

The process is linked to Innovation Labs – essentially a short-term incubator run in various regional locations where promising ideas can be worked up jointly by BBC staff and developer before being pitched to senior managers for possible adoption.

As we saw in Chapter 3, similar models are used by agencies like the UK's Ordnance Survey which is partnering up with a wide range of firms such as Nokia, Philips and Garmin and also opening up its website to invite users to suggest ways forward for joint developments. Lego has also developed extensive links with user communities following its success with an open innovation approach with the Mindstorms product.

Using alternative measurement and evaluation criteria

Within any selection system there is a need for criteria – and general acceptance of these as a good basis on which to take decisions. But this is difficult to do under conditions of high uncertainty – and so often the problem is resolved by adapting existing systems which may be only partially effective. For example, Reckitt Benckiser employs conventional criteria but increases the hurdle rate in order to mitigate the risk associated with uncertainty. Kodak relaxes conventional criteria to recognize that DI needs room for moulding and maturing; and Unilever applies broad boundaries (maximum permissible losses) in which DI can be nurtured.

Other organizations are experimenting with deploying alternative criteria within their decision systems – for example using approaches such as discovery-driven planning where higher uncertainty is involved along technical, market or other dimensions. The idea here is to use learning loops rather than stage gates, and rather than a simple pass/fail decision the discussion at each loop is around what we know and what we need to explore further – where to target the next stage of learning. Such models link to resource allocation in the same way as stage gates but have the advantage of allowing further exploration to proceed.

Mobilizing networks of support

The trouble with radical ideas is that quite often they can be revolutionary! They are going to upset some apple carts, disturb someone's equilibrium and generally pose problems which challenge the quiet life, the comfort zone, 'the way we've always done things'. So it follows that to get over this formidable set of obstacles entrepreneurs/intrapreneurs are going to need a great deal of personal energy, enthusiasm and passion to move their ideas forward. But they could also benefit from a little – or a lot – of help from their friends, especially if those happen to be powerful sponsors at high levels who can help promote their cause or ease some of the tensions it sets up.

Much of the literature around radical innovation identifies the role of champions of various kinds. It's possible to identify several types of champion: technical champion, project champion, senior management champion, business unit champion – and these can be combined in the same individual, e.g. James Dyson, or in a team/tandem arrangement, e.g. Art Fry and Spencer Silver at 3M. In their work on radical innovation in the US, O'Connor and Veryzer (2001) observed three distinct roles of individuals that help formulate, articulate, sustain and implement DI opportunities: ruminators, champions and implementers – each covering the search, selection and implementation phases of innovation.

- *Ruminators* – contemplative, experienced and progressive people with the ability to bring together disparate information by looking far beyond their own business boundaries. Key to search.
- *Champions* – promote the opportunity identified by the ruminator. They are entrepreneurial in obtaining the necessary resources and effective at selling or justifying the vision. Key to selection.
- *Implementers* – often volunteers who enjoy working on more risky projects, particularly if they feel they have an opportunity of working on technology that may 'change the world'. Key to implementation.

The challenge lies in developing ways to engage and use champion roles within DI in some kind of planned fashion rather than hoping for their emergence. One approach is to make formal links with senior managers whose task becomes that of sponsor for DI projects, i.e. senior management champion. Another approach is to identify and use individuals with a high-profile reputation, i.e. technical champion.

For example, a basic element of BT's Wakaba (Japanese for 'green shoots') programme to support innovative ideas within the company is the creation of partnerships – each project has a senior management mentor associated with it. Every eight weeks the ongoing innovative projects are reviewed by a jury of top executives and the mentors represented at this session provide advice and guidance to help shape and take ideas forward. This process ensures the awareness and the involvement of the top management in the innovation activities as well as providing support for the innovation teams. O2 uses a similar approach; in the early phase ideas are presented informally to senior staff and after projects have been chosen, they are allocated to a champion, who acts as a sponsor and advocate to support the project.

In some cases the organization may co-opt outsiders who help with the innovation process, in terms of both bringing in different perspectives and providing support and championship for interesting ideas. For example the UK charity Cancer Research uses a process of bringing in external experts as 'dragons' who then influence the inertia and risk averseness of internal people.

Using alternative decision-making pathways

Smart organizations recognize that innovation is risky and so they put in place systems not only to select and build a balanced portfolio of innovation projects but also to review their progress as they make their way from being an exciting gleam in the eye through to full-scale implementation on the internal or external market. There is usually some variant on the innovation funnel – a front-end sieve to select and build a balanced portfolio of projects which match business needs and then a series of stage gates to review progress against increasingly tight criteria and objectives.

At the lower end of the risk spectrum there are often fast-track arrangements – simplified structures which allow quick decisions and rapid implementation of simple ideas – the kind which often emerge, for example, in employee involvement programmes. But what about the other end of the risk scale – the radical projects which simply don't fit the mainstream stage-gate/funnel system? Quite correctly – since such systems were designed to manage risk and enable decisions based on market and technological facts marshalled into clear business cases – they would throw out ideas which are vague, hazy, speculative and lacking a clear business case. Passion and vision are all very well but innovation funnels are not usually designed to respond to such woolly proposals.

To help deal with this and to provide a pathway for developing radical ideas at least to the stage where they can stand up for themselves in the mainstream innovation funnel process, many organizations have experimented with parallel or alternative structures for radical innovation. They vary in shape and form but essentially have a 'fuzzy front end' which allows for building a potential portfolio of higher-risk ideas and options, and some mechanisms for gradually building a business case which can be subjected to increasingly critical criteria for resource allocation – essentially a parallel funnel structure. These systems may rejoin the mainstream funnel at a later stage or they may continue to operate in parallel (see Fig. 2). And of course they may lead to very different options apart from progression as a mainstream project – spin off, license out, buy-in, etc.

It is clear that extensive experimentation is going on within firms to try to develop alternative approaches and structures. For example, the UK's Ordnance Survey uses a model based on the popular TV series *Dragons' Den*. A panel of senior executives convene periodically to assess competitive funding bids for both conventional and discontinuous projects. Ideas generated by employees are initially assessed against predefined criteria by 'innovation angels' who then select and refine projects for presentation. The idea is then pitched to the 'Dragons' Den' which decides on whether to support it with ring-fenced funds. Not only are the projects selected using a forum that bypasses the corporate immune system but they also gather considerable executive support from the outset.

Other companies such as O2 adopt a more informal approach by using presentation rounds. These are early-stage forums in which both conventional and discontinuous ideas can be pitched to senior staff. In contrast to 'Dragons' Dens', no formal screening criteria are applied and the competition is not to win funding. Instead, successful projects win the interest and support of the senior staff and then are allocated a champion (who acts as a sponsor and advocate) to help take the idea further and assist in securing resources.

Key to both of these is the provision of either discretionary or dedicated developmental resources, which are separate from the traditional R&D or innovation budgets – these are essentially the 'dragons' teeth' and underwrite the utility of the parallel pathways.

Another interesting development is the use of internal markets to assess ideas. Building on the principles of crowdsourcing and the wisdom of crowds, such models provide a radically different way of assessing – and also building support for – radical ideas. The key here is to open the evaluation to a broader set of people to get an aggregation of opinions. This principle underlies the growth of many businesses working around the mass customization theme – for example the collective customer commitment at Muji (a consumer and household goods manufacturer/retailer) or aggregated evaluation of T-shirt designs at Threadless (www.threadless.com) or the Spreadshirt marketplace (www.spreadshirt.net).

Various approaches are being explored to utilize this concept – for example some companies are experimenting with what can be termed a 'virtual stock market' (Spann and Skiera, 2004). In this approach a group of people trade virtual shares of new product ideas on a virtual stock market. Virtual shares can represent multiple future events, for example the specific sales of a new product at a determined timeslot. The value of the shares depends on the realization of the market situation. Thereby the assessments of future developments are revealed. This tool can be positioned between evaluation by experts and consumer research (Spann, 2002). In addition to gaining market insights, this approach can help to find individuals who have a specific talent in forecasting future sales. They can be identified by the value of their virtual portfolio (Spann *et al.,* 2007).

Another approach is to use open evaluation platforms which enable individuals within the business to evaluate a product quantitatively or qualitatively and to make suggestions about how to take the idea further. For example, German car roofing system supplier Webasto uses an intranet platform which allows the entire company to become part of the selection process – and to innovate while selecting. In addition to the motivational benefits of involving all employees in the innovation process this means that evaluation is made by an aggregation of hundreds of people with different backgrounds.

In Swedish paper products company SCA there has been extensive parallel development of systems for managing normal innovation and radical innovation via different routes. An important element in their DI model is the recognition of the need to capture and retain ideas which may not find immediate application but might form the basis for future development, licensing out or other development routes. The origins of this parallel model lay in the recognition that their existing idea management system did not mirror the changed innovation scope of their business which was seeking more radical options. If a business idea was submitted it used to be rejected since the managers of the system did not have the competence or authority to evaluate business ideas. These ideas were then directed to the market organization, which was often too busy to develop such initiatives further.

Central to the system is making a distinction between inside-the-box and outside-the-box innovation ideas. Inside-the-box ideas are defined as incremental technological innovations with little market novelty and initiatives which are within the current competence area of the firm. Those ideas which are completely new for the firm, in either the technological or business dimension, are defined as outside-the-box initiatives.

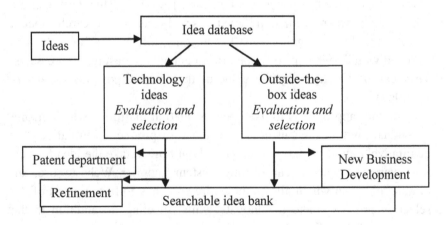

Fig. 2. DI model.

When an idea is submitted, it is first of all classified as either inside the box or outside the box, and then it takes different paths depending upon its nature. The ones which are inside the box go either to the patent department for further investigation or to the market organization. Those ideas are treated like other project initiatives within the firm. The ideas which are regarded as outside the box take a different path. They go to a recently started unit called New Business Development (NBD) which lies outside the rest of the organization and aims to evaluate, incubate and develop those ideas. Here, the evaluation process differs in many respects from the assessment of incremental innovations. The criteria are less rigid here; rather than evaluating an idea according to the current capabilities of the firm, the initial screening here attempts to define gaps in capabilities and find ways to solve the potential problems those gaps are associated with. Moreover, instead of evaluating ideas according to their risks, an iterative approach is employed aiming to identify and reduce risks. When these ideas have been developed further they are either handed over to the main organization of the firm or launched as independent ventures.

Deploying alternative funding structures

If ideas are the spark for innovation, then the fuel which enables the innovation engine to burn and deliver power is money. Resources are essential to allow further exploration of technical or market options, to develop and test ideas, to commit to full-scale preparation and launch and to support innovations in the long term as they mature and continuously improve. But simply throwing money at innovation is not a good idea – and is a very fast way of losing it!

Not surprisingly, smart organizations have developed sophisticated systems for resource allocation and decision structures and rules to trigger (and sometimes stop) the flow of resources to innovation projects. But just as the external financial markets recognize a place for venture capital finance available for higher-risk and potentially higher-reward projects, so increasingly organizations are developing alternative and parallel funding arrangements which provide access to funding on different terms.

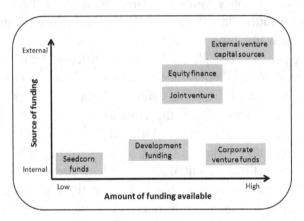

Fig. 3. Different funding models.

There is a wide range of models for doing this which we can position on the diagram in Fig. 3. One axis is the amount of funding, from small development increments to full-scale big bets. And the other is the extent to which this is internal funding as opposed to external.

In a short survey of UK participants in the DI Lab two thirds of them acknowledged issues related to the accessibility of conventional sources of funding and thus allowed DI to tap special dedicated or discretionary budgets. Using a special funding approach gave those working on the projects access to a more reliable funding stream. Their projects did not have to fight so hard for funds and could stay under the radar in terms of the more formal organizational decision system. In many cases such projects also had a top-level champion who could sometimes provide additional access to resources.

By contrast, partnering brings in resources – and also a different perspective – from an external organization. It enables financial risk to be shared and ensures that an incubating DI is given appropriate focus and not left in 'development hell' or on the back-burner. Organizations such as Kodak and Unilever identified partnering as a real option to offset risks associated with dedicated funding and provide a mechanism for more diverse opinions and specializations to be heard.

Although many companies might have access to government funding for early-stage innovations, ideal for DI projects, only the BBC and Ordnance Survey acknowledged this potential source of early-stage funding.

As we've seen, many organizations develop a parallel structure or track for ideas which lie outside the mainstream – by setting up some kind of dual structure. This can take many forms, including special project teams, incubators, new venture divisions, corporate venture units and skunkworks. Some have more formal status than others, some have more direct power or resources whilst others are dependent on internal sponsors or patrons. Whatever the particular arrangement the underlying purpose of such dual structures is to protect new and often high-risk ideas from the mainstream organization until they have achieved some measure of commercial viability. But, as AIM Fellow Julian Birkinshaw and colleagues point out, such units are hard to manage effectively. Their research suggests that they work best when they have CEO-level support, clear objectives and their own separate sources of finance, and they work least well when parent company managers meddle in the evaluation and selection of ventures, and when they are expected to support multiple (and changing) objectives (Buckland *et al.*, 2003).

The other issue with such dual structures is the need to bring them back into the mainstream at some point. They can provide helpful vehicles for growing ideas to the point where they can be more fairly evaluated against mainstream criteria and portfolio selection systems, but they need to be seen as temporary rather than permanent mechanisms for doing so. Otherwise there is a risk of separation and at the limit a loss of leverage against the knowledge and other assets of the mainstream organization.

Using alternative/dedicated implementation structures

Part of the difficulty of DI selection is that ideas are not well developed when they first come up for consideration. So, one strategy for dealing with this is to allow them to incubate elsewhere – offline or at least away from the harsh environment of the normal resource allocation system. In essence this strategy bridges both the selection and implementation challenges and makes use of different mechanisms for incubation and early-stage development.

In seeking to develop capabilities beyond their core competencies, many companies have developed bespoke structures and processes to deal with DI opportunities. A good example is the famous skunkworks at Lockheed Martin, but there are many variants on this model involving dedicated teams with a different DI remit. In trying to open up new market and technology space to move beyond its current product range, Coloplast, the Danish medical devices firm, established a small group, Nebula – New Business Lab, with the remit to explore and bring back new options. These could be acquisitions, licences for new technologies, new alliances and partnerships or established product ideas. The group also had the mandate to explore licensing and spinning out. Unipart – the UK services and logistics company – has a similar operation called Green Shoots.

Other variants include setting up external ventures where such incubation can take place – for example, Siemens makes use of satellite small- and medium-sized enterprises (SMEs) in which it has a share to act as incubator environments to take forward some of its more radical ideas. Others take stakes in start-ups to explore and develop ideas to the point where they might represent formal options for full acquisition – or spin out.

Another approach is to use third-party consultants as a short-term environment in which more radical ideas can be developed and explored. IDEO and others have been playing this role on behalf of several firms and the consultancy ?What If! now has its own venture arm in which it takes stakes in radical ideas which emerge from its consulting activity.

In many cases the venturing and the dedicated funding themes are linked in some form of new venture fund. For example, Nick Allen at Unilever Ventures explained how their quasi-autonomous division is responsible for assessing, selecting and investing in DI opportunities originating from within and outside Unilever. Charged with a budget of $250 million it is essentially a corporate venture fund that co-invests in businesses outside the usual scope of Unilever operations. It has an exit horizon of five years and beyond not losing more than $50 million/year is relatively unconstrained. Unilever's approach is also ideally suited to engaging in partnerships. These confer a host of benefits including risk-sharing, a higher probability of project success through shared skills/experience and a greater level of commitment than found in solo ventures. Furthermore the reduction in risk and uncertainty associated with effective partnerships may lead to a broader range of DI opportunities being considered and selected. At the end of the five-year investment cycle the mature businesses will either need to be sold off or bought out entirely and incorporated into Unilever's corporate structure.

However, despite being effective vehicles for identifying and exploring DI, the operational, organizational and strategic disconnect of such venture works and their projects from the corporation raises some serious issues, not least the feasibility of assimilating a mature but discontinuous business into the parent company.

SAP has set up a venture unit called SAP Inspire to fund start-ups with interesting technologies. The mission of the group is to 'be a world-class corporate venturing group that will contribute, through business and technical innovation, to SAP's long-term growth and leadership'. It does so in a number of ways, including:

- Seeking entrepreneurial talent within SAP and providing an environment where ideas are evaluated on an open and objective basis
- Actively soliciting and cultivating ideas from the SAP community as well as effectively managing the innovation process from idea generation to commercialization
- Looking for growth opportunities that are beyond the existing portfolio but within SAP's overall vision and strategy.

Mobilizing entrepreneurship

At its heart the DI challenge concerns entrepreneurship – seeing opportunities and making them happen in the form of radical innovation. So it makes sense to explore options for helping the process forward, which build on core principles of entrepreneurship – such as being able to pitch an idea with passion and enthusiasm. Whilst many of the mechanisms mentioned help with the selection phase, another strategy is to try to identify and work with entrepreneurs inside and outside the organization and allow their natural capabilities to help select and implement discontinuous innovation ideas. This is at the heart of many famous programmes such as 3M's 'intrapreneuring' or, more recently, the free time allocated to Google's engineers to explore new ideas of their own. Procter & Gamble are trying to take their open innovation model forward partly through the use of technology entrepreneurs whose role is to identify and also help promote and sell internally new ideas. Their Tide to Go product – essentially a stain remover in a pen – was the brainchild of one such entrepreneur, Roy Sandbach, who developed the original concept whilst experimenting at home. It took several passes through the corporate decision system over a five-year period but eventually his enthusiasm and skill brought it into full-scale development and launch. Shell's GameChanger is another vehicle which has at its heart a cadre of internal entrepreneurs who not only have the tools and techniques to identify promising DI opportunities but also have the personal skill sets to try to take them forward inside a conservative organization.

A number of organizations are trying to make explicit use of this approach to help with all stages of the DI challenge – search, select and implement. Creating the culture to enable this is not simple; it requires a commitment of resources but also a set of mechanisms to take bright ideas forward, including various internal development grants and an often complicated and fickle internal funding process. Many such schemes have a strong incentive scheme for those willing to take the lead in taking ideas into marketable products at their core. An additional incentive is often the opportunity to not only lead the development of the new idea but also get involved in the running of the new business.

Fostering a culture of bootlegging (Augsdörfer, 1996) can also help since it creates a difficult environment in which strong ideas can surface through the energy of entrepreneurs in spite of apparent rules and constraints. BMW has a strong commitment to bootlegging – encouraging people to try things out without necessarily asking for permission or establishing a formal project. In BMW these are called Uboot projects. This approach means that people deploy their natural entrepreneurial abilities and often come up with creative solutions.

Novozymes is building an internal network of entrepreneurs. Besides identifying internal people it also recruits people with entrepreneurial spirit from the outside – often people who had built up their own businesses. While aware that these people may be very different from existing employees and want to leave after a short period of time, it decided that even a couple of years would be enough time to provide inspiration and learning.

Conclusion

Innovation strategy is not an exact science. By its very nature the process of choosing where to place scarce resources when we don't know the outcomes of the projects we decide to run has a lot in common with betting at the racetrack. But over time smart organizations develop systems to help them with this – using frameworks and techniques which help them convert the raw uncertainty into a degree of calculated risk and spread this risk across a portfolio of projects. For some time we have known the system for selection and resource allocation when the race meeting involves the steady state of innovation – essentially 'doing what we do but better'. The frontier has moved to trying to develop a parallel and workable system for dealing with the challenges of high-uncertainty innovation possibilities when the races are along the 'do something very different' track. But, as this chapter suggests, whilst we haven't yet got a fully developed system there is a growing body of experience to suggest that firms don't have to rely on impulse alone.

References

Augsdörfer, P. (1996). *Forbidden Fruit*. Avebury, Aldershot.
Buckland, W., Hatcher, A. and Birkenshaw, J. (2003). *Inventuring: Why Big Companies Must Think Small*. McGraw Hill Business, London.
Cooper, R. (2001). *Winning at New Products, 3rd Edition*. Kogan Page, London.

Machiavelli, N. (1935). *The Prince, (Il principe)*. Translated by Ricci, L., revised by Vincent, E.R.P. Oxford University Press, Oxford.

Neyer, A.K., Doll, B. and Möslein, K.M. (2008). Service Innovation: Der Beitrag des Prototyping als Instrument der Innovationskommunikation. *Zeitschrift Führung und Organisation*, 4(77), 208–214.

O'Connor, G.C. and Veryzer, J.R.W. (2001). The nature of market visioning for technology-based radical innovation. *Journal of Product Innovation Management*, 18, 231–246

Spann, M. (2002). *Virtuelle Börsen als Instrument zur Marktforschung*. Gabler Verlag, Wiesbaden.

Spann, M., Ernst, H., Skiera, B. and Soll, J.H. (2009). Identification of lead users for consumer products via virtual stock markets. *Journal of Product Innovation Management*, 26(3), 322–335.

Spann, M. and Skiera, B. (2004). Einsatzmöglichkeiten virtueller Börsen in der Marktforschung. *Zeitschrift für Betriebswirtschaft*, 74, 25–48.

Chapter 12

Selecting Discontinuous Innovation in Practice

Elliot Cox, James Eedes, Syed Jafri, Otome Oyo
formerly Imperial College, Tanaka Business School, UK

Introduction

As part of the selection phase of the Innovation Lab research, a team from Tanaka Business School at Imperial College London were asked to research how discontinuous innovation (DI) is selected in practice in the UK. This report presents the findings of this research and offers observations and insights from which other organisations might learn.

Representatives from nine UK organisations were interviewed. The organisations were the BBC; the UK Department of Health (DoH); GlaxoSmithKline (GSK); Kodak; O2; Ordnance Survey; Reckitt Benckiser; Royal Bank of Scotland (RBS); and Unilever Ventures. Because of the small sample size, this report has no pretence of speaking for all UK companies but rather seeks to reflect anecdotal lessons and experience from the sample group, consistent with the spirit of the Innovation Lab.

The interviews encompassed the following four areas related to the selection stage of DI:

- How is DI presented in your firm?
- What mechanisms and criteria are used to select and assess DI opportunities?
- How are DI opportunities funded?
- How does your firm respond to discontinuous innovation?

Our findings suggest that firms regard DI in two distinct ways:

- A potential threat to their existing business model and thus something to be mitigated against by developing projects that act as long-term product/market hedges (i.e. reserving the right to play) (Courtney *et al.*, 1997)
- A potential means of entering, defining and exploiting new markets.

In practice, this attitude towards DI is a good predictor of the types of mechanisms firms use to assess and select DI projects. We found that companies that view DI proactively, as an opportunity rather than a threat, devote considerably more time and resources to developing 'bespoke' DI-compatible appraisal mechanisms.

Our interviews revealed that although there are a multiplicity of types of structures, processes and people involved in selecting DI projects, three general methodologies are discernible: *conventional*, *hybrid* and *bespoke*.

Regardless of the methodology employed, we found that the mechanisms used by firms to evaluate and select DI all had to deal with three major challenges:

- *Uncertainty of DI technology* – since DI usually requires expertise beyond core competencies it is associated with higher technological risk than conventional projects.
- *Uncertainty of DI funding* – DI projects often necessitate a long-term/open-ended engagement, thus overall funding requirements are often unclear, especially in the early stages of the project.
- *Uncertainty of DI returns* – DI addresses unfamiliar or emerging markets which are difficult to size or segment. Potential revenues from these markets are thus subject to significant uncertainty and consequently conventional criteria such as return on investment and internal rate of return (IRR) become difficult to predict.

Conventional selection mechanisms

In all but one case, firms stated that to some degree they used conventional, pre-existing mechanisms (processes and procedures already in place to assess investment opportunities, such as stage-gating or innovation funnels) to select DI projects. Indeed, despite research suggesting that these methods have limitations when considering DI opportunities and are only effective in the assessment of conventional innovation, just under half the respondents admitted to relying on these evaluative mechanisms alone.

Conventional mechanisms have some advantages over hybrid or bespoke mechanisms but they also have disadvantages. See Table 1 for details.

Table 1. Observations and benefits of conventional DI selection mechanisms.

Observation	Advantage/ Disadvantage	Comments
Accepted methodology	Advantage	Proven track record with multiple proponents. Implementation staff structures and processes already in place
Low cost	Advantage	Low marginal cost of considering a new project – 'efficiencies of scale'
Produces adoptable projects	Advantage	Criteria for funding favour sustaining innovation which is easy to implement
Rigid framework	Both	Advantage: Clear project requirements for proposals to be considered – regarded as fair and open Disadvantage: Modification of project proposals to improve fit is common. Selection bias against some types of project
Bias against DI	Disadvantage	More likely to accept clearly understood continuous projects
Favours corporate immune system	Disadvantage	Optimal forum for sceptics to kill DI project using accepted mechanisms for assessment
Single projects	Disadvantage	Implementation of a risk-reducing portfolio approach which suits DI projects best

A number of reasons for pursuing the conventional approach instead of special mechanisms were offered.

Reckitt Benckiser didn't believe that an innovation that would irrevocably alter the competitive landscape and disrupt their current business models was likely to occur in Reckitt Benckiser's mature core markets. This meant that there wasn't a good argument to support spending scarce resources on constructing elaborate procedures and processes just for DI.

O2 was confident that in the event of a DI, the company would be capable of 'fast following' and thus the early funding of multiple discontinuous ideas was unlikely to yield significant benefits over the later funding of a single proven discontinuous project.

Some companies were simply more comfortable with a risk-averse attitude to innovation, resulting in a natural proclivity towards projects that exploited existing capabilities and markets over those that required new competencies or new market entry, hence the logic that such ideas fitted in with conventional selection mechanisms.

When combined with evidence (Day, 2007) to suggest that conventional mechanisms such as innovation funnels or multi-step stage-gate processes have a selection bias against DI projects, it isn't surprising that these companies tended to be innovative with a small 'i'.

However, firms that used conventional mechanisms but who viewed DI in opportunistic terms employed their selection mechanisms differently from those that regarded DI as a threat to be mitigated. They recognised the shortcomings of conventional mechanisms (see Table 1) and attempted to compensate for them by subtly altering the interpretation of selection criteria and procedures.

The European R&D director of Kodak is given considerable discretion to assess, fund and champion DI. He does this by either 'authorizing below the radar development, presenting the project to heads of strategic business units (SBUs) and the US-based selection team or even demonstrating a prototype to the CEO'.

DI is still assessed using the same mechanisms as conventional projects but is cut more slack and allowed to mature for longer before being forced to compete against them. When DI projects are brought out into the open, a more concerted effort is made to accrue top-level buy-in from SBU chiefs and the CEO to counteract the procedural bias against them.

Hybrid selection mechanisms

Just over half of the organisations interviewed felt that they needed to address the selection bias of conventional mechanisms by developing robust selection frameworks for DI. However resource constraints or political considerations prevented most from deploying fully bespoke solutions. Instead, they were forced to implement supplemental selection procedures which operated in parallel to the conventional mechanisms outlined earlier.

At this point we would like to refer back to the two case examples of Ordnance Survey and O2 provided in the previous chapter, which show very clearly how radical projects can get organizational support in firms. First, the 'Dragons' Den' mechanism at Ordnance Survey helped to select conventional and discontinuous innovative ideas and concepts from around the business. The forum was open for all employees to pitch their ideas, but the 'dragons' were senior executives who had to agree which concepts to invest. Once accepted the panel would provide sufficient funding and executive advice to ensure that the project would overcome corporate innovation barriers. The approach at O2 was less formal, and instead ideas were put forward in presentation rounds. Both, successful continuous and discontinuous concepts of the first round would subsequently be presented to a more senior level. In comparison to the 'Dragons' Den' approach, no formal selection criteria were applied but a champion did accompany the project. Main criteria for success in both firms was the commitment of discretionary or dedicated development resources, which were separate from the main or traditional R&D/innovation budgets – a kind of skunk works.

Bespoke selection mechanisms

For some respondents, the need to anticipate and deal with disruptive innovations which could either challenge their market position or present new growth opportunities is much greater. In seeking to develop capabilities beyond their core competencies, their companies have developed bespoke structures and processes to deal with DI opportunities. These take the form of special external vehicles which operate outside the existing corporate structure.

We refer here to an example given in the previous chapter of Unilever Ventures. With a budget of $250 million, they invested in a quasi-autonomous division that is responsible for the assessment, selection and funding of discontinuous initiatives. These initiatives can come from inside and outside of the company. Partnering is explicitly encouraged with the objective of sharing the risk, increasing the number of projects and, as they found out, heightening the probability of success as skills and experience are shared. They also discovered that the level of commitment from participants was greater when working in teams. The corporate venture fund has an exit horizon of about five years and an edict of not losing more than $50 million/year. Once the ventures reach these limits the businesses will either be sold off or bought out entirely. The Venture Works approach is effective for identifying and exploring DI. However, and as we already mentioned, its operational and strategic disconnect from the organization does raise serious issues such as the feasibility of assimilating discontinuous business into the company.

To date, none of the companies interviewed have attempted such a re-integration: in the closest example – Dove Spas (a successful service business founded by Unilever Ventures) – integration concerns were avoided by switching to a franchising model. Today, franchisees, operating under the Dove brand and Unilever's watchful eye, manage a number of spas throughout the country. Unilever profits from the DI but has avoided the challenge of integrating a service business into its fast-moving consumer goods (FMCG) portfolio.

Summary of DI selection mechanisms

The mechanisms used by companies to assess and select DI projects are closely correlated with how they fundamentally regard DI. Our study identified three broad groups of mechanisms – conventional, hybrid and bespoke. A summary of mechanism characteristics is given in Table 2.

Table 2. Summary of observed mechanism characteristics.

Characteristic	Conventional	Hybrid	Bespoke
Autonomy	Low	Medium	High
Political risk	Low	Moderate	Moderate
Bias against DI	High	Medium	Low
Cost	Low marginal cost	Moderate	High
Skills	Standard	Standard	Specialised and different
Exploration potential	Low	Medium	High
Exploitation potential	High	High	Variable

- *Conventional mechanisms* – these evaluation tools have an inbuilt bias against DI and tend to be used by companies which view DI as a means of abrogating future threats rather than exploiting future opportunities. In those organisations where DI is seen as a potential growth driver, the conventional selection criteria and processes are subtly altered to mitigate against anti-DI bias.
- *Hybrid mechanisms* – these mechanisms are used by companies who recognise the value of DI but are still subject to political or resource constraints. They take the form of parallel executive selection panels that review both continuous and discontinuous ideas and fund successful projects through either discretionary or dedicated funds. Examples include 'Dragons' Dens' and other informal presentation exercises.
- *Bespoke mechanisms* – a small number of companies have the desire and resources to fully explore highly discontinuous projects in a custom-tailored environment. They establish quasi-independent

venture arms which act as vehicles for selecting, funding and maturing DI away from the main corporation. Although these allow a broader range of projects to be undertaken (often in partnership), questions still remain regarding the feasibility of eventually reintegrating them back into the main business.

DI selection criteria

Whereas mechanisms describe the formal (systematic) or informal process a DI opportunity is passed through during assessment and selection, criteria are the variables by which DI opportunities are judged within these mechanisms.

Discontinuity does not invalidate conventional criteria for assessing and selecting opportunities to be pursued by the firm. Indeed, when questioned what criteria were applied when selecting DI opportunities, most respondents initially replied that opportunities must achieve minimum rates of financial return – the commercial upside must justify pursuing the opportunity in preference to other choices.

The problem that quickly emerges, however, is that by its nature, DI is very difficult to evaluate and compare using conventional criteria because the opportunity is inherently uncertain and unpredictable.

Most times, firms lack any frame of reference, such as past projects or market research, to quantify key parameters of the DI opportunity. Forecasts of demand, costs and profits were either unreliable (which increases the risk to key decision-makers such as the CEO and CFO) or were time-consuming and complex to model (which slows and even jeopardises the progression of the DI opportunity through the selection process).

Based on our interviews, it is evident that firms circumvent the problem in crude ways.

Reckitt Benckiser stated that the firm employs conventional criteria but increases the hurdle in order to mitigate the risk associated with uncertainty. Kodak relaxes conventional criteria to recognise that DI needs room for moulding and maturing. And Unilever applies broad boundaries (maximum permissible losses) in which DI can be nurtured.

Determining suitable criteria for DI selection is an arena where both the academic literature and practitioners fail to find consensus. Instead, overarching frameworks or approaches are offered that companies might employ.

Christensen *et al.* (2002) suggest that 'a relatively low number of questions or criteria' should be employed. Concerned by the raft of criteria found in their own research, they concluded that 'such a dizzying array of criteria makes it difficult for managers to evaluate proposals and engage in fruitful discussion'.

On the other hand, Tidd *et al.* (2005) suggest a broad but balanced set of considerations including 'risk, reward, novelty, experience... to create a broad portfolio which helps with both the "do what we do better" and the "do different" agenda'.

Both approaches raise different problems: too few criteria do not sufficiently remove uncertainty and too many criteria stall decision-making because often there are too many unknowns.

In terms of a generic model, the research identified three broad themes that determine what criteria firms apply (Fig. 1):

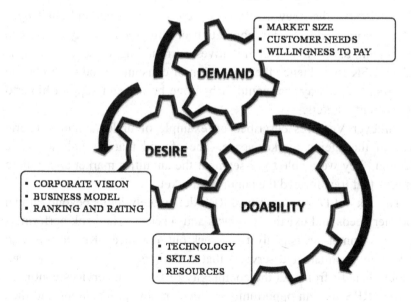

Fig. 1. DI selection criteria employed in UK companies.

- *Demand* – is there a viable market for the product or service?
- *Desire* – does DI fit with the corporate strategy?
- *Doability* – can DI be implemented successfully?

Demand

Demand refers in a very broad sense to the market space that the DI opportunity covers – are there sufficient customers in accessible markets who are willing to pay a profitable price for the product or service? Demand covers:

- The number of potential customers
- Customer needs, wants and desires
- Willingness to pay for products or services to satisfy that need
- The condition or pulse of the market – is the market changing, how is it changing, what are the factors affecting this change and how does that change affect the current and future position of the company?

GSK stated that they assess global consumer trends and challenges such as caring for an ageing population or childhood obesity as well as government regulations and initiatives surrounding these issues. This enables GSK to influence the innovation of consumer products to tackle these issues in a way that couldn't be done before and support hitherto non-existent markets.

Unilever Ventures described an example of understanding generic needs of the ageing market space. They found that through scientific selection, they were able to re-segment the annuities market and build a business that transformed the annuities market.

To seek out DI opportunities, RBS deliberately looks beyond known customer needs and existing products and services. The bank performs a 'customer unmet-needs analysis' to seek out new ideas. Key to this is to think about products and services that customers don't know they want or could benefit from. As the complexity of financial services continues to grow, RBS sees an opportunity to develop new propositions and then sell the benefits to customers.

Although no firms interviewed had precise criteria for the required minimum size of the addressable market (it varies on a case-by-case basis), in all cases the viability of the market was a top-level prerequisite. However, it was noted that the more discontinuous the innovation, the greater the level of uncertainty regarding the exact size and nature of the demand. Figure 2 summarises the various demand concerns of DI and observed processes of mitigation.

Measuring and evaluating demand is a key component of the selection mechanism. Unilever Ventures, for instance, put budget and resources behind ideas to test the demand; RBS uses prototyping (which, according to the Director of Innovation for UK Corporate Banking, is a new and different approach now being employed by the group).

Where resources are not made available to measure the market, DI opportunities can get bogged down by indecision.

Doability

Doability refers to the physical, organisational and financial resources and capabilities of a firm to undertake DI, especially focused on what new resources and competencies are needed and how these will be acquired and at what cost.

The BBC observed that 'Doability and discontinuity are not natural bedfellows' (Mcbain, 2007). True, DI implies an entirely different way of delivering value to customers and is, therefore, necessarily less 'doable'. If the same outcome could be achieved by utilising existing resources and know-how, the innovation – at least semantically – would be continuous.

'Can we do it?' therefore becomes a key criterion for selecting DI. There are two elements to the question:

- First, what resources are needed to pursue the DI opportunity, and can it be implemented cost-effectively? This has a strong quantitative dimension, determining the actual costs of implementation such as investment in new plant and machinery or acquisition of another firm.

- Second, can the firm achieve the necessary change in orientation or culture to successfully implement the DI opportunity? This is far more difficult to predict.

Unilever Ventures, for instance, is a testing ground which helps to fully understand the financial costs of a DI opportunity; however, merging a venture into the wider group poses an integration risk.

Desire

Desire refers to the underlying motivation to pursue or resist DI, manifested in such mechanisms as the corporate vision or mission or determined by factors such as the firm's current strategic direction. The firm's desire for DI is intimately linked to the influence and inclination of its high-level champions, such as the CEO, and its corporate immune system, which can put in place explicit or implicit hurdles for DI to meet.

After the takeover of O2 by Spanish telecoms giant Telefonica in 2005, the management of O2 shifted its focus to meeting performance expectations of its new parent company. The uncertainty and inherent risk of true DI was incompatible with the relationship that was established. Today, O2 explicitly states that its strategy is to be a fast-follower.

In contrast, RBS has increased its appetite for innovation – by hiring key staff, for instance – predominately because it has a strongly innovation-minded group CEO at the helm.

Desire is also influenced by industry context. Notwithstanding the supportive attitude of the RBS group CEO towards innovation, RBS exists in a highly regulated and traditionally conservative industry. An important and constraining DI criterion for RBS is that any project must be compliant with strict regulations. Similarly, RBS faces severe downside risks – if a project with its brand attached fails, it risks eroding customer confidence in RBS. In banking, that confidence is absolutely crucial.

Unilever is a multi-product portfolio company with a large number of brands. Its willingness to gamble on a new brand has little consequence and downside risk for existing brands – if a new brand fails it does not reflect on other new brands and overwhelmingly customers probably will not even be aware that the new brand was developed by Unilever.

Although not a clear-cut observation, there is a strong sense that DI is always at risk of losing out to conventional investment choices because firms can more confidently predict outcomes to continuous innovation (based on internal and industry precedents as well as key decision-makers' intuition or gut feel) whereas DI, whatever its promise, is inherently more uncertain and therefore more risky.

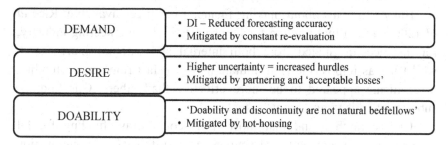

DEMAND	• DI – Reduced forecasting accuracy • Mitigated by constant re-evaluation
DESIRE	• Higher uncertainty = increased hurdles • Mitigated by partnering and 'acceptable losses'
DOABILITY	• 'Doability and discontinuity are not natural bedfellows' • Mitigated by hot-housing

Fig. 2. Summary of concerns around DI and observed mitigation.

Summary of DI selection criteria

There is neither academic nor practitioner consensus on what criteria to apply when assessing and selecting DI opportunities. The nature of DI is uncertain and risky, and quantification of unpredictable outcomes, particularly financial, is problematic. Furthermore, firms necessarily have no precedent to draw on and relevant market data is most times unavailable. Some of the firms interviewed address this either by increasing the required hurdle rate of projects or deliberately easing conventional selection criteria to permit a DI opportunity to germinate and become clearer.

Although there is a generic framework for selection criteria – is there a market? (demand); can we do it? (doability); and do we want to do it? (desirability) – there appears to be no best practice on how to answer these questions accurately. What is apparent is that if there is no allowance given for the uncertainty of DI, these opportunities are overtaken by more certain and predictable conventional innovation opportunities.

DI Funding

Funding is the ultimate litmus test of a firm's commitment to DI. Even before implementation, investment is often needed to fully assess or test an idea. Mechanisms and criteria can be window-dressing – a pretence of commitment to DI – but funding is the clearest indication of intent.

But it isn't just about making financial resources available. Rice *et al.* (2002) found that funding for DI projects in the engineering industry, for instance, originated from both internal and external sources and, whilst it was impossible to formulate hard and fast rules, some funding mechanisms appeared to be more effective than others. Our findings substantiate this view to some extent.

Our research found that most firms could draw funding for DI assessment from conventional sources such as the R&D or innovation budget. This stems from the fact that in these cases R&D departments or heads are explicitly or implicitly encouraged to direct a proportion of their resources towards DI. However, as many as two thirds of the interviewees recognised shortcomings in these conventional funding arrangements and thus also drew on a variety of special internal funding options such as a CEO's discretionary fund. Figure 3 outlines the range of DI funding options employed in the UK.

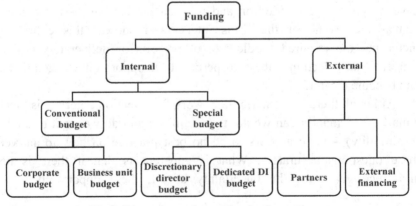

Fig. 3. Discontinuous innovation funding options.

The popularity of each source of funding for DI can be seen in Table 3. Most companies stated that they could access two or three sources of funding for DI, allowing greater flexibility but potentially increasing protective behaviour if budget holders realised that funds could be secured elsewhere.

Table 3. Popularity of DI funding options and potential for resistance.

Company	Cor-porate budget	SBU budget	Discretionary director budget	Dedicated DI budget	Partner-ing	External funding
Kodak	√			√	√	
Unilever				√	√	
BBC	√	√				√
GSK	√		√			
RBS	√		√			
Reckitt Benckiser	√	√	√			
O2	√	√				
DOH	√					√
Ordnance Survey	√	√	√			
Popularity	**8**	**4**	**4**	**2**	**2**	**2**
CIS resistance	High	High	Low	Low	Variable	Variable

Conventional sources of funds

Conventional sources of funds include allocated budgets with prescribed spending guidelines, such as an R&D or innovation budget. Although in some cases the guidelines stipulate the amount of DI spend, it appears commonplace that DI loses out to other spend requests when budgets are under any kind of pressure.

Kodak stated that their approach to funding the corporate budget is to spend 5–6% of revenues on general research and 1% on corporate research: 'We don't have to fund project by project so we have our own portfolio management process to make sure some of it is disruptive'. This sounds positive and progressive but in tough times, Alan explained, priorities shift to achieve short-term business objectives; thereby putting DI on the back-burner.

Other firms found that strategic business unit budgets are equally unpredictable and difficult to source funds from.

Ordnance Survey revealed that a sum of £2 million per year is spent on research and silos carry incremental budgets for continuous innovation. On silo budgets, David observed that 'you can have meetings with budget holders but if it doesn't fit with the current business you are relying on their charity'. Strategic business unit budgets would typically be used when DI is investigated at a local (geographic or silo) level. Reckitt Benckiser, for example, acknowledged that even if the CEO was championing a project, it would still require buy-in on a country level in order to go ahead.

Some elements of conventional funding can carry concerns for proponents of DI:

- By its nature, DI is an unknown quantity. The lack of specialist knowledge in DI arenas increases uncertainty with regard to funding expectations. This leads to DI being at a disadvantage compared to continuous innovation when it comes to arguing for funding approval.
- DI would have to compete with continuous innovation for funding from conventional sources. This may cause issues, especially in the case of reactive DI, or the event of 'the rug being pulled'.
- Stulz (1999) surmised that 'the rug being pulled' would make the raising of funds for projects more expensive and more difficult. It is highly likely that attempting to raise funds specifically for DI under these circumstances would be even more so.
- If a project is likely to meet resistance in the form of restricted or withheld funds, it is most likely to do so when seeking funds from conventional sources. DI is less well understood, may threaten the status quo or may absorb scarce resources, and is therefore likely to meet resistance through the withholding of funds.

Conventional funding was found to be the most popular source of funds for DI primarily because the access mechanisms tend to be well understood. It also tended to be accepted that a proportion of the efforts of the research/innovation departments would be focused on blue-sky or off-the-wall thinking; therefore, very early 'search' stage funding may be utilised from such conventional sources. However, it was also recognised that conventional sources were likely to be the least effective approach due to them being influenced by the corporate immune system (CIS).

Special sources of funds

Two-thirds of organisations acknowledged issues related to the accessibility of conventional sources of funding and thus allowed DI to tap into special dedicated or discretionary budgets.

Unilever revealed that Unilever's Venture Works is funded through a lump sum of £250 million over a five-year period. Open access is granted and the only monetary control enforced from on high is that no more than £50 million be lost in a given year.

Reckitt Benckiser stated that their most discontinuous project recently was implementing an environmental sustainability programme across their entire supply chain and product range. For this, the CEO, on advice from the Environment Director, used his discretionary budget to fund the programme.

Using a special funding approach enabled those working on the project access to a more reliable funding stream. The project would not have had to fight so hard for funds and could have been kept under the radar if deemed necessary. On the other hand, if a top-level champion was required to support the DI, the champion may have been required to put their money where their mouth is.

Two concerns relating to special DI funding sources should also be considered:

• *Guaranteed funding might carry risks* – although not evident in our findings, Christensen *et al.* (2002) proposed that ring-fencing too much cash would allow those running a venture to follow a flawed strategy for too long.

- *Decisions may lack rigor* – bypassing the CIS removes the opportunity for a more diverse set of perspectives to contribute to decision-making, potentially leading to poor selection.

Both Kodak and Unilever recognised the risks surrounding dedicated DI funding and put in place methods of mitigating them. Unilever impose a maximum loss per year on its Venture Works and both companies seek to *partner*.

Partnering and other external funds

As identified by Unilever and Kodak, partnering can bring benefits. It brings new thinking, it shares the financial risk, it drives effort and focus, ensuring initiatives don't fade away or get shelved.

And although all companies are likely to have a rightful access to Government funding for early stage innovations, only the BBC and Ordnance Survey acknowledged this potential source of early stage funding for innovations and specifically for DI projects (see also Chapter 11). Rice *et al.* (2002) recognised that such external funding is not likely to be available past early-stage research.

It is important to note that partnering also lends itself to a reduction in control, ownership and secrecy:

- *Loss of control* – sharing financial risk and allowing external parties to have a say clearly reduces the control an organisation may want over a DI project.
- *Loss of ownership* – partnering requires legal agreements over subsequent IP.
- *Loss of secrecy* – building relationships with external parties relies on trust. Public knowledge of a firm's DI research may cause concern among stakeholders.

The organisation should always weigh up its options and consider the benefits as well as the risks.

Unilever indicated that they militate against the issue of secrecy by selectively partnering only on projects that benefit all parties. For example, Unilever are partnering with some of its competitors on the development of a common standard for radio-frequency identification (RFID) technology that will improve supply-chain efficiency for all.

DI funding summary

Conventional sources of funds, such as corporate or business unit budgets, are widely employed and accepted in the UK for DI but carry a higher propensity for uncertainty of sustained funding, tend to be subject to conventional and inappropriate criteria, and have an increased chance of meeting resistance from the CIS (see later section).

Special sources of funds, such as discretionary director budgets or dedicated DI budgets, are recognised as being more reliable and reduce the scale and scope of potential resistance but do not mitigate financial, operational or strategic risk.

Seeking funds from external, uninvolved sources such as the government for subsidies or grants is a valuable source of support but tends to only be available for early-stage research.

Partnering or collaboration is an option that tends to work in practice alongside access to dedicated internal funds and is employed mainly for product or process DI. Partnering brings a different perspective, reduces financial and operational risk and can be reliable. However, with the reduction in risk comes dilution of control, secrecy and ownership. This approach is not suited to positioning, or to paradigm or business DI (Bessant *et al.*, 2004).

An important point to note is that, however DI is funded, the company should be patient and flexible with funding – at the outset, DI sometimes does not offer much apparent market potential (Christensen, 1997); but what at first looks unappealing could hold the key to the future.

DI Influencers

With respect to DI two opposing forces of influence sway the selection decision: supporting the project are so-called champions; resisting the project is the CIS.

Champions

By its nature, discontinuous innovation is demanding, covering radical shifts in products, processes, positioning or paradigm (Tidd *et al.*, 2005) and often bearing uncertain or risky benefits and outcomes. Because of this, building support to bring DI through selection to implementation is often necessary.

Our research underscores that internal organisational resistance is prone to slowing or derailing DI and can strike either explicitly or implicitly.

- Explicit resistance is when projects are rejected by clearly identifiable individuals for clearly articulated reasons, permitting proponents of DI to address the resistance head-on.
- Implicit resistance cannot be attributed to any one individual and does not necessarily centre on known or even rational reasons for resistance, such as when the organisational culture pushes back against unsettling, disruptive change.

With any process carrying a high degree of uncertainty and propensity for resistance, individual initiative, commitment, creativity and persistence are key (Rice *et al.*, 1998).

The role of champions

Spanning the search, select and implement phases of innovation, O'Connor and Veryzer (2001) observed three specific and distinct roles that would be required to help design, present, sustain and implement DI opportunities: ruminators, champions and implementers. See also Chapter 11, page 244 for further detail.

In the selection phase of a DI opportunity, the champion is the key; this was a common theme emanating from all interviewees. Any project selection will require an individual or a set of individuals to get the message across and steer the DI through resistance and decision-making to selection and implementation. Champions, either formal or informal, are essential to increase the chance of selection success.

The attributes of champions

Champions are not necessarily heads of innovation or indeed C-suite executives. Rice *et al.* (1998) identify several types of champion: technical champion, project champion, senior management champion, business unit champion and in some cases a single individual champion who takes on multiple championing roles.

From our research, we propose that champions display one or more of the following attributes: *authority, knowledge* and *credibility:*

- *Authority* – the most effective means of ensuring a DI project is selected is to have a person with authority on side. Ideally, this would be the CEO and/or CFO and would be influential in the final go/no go selection.

At RBS, top-level support for innovation is a given – the group CEO is a strong supporter, says the Director of Innovation for UK Corporate Banking: 'The challenge is less at senior level and more about getting the troops engaged. In such a big organisation, to get the message out across the group in a consistent way is quite a challenge.'

- *Knowledge* – most effective at narrowing down the range of opportunities to the most feasible for final selection. Commonly this would be key individuals from the research or innovation teams.
- *Credibility* – after narrowing the range and before the final selection, individuals with a high-profile reputation would target pockets of

resistance to ensure the final selection is made without undue influence from the corporate immune system.

Kodak revealed that the research department tactically recruits key individuals in the group to champion an idea through the organisation prior to final selection:

> I know people who I need to warm up with ideas and get them excited. They are in those jobs because they're good at championing things through, which comes down to personality and track record. When this particular person has a mission and gets behind an idea, people listen.

DI champions summary

However effective the mechanisms, criteria and funding utilised to select a DI, decisions are still made by people and are influenced by people. Any project selection will require an individual or a set of individuals to get the message across as to why a particular DI project should become reality. In some cases, people need educating on the situation, in others resistance is met which needs to be addressed. Whatever the situation, a champion is required.

Effective champions carry authority, knowledge or credibility; or a mixture of the three. Without one or more of these attributes the final selection to take a DI to implementation is a difficult task. Having individuals in the organisation on side with the highest level of each attribute is likely to be most effective for DI selection.

Corporate immune system (CIS)

The academic definition of the CIS is that of a powerful and vocal set of individuals that, when presented with a 'foreign or strange' idea, 'will isolate it, weaken it, or kill it outright ... even if the change is good' (Wolford, 1997). Our research suggests that for many, if not all firms, the CIS is a very real political force that exercises considerable influence in the selection and funding of innovation.

In many situations the CIS is a constructive force that helps to focus scarce R&D resources on projects that build on proven competencies, are a good strategic fit and most important are deliverable. However, with respect to DI, the CIS is usually dysfunctional, serving to resist, delay or undermine a project regardless of its merits (Fig. 4).

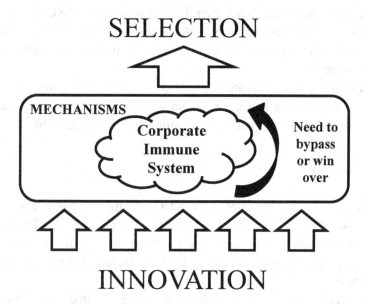

Fig. 4. Representation of the CIS.

The inevitability of such a response from the CIS was acknowledged by several respondents. A representative from the BBC said: 'I'm quite realistic that you can't expect 100% of the organisation to be comfortable with a discontinuity … people don't work like that'.

To overcome this, all the firms interviewed recognised that on occasion the CIS needed to be restrained, bypassed, overridden or 'brought on side'. This is relatively straightforward during the implementation phase of a project where a decision has been made and C-suite buy-in secured, but much more of a problem during the selection process. At this stage, the project has few if any champions, its funding requirements and the returns on investment are unclear and it is competing with a variety of conventional projects, many of which already have strong support from the CIS. In the face of these challenges our study has identified three approaches taken by proponents of DI:

- *Circumvention* – the CIS is bypassed by developing independent selection and funding mechanisms such as Venture Works. Operating semi-autonomously with different strategic targets and staff, we found that they were relatively immune to the CIS.
- *Defence* – the recruitment of high-value champions who are prepared to publicly support the project was a feature common to all respondents.
- *Engagement* – integrating members of the CIS polity into the innovation teams and giving them a forum to express constructive criticism and develop effective solutions diluted opposition.

Circumventing the CIS

As discussed earlier, the selection mechanisms most conducive to DI are those that bypass the usual channels of CIS dissent. Traditional mechanisms such as the stage-gate processes, which aim to filter and prioritise projects, can be abused by the CIS. Developing new forums for assessment can help to counteract this.

A representative from Ordnance Survey stated that prior to implementing the 'Dragons' Den', the reams of red tape meant that a decision he worked through took 13 iterations through various governance boards. It took a great deal of energy to get any idea through, let alone DI. He said: '"Dragons' Den" was so successful we hit our year's quota of adopted ideas in two sessions … the traditional approach could take seven months.'

An equally successful method of bypassing the CIS is to set up a Venture Works, as Unilever has, outside the core operations of the organisation where DI can be hot-housed and worked on away from the glare of the CIS.

It should be noted that having effective CIS-busting mechanisms in place does not mean that decisions in favour of DI will be made. Ordnance Survey's 'Dragons' Den' brought 'too many' DIs to the fore and threatened to kill several 'sacred cows'. At this point, the management team decided to reign in this DI selection mechanism, preferring to take the slow road to change.

If the CIS is avoided in the selection phase, there is a possibility that the CIS may attempt to influence proceedings more fervently in the implementation phase.

Recruiting champions to defend against the CIS

If the CIS is particularly resistant, and selection mechanisms are unable to adequately ameliorate its effects, then it remains up to the champions to counter its influence. All the respondents employed champions to combat the CIS. In order to fulfil their role effectively, they were often executives with high levels of organisational authority, specialist knowledge and/or significant social capital and credibility.

The representative from Kodak recognised that a satellite research team being in Cambridge, UK, when the corporate R&D facility is in Rochester, USA, means that conscious efforts must be made to walk DI opportunities round the offices of influential individuals at Rochester. He has a list of 'the usual suspects' who have great credibility and can carry projects through, cutting through the CIS. He said: 'A new project didn't go through the normal filter because this person brought it in with a lot of credibility.'

He went on to suggest that with particularly sensitive or ground-breaking DI, 'At the end of the day, it needs the CEO coming into the office and seeing something and a light going on in his head.'

It is worth noting that champions of DI that challenge the CIS on an organisational level are not necessarily the same individuals that support individual DI projects.

For instance, at RBS, the CEO is a leading proponent for a more innovation-friendly corporate mindset but doesn't get involved in individual project selection.

Furthermore, champions don't always have to be members of top-level management – at the BBC less senior individuals with knowledge

or credibility – 'Trojan Mice' – are employed to sneak under the radar
and seed support in a less formal and confrontational way.

Engaging with the CIS

Essentially a reworking of the old adage 'If you can't beat them, join
them', it is at its heart an attempt to realign the objectives of the CIS by
integrating leading dissenters into decision-making vehicles tasked with
DI project selection. By forcing key CIS advocates to consider problems
within the larger framework of long-term group corporate strategy, the
influence of the CIS is reduced and realigned.

Ordnance Survey revealed that each silo in the organisation,
although extremely effective in achieving its own objectives, was
dysfunctional. However, the CIS was dysfunctional only because there
was no overarching organisational objective to be working towards. A
representative said: 'We're all ruthlessly efficient in our silos but there
was nothing spanning the whole business; so we've set up a product
strategy team that works across the silos [and is responsible for
examining and facilitating DI projects].'

This realignment can occur across the entire organisation. For
example, RBS stated that their head of innovation is just as focused on
changing the culture of the organisation to make it more innovation
friendly than he is on any one innovation project, thereby attempting to
prevent the CIS from forming.

To focus the group on identifying, selecting and implementing
'breakthrough' innovations, an outsider was recruited. RBS's Group
Head of Innovation is an entrepreneur with a background in banking. He
has employed people from very different backgrounds, to avoid
entrenched ways of thinking. The objective was to find people without
any 'baggage', who can 'see things from an entirely different
perspective'. His job is as much to champion individual opportunities to
key decision-makers as it is to champion an innovation mindset across
the group. A representative said: 'The group Head of Innovation is
putting in place a framework that everyone can buy into so that we all go

in the same direction and following it through, we are more likely to achieve a tangible outcome.'

RBS isn't just trying to overcome risk aversion typical to banking; it is also trying to reverse staff scepticism to the process. The representative said: 'People have been stung before. We've tried to set up things like this before where ideas have come through and they have disappeared into a black hole.'

CIS summary

It is natural for there to be some resistance to radical ideas within any organisation; however, sometimes this resistance is disproportionately influential and acts to impede the adoption of worthwhile projects – at its most virulent it is often characterised as the CIS.

Our research indicates that the CIS is a ubiquitous, pervasive and powerful force in all the companies studied. Although it may have a valuable role in the evaluation of conventional innovation, it has a singularly negative effect upon the selection and assessment of discontinuous innovation projects.

We found that proponents of discontinuous innovation projects use three main strategies to counteract its malignant influence – circumvention, defence and engagement.

- *Circumvention* – the establishment of separate bodies for assessing discontinuous innovation ideas enables the usual forums' dissent to be bypassed. These structures may be internal ('Dragons' Dens') or quasi-external (Venture Works).
- *Defence* – the recruitment of champions with high levels of organisational authority, specialist knowledge or significant credibility was a common and effective tool for countering criticism from the CIS.
- *Engagement* – recruiting leading dissenters into assessment groups and charging them with finding innovative ideas often attenuated the levels of resistance from the CIS.

Conclusions and Recommendations

It is clear from the research that firms adopt very different approaches to assessing and selecting what they consider DI opportunities:

- *Mechanisms* – the firms interviewed utilise a range of structural and procedural mechanisms to select DI opportunities for implementation. A trade-off exists between utilising pre-existing conventional selection mechanisms, which tend to undermine DI ideas early, and utilising a parallel, bespoke selection mechanism (set up for DI), which is costly but is best for germinating a DI idea.
- *Criteria* – firms need to make allowance for the inherent uncertainty of DI; if not, DI often risks unfavourable comparison with more predictable investment opportunities. However, with little academic or other guidance, firms have resorted to make-do solutions. Establishing the appropriate criteria by which to assess DI, especially when conventional financial returns are difficult to quantify, appears to be one of the most obstinate obstacles to selecting DI.
- *Funding* – allocating financial resources to the assessment of DI (for market research, for instance) is the surest indication of commitment but it is how funding is committed and from what source that matters. A dedicated or highly discretionary budget is necessary to avoid resources being allocated to easier, more predictable opportunities ('low-hanging fruit').
- *Influencers* – far more than other innovation, DI faces resistance from the CIS; this can be overcome by structures (by hot-housing ideas in autonomous, external units, for instance) but far more important is the role of champions to motivate an idea and overcome resistance. As important as a champion is, so is the institutional climate for DI. Unless the tone has been set by senior management, DI ideas risk never getting off the drawing board.

A diagram of DI selection components is shown in Fig. 5.

Search ⟶ **Select** ⟶ **Implement**

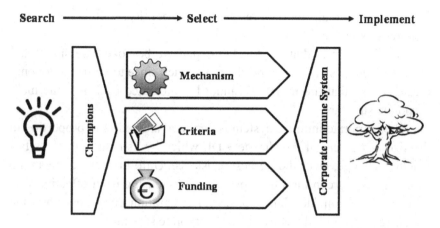

Fig. 5. Diagram of DI selection components.

In overall assessment, it is evident that DI is more difficult, complex, costly and time-consuming – and therefore more risky – than continuous innovation. Whereas the *search* for DI opportunities can be pursued autonomously with relative ease, *selection* runs into rational (i.e. uncertain returns) and irrational (i.e. fear of change) obstacles. Despite official commitment to DI, many interviewees felt that true DI would only be possible if the firm was under threat – under normal circumstances there were too many hurdles to overcome. While some firms clearly explore DI opportunities (or at least radical innovation) more earnestly than others, none of the firms interviewed had a successful blueprint. Clearly, more work is needed to establish best practice.

We found a wide variance in each firm's understanding and working definition of DI. Rather than a consistent definition, we found a shifting characterisation that spans the radical end of incremental innovation through to paradigm-shifting change that fundamentally changes the structure of the industry.

Allowing for this variance (albeit unscientifically), it is possible to draw a number of headline conclusions.

DI, by any definition being more disruptive, needs to be assessed differently from continuous improvement. DI needs allowance to account for its inherent uncertainty. Fully developing this level of flexibility in assessment mechanisms requires significant political will, expertise and resources, which are often lacking.

For those firms that do develop expensive bespoke assessment and selection vehicles, a balance needs to be struck since too much autonomy creates a risk that the initiative cannot be integrated back into the main corporate structure.

The corporate immune system is very real and exists in proportion to the size and extent of the change – DI, which by its nature involves far-reaching change, faces the sternest resistance. Unfortunately, there are no shortcuts to overcoming this resistance. Hot-housing is an effective way of germinating an idea but it poses an integration challenge when the idea is reversed into the conventional corporate structure.

Champions are essential to steer a DI opportunity through selection; without a strong motivator for DI, it will almost inevitably stall in response to explicit or implicit resistance. But such champions are exceptional individuals, possessing the vision to recognise the DI opportunity, the entrepreneurial flair to know how to make it happen and the social capital and influence to win over doubters. However, often it's outsiders who are able to see the opportunity, individuals who are unencumbered by preconceived ideas and legacy thinking but who lack the internal influence to convince key decision-makers. To succeed at DI, firms need to identify and empower champions, recognising that different individuals may champion an idea at different stages of the selection process.

As with anything disruptive, success ultimately depends on the support of the chief executive. It is clear that no design of the mechanisms, criteria, structure and processes will ensure DI success unless the most senior management is already on board, even if just in principle. To ensure passage through the selection process, it is necessary that the CEO has already set the tone by encouraging and promoting the search for DI opportunities, which in turns starts to break down the CIS and the bureaucratic red tape that prevents ideas percolating through to decision-making.

References

Christensen, C. (1997). *The Innovator's Dilemma*. Harvard Business School Press, Cambridge, MA.

Christensen, C., Johnson, M. and Dann, J. (2002). Disrupt and prosper. *Optimize*, November, 41–48.

Courtney, H., Kirkland, J. and Viguerie, P. (1997). Strategy under uncertainty. *Harvard Business Review*, Nov–Dec, 67–79.

Day, G. (2007). Closing the growth gap: Balancing big 'I' and small 'i' innovation. A Knowledge@Wharton research paper. Available at: http://knowledge.wharton.upenn.edu/paper.cfm?paperID=1344. [Accessed 21 March 2011.]

Mcbain, H. (2007) Interview on how BBC selects discontinuous innovation. Interviewed by Elliot Cox and James Eedes [in person] BBC Television Centre, London, 1 May 2007.

O'Connor, G.C. and Veryzer, R. (2001). The nature of market visioning for technology-based radical innovation. *Journal of Product Innovation Management*, 18, 231–246.

Rice, M., Leifer, R. and O'Connor, G.C. (2002). Commercialising discontinuous innovations. *IEEE Transactions on Engineering Management*, 49(4), 330–340.

Rice, M., O'Connor, G.C., Peters, L. and Morone, J. (1998). Managing discontinuous innovation. *Research Technology Management*, 41, May/June, 52–58.

Stulz, R. (1999). What's wrong with modern capital budgeting. Address to Eastern Finance Association. Available at: http://papers.ssrn.com/sol3/papers.cfm?abstract_id=168068. [Accessed 21 March 2011.]

Tidd, J., Bessant, J. and Pavitt, K. (2005). *Managing Innovation: Integrating Technological, Market and Organisational Change, 3rd Edition*. John Wiley and Sons, Chichester, p. 90 and p. 366.

Wolford, D. (1997). Overcoming the corporate immune system. Interview. *Getting Results: Plant Edition*, 42(8), 5.

Chapter 13

Innovation Buy-In at Schneider Electric: The KIBIS Method

Sylvie Blanco, Valérie Sabatier, Corine Genet
Grenoble Ecole de Management, France
Bernard Cartoux
Schneider Electric, France

Introduction

Business survival in the face of rapidly changing environments depends on the dynamic capabilities of an organization, including 'the capacity to manage threats through the combination, recombination and reconfiguring of assets inside and outside of the firm's boundaries' (Augier and Teece, 2009).

As a potentially disruptive phenomenon, innovation may demand that managers are able to orchestrate accessible resources in a new way and invent new business models and organizational forms (Johnson *et al.*, 2008). However, empirical observations highlight numerous failures of big companies such as Xerox, Polaroid, and RCA in making these changes – an issue which has remained true in more recent cases too. Post-event rationalization allows the reasons for failures to be explained, but is not of much help to those who are currently in such a situation. Actually, despite the extensive literature exploring dynamic capabilities, ambidexterity, radical innovation and new business models, little practical guidance is available to help managers invent new business models within the confines of their organizations. In particular, the decision process of the design of a new business model disrupting the firm's existing business models is a major stumbling block. This buy-in challenge can be extremely risky for managers and their companies, and they could feel ill-equipped to make decisions on whether to invest and also how to allocate resources in potential innovations if they are perceived to be 'different' from the mainstream.

Our aim here is to better understand the buy-in of innovation projects in order to offer actionable, procedural knowledge to managers and to provide new theoretical insights to academics. Since the buy-in is subjective and barely observable, we have adopted an active research methodology employing real-case experimentation with practitioners in the process of selecting innovative projects and new-to-their firm business models. In this approach, we do not assume that the strategic selection is the role of top managers, but rather a matter of co-constructing a satisfactory fit between feasible business models for the established organization and appropriate business models for creating and capturing value based on potential innovations. This research process helped us to design the KIBIS method (Kickstart Innovation in Business Strategy), an experimental method of real-life innovation projects from Schneider Electric that was progressively developed with Schneider managers over a period of 18 months. This chapter will present KIBIS and highlight the Drill-It-Right innovation case, addressing the relevance of the issue of buy-in innovation projects within a large company.

KIBIS: Conceptual Framework and Method Overview

Literature review: Selected insights about the buy-in challenge

In-depth confrontation of theoretical insights with practical observations about the strategic selection problem led us to focus our research on the following question: how can the implicit way business managers buy-in to significantly different innovation proposals be explicitly revealed? Two theoretical concepts appear to be relevant as potential sources of understanding and actionable knowledge, as the managers at Schneider Electric needed a representation of the potential tensions and synergies created by the innovation project, and a way to make sense of this innovation.

Business managers use simplified and actionable ways of viewing what the business is and what it could be in order to forecast the impact of the innovation project. Using a general framework of a business model appears to be appropriate because it simplifies the representation of business by considering the customer value proposition, the profit model, the extended value chain and the necessary resources, and it functions as a guide and an invitation to rethink and challenge each component of the business model.

In the information processing view of organizations, the buy-in challenge can be qualified as uncertain, ambiguous, multifaceted and subject to cognitive biases and to emotional and political dimensions. Managers enter a process of *sensemaking* (Weick, 1995) and engage in formulating a set of heterogeneous decisions and actions such as resource allocation for experimentation and learning within new organizational structures, thus allowing the funding of failures! Improving this process should start with raising practitioners' awareness of the problems they face with their existing practices.

Business model as an integrative framework for the buy-in process

In considering business models, we adopt the definition of Smith *et al.* (2010):

> By business model, we mean the design by which an organization converts a given set of strategic choices – about markets, customers, value propositions – into value, and uses a particular organizational architecture – of people, competencies, processes, culture and measurement systems – in order to create and capture this value.

It leads us to define four blocks (see Fig. 1) that need to be considered by a management team to strategically select an innovation project: the value proposal, the extended value chain, the resources and structure required, and the profit model.

Discontinuous Innovation

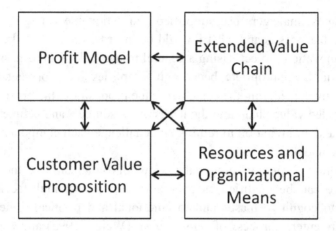

Fig. 1. A simplified representation of the business model.

The customer value proposition. This highlights the way the company delivers value to customers: 'A business model reflects management's hypothesis about what customers want, how they want it, and how an enterprise can best meet those needs, and get paid for doing so' (Teece, 2010). This block is comprised of three parts: the offer, the market segment and the comparative advantages of the new offer.

The extended value chain. Because a business model transcends the boundary of the firm (Amit and Zott, 2001), part of the business model can be carried out by another organization (Lecocq *et al.,* 2006). To deliver the value proposition, a network of partners and suppliers may be involved (Osterwalder *et al.,* 2005). The position of the firm within the value network linking suppliers and customers, potential partners and competitors is key information (Chesbrough, 2010). The management team must list the participants involved in the production and the supply chain, those involved in the commercialization and those participating in the creation of the innovation, and then it must describe its own key processes, i.e. commercialization, the supply chain, manufacturing and innovation.

The resources and the organization. To deliver the value proposition to customers, the firm mobilizes a network of partners and suppliers and internal resources that are embedded into a particular organizational architecture of people, competencies, processes, culture and measurement systems. For the management team, delivering the value proposition to customers requires identifying key organizational items: human resources, immaterial resources, material resources and an adapted structure of the organization.

The profit model. The business model is a framework for conceptualizing a viable profit-generating business logic (Brink and Holmén, 2009). The balance between creating value for customers and capturing part of this value is the profit model. It requires detailing the revenue mechanisms by which the firm will be paid for the offering and estimating the cost structure so that profit sources can be identified.

The sensemaking process

As a cognitive process, the selection can be described in three major sequences: sensing, categorizing and interpreting. We apply it to the buy-in of discontinuous innovation so that we can produce a preliminary hypothetical representation of the way managers practice the strategic selection:

- *Stage 1: Sensing* – perceiving a stimulation indicating that there might be a problem with an innovation proposal such as no added value to the business (lack of synergies) or tensions (cognitive dissonance with established beliefs and practices). Examples and types of synergies, as well as tensions, such as reinforcing, renewing, increasing, extending, performance, growth, revenues, risks, client relationships, distribution channels and technologies, are listed to inspire managers.
- *Stage 2: Categorizing* – using known stereotypes to better qualify and understand the problem which has been identified. We suggest creating categories in a compatibility matrix based on the level of perceived tensions and synergies between the established business model and the innovation proposal. A four-square matrix separating the level of synergies and tensions is the starting point since four major situations are suggested by the literature.

- *Stage 3: Interpreting* – determining the problem and possible solutions so that decisions can be made and actions formulated with the required resources identified.

The KIBIS method will use the representation of a business model and the three consecutive steps of sensemaking to help the group forecast the impact of the innovation project and make decisions concerning the development, or cessation, of the project.

Overview of the KIBIS approach

A KIBIS session joins two groups of shareholders: business managers from the innovation committee in charge of selecting projects and innovation teams presenting potentially discontinuous innovations, since the buy-in problem involves the interface between these two groups. A facilitator of the session helps all the participants share their views and proceed through the different steps of the approach.

At the beginning of the session, the facilitator reminds the participants of the innovation proposal under selection and of the KIBIS approach to be used. He presents the business model (see Fig. 2) and its components, and he may review, if necessary, the existing business model of the firm.

First, in the sensing stage, each participant identifies and writes on small pieces of paper both the tensions and the synergies that they perceive exist between the innovation project and the business model. These papers are positioned on a large and common business model map. When each participant is ready, synergies and tensions are shared and discussed so that each participant enriches their understanding of the problems.

PROFIT MODEL	EXTENDED VALUE CHAIN
Revenues:	Production and supply chain:
Costs:	Commercialization:
Profitability:	Innovation:
CUSTOMER VALUE PROPOSITION	**RESOURCES AND ORGANIZATIONAL MEANS**
Offer:	Human resources:
Market segments:	Immaterial and material resources:
Comparative advantage:	Structural resources:

Fig. 2. The business model map.

The next step, categorization, aims at qualifying the problem. The discussion session between participants allows each person to individually position the innovation proposal on the compatibility matrix presented in Fig. 3.

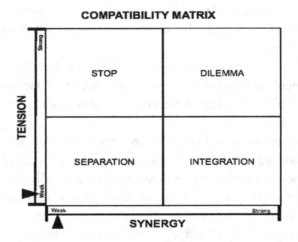

Fig. 3. The compatibility matrix.

This matrix allows them to categorize the type and intensity of disruption they perceive accompanies the innovation project. The positioning of these perceptions on the matrix will converge or diverge among the participants. This affords the opportunity for the participants to discuss the meaning of each case of the matrix in order to cross-validate the way they position the innovation. Their discussion is supported by theoretical insights brought by the coordinator of the activity. For example, in a discussion of the 'Dilemma' situation which is often cited for potentially discontinuous innovations, participants are reminded of strong tensions and strong synergies.

In the case of both strong tensions (such as market cannibalization) and strong synergies (such as a good increase in the commercial margin on the basis of existing clients), the management team is presented with several options and experimentation is highly recommended.

- First, the innovation can be adopted and developed within the organization. The company must have dynamic capabilities (Teece *et al.*, 1997; Eisenhardt and Martin, 2000) to unlearn routines and build new competencies because tensions may destroy existing competencies and resources. Drawing the roadmap should help them to define a learning plan and identify who in the organization will be in charge of each step. This is crucial, requiring autonomy but also strategic support.
- The second option is to externalize partly the innovation experimentation in order to maintain control of the choices and results and to be able to integrate the innovation if tensions are sufficiently reduced.
- The third option is to disrupt the disruption (Charitou and Markides, 2003) and develop another innovation that will overtake this one. The process of evaluating tensions and synergies will restart.
- The fourth option is to study the innovation again: if the management team cannot find a consensus because tensions are too strong but synergies are too attractive, complementary studies on markets, technological feasibilities, compatibility, etc., need to be done. However, this option often leads to 'wait and see' decisions.

Then, they enter into the final stage, the interpreting stage, to make decisions about possible routes and to define a set of actions to undertake within organizational settings. Relying on the literature, mostly O'Reilly and Tushman (2004), we suggest that they consider both the required and readily available levels of organizational autonomy and strategic/ hierarchical supervision. This enables them to identify four potential organizational settings: functional teams, cross-organizational teams, new business units and independent teams.

Thanks to KIBIS, innovation teams can enrich their proposals with organizational and 'roadmap' arguments, while business managers can better understand the proposals and their potential impact on their business. Resulting, decisions made are enlightened and the options put forward will be potentially novel compared to traditional proposals.

KIBIS at Schneider Electric: The Drill-It-Right Case

This case study was made possible by the collaboration of Schneider Electric, a multinational company, and the Grenoble Ecole de Management. Our team of professors worked with B. Cartoux, who was responsible for the innovation platform of the major business unit of Schneider. For 18 months, we co-developed and tested the KIBIS method on different real-life projects with innovation teams and business managers. The approach is now a systematic step in Schneider Electric's innovation pipeline, having been disseminated throughout the entire company.

Schneider Electric: Business and innovation

As a global specialist in energy management with operations in more than 100 countries, Schneider Electric offers integrated solutions across multiple market segments, including leadership positions in utilities and infrastructures, industries and machine manufacturers, non-residential buildings, data centres and networks, and in residential buildings. Focused on making energy safe, reliable, efficient, productive and green, the group's 110,000-plus employees achieved sales of €19.6 billion in

2010 through an active commitment to help individuals and organizations make the most of their energy.

Schneider Electric makes energy safe (with power and control), reliable (with critical power and cooling), efficient (with energy efficiency controls), productive (with industrial building and home automation) and green (with renewable energy and solutions). The power and control division develops products, equipment and systems covering all phases of transmission and electrical distribution, which are classified according to their voltage levels. Low-voltage and ultra-terminal products such as circuit breakers, switches, security lighting systems, prefabricated busbar trunking systems and modular switchgears are designed for the construction market; medium-voltage equipment is used for transforming energy and transmitting it to end users.

Schneider Electric has always been driven by an international, innovative and responsible mindset to shape the transformation of its industry. The energy challenge is a major driver for innovation today. Energy demand is expected to double following demographic, economic and industrial growth across the world and, at the same time, we should reduce greenhouse gas emissions to avoid the dramatic consequences of climate change. Three energy trends drive the company's strategy: energy efficiency as the mainstream; new economies as the world's economic engine; and the smart grid (to balance production and energy consumption). In this context, the business priorities include expanding product leadership, boosting its solutions business and making the grid smarter for customers. To achieve such objectives, Schneider Electric constantly innovates in its core business, in energy management solutions for every market and every customer. Innovation and R&D amounts to 4–5% of sales and contributes by:

- developing solutions that not only optimize efficiency and reduce costs, but also deliver increased simplicity, ease of use and environmental benefit; and
- providing new responses by incorporating high-technology products, services and software (386 patents in 2009; 8,600 R&D engineers in 20 countries).

A real-life innovation project: Drill-It-Right

At Schneider Electric, innovation platforms are dedicated to specific business units. The Drill-It-Right innovation was born from a challenge levelled by a team of the core business' power business unit: how is it possible to drill a hole in the door of a cabinet exactly in front of the rotary handle of the device inside the cabinet?

The main customer concern was the difficulty of accurately determining the position of a drilling hole in an enclosure door.

Causes:

- On the unit switchboard, the position of the drilling hole is not known beforehand
- Enclosures and their doors have rounded edges that make it difficult to transfer dimensions
- The axis of the handle has a lot of play
- The alignment of the handle with the axis must be very accurate.

Impacts and pain points:

- The customer makes a mistake when drilling the hole and must order another door;
- The handle axis of the breaker is not aligned properly and the breaker doesn't trigger properly.

Palliatives:

- Lay down the enclosure on the ground so that the handle axis is vertical and is not subject to gravity during the drilling determination
- Take into account very accurately the shape of the edges when transferring the dimensions onto the door.

Limits of palliatives:

- Impossible to lay down a cabinet when it is too big
- Huge waste of time during the drilling phase.

This operation is complicated and can be subject to frequent errors, forcing Schneider's customers to order new doors. Schneider Electric's project engineers became aware of this problem thanks to the close relationship they maintain with their customers. As a result, they designed and tested an innovative tool: the Drill-It-Right. At first, it was sold with the TeSys U rotary handle as the Laser Square (http://www2.schneider-electric.com/documents/panelbuilders/en/shared /tesys.pdf).

Presentation of the Laser Square

Essential for accurate and careful alignment of the rotary handle and circuit-breaker, the Laser Square is much more than a mere accessory! Simplified handle alignment, guaranteed drilling, accuracy, compact tool, easy to use.

Fig. 4. Laser Square.

Description of the Laser Square

Operating mode of the Laser Square:

• With the unit's door open you point the laser beam at the item inside that's to be connected to the cupboard door when the door is closed. Following this, close the unit's door.
• You draw on the door where the laser line is.
• You repeat the first three steps to have another line.
• The intersection of the two lines gives you the drilling point.

As a result of receiving such a high satisfaction rating, the increase in demand brought into question the power innovation platform. The main question was the market potential for this tool. After the idea entered the exploration stage, an evolved concept emerged: the professional Drill-It-Right.

Description of the professional Drill-It-Right

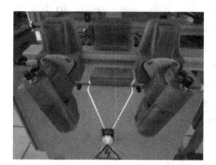

Fig. 5. A comparison of the professional and promotional tools.

Table 1. Comparison of the professional and promotional Laser Square tools. (NOK is used for Not Okay.)

	Laser Square	Professional tool
Front door drilling	OK	OK
Top and lateral drilling	NOK	OK
Squareness accuracy	3–4 mm per every 1.5 m	1 mm for all lengths
Calibration possibility	NOK	OK by using the mirror and the millimetre screw
Rotation of the laser heads	NOK	OK in the two rotating ways to avoid blind spots
Magnetization	Weak and non-disengageable	Strong and disengageable, mechanism to focus the tool with precision.
Precise positioning	NOK without another tool	OK with the integrated tape measure.
Positioned on a loose door	NOK	OK to position without another tool
Kind of laser	Class 2	Class 3
Battery running time	1 hour	50 hours

Three prototypes of the professional tool were tested successively, picture demos posted on the Internet for feedback and its acceptability assessed with industrial partners. Finally, a promising proposition for the customer was identified and qualified through three criteria: time and ease of drilling electric cupboards; economic savings thanks to fewer errors in drilling, which avoids the need to purchase new doors for cupboards (from €2,000 to €5,000 each); and technical efficiency, which enables more holes to be drilled in the same space. Customer feedback in different market segments highlighted that they were ready to buy a professional tool at an average price of €250. However, a few uncertainties and expectations remained to be explored: level of precision; avoidance of the necessity of complementary tools for metering; and extending the tool's potential applications (i.e. to be used on items other than cupboards).

This positive feedback resulted in an economic analysis before the innovation project was presented to the innovation committee for selection. The key figures were:

- Required total investment (technical development and studies): €270,000
- Total cost of production: €72 per unit
- Component production done by an existing partner
- Expected market for the next three years: 3,000 units, €250 per unit
- Expected profit: €1.26 million
- Patent: ongoing application
- Other external markets and applications, kitchen installers: to be determined.

The innovation committee, however, did not select this project and decided not to invest. They determined that the required total investment was too low for the corporate level and that it should be negotiated at the business unit level. The Laser Square could address all the business unit's needs, but the unit refused to invest using its own funds.

Understandably, the team was highly disappointed and wondered about the internal path to value innovation for a product that had positively passed customer tests and which required low investments.

Cartoux could accept the negative answer but could not afford the disappointment of good employees. He decided to try KIBIS – first with the innovation team in order to see whether the project could be presented in a better way.

KIBIS workshops on the Drill-It-Right

The first session was conducted with the innovation team. The researchers served as the facilitators. They explained the framework, the process and supported the steps of the session. The innovation project leader, who was greatly motivated by such a workshop, presented the innovation to his team, but also to other people from the power and industry business units who shared the same innovation platform. Representatives of the marketing and the financial departments were also present. The innovation project leader presented the following:

- The innovation proposal, with a focus on the professional solution and a comparison with the existing promotional tool
- He highlighted that three features had been drastically improved, including precision, type of laser and attractive strength, and eight features had been added based on customer input
- Customer perceived uses and value added
- Economic analysis with foreseen profits at a low level of risk. The range of potential new markets had widened.

At the end of his presentation, a few questions were raised about potential positioning in other markets. Then, participants entered the first stage of the process: sensing problems. They highlighted synergies in green and tensions in red on the business model map (Table 2).

Table 2. Synergies and tensions of the Drill-It-Right.

Dimensions of the business model	Synergies	Tensions
Profit model	Customer acceptance is validated	The total potential value is not significant for the company (too small) The profit model is not credible More guarantees are required Low margins
Extended value chain	Commercialization is easy for us Fits our image of taking care of customers The problem came from the customer .	Not our job Customers buy these tools from other providers
Customer value proposition	The innovation allows another product to be sold Improves the implementation of our complex solutions (complementary) New markets	These tools highlight our products' faults It communicates our weaknesses Competition will be happy! Easy to imitate
Resources and organizational means	No technological problem Industrial tools are known (competencies are available)	No practice of selling IP Who will produce?

Finally, even though all participants did not come to full agreement, Stage 2 was engaged.

The categorization, after collective discussion on tensions and synergies, did not converge. All four squares of the compatibility matrix had been chosen. However, 'Stop' and 'Dilemma' were the most representative choices. Another discussion followed, and the participants finally agreed to converge on the 'Stop' option.

The innovation team was stunned by this decision, but they also understood why the innovation committee rejected the project. They asked the facilitators whether 'Stop' meant that nothing more could be done.

It was at this time that the innovation project leader introduced Stage 3. It began with the presentation of the theoretical options associated with the 'Stop' position. However, since the position of the project was closed to the 'Separation' situation, both the alternatives 'Stop' and 'Dilemma' were detailed. Two options were identified and two sets of actions were generated by the participants. They then identified people to lead these actions and try to determine the team and the organizational settings for each option. That two-hour session ended with a new roadmap of actions and a better understanding by the participants of the mechanisms of decision-making. They also better understood the impact of the innovation project on the business model of the company.

On the basis of these results, the innovation proposal was revised and the innovation team suggested a new KIBIS workshop involving the innovation committee. The sensing stage led to the same results as the previous experiment. The categorization stage had a similar result except for the time involved, which was significantly shorter.

Then, the group entered the interpreting stage. They rapidly chose one of the options. The organization did not appear to be able to integrate such a transversal project; that would require convincing foreign business units and acquiring strong support from the top executive management. Compared to other Schneider Electric projects, the Drill-It-Right was too small a project to be acceptable. At the same time, the participants wondered whether they should think about creating a licensing unit for their patents.

Follow-up and evaluation

Unsurprisingly, the participants were motivated to participate and discuss the innovation project because this was an important issue regarding their jobs and their company. They wished to go on with other projects. One of the participants of the innovation committee workshop stated: 'The KIBIS game gives us a framework to decide collectively instead of relying on intuitive and individual credo.'

An internal communication plan was implemented to propose a method for other innovation platforms. Figure 6 shows the communication on the internal journal of the company.

Inside the innovation engine... Business model analysis

KIBIS, Kickstart Innovation in Business

KIBIS has been elaborated for innovation teams and their executives to evaluate the opportunity of the innovation for SE. Half a day of teamwork brought the following results:

• The evaluation of the acceptance of the innovation in the existing organisation.

• The synergies and the tensions raised by the innovation.

• The corrective actions to help decide whether to continue with or withdraw the project.

The KIBIS approach shows the interactions with the existing business models of the firm. Used by the business managers, KIBIS makes objective the go/no go decision, formalizes the key points to be followed by the management during the downstream process of transforming innovations into business.

Fig. 6. Inside the innovation engine (Cartoux, 2011).

The decision has been taken to improve the method according to Schneider Electric's peculiarities and to disseminate it within the whole company. A specific training module is being conceived. Complementary reflections are surfacing about key strategic questions triggered by the KIBIS workshops. For instance, the workshops raised the attention of the finance department who felt support for their ability to forecast profits and expenditures. Also, improvement of the job codes by the HR department could be an impact. Finally, the innovation team discovered a tool to prove the status of non-core innovation from an internal point of view.

Discussion and Implications

The analysis is structured according to three levels of objectives: usefulness and practicability of the approach, learning of new innovation management practices by practitioners and theoretical enrichment for researchers.

Usefulness and practicability of the KIBIS approach for practitioners

This approach has been perceived to be useful by both the top management and those within the innovation process and platforms. It is currently promoted within the organization, which is about to deploy it more widely and implement it more systematically. Beyond explaining a well-known problem, the approach brings a solution when all stakeholders do not know how to proceed and therefore new practices are not looked for. From the innovators' standpoint, the approach allows them to identify and prepare for the key questions that may arise and then check the innovation at the selection stage. Hence, a clear mutual understanding seems to be possible between the innovators and strategy planners, each of whom perceives themselves as potentially useful in this process.

More precisely, the short introduction-training session has allowed participants to understand their selection difficulties and to improve their knowledge of this process. They have recognized that it has increased their motivation to learn how to work better or differently and also to acquire new innovation management expertise that might increase innovation success. The short training on key concepts is perceived as part of an event and not a training programme so that they feel they can freely interact. As Vandenbosch and Huff (1997) suggested, it appears necessary to train people on the concepts and constructs they will have to implement. The development of preliminary knowledge is a necessary condition for the participants to be motivated and effective in their tasks. However, this stage may differ depending on the participants: shorter for top management who are used to concepts such as a business model, and longer for R&D people who are generally more focused on the technical developments.

Following the KIBIS approach is useful for various reasons: it provides the opportunity to be more effective by bringing in procedural, actionable knowledge to face ambiguous problems. Moreover, participants not only become aware of their own biases, but also of the added value of sharing them with their colleagues. This tends to favour collective intelligence behaviours and processes. People need to share their own representations and knowledge to enhance mutual success and enrichment instead of defending an individual or local, outdated vision. Participants also discover that their common frames, namely business models, are ultimately implemented with different meanings and understandings. All participants of a KIBIS session get a better understanding of the problem and of the process and steps of the buy-in of innovation projects. The different concepts of tensions, synergies, compatibility matrices and organizational settings for implementation are all perceived as useful at different levels. Another major point is that the organizational issues related to the integration of innovation become more explicit than before. Participants notice that the issue of which organizational settings to promote has not been tackled explicitly and in a structured way before. Whilst they discover what 'doing business as usual' means, they also come to understand that, within the same company, not all services and business units proceed in the same way. New sources of collective intelligence appear.

Within this process, both the business model and the matrices appeared to be appropriate and actionable frameworks for the purposes of knowledge integration, thus acting as a driving force for their innovation process. These also act as a way to reinforce a company-wide vision as well as the credibility of the selection process which is quite unappreciated by both innovators and top managers. However, the links between the compatibility matrix and the decision to invest in the innovation project could be reinforced and suggest a new research avenue.

This new method can be applied to diverse situations, by considering the field, the organization or the type of innovation. Surprisingly, we also noticed the usefulness of the approach for gathering information that might seem incremental to most people. Cases like this one show that some projects need new or different business model approaches that have never been anticipated before.

Theoretical learning

This approach is also very useful for researchers wishing to better understand the selection-integration of innovation projects within established organizations from a decision-process standpoint. Selection appears to be an iterative learning process and should necessarily include some experimentation plans to cope with the intrinsic ambiguity and uncertainty of innovation in the early stages of its development. The model and its implementation constitute a good means of research with which to observe a subjective and informal process, the existence of which practitioners are not even aware. As a result, this approach allows confirmation of our hypothesis that the strategic selection and implementation of innovation benefits from a collective intelligence approach.

The approach also questions the more sequential and technical approaches leading to launching innovation projects handled with traditional managerial strategies. Even though the method can be greatly improved, its foundation is robust and repeated implementation of KIBIS may allow us to provide the research community with advanced understanding and solutions. For instance, this selection-integration task can be assimilated to opportunity amplification processes so that all managers can be made aware of it. They should be given methods and tools to activate knowledge integration through field interactions and actions. For instance, the Drill-It-Right case highlights the necessity to conjecture about the appropriate methods to explore a market and the knowledge to be produced in relation with it. One should be able to differentiate between actions which allow an offer to be validated and those which enable the exploration of new fields and applications that could be bought-in at the organization's corporate level.

In regard to knowledge integration, prior knowledge in the form of expertise, privileged relationships with the environment and also organizational position affects the use of this approach. Individuals feel guided and more effective in their information selection thanks to the heuristic method. Nevertheless, as Kiesler and Sproull (1982) suggested, cognitive biases also apply here. For instance, the relevance of information depends on the knowledge individuals have about actors and issues related to the innovation and the business model. We have also observed that some people judge information as irrelevant simply because it does not enter their specific domain of expertise or because of their organizational position, as mentioned by Walsh (1988). Hence, prior knowledge may act as an important obstacle even through collective intelligence processes.

Conclusion

Finally, this research opens pathways upon which to explore the creation of innovative activities through a new frame of reference, thus allowing us to further understand this complex process. This is undoubtedly an important stage in the production of actionable knowledge for innovation managers under the shape of sensemaking activities. For instance, a methodological guide about how to select and integrate innovation, based on individual and collective learning, on knowledge integration through actions and reflection could be a valuable research output. In that sense, we are currently focusing part of our research on heuristic methods for innovators and R&D personnel to explore the potentialities of their ideas. This exploratory research opens the path for a series of other research questions to be addressed in the field of the strategic management of R&D and innovation. Beyond this exploratory phase of research, we are also wondering about how to develop and disseminate such a methodological approach toward decision-makers so that SWOT matrices can be used in relevant situations and replaced by more appropriate models and templates built for innovation.

The KIBIS method, following a process of sensemaking, with its phases of sensing, categorizing and interpreting, and use as a framework the business model concept, helps to inform decisions in the development of innovation projects. Designed with, and for, managers of innovation, it links theoretical concepts for research in innovation and technology management with practical issues found in the existing business model, while investing in the future businesses of companies.

References

Amit, R. and Zott, C. (2001). Value creation in e-business. *Strategic Management Journal*, 22(6–7), 493–520.

Augier, M. and Teece, D. (2009). Dynamic capabilities and the role of managers in business strategy and economic performance. *Organization Science*, 20(2), 410–421.

Brink, J. and Holmén, M. (2009). Capabilities and radical changes of the business models of new bioscience firms. *Creativity and Innovation Management*, 18(2), 109–120.

Cartoux, B. (2011). Power Innovation. *Schneider Electric internal journal, Know+*.

Charitou, C.D. and Markides, C.C. (2003). Responses to disruptive strategic innovation. *MIT Sloan Management Review*, 44, 55–63.

Chesbrough, H. (2010). Business model innovation: Opportunities and barriers. *Long Range Planning*, 43(2–3), 354–363.

Eisenhardt, K.M. and Martin, J.A. (2000). Dynamic capabilities: What are they? *Strategic Management Journal*, 21(10–11), 1105–1121.

Johnson, M.W., Christensen, C.M. and Kagermann, H. (2008). Reinventing your business model. *Harvard Business Review*, 86, 50–59.

Kiesler, S. and Sproull, L. (1982). Managerial response to changing environments perception on problem-sensing from social cognition. *Administrative Science Quarterly*, 27, 548–570.

Lecocq, X., Demil, B. Warnier, V. (2006). Le business model au coeur de la croissance de l'entreprise. *L'Expansion Management Review*, 123(Hiver), 96–109.

O'Reilly, A. and Tushman, M.L. (2004). The Ambidextrous Organization. *Harvard Business Review*, 82(4), 74–81

Osterwalder, A., Pigneur, Y. and Tucci, C.L. (2005). Clarifying business models: Origins, present, and future of the concept. *Communications of the Association for Information Systems*, 16(1), 1–25.

Smith, W.K., Binns, A. and Tushman, M.L. (2010). Complex business models: Managing strategic paradoxes simultaneously. *Long Range Planning*, 43(2–3), 448–461.

Teece, D. (2010). Business models, business strategy, and innovation. *Long Range Planning*, 43(2–3), 172–194.

Teece, D.J., Pisano, G. and Shuen, A. (1997). Dynamic capabilities and strategic management. *Strategic Management Journal*, 18(7), 509–533.

Vandenbosch, B., Huff, S.L. (1997). Searching and scanning: How executives obtain information from executives information systems. *Management Information Systems Quarterly*, 21(1), 81–107.

Walsh, J.P. (1988). Selectivity and selective perception: An investigation of managers' belief structures and information processing. *Academy of Management Journal*, 31, 873–896.

Weick, K.E. (1995). *Sensemaking in Organizations*. Sage Publications, Thousand Oaks, CA.

Part III

Chapter 14

Implementing Discontinuous Innovation

John Bessant
University of Exeter Business School, UK

To state the obvious, radical innovation isn't easy. It involves taking a leap into the unknown – and is particularly difficult for established organizations who have a track record of success which they don't want to put at risk. So how does an organization jump the track? How can it switch off its immune system and open itself up to new – and potentially dangerous – inputs? How can it reframe, let go of its old ways of looking at the world and take on something which is very new – but by definition untried and risky?

These are not academic challenges but the very stuff of innovation management – the essence of what it means to lead strategically. Put very simply, innovation is a survival imperative. If organizations don't change what they offer the world – products and services – and the ways in which they create and deliver those offerings (processes), then they risk being left behind and at the limit disappearing. History shows us an almost Darwinian pattern of the rise of new entrepreneurial and agile organizations which mature, become comfortable, then fat and gradually lose their edge. Middle age gives way to a kind of sclerosis where change is reduced to smaller and smaller increments until one day the organization is upstaged by external events and unable to move fast enough to cope. It is the new kids on the block who exploit the new technology, pick up on the new market trends and work out new and more appropriate business models.

Organizations do have the capacity to reinvent themselves. Not many survive beyond a fairly short life span but a handful of organizations do last beyond decades, joining the centenarians and even – in a very few cases – lasting over several centuries. But close analysis shows just how much these organizations have had to change in order to reinvigorate

315

themselves. For example, Swedish firm Stora, which merged with Enso-Gutzeit Oy in 1998 to form Finnish company Stora-Enso, was founded in the 13th century and is still a successful business today – but it has survived not by remaining in the original business of copper mining but by changing. German tourism giant TUI is coming up for its 100th anniversary – but when it was founded in 1917 it was the Prussian state lead mining and smelting company. Mining and melting rocks is a long way from the tourism, travel and services business of today. And Nokia began life as a timber and paper company, not the global mobile telecoms player it has become, nor the mobile media and services business it is transforming itself into.

Importantly, studies of longevity in organizations suggest that it isn't simply a matter of 'out with the old and in with the new'. What long-term survivors do is manage crises in ways which incorporate past strengths rather than replacing them. There is, of course, a need to take on new knowledge but there is also a process of letting go of what no longer matters. And most important there is a synthesis, a blending of old and new, rather than a wholesale switch from one field to another. It's about learning new tricks but it also reflects a capability to manage the learning process.

In Part III of the book we look at a number of case examples from organizations within the Discontinuous Innovation Lab which focus on the implementation challenge. The first case (by Berg Pekka, Pihlajamaa Jussi, Poskela Jarno, Vanharanta Outi and Patana Anne-Sisko from the Finnish Lab) discusses how an enterprise can improve its preconditions for developing discontinuous, business-renewing innovations. In particular they focus on strategic flexibility, a culture that supports innovations, and how to measure discontinuous innovation. The second contribution (by Frank Gertsen and René Nielsen) deals with the Danish firm Coloplast; the twist in this case is that it required a new and somewhat complicated renegotiation of ownership between Coloplast and Aalborg University. The next example is written by Dorothea Seebode and Gerard Harkin from the perspective of the project team charged with implementing radical change within the giant Philips corporation. Here, the core theme is the challenge to appropriately communicate with senior management and to maintain their interest and support and engage with them as partners rather than simply sponsors. German consultant UnternehmerTUM helps academics to start their company and in the next case Manuel Götzendörfer describes how their business design approach is put into practice at a retail shop.

We conclude with two further short case examples. The first one by Peter Meier and Stefan Uhrlandt is about how the implementation of discontinuous innovation has made a change in Ethicon's organization necessary. In the second, Monica Streck and Marcus Roßbach show how InfoGate, a virtual information desk, has disrupted the services at Munich Airport.

Chapter 15

Strategic Flexibility, Culture and Measurement as Organisational Enablers

Berg Pekka, Pihlajamaa Jussi, Poskela Jarno, Vanharanta Outi and Patana Anne-Sisko

Aalto University School of Science, Finland

Introduction

This chapter is based on the results of the Innovation Lab of the Innovation Management Institute (IMI) of Aalto University School of Science and the SC Research Unit of Lappeenranta University of Technology. This project was funded by Tekes, the Finnish Funding Agency for Technology and Innovation. It was implemented during 2008–2009 and involved 17 Finnish enterprises from several industrial and service branches. The objective of the Innovation Lab project was to create new understanding and concrete operational models and tools for the effective and successful development of discontinuous innovations in companies. However, instead of processes and methods, organisational enablers and management practices emerged strongly from the interviews. Obviously, various tools and models cannot be effectively utilised in business development without strategic intent and supportive culture. In this chapter, we will review the project results to discuss how an enterprise can improve its preconditions for developing discontinuous, business-renewing innovations. We will pinpoint some factors pertaining to strategic flexibility and a culture that supports innovations as the companies expressed their need to develop these sectors. We will also deal with measurement as a method to support the decision-making process in the context of radical innovations. The business examples described in the chapter are mainly based on the business interviews conducted during the Innovation Lab project.

Strategic Flexibility

It is generally accepted that firms must establish strategic commitment to innovation to cope with a dynamic and changing environment (Cottam *et al.*, 2001). The front end of innovation in particular, where innovation strategies are developed, contributes to organisational learning and strategic renewal in the firm (Koen *et al.*, 2002; Reid and de Brentani, 2004). The way in which strategies for innovations are formulated and implemented can also make a difference in terms of financial success. Successful companies are reported to invest six times more time on creating, cultivating and implementing innovation strategies compared with the reference group of low-performing companies (Ebert *et al.*, 2008). However, the strategies that companies create may cause rigidities that inhibit strategic renewal, despite the continuous need for innovation. The strategy must be renewed continuously and the renewal must be justifiable by changes in the market, which can often be rather irrational. Strategic planning typically includes the following phases: setting of goals and objectives, charting of current situation, charting of alternative courses of action, choice of approach (i.e. strategy), implementation of strategy and monitoring and assessment of the operation.

While organisations have developed efficient practices to develop more incremental innovations, it has been noticed that these same structures and processes inhibit development of discontinuous innovations (Lynn *et al.*, 1996; Cooper, 2003; Bessant *et al.*, 2005; Phillips *et al.*, 2006). The shift to consciously renewing innovations requires clear strategic intent, visualisation and deployment of objectives, abolition of old beliefs, open interaction and a working atmosphere based on values, and the development of new operational models to support them. All this requires flexibility and a new kind of thinking in the strategy work, the development of management and supervision, as well as new procedures to complement the approach geared towards promoting the continuity and effectiveness of operations. It is important to create operational models that, on the one hand, support and enable the processing of new radical ideas and, on the other hand, maintain the development work to support the basic business operations. It is also important that no rivalry arises between the two strategic focuses and that they complement each other instead.

What, then, inhibits strategic renewal? The previous literature has already explored various innovation traps and flaws of strategic decision-making, and they can be divided into three different temporal zones: (1) traps from historical burden, (2) traps from present decisions and (3) traps from future uncertainties. These traps should be identified and brought up in discussion during the strategy process (Poskela and Vänskä, 2009; Poskela and Martinsuo, 2010).

Traps from historical burden:

- *Portfolio trap* – since organisations mainly focus on innovations geared towards continuous improvement, resources for risk-prone and business-renewing innovations may easily be under-allocated (Cooper, 2003; Hamel and Välikangas, 2003).
- *Cognitive trap* – people tend to base their decisions on past experiences and thus inherently resist anything new, if it contradicts the established approach (Hamel and Välikangas, 2003; Roxburgh, 2003).

Traps from present decisions:

- *Structure trap* – in practice, processing both continuous and discontinuous innovations may cause problems (Bessant *et al.*, 2005; Kanter, 2006).
- *Competence trap* – innovations aiming at the renewal of business require the organisation to have diverse skills and competences. Many promising ideas may fail due to the lack of expertise. Discontinuous innovations would need more than just technological competences (Kanter, 2006).

Traps from future uncertainties:

- *Performance trap* – when profit margins and growth figures are well ahead of those of competitors, the mainstream business seems safe and takes all the attention. It always seems difficult to optimise the timing for discontinuous innovation (Hamel and Välikangas, 2003; Roxburgh, 2003; Välikangas and Gibbert, 2005).

- *Business model trap* – unwillingness to consider new business models may hamper the exploitation of new ideas, as the existing business model may not be the right way to launch them in the market (Hamel and Välikangas, 2003; Välikangas and Gibbert, 2005).
- *Customer trap* – focusing on the mainstream customers may lead to ignorance regarding the future mainstream as it can easily cause blindness to emerging needs and new entrants (Christensen, 1997; Hamel and Välikangas, 2003).
- *Commitment trap* – investment decisions are often problematic. The high risk and insecurity involved in radical innovations may initially prevent people from committing to decision-making. On the other hand, a very appealing innovation may be accepted too lightly (Roxburgh, 2003; Välikangas and Gibbert, 2005; Kanter, 2006).

Good practices for developing a more flexible strategy

As already stated, creative and flexible thinking is a central starting point for the management of business-renewing innovation. The strategy process itself seems to contain some features of discontinuous innovation, because it involves the need to change the present routines of strategy work. Following is a description of things and operational models identified during the Innovation Lab project, which will help break the conventional boundaries, bring new perspectives to decision-making and thus develop strategic flexibility (Poskela and Vänskä, 2009).

Ways to avoid historical burden:

- *Proactivity* – for the development of strategic flexibility, it is important to be proactive and get as many new ideas for the discussion as possible. A good means to this end is coaching people working at the customer and market interfaces to be more sensitive in recognising new possibilities.

- *Utilisation of new customer- and user-oriented approaches* – bringing new ideas and thoughts to the strategy discussion will not be enough if the team working on the strategy is not also willing or ready to evaluate the business environment from new perspectives. This does not mean abandoning the so-called normal strategy process altogether. New customer- and user-oriented approaches and, for instance, approaches based on the Blue Ocean Strategy allow collected information to be analysed in a new way and new complementary viewpoints to be found (Kim and Mauborgne, 2005). People's understanding about the customers and users can be increased, for instance, by systematic collection and analysis of customer information, and involving the customer in a new way in the company's innovation process.
- *Renewal through making and sticking with radical decisions* – companies often invest too much on incremental initiatives and underfund breakthrough projects (Hamel and Välikangas, 2003), which leads to the portfolio trap. The decision of how much to invest in discontinuous innovations is a strategic decision. One mentioned approach, which is also known in the literature, is the use of strategic buckets and separate decision criteria for incremental and discontinuous innovations (Cooper, 2003).

Ways to alter the present decisions:

- *Renewal through mixing people* – the traps from present situations were overcome in the studied companies by, e.g., involving people known to have different views in the strategy process, use of extended management teams and involving people from different levels of the organisation.
- *Renewal through creativity* – it is often characteristic of different design teams that the decision-making is rather straightforward, and alternative ideas are not produced and analysed adequately. One means to avoid this problem is to systematise the processing of issues in a new way. Routines can be broken by the use of various creativity tools that can be used for the systematic production of new alternative solutions and to support decision-making. At their best,

creativity tools can be used to change old working procedures, break conventional models of thought and create fresh approaches to the development of business operations. If the company already uses creativity tools that support the innovation process, they can also be applied to the strategy process. Experiences from the use of external consultants have also been good, in particular if no staff members were familiar with the use of the tools or leadership of team processes.

Ways to harness future uncertainties:

- *Systematic production of new ideas for the strategy process* – new ideas can be created, for example, by utilising forums outside the management team and internal interest groups. Besides parties inside the company, these can include partners, customers, investors, and various experts and consultants.
- *Production of alternative strategies* – a more radical approach is the production of alternative strategies. This involves concrete comparisons of different views and, if successful, produces new solutions. Alternative strategies can be produced, for instance, by selecting people from inside the company who desire to get publicity for their views. Strategies may also be produced by consciously utilising new scenarios.
- *Idea competitions and anticipation procedures* – companies have also successfully implemented competitions for future ideas and launched various anticipation procedures to recognise weak signals and trends and to draw up alternative scenarios.

The following themes were brought up during the Innovation Lab project in the discussion with companies concerning the key success factors and development areas related to strategic reform and flexibility.

Success factors:

- Setting a new direction for strategy and changing the way of thinking with the help of external parties where necessary

- A comprehensive overall view of the business operation and environment
- Using scenarios as part of the strategy process
- Involving the staff in the design of strategy
- Strategic planning to be guided by strong faith and vision of objectives
- Choosing the right growth segments (products, customers, geography)
- Communicating intent clearly to the entire organisation
- Focusing on the implementation and securing of strategically selected things
- Structural changes in the organisation
- Identifying and developing required competences.

Special areas to be developed:

- Understanding when the perspective has broadened sufficiently
- Maintaining a focus on discontinuous innovations irrespective of economic fluctuations
- Ability to react and readiness for change
- Increased emphasis on market, customer and user orientation.
- Finding the top performers required for reform
- Ensuring the sufficiency of resources
- Unlearning conventional ways of thinking and acting.

To pursue business renewal, strategy processes must include practices that promote both seeing and enacting discontinuous innovations at the same time. The findings propose that the traditional strategy processes and structures can be altered to promote repeated discontinuous innovations. Higher-level management activity to allocate resources and to define broad frames and targets for development work has been noticed to be critical in terms of strategic renewal in the front end of innovation.

Example: Strategy renewal – converting a product-driven strategy into a market-driven strategy

Company A was the market leader in its existing product range. Business was very profitable but seeking strategically significant growth was not economically possible in the present market. The company had also established process conventions in every division that supported the present operation adequately. Business-renewing innovations had been sought systematically to promote growth, but the main reasons for their adoption in the organisation proved to be, on the one hand, a strong division-specific profit-making culture that supported the conventional operations, and, on the other hand, the lack of operational models and business logics transcending the borders of divisions.

The company launched a strategy reform that was based on market surveys conducted by external experts and internally resourced development work. As a result of the development work, the previous product-driven strategy was replaced by a market-driven one. The company identified and defined for itself the market segments in which it wanted to operate and grow. The new strategy re-segmented the market and made it possible to gain a deeper understanding about the customers and their business operations. Earlier the company had developed technologies and products for which it sought customers. The new mode of operation is based on trying to satisfy the customers' needs by providing solutions based on the company's own expertise and strengths. The new operational model also means a more limited number of application areas and a stronger focus on them. In terms of discontinuous ideas, the new strategy broadened the innovation potential by introducing a stronger focus and supporting new solutions. According to the present procedures, financing decisions are made by the persons responsible for market segments instead of the persons in charge of product lines, which means that the internal payer can be found more easily across product divisions, and it is possible to make better use of internal expertise. The new responsibility model also allows new kinds of conceptual and business model innovations to be created.

A culture to support the development of innovations creating new business opportunities

In the foregoing we referred to the effects of discontinuous innovations from the point of view of organisation management, modes of operation and structures. Changing the operational culture or introducing new elements to the existing culture may sometimes require extensive and systematic development and a change process. Researchers have identified a number of factors with a positive effect on a culture that favours discontinuous innovations. One of the key concepts here is innovativeness. In general, an organisation is considered innovative if it has the ability to show enthusiasm in creating new profit-making operations. Innovative operations do not always lead to innovations, but they are characterised by being able to create the preconditions for innovations.

When developing the innovativeness of an organisation it is useful to identify the factors affecting it. It is often thought that innovativeness is merely the ability of individuals to produce new creative ideas and thoughts. In reality, however, innovation has been found to consist of two mutually complementing components: creativity and implementation ability, both of which can be developed systematically (Fig. 1).

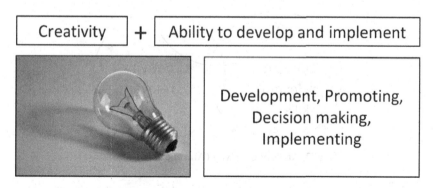

Fig. 1. Components of innovativeness (Tuominen, 2006; Lempiälä, 2008).

The creativity component is composed of an individual's professional competence, creativity skills and motivation (Fig. 2). All of the three components of creativity can be consciously developed:

- Professional competence is enhanced by such things as education, job circulation and attending conferences in the field
- Creativity skills can be developed, for example, by learning to use creativity tools and getting to know various creative processes
- An individual's motivation consists of both internal and external motivation. Internal motivation can be promoted, for instance, by offering the individual meaningful and challenging tasks, freedom for self-fulfilment and a safe work atmosphere. External motivation, in turn, is strengthened by various wage policies and incentives. Besides monetary rewards, so-called immaterial rewards are also important. They may include entrusting individuals with responsibility, giving them recognition and permission to use their time for refining their own ideas.

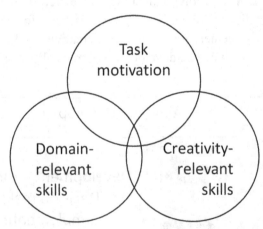

Fig. 2. Areas of creativity (Amabile *et al.* 1996).

Implementation ability can be widely defined as the organisation's ability to manage and develop new ideas systematically and with determination. Implementation ability covers all such formal and informal conventions, processes, structures and tools by which the organisation supports and provides the preconditions for the work of individuals, groups and teams. The balance and priorities of creativity and implementation ability can be used to influence the nature of innovations in the organisation. A culture of continuous development often stresses the implementation ability and efficiency while a culture focusing on discontinuous innovations generally requires a stronger emphasis on creativity.

Development of an innovative business culture

The development of a new business culture and related implementation ability is often a long and stepwise process where changes take place on many levels and are due to the combined effect of many factors. A challenge in the development of the innovation culture is unlearning the old and deploying alternative and creativity-enhancing operational models as good practices approved by the entire organisation. It is important to strike a balance between formal practices supporting the necessary systematic development, on the one hand, and freer informal practices supporting renewal, on the other hand. The development of the innovation culture is thus a change process that concerns the entire organisation and ensures its competence, functionality and motivation to implement a strategy corresponding to the new intent. Identified cultural features that promote innovativeness include encouraging people to take risks, a climate of excellence, rewarding success, accepting failure, accepting constructive task-level conflicts, learning orientation, market orientation, entrepreneurial spirit, participant decision-making and distribution of power (Amabile *et al.,* 1996; Koberg *et al.,* 1996; Tuominen, 2006).

Culture is reflected, for instance, in visible signals by which people express themselves and interact with each other. This is mirrored in formal structures such as organisation charts, processes, technology, etc. Important things to be considered here are the organisation's values, coherence of the community, informal organisation and its structures. To bring about a change, management must have a clear overall idea and the ability to assess the areas of development that are necessary for their own organisation. Figure 3 illustrates the factors of the innovation culture identified in the Innovation Lab project, which can be used as a checklist in assessing and developing one's own innovation culture to support discontinuous innovations.

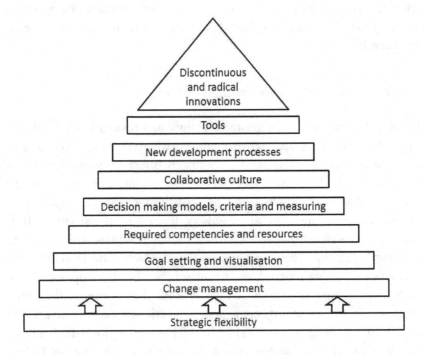

Fig. 3. Building blocks of an innovation culture supporting discontinuous innovations.

Management as a Motor of Culture Change

A successful culture change always arises from successful management leadership and supervision. A few things that should be considered in the management of a culture change are listed below:

- It is important that senior management plays a visible role in the process, sends clear signals about the importance of the change to various parts of the organisation, and helps resourcing and directing measures for realising the benefits to the organisation.

- Management's support helps lend credibility to the measures taken by middle management responsible for the implementation of results and practical work.
- Management should also communicate the things to be deployed to the staff and help all staff members to understand their own role in the introduction process and the significance of their decisions in the attainment of results. Values that are not shared can be dysfunctional (Drucker, 1999).
- In the management of change it is also always necessary to be prepared to face resistance and defend the change.
  - Organisations typically have a desire for stability, which is always to some extent shaken by the change. This often induces instinctive resistance for which management should get ready in advance.
  - Underlying this resistance are familiar and trusted conventions that are difficult to give up, as well as fear of the unknown and of losing one's own benefits or status. Another cause of resistance may often be the fear of not being able to cope with the change and not learning the new things required.
  - Typical causes of resistance to change are misunderstandings and differences in opinions arising from lack of information or poorly communicated objectives. The need for the change must be understood at both the individual and the enterprise level.

The following success factors and problems in the development of an innovative business culture were brought up in the discussion with companies during the Innovation Lab project.

Success factors:

- Persistent support of senior management, encouraging risk-taking and permitting failures
- The manager's good self-knowledge and ability to envision possible new futures
- A value-based management principle that encourages innovativeness
- Freedom and support given by management

- Management's positive attitude
- Transparent operations and interaction with the entire organisation.

Challenges:

- Organizations believe that it is possible to synchronise radical innovations with quarterly economic cycles
- The progress from vision to practical realisation has not been defined clearly enough in the strategy process
- The organisation lacks courage to take controlled risks (lagging behind because of slow decision-making)
- The organisation is unable to delegate responsibility to the resources behind the so-called gurus
- Many collective decisions are made because responsibilities and duties have not been defined clearly
- The hierarchical management model of the organisation prevents creativity and the advancement and development of ideas.

Objectives and how to visualise and communicate them

The objectives and purpose of the development must be communicated clearly to the organisation. A change always causes resistance and uncertainty which can be prevented by correctly timed and open communication. Such communication also promotes commitment and gives the organisation an impression of planned and controlled development. It is recommendable to take the values related to the new strategic intent as a starting point of the cultural change and to create a vision (Kotter, 1997) that clearly depicts the change and culture at which the development aims.

Before communicating and launching the practical measures related to the change, a clear idea of the existing innovation culture of the organisation must be formed and the need for the development measures required for the new desired culture be analysed.

The existing innovation culture may be analysed with the aid of the following questions:

- How does the existing intent of the organisation take into consideration and communicate discontinuous innovation activity and promote the selection and advancement of innovations?
  - Norms, rules and directives.
  - Portfolios, templates.
  - Target indicators and incentives.
  - Speaking the same language?
- How is the staff presently encouraged to engage in so-called out-of-the-box thinking?
  - Are they encouraged to forget limitations and existing conditions?
  - Are they encouraged to take risks?
  - Is the selection and refinement of discontinuous innovations promoted by rewards?
  - Is internal entrepreneurship encouraged?
  - Is some free time allocated for this purpose?
- Are factors related to the feelings of confidence and security given special consideration?
  - Do the staff feel secure enough to engage in new/radical things?
  - Are they willing to take risks?
  - Are they willing to do new things?
- What kind of operational models are involved in the existing decision-making culture?
  - How interactive are the modes of operation?
  - How have the promotion, possibilities and significance of networking been taken into account?
  - Has the allocation of resources been flexible?
  - Does the organisation include strong persons (champions) who advance ideas?
- How does your organisation maintain the ability to promote decision-making and implementation related to discontinuous innovations?
  - Are things related to creativity and innovativeness dealt with in training?
  - Does the organisation have the ability to copy the best practices (function transfer)?
  - How does the organisation support learning?

Experts external to the company may also be utilised in the analysis to increase the objectivity of the results. When the gaps between the present and desired innovation culture have been surveyed, a plan is made that covers the things to be developed, their contents, method of implementation and schedule. Based on the results of the analysis, various development, training and recruitment programmes can be designed to ensure adequate and correct inputs into the development. The analysis also helps to specify the contents of the communication.

For example, the following stepwise structure can be used as a tool for communicating on the change:

- Why is the change necessary?
- What are the organisation's desired direction, state of mind and intent targeted by the new premeditated development process?
- What does the change require?
- What are the things to be changed?
- How will the changes be implemented?
- How does management support the implementation of the change and the development of the organisation's abilities?

Required know-how and ensuring of resources

Discontinuous innovations usually require a degree of development of the organisation's competences and resourcing. This can be accomplished by internal resource transfers, recruitment of new people, utilisation of external network partners or training of existing staff. Typical fields of competence to be developed are:

- Various professional substance competences
- Creativity skills and methods
- Interaction skills
- Group and team activity
- Training of superiors
- Anticipation methods.

For important key areas, some personnel could be trained to lead various group processes that support creativity, participation and interaction, and thus use their own example to create practices to support the culture. The scope of the provided education and training may vary extensively depending on the company and the scope of the change. The measures taken in the companies interviewed for the study varied from new themes introduced to the meeting agenda to massive training programmes covering the entire organisation. In the following, we will describe some success factors and challenges related to the resourcing of discontinuous innovations at the individual, group and organisation level which were brought up in the discussions during the Innovation Lab project.

Success factors:

- *Individual level*
  - Good theoretical education that allows linking things to the reality
  - General education and curiosity towards the world
  - Coming from 'another world' (helps create new points of view)
  - Extensive and versatile experience and know-how.

- *Group level*
  - Ability to tolerate different ways of thinking
  - Genuine curiosity and the ability to wonder
  - Philosophy of questioning
  - Good cooperation skills (the ability to 'play together')
  - Broad expertise.
- *Organisation level*
  - Organisational changes
  - Circulation of the staff, for example, from a research centre to business operations
  - Working in cooperation with the international network
  - Use of external competence resources
  - Recruitment of new people.

Problems:

- Lack of top performers
- Distribution and adequacy of resources
- Small units often have scarce resources and a narrow view of the operation
- Constant workload does not leave enough time for development
- Fragmented and compartmented organisation where information does not flow between different functions and no synergy is created.

Interactive environment

An important element in the development of a culture that supports discontinuous innovations is the creation of interaction and an open conversational atmosphere, both within and between organisational levels. An interactive culture also includes active dialogue at the company's external interfaces with customers, users, partners, research institutions and different influential parties.

Conversational and open interaction consists of factors such as the following:

- *Building of confidence, security and freedom of thinking* – for the working environment to be called innovative, the general communication culture and interaction in the company must be open and permissive. Trust is composed of institutional trust, which can be understood as confidence in the structures, processes and practices of the organisation. This supports interaction and social confidence in the organisation. Trust is the final outcome created as a result of the operation. Trust can be built by numerous means, such as:
  - Transparent and understandable strategy communication and good personnel administration
  - Permitting errors
  - Open attitude to different modes of operation and confidence in the skills and competence of individual employees.

- *Versatile utilisation and refinement of the organisation's internal information, know-how and various ideas and points of view* – cross-organisational teams make it possible to introduce different interpretations and points of view to the discussion. The teams also enable sharing and combining so-called tacit knowledge, which makes it easier to identify new opportunities and produce new solutions.
- *Increased understanding and utilisation of bottom-up and top-down information* – management's messages and steering signals may be interpreted differently from what was meant. On the other hand, many new ideas may be created in the organisation that may even challenge the existing strategy. Two-way open communication promotes steering and innovativeness in the organisation and allows the whole organisation to participate in the renewal of the strategy.
- *Identification of new opportunities, trends and discontinuities outside the company* – systematic monitoring of markets and technological development, and analysis and active interaction with different people increases the sensitivity to identify discontinuities and react to them.
- *Opening a wide window with multiple perspectives into the business environment* – a broad external communication interface on different organisational levels promotes understanding of the market and enables the identification of new development ideas. Different functions of the company view the business environment from their own perspectives and form their own interpretations of it. Open interaction and, for example, the use of cross-organisational teams promote the combination of new perspectives and the identification of new opportunities.

A culture that supports discontinuous innovations emphasises the significance of informal interaction in the identification and refinement of thoughts and ideas. The more social interaction is created between different people, the higher the potential to combine ideas and know-how and to make latent possibilities visible.

The emergence of social interaction preceding renewal may be promoted, for example, by the following means:

- Unprejudiced personnel selections (young, new persons)
- Introducing different educational and cultural backgrounds to the organisation
- Technology to support virtual communication, such as Web cameras for computers
- New meeting forums to gather people from different functions
- Spatial arrangements to facilitate unexpected and unplanned meetings
- Gathering the 'right group' for each project and also placing the group at the same physical location
- Job circulation that creates interaction with new colleagues.

Rewarding to support motivation

The development of discontinuous innovations increases the need to tolerate uncertainty and to take more conscious risks. This is concretely reflected in decision-making, in the criteria behind the decisions, and the measurement and rewarding of results. Regarding the decision-making criteria it is typical that conventional criteria do not work and the situation calls for an educated guess based on the measurable factors that best describe the new situation. Through the measurement of results, the pressure is also directed to the profit goals of individuals and to the related reward system. Of vital importance here is the role of the managers and superiors and their consistency between the communication of objectives and the steering, monitoring and measurement of the operations. Contradictions create uncertainty in the organisation and directly influence people's experience of trust and security. This, in turn, weakens either internal or external motivation and decreases creativity. In unclear or conflicting situations people typically tend to secure their own position, which often leads to increasing mediocrity of innovations, as everyone advocates ideas and projects that involve minimal risk and uncertainty.

The development of a business culture that supports discontinuous innovations is essentially linked to measurement and rewards to support operations. Rewarding tools are usually divided into monetary and immaterial rewards. Typical monetary rewards are the basic pay, performance pay and various bonuses for initiatives, ideas and inventions. Monetary rewards always involve the demand for fairness. The reward system must be governed by clear rules that take into account such things as the roles of individuals and groups as owners, developers and those responsible for the commercialisation of ideas. Material rewards influence the external motivation behind the individual's innovativeness. Immaterial rewards may apply to things such as the contents of the work, development and education prospects, career development, feedback and recognition, possibilities to participate and have influence, work and working time arrangements, and the quality of the employment. Immaterial rewards influence the internal motivation behind the individual's innovativeness.

It is important to communicate clearly the rewarding strategy to support discontinuous innovations to the organisation, since innovative operations in organisations being renewed affect the entire staff in one way or another, and separating innovativeness and creativity from the basic tasks may be difficult. The challenges involved in rewarding are also increased by the different attitudes of individuals towards different means of rewarding. Some are motivated by their superior thanking them privately, while others need public recognition or monetary rewards. In practice, reward systems are actually combinations of so-called traditional performance indicators and specially defined indicators for measuring innovative operations. Knowing the staff makes it easier to identify the most appropriate rewarding means to increase motivation.

Processes to support the implementation ability

Failure in the development of discontinuous innovations aimed at the renewal of business operations is often due to the lack of suitable decision-making and implementation processes for advancing the idea. For the ability to implement discontinuous innovations, it is important that the organisation has described and sufficiently formalised processes and procedures to enable the processing of high-risk ideas. This issue is closely related to so-called strategic buckets and allocation of resources in budgeting. The resources budgeted for innovations may be divided into different buckets by a strategic decision according to their risk (Fig. 4) (Cooper *et al.*, 2001).

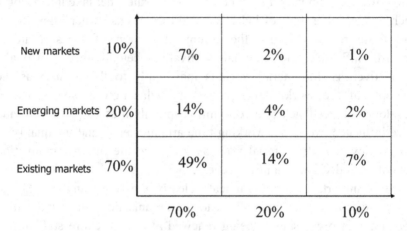

Fig. 4. Example of strategic resource allocation (strategic buckets) (Cooper *et al.*, 2001) for making ideas transparent and evaluating and refining them (creativity tools).

New tools and virtual environments for ICT and social media, such as Second Life, offer new kinds of new-generation opportunities to participate in different innovation-producing environments. Utilising these tools, especially in the area of social media, is surely a future possibility from the point of view of discontinuous innovations and part of a new-generation innovation culture and interaction with users, customers and other interest groups.

If used correctly, the tools are useful in supporting the formation of a dynamic culture. An obstacle to the use of these tools has turned out to be, in some cases, their formalising effect on processes (e.g. in the case of idea management tools), and, in others, the lack of facilitators and a high threshold to introduce various new-generation interaction tools.

As was stated in the beginning, the change of the innovation culture is a broad and multifaceted process. However, this should not be an excuse for not starting the culture change in the first place. Management should understand the whole set of things affecting innovativeness and the culture behind discontinuous innovations, and make a determined decision to gradually build an environment that supports the new strategy through prioritised changes. The change takes place in small steps and experiences of success when you get the whole organisation sufficiently involved in the change.

Example: Change and deployment of strategy in company B

The objective of the company was to change the character of the business from ensuring continuity towards reforming the operation. Underlying the strategic planning, on the one hand, was a social obligation to offer basic services, and, on the other hand, was the company's role in contributing to the development of the sector. At the same time, the consumption habits of the service customers were changing radically. The company traditionally had a strong belief in linear growth and support for incremental innovations. Customer orientation was considered a strange concept and the internal technology development produced solutions 'upon order' instead of actively thinking of something new that could be offered proactively. The objectives of the new strategic planning included, among other things, a change in the culture and attitudes, stronger customer and user orientation, networking on the distribution side, as well as premeditated investments in discontinuous innovations.

External consultants were utilised to some extent in the reform, but the new policy definition was mainly based on the company's own management team's discussions. In a new operational model, the organisation was not specifically authorised to carry out discontinuous innovations but the innovations were based on meeting customers' expectations. The management in charge of the company vision was mainly responsible for devising controls for the continuity of discontinuous innovations but partial responsibility was shared by all units. No annual budget was allocated to 'Gyro Gearloose' projects. However, a chronological target was set for new offerings, which meant moving resources from linear services to the new ones according to the devised plan. In practice this meant investing 5–12% of the development budget in discontinuous innovations.

The deployment of the strategy was planned to be implemented by a centralised process over two years. A key element in the deployment is the major responsibility assumed at the implementation level. This takes place by inviting every area of expertise to think what should be done to develop better relations and interaction with the customers. The people in charge are deeply involved and an attempt is made to make the process conversational and to break conventional roles. Suitable creativity tools have also been utilised in discussions with the customers. The message to the organisation is that 'blunders are allowed'; in other words, risks must be taken and experimenting is expected.

The structure of the organisation has been changed from product group-driven to content- and competence-driven, and the formed competence centres have internal responsibility for developing their own know-how. This means, among other things, recruiting many new people, training superiors and training that influences attitudes and modes of operation in the entire organisation. The key success factors of the change have been identified as follows: anchoring the things to be done to the company's values, and an open and conversational working atmosphere (vertical/horizontal) and management culture.

Measurement in the Discontinuous Innovation Context

Measurement: Introduction

The current measurement and reward systems are built to support efficient development and high productivity. However, discontinuous and radical innovation should be measured differently from more conventional projects, since forcing people to follow rules designed for measuring incremental change will suffocate innovation (Stringer, 2000; Simon *et al.*, 2003). The measurement system is designed for evaluating actions aiming to produce profit in the short-term period. Thus the same measures are not valid for evaluating actions in radical innovation projects, which differ quite a lot from traditional projects and which have longer time spans. Usually radical innovation projects change direction several times from idea conception to implementation. In the very early phase of the project the focus should be on learning, focusing and redirecting instead of reaching milestones. Strict financial analysis or justification too early in the project can be misleading because of the problems with market analysis (Simon *et al.*, 2003). However, in spite of the uncertainty, there should be processes which create a sense of urgency. As such there could be specified milestones which will determine whether the funding will continue. Reward systems should take into account the differences in radical and incremental innovation projects so that the system allows equal rewards inside the organisation (Simon *et al.*, 2003).

The new measurement method proposed next comprises five stages:

- Nature of companies' discontinuous innovation environment
- Selection of measurement criteria (RIM Model)
- Selection of data sources
- Data collection
- Analysis of results.

We call this five-stage entity the Radical Innovation Measurement Method (RIM Method). In this chapter, in the description of the method we concentrate on the argument dealing with the nature of companies' discontinuous innovation environment and selection of the measurement criteria. This latter we call the Radical Innovation Measurement Model (RIM Model).

Nature of companies' discontinuous innovation environment

There are suggestions based on research as to how to overcome some of the challenges dealing with the nature of companies' discontinuous innovation environment. The following themes should be considered in order to create success in discontinuous innovations.

The organisation should be challenged to do more than it currently does. Unconventional thinking and the need for new products should be made explicit and it should be made a strategic imperative (Stringer, 2000). Goals should be set so that they prompt extraordinary results. However, the goals should be close enough to avoid paralysing the organisation and be in line with and enable the current business objectives and strategies. Yet many radical innovation projects will not be successful, and therefore the financial expectations should be based on the portfolio instead of individual projects (Simon *et al.*, 2003).

There needs to be an active process which spins the knowledge and ideas from all parts of the organisation as if everyone in the organisation were participating in the innovation process. It is essential to do this within the context of the organisation's capabilities with an understanding of appropriate markets and how the products are used. Furthermore, there should be awareness of the progress in a technology platform to enable the use of it in new product applications. In any case a reduction in information cycle time is crucial for radical innovation. Therefore, information networking both within the organisation and outside of it allows more rapid identification of problems, solutions and opportunities (Simon *et al.*, 2003).

Successful recruitment focuses on curious, particularly entrepreneurial individuals. Rather than problem-solvers they ought to be solution-finders. Before one is able to create a radical innovation, it is important to understand the issue fundamentally. Therefore, those recruited should be especially skilful in this area. Rather than experts in only one area, they preferably should have a more robust mix of skills. A combination of business and technical insight, experience in external partnering and acquisition has been found to be a successful mix (Simon *et al.*, 2003).

Senior management has an important role as a provider of support. They should be involved in the project, committed to it and passionate to keep the project alive and champion the people all the way to the end of the project (Simon *et al.*, 2003). Instead of using a control-based approach to managing, radical innovation favours a mentality of monitor and redirect. Monitoring can be done through checking off assumptions as they are tested. What's learnt from these experiences could then be documented along with the decisions made based on these results. It has been suggested that radical innovation evaluation could be based on the amount that was learned compared to the amount of money invested in the project, rather than tracking task completion against the budget and schedule. These results ought to be distributed within the whole organisation so that the benefit of the learning can reach more than a few people (Leifer *et al.*, 2001; see also Stringer, 2000).

The teams could be protected so that the concepts have a chance to incubate and develop. It could be done by providing an isolated environment from the organisation to minimise the distractions and pressures. It has been even recommended to spin the teams out from the conventional internal organisation (Simon *et al.*, 2003). However, the problem might be that these projects are not regarded as part and parcel of the organisation. Having a crisp and clear vision for the entire business and efficiently explicating it throughout the organisation is a tool to overcome some of these difficulties (Stringer, 2000).

The spirit of persistence and patience is imperative in the team. It is mediated by senior management through their actions, such as staffing the teams appropriately and sustaining the support even in tough financial phases. The role of senior management is cheerleading, since the radical innovation projects can be frustrating for the people involved. The development of the project is characterised by a series of starts and stops along with ups and downs. During the low points management's supporting role is crucial (Simon *et al.*, 2003).

Selection of measurement criteria (RIM Model)

Based on earlier research (SFS-ISO 9001, 1988; Hannukainen, 1992; Paulk, 1995; QS 9000, 1998; ISO/CD2 9000 Draft, 1999; Berg *et al.*, 2002; Berg *et al.*, 2004), the structure of the RIM Model lies on the structure of the Quality Maturity Method (QMM) and assessment method for national technology programmes in Finland. The mentioned methods consist of a three-step procedure for the setting of objectives where the objectives of a technology programme are divided into impacts, outputs and activities. The business viewpoint in the QMM model corresponds with the impact of the national technology programmes' assessment model; the product viewpoint in the QMM model corresponds with the outputs of the national technology programmes' assessment model; and finally, the implementation viewpoint in the QMM model corresponds with the activities of the national technology programmes' assessment model.

In the selection of the measurement criteria the two most crucial questions are as follows:

- What are the objectives of measurement?
- How can objectives be made measurable?

After we have linked objectives with attributes we get the entity of measurable criteria. In the selection of objectives we have several challenging issues to take into account. What is the reliability of the potential objectives? Is there any reference data related to the objectives collected in an earlier measurement of the same company or in other partner companies? What things other than product development have an effect on achieving the impacts? Also, it is important to see the entity of measurement criteria and interrelationships between the different factors (Khurana and Rosenthal, 1997).

Table 1. Main innovation process objectives, Radical Innovation Measurement Model (RIM Model).

Main objective	Sub-objective
Social environment	Innovativeness Creativity Ability to implement
Input	Market growth Market orientation Customer understanding
Innovation process	Opportunity identification Data collection Idea generation Pattern recognition Concept idea/formal project plan
Outcome	Goods Services Customer interaction
Impacts	Market share Profitability Customer satisfaction
Physical (artefact) environment	Spatials ICT systems Other artefacts (process descriptions, templates)

Our idea is a framework of the model for measuring the innovation front end. It contains in the first draft five assessment viewpoints as follows: input, process, outcome (including impacts), social environment and physical environment. The connection with these elements in the measurement of innovation activities as a whole has been weak. The sub-objectives of these three assessment areas are presented in Table 1, which contains a list of objectives mentioned earlier.

Criteria to be assessed become concrete and measurable when the party responsible for the assessment makes decisions on the assessment criteria, corresponding attributes of measurement and the emphasis on qualitative and quantitative data. Attributes can be subjective or objective. We can have a notional scale with purely subjective measures at one end or measures based on absolute standards at the other (Ward, 1996). Our ideas for objective and subjective attributes are presented in Tables 2 and 3.

Table 2. Objective attributes.

Attribute category	Attribute
1. Currency unit	Turnover Increase in turnover Adherence to budget Economic performance in relation to competitors Production costs Net profit/ROI Development of quality costs by products
2. Pieces	Patents, publications
3. Persons	Number of personnel
4. Time (years, months)	Adherence to timetable Repayment time Throughput time of products
5. Percentage	Change in market share Product renewal rate Share of demanding products
6. Technical attributes	Technical performance in relation to competitors

Table 3. Scaling list for subjective attributes.

Importance	Input
Very important 4 Important 3 Rather important 2 Of little importance 1	Too large input 4 Proper input 3 Too small input 2 Insufficient input 1
Goal setting Very successful 4 Successful 3 Some success 2 Poor 1	**Attainment of set goals** (You can use % here too) Very successful 4 Successful 3 Some success 2 Poor 1
Changing of set goals Very big changes 4 Big changes 3 Some changes 2 Little changes 1	**Benefits** Very big benefits 4 Marked benefits 3 Some benefits 2 Little benefits 1
Difficulty Lot of problems 4 Fair amount of problems 3 A few problems 2 No problems 1	**Successfulness** Extremely successful 4 Very successful 3 Moderately successful 2 Unsuccessful 1

Measurement: Conclusions

We conclude that the framework of the model for measuring the innovation front end in the discontinuous context in the first draft contains five assessment viewpoints. They are input, process, outcome, social environment and physical environment. The connection with these elements in the measurement of innovation activities as a whole has been weak, but now these will be covered by a new approach, the RIM Method. In our research we are now in the process of studying the first managerial implications of the RIM Method for Finnish, German and US companies.

The following subjects should be taken into consideration in the application and further development of the model:

- The current situation and the nature of the each company should be taken into careful consideration in the applications of the model. The subjects described in the model are not suitable for all companies but the appropriate tools could be chosen for an individual company.
- The model should be defined as a practical tool for managers. This assumes cultivating the model description into a concrete workbook. It should also be noted that the model is primarily a tool for internal assessment (evaluation) which is also clearly related to external audits of companies.
- The reliability of the data collected by the model should be considered critical. This is especially important when the data collected in internal assessments is also used as basic data for the external audits. Special consideration should be given to the sources of information used in the internal assessment: how much information is collected from external experts and from other objective data sources.
- Defining the criteria to be assessed is the most critical stage of the measurement. The central issue is to define sub-criteria supporting the main criteria for a single case. That would enable a clear interpretation of the criteria from two viewpoints: from the viewpoint of the innovation front end and from the viewpoint of discontinuous innovation.
- The linking of national and branch-specific strategies to companies should be improved. Corporate strategy work performance could be intensified by inviting experts who have participated in defining national R&D strategies and technology policies to be heard at the top of the companies. National strategies are seldom written in an easily understandable language. Having the experts speak to management would enhance the linkage remarkably.
- Special consideration should be given to impacts on the structures of the branch. Networking in the branch should be studied more.

The impacts on the branch could in the future be divided according to the following main criteria:

– clusterisation of the branch, including changes at the interface and new cooperation parties
– internal impacts on the branch, such as profitability and export
– networking and cooperation
– organisational changes inside organisations.

The developed model is flexible and can also be applied extensively to purposes other than companies. Application targets worth studying are research and development programmes of different ministries at the national level. The model could also be applied to internal research, technology and development programmes of enterprises, research institutes and other organisations. The study has been mainly targeted thus far at the manufacturing industry from the viewpoint of production of goods. The initial observations show that the new measurement model might be useful in other industrial areas, such as the service sector, as well.

Final motto: 'It is not enough to do things right; the right things must be done.'

References

Amabile, T.M., Conti, R., Coon, H., Lazenby, J. and Herron, M. (1996). Assessing the work environment for creativity. *Academy of Management Journal*, 39(5), 1154–1184.

Berg, P., Leinonen, M., Leivo, V. and Pihlajamaa, J. (2002). Assessment of quality and maturity level of R&D. *International Journal of Production Economics*, 78(1), 29–35.

Berg, P., Pihlajamaa, J., Nummi, J. and Leinonen, M. (2004). Measurement of the quality and maturity of the innovation process: Methodology and case of a medium sized Finnish company. *International Journal of Entrepreneurship and Innovation Management*, 4(4), 373–382.

Bessant, J., Lamming, R., Noke, H. and Phillips, W. (2005). Managing innovation beyond the steady state. *Technovation*, 25(12), 1366–1376.

Christensen, C.M. (1997). *The Innovator's Dilemma: The Revolutionary Book that Will Change the Way You Do Business.* Harper Business Essentials, New York.

Cooper, R. (2003). Your NPD portfolio may be harmful to your business's health. *Research Technology Management*, 47(1), 31–43.

Cooper, R., Edgett, S. and Kleinschmidt, E. (2001). Portfolio management for new product development: Results of an industry practices study. *R&D Management*, 31(4), 361–380.

Cottam, A., Ensor, J. and Band, C. (2001). A benchmark study of strategic commitment to innovation. *European Journal of Innovation Management*, 4(2), 88–94.

Drucker, P.F. (1999). Managing oneself. *Harvard Business Review*, 77, 65–74.

Ebert, J., Chandra, S. and Liedtke, A. (2008). *Innovation management. Strategies for success and leadership.* A.T. Kearney Inc., Chicago, IL.

Hamel, G. and Välikangas, L. (2003). The quest for resilience. *Harvard Business Review*, 81(9), 52–65.

Hannukainen, T. (1992). *Laatuyritykset: Laatujohtaminen maailman valioyrityksissä.* Metalliteollisuuden Keskusliitto, MET, Tampere.

ISO/CD2 9000 Draft (1999). *Quality management systems – fundamentals and vocabulary.*

Kanter, R.M. (2006). Innovation: The classic traps. *Harvard Business Review*, 84(11), 72–83, 154.

Khurana, A. and Rosenthal, S.R. (1997). Integrating the fuzzy front end of new product development. *Sloan Management Review*, 38, 103–120.

Kim, W.C. and Mauborgne, R. (2005). *Blue Ocean Strategy: How to Create Uncontested Market Space and Make Competition Irrelevant.* Harvard Business School Press, Boston, MA.

Koberg, C.S., Uhlenbruck, N. and Sarason, Y. (1996). Facilitators of organizational innovation: The role of life-cycle stage. *Journal of Business Venturing*, 11(2), 133–149.

Koen, P., Ajamian, G., Burkart, R., Clamen, A., Fisher, E., Fountoulakis, S., Johnson, P.P. and Seibert, R. (2002). 'Fuzzy front end: Effective methods, tools, and techniques', in Belliveau, P., Griffin, A. and Somermeyer, S. (eds), *PDMA Toolbook for New Product Development.* John Wiley & Sons, West Sussex.

Kotter, J.P. (1997). Leading by vision and strategy. *Executive Excellence*, 14(10), 15–16.

Leifer, R., O'Connor, G. and Rice, M. (2001). Implementing radical innovation in mature firms: The role of hubs. *The Academy of Management Executive*, 102–113.

Lempiälä, T. (2008). *Aamuhämärän ratsastajat – koordinaatteja innovaatioprosessin sumean alkupään johtamiseen.* Unpublished manuscript.

Lynn, G.S., Morone, J.G. and Paulson, A.S. (1996). Marketing and discontinuous innovation. *California Management Review*, 38(3), 8–37.

Paulk, M.C. (1995). *The Capability Maturity Model: Guidelines for Improving the Software Process.* Addison-Wesley, Reading, MA.

Phillips, W., Lamming, R., Bessant, J. and Noke, H. (2006). Discontinuous innovation and supply relationships: Strategic dalliances. *R&D Management*, 36(4), 451–461.

Poskela, J. and Martinsuo, M. (2010). *Escaping strategic rigidity to pursue business renewal through discontinuous innovations.* Unpublished manuscript.

Poskela, J. and Vänskä, J. (2009). Escaping strategic rigidity to pursue business renewal through discontinuous innovations. *Proceedings of 10th International CINet Conference.*

QS 9000 (1998). *Quality System Requirements, 3rd Edition.*

Reid, S.E. and de Brentani, U. (2004). The fuzzy front end of new product development for discontinuous innovations: A theoretical model. *Journal of Product Innovation Management*, 21(3), 170–184.

Roxburgh, C. (2003). Hidden flaws in strategy. *McKinsey Quarterly*, 2, 26–39.

SFS-ISO 9001 (1988). Laatujärjestelmät. Malli suunnittelussa tai tuotekehityksessä, tuotannossa, asennuksessa ja toimituksen jälkeisissä palveluissa toteutettavalle laadunvarmistukselle. Suomen Standardoimisliitto.

Simon, E.S., McKeough, D.T., Ayers, A.D., Rinehart, E. and Alexia, B. (2003). How do you best organize for radical innovation? *Research Technology Management*, 46(5), 17–20.

Stringer, R. (2000). How to manage radical innovation. *California Management Review*, 42(4), 70–88.

Tuominen, T. (2006). *Innovativeness and creativity in organisations. Literature review.* IMI Working Paper, Helsinki University of Technology.

Välikangas, L. and Gibbert, M. (2005). Boundary-setting strategies for escaping innovation traps. *MIT Sloan Management Review*, 46(3), 58–65.

Ward, A. (1996). Measuring the product innovation process. *Engineering Management Journal*, 6(5), 242–246.

Chapter 16

Coloplast: Fixing Broken Hearts?

Frank Gertsen and René N. Nielsen
Aalborg University, Denmark

A Hard Stone in the Shoe

The fact that about 20% of the Western world's population dies from heart attack makes this the most common cause of death, and for a quarter of these incidences it happens entirely without warning (Schmidt, 2011). Diagnosing this condition is a rather costly affair and the current gold standard (catheter-injected contrast and live X-ray) is invasive, furthermore, 30–40% of patients checked turn out not to suffer from coronary artery disease (CAD). Indeed this problem is a considerable stone in the shoe – a challenge for innovation. Could something be done about it? Would it be possible to develop a less expensive diagnosis of signs of CAD allowing for preventive action?

While pondering the subject of their master's theses, two students Samuel Schmidt and Claus Graff at Aalborg University's Department of Health Science and Technology were alerted to this question (and many other possible medical challenges for that matter). One of their supervisors had provided them with an electronic stethoscope from 3M, manufactured – at that time – by Bang & Olufsen Medicom, and some ideas for a heart-sound project. But, as Samuel explained: 'I have never done what the supervisors suggested us to do; one could always find something that felt exciting for oneself,' He continued: 'So, we looked into the literature, etc. Then, incidentally we came across an old article from the seventies, which showed that in rare cases they [the surgeons/researchers] had heard this sound.' The sound referred to was a weak murmur caused by turbulence in the blood stream of an occluded artery surrounding and supplying blood to the heart. The students then concluded: 'If it could be occasionally heard, with signal processing, we must be able to find it.' Thus, the technical task was to record the weak murmur of blood flow in the coronary arteries and segregate it from other loud sounds in order to analyse the murmur sound and reveal any potential stenosis. The key challenge was segregating a sound which is more than 60 dB (up to 1,000 times) weaker than surrounding sounds (in particular the heartbeat), and achieving sufficient quality to enable sound pattern recognition for the detection of stenosis.

Further investigation into this problem revealed that the basic idea was not new at all and more recent attempts had been made, particularly in the United States, to pursue the same idea,[a] and even to develop the idea into a commercial product, but apparently without success. Samuel said: 'They also achieved some reasonable results, but they have not gotten further on with it, so we thought we would give it a try.'

As in most cases of invention someone has been there before but there is a chance that improvements, re-combinations of existing means and changing needs may enable a better and more timely solution to the needs of today's market. In addition, students exploring ideas have everything to gain, that is, if they don't succeed with usable results, they will succeed with learning (arguably, the same is essentially true for companies, but resources and time for learning are scarce and learning is rarely a target in itself). So, despite some initial scepticism from the supervisors and a certain sense of 'mission impossible', the students pursued the idea and achieved very promising results in terms of a

---

[a] Henrik Zimmerman (project participant, PhD student at Aalborg University) reported: 'A direct relation between the murmur originating from occluded coronary arteries was reported by a case study in 1967 (Dock and Zoneraic, 1967). The case study described how surgeons who perform coronary angiography were encouraged to look for a murmur before surgery; however, during a period of eight months only one case was brought to their attention... The same paper also refers to earlier studies dating back to 1885 where murmurs from the heart were noticed. The case described by Dock and Zoneraic (1967) was later used for further research which was carried out in the early eighties. Recently a large study has been carried out to prove that a transducer specifically made for the purpose would make it possible to make a diagnosis of CAD based on sound (Semmlow and Rahalkar, 2007).'

technical solution and tests on a (limited) number of patients. The diagnostic method involved a digital stethoscope, wireless connection and a computer with software including algorithms for analysis. The sound was recorded by the stethoscope at the chest of the patient and the sound was rinsed from noise before entering the calculation in the specific algorithms designed to recognize and visualize patterns known to be associated with CAD.

The promising student work was followed up by Samuel in temporary research positions and later in a PhD project at Aalborg University. The proof-of-concept study was positive in terms of diagnosing patients who did or did not have the disease and patents were filed by the university's innovation department.

In order to make progress and turn the idea and patents into a commercial product, different potential partners were contacted and introduced to the idea of a non-invasive tool for diagnosing CAD.

Coloplast A/S

Coloplast A/S is a Danish medical device company with an annual turnover of €1.3 billion (2010), employing more than 7,000 people in the manufacture, sale and distribution of their products. The company focuses on:

> ... products and services that make life easier for people with very personal and private medical conditions. Working closely with the people who use our products, we create solutions that are sensitive to their special needs. We call this intimate healthcare. Our business includes ostomy care, urology and continence care, and wound and skin care... (Coloplast, 2011).

Coloplast A/S was established as an independent company in 1957 with a gazelle-like growth rate of 40–45% per year. The company's conception is a story of radical innovation:

> It all started back in 1954. Nurse Elise Sørensen was concerned by the dramatic change in her sister's lifestyle following an ostomy operation. Thora no longer dared to go out, fearing that her stoma would leak in public. Elise was determined

to help her sister out of her isolation. She came up with the idea of an ostomy bag with an adhesive ring, which would make it fit tightly to the skin. This would prevent leakage and give her sister – and thousands of people like her – the chance to return to their normal life. (Coloplast, 2011).

One summer's day the same year, Elise went to meet Aage Louis-Hansen, a small producer of printed plastic bags, and she introduced him to what she thought was a brilliant idea and asked if he wanted to produce it. His immediate answer was 'No!'

Here the history of Coloplast could have ended – even before it started – were it not for another woman in a more persuasive position. When he got home, Aage told his wife, a former nurse, about the meeting. Johanne Louis-Hansen eventually convinced her husband that he should take a second look at the invention. Nurse Elise Sørensen was invited to the company and the first experimental bags were made. A patent application was filed and a license agreement signed which allowed Johanne and Aage to produce and sell the product.

Coloplast has expanded its business and earned a reputation for excellence in its incremental continuous innovation and involvement of users in the search for ideas for improvements and new products. This includes dialogue with stoma care nurses through Coloplast Ostomy Forum, dialogue with international surgeons through Stoma Research Board, dialogue with end users through Coloplast User Panel and observation of usage situations in the Usability Lab.

In support of new product development, Coloplast has adapted commonly accepted product-development models. In 1996 a stage-gate model (see e.g. Cooper and Kleinschmidt, 1993) called Accelerated Ideas to Market (AIM) was introduced. The model was used and regularly modified until 2006, when it was extended by a front-end Coloplast Innovation Cycle (CIC) and a downstream roll-out activity. Internally the model is known under the acronym 'FIGARO' (From Innovation to Accelerated Global Roll-Out) (see Fig. 1).

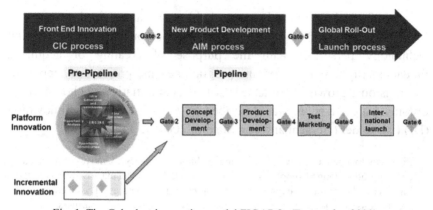

Fig. 1. The Coloplast innovation model FIGARO. (Enemærke, 2009).
Reproduced with permission.

FIGARO is a company-specific, carefully documented and theory-based second-generation stage-gate (Cooper, 1994) system for new product development. The model was introduced for several reasons, but two of the main reasons were to make sure that the firm was working with the right ideas and to shorten the time for innovation (Enemærke, 2009).

Peter Samuelsen[b] (2011) added: 'FIGARO is an innovation model designed to support all business units in their evolutionary development and as such it is a tool.' Such systems of innovation processes are often inappropriate for path-breaking types of innovation, as, for instance, expressed by Bessant *et al.* (2010): '... because such systems were designed to manage risk and enable a decision based on market and technological facts, they bear the risk of not supporting ideas that are vague, hazy and speculative.'

In Pursuit of Radical Innovation

In pursuit of more radical innovations that could stretch the scope of the current business and meet the growth and renewal ambitions of the company, Coloplast launched two initiatives during the last decade.

---

[b] Research Director of Coloplast Research and VP of Coloplast Incubation at the time.

In 2005 Nebula (New Business Lab) was initiated in the form of a small (seven-person) multidisciplinary team of business personnel and technology personnel with the purpose of creating or acquiring fundamentally new front-loading programmes and projects in support of the division's growth (Samuelsen, 2011). This initiative, anchored in the Ostomy Care Division, was described by the Discontinuous Innovation (DI) Lab folder (Bessant and von Stamm, 2007) as follows:

> In trying to open up new markets and technology spaces to move beyond its current product range Coloplast established a small group, Nebula – New Business Lab, with the remit to explore and bring back new options. These could be acquisitions, licences for new technologies, new alliances and partnerships or established product ideas. The group also had a mandate to explore licensing and spinning out business units.

The positive experience from this initiative included (Christensen, 2006) identification of a high number of projects constituting a diverse portfolio of projects at varying stages and of different origins (from ideas to acquisitions). Also, many processes were initiated (vision/strategy/innovation), Market Attack Teams (MATs) were established, and there was a high level of energy, a new spirit and good commitment. Despite the positive experience, this initiative encountered a number of challenges which, after two years, brought Nebula to an end. The internal challenges included a biased focus (too much focus on tools rather than on HR issues such as skills, entrepreneurial competences and team composition). Related to this, diverging individual agendas existed (e.g. fast money, future technology, safe projects, risky development), the strategic scope was wide but without *a priori* vision and strategic direction, leading to too many projects since there were no criteria for selecting/killing projects. The challenge external to Nebula was the governance structure, since the unit was a divisional – not a corporate – entity, so in a sense it had to work partly undercover with different views of the future, which were not aligned with the company strategy and thus not embedded in top management. Working under these conditions also made it difficult to hand over projects to the existing R&D organization. The lack of embeddedness of Nebula and the nature and difficulty of the projects resulted in (as expected) a long time-to-market and potential lack of technology fit.

A second attempt to create future business opportunities was made by the establishment of a corporate venture unit (Coloplast Incubation) in 2007. Peter Samuelsen (Samuelsen, 2011), a Coloplast employ, said:

> Incubation was established during restructuring of all R&D activity, including a shut down of the corporate research department. The research department had a number of ongoing research collaborations reaching out to external partners in order to adopt new technologies. A number of these collaborative projects were moved to Incubation, in which three focal areas of technology were defined and supported by projects and investment: sensors, tissue engineering [stem cells], and nano technology [delivery spheres].

These initiatives reflect a strategic intent and emphasize that management sees a need for moving beyond evolutionary development of the current business, however important that might be in itself. An interview with Claus Bo Christensen (former Coloplast senior medical technology specialist) and Peter confirms that management was initially supporting the search for potential radical innovations.

In Incubation there was generally an open approach to innovation. A great part of the work was dedicated – especially through networking – to searching the environment for potential innovations. The search was directed towards new technologies within the three focal areas mentioned earlier. The intention was not merely to license or acquire such technologies but rather to engage with partners in order to co-innovate. Peter said: 'It was not just about investing, we also wanted to absorb and develop the technologies through collaborative projects.' The case described in this chapter should be viewed from this open innovation perspective.

Match Point

Peter and Claus Bo were visiting Aalborg University to follow up some ongoing projects. Whilst there, they grabbed the opportunity to meet for lunch with Egon Toft (then Vice Dean, Professor, Dr. Med.), whom Peter knew and had met on other occasions since they both participated in The

Electronic Patch,[c] a so-called Innovation Consortium funded by the Danish government focused on enabling continuous surveillance of patients with, e.g., heart diseases. In fact, the Coloplast link to Aalborg University had been built gradually over a longer period of time. Amongst other things, the lunch led them to talk about a new invention, a promising method for diagnosis of CAD, which had previously been exposed when Samuel Schmidt and Claus Graff (at that point students working on the invention) won the prestigious Danish Medico Award 2007.

Peter and Claus Bo immediately sensed that the invention and the university staff's competences related to it were complementary to Coloplast's competences within adhesives, clinical trials and commercialization competence, and Egon seemed to agree. Claus Bo said:

> They could see it [the invention] was interesting in many ways and could really contribute something new, but there were also some obstacles for them to overcome before they could get on with it. But we thought it was just obvious to combine their invention and competences with some of Coloplast's core competencies.[d]

Importantly, this did not remain a vague idea. Peter, Claus Bo and Egon chose to initiate a collaborative process aimed at transforming the invention into an innovation with significant market potential. That was, to develop a diagnostic method based on an adhesive patch applied to the patient's chest which uses advanced listening technology and a computer program with algorithms that can analyse the sounds for early signs of CAD.

One of the first steps in this process was to identify additional partners that could contribute the resources and competences crucial to turn the idea and invention into an innovation with a strong value

---

[c] Project period 2007–2009. For more information, see www.eplaster.dk.

[d] From an interview with Peter Samuelsen and Claus Bo Christensen conducted on 16 September 2010. The quotation has been translated into English and in this process slightly edited.

proposition. Here the acoustic section of Aalborg University was involved because their acoustic competences were needed in order to improve the design for achieving better sound from the coronary arteries.[e] For field tests, Rigshospitalet – Copenhagen University Hospital[f] was invited. In unison these partners drew up a joint application to the Danish National Advanced Technology Foundation and obtained public co-funding (approx. €800,000 out of a €1,600,000 total budget), which was vital for the project.

When joining such collaborative innovation projects there are bound to be difficult but inevitable negotiations related to input of resources and efforts vs. future ownership of any achieved economic value. Peter and Claus Bo represented Coloplast in these negotiations and they reached a settlement with administrative representatives of Aalborg University who negotiated on behalf of the researchers. Interviews revealed that Peter and Claus Bo were quite satisfied with the negotiation process and the outcome, especially in comparison with their experiences of similar negotiations with other universities in Denmark. Several of the university partners were, on the other hand, somewhat more doubtful about how favourable a negotiated result they had achieved. These doubts among the university partners did not, however, change the fact that they were generally pleased about participating in the project and its subsequent development.

Based on the negotiations and the granted public co-funding the innovation project was set up with Claus Bo in a coordinating role as project manager, a project group and a representative steering committee, as well as a meeting structure, etc. The work was defined by work packages each managed and developed by the partner with the appropriate (core) competence profile, and the desired momentum of the project was agreed upon in a timetable. Generally this project setup

---

[e] One weakness of the preliminary measurements was the poor resolution of the stethoscope, which reduced the accuracy of the diagnosis.

[f] This partner was substituting the originally intended partner, Aalborg Hospital/Aarhus University Hospital, during the application process, due to changes related to the establishment of a medical faculty at Aalborg University.

seemed well chosen for this specific project. Except for some delay in the final stages, the different work packages largely developed as planned and the overall project progressed roughly in line with the project schedule, which is often not the case for radical innovation projects (Leifer *et al.*, 2000).

A Few Stumbling Stones on the Road

Each partner entered the project with specialized skills and competences that have been crucial for the achieved progress within each work package and, in total, it is the complementary differences in the partners' competences that constitute the innovation potential in the project. This does not mean, however, that the partners have not experienced any challenges in their collaborative innovation process.

In an interview, a corporate participant stated that there have definitely:

> ...been some cultural differences ... [and there] are some different levels of ambition and requirements for how university faculty qualify themselves and how we from a business perspective need to think in terms of markets and sales. We can build the world's most expensive equipment, but if we do, we simply will not be able to sell it ... There we have ... a conflict of interest.

This statement seems to be in accordance with the rather widely held view that universities and companies are, roughly speaking, characterized by different – partly opposing – institutional purposes, norms and cultures. University faculty members naturally tend to maintain a focus on producing new, thoroughly researched academic knowledge, while corporate employees are more focused on practical applicability, costs and temporal progress of the project.

But in the concrete case (and maybe in others too) this widely held view might not hold true. A university participant expressed that they did not enter the project primarily to do academic research. Instead, they were interested in practical problem-solving related to the project and in solving practical problems as quickly and as cost-efficiently as possible.

A recurring dispute concerned different stances as to which work process was the most efficient in producing the desired end: a marketable product. The acoustic group of academics were focusing on proving the core principles by building a prototype based on leading-edge knowledge and technology (to optimize the clinical test) and then subsequently reducing unnecessary performance features and costs. Thus, a university participant argued: 'A systematic course as we are used to in research is not in conflict with getting results fast and cheap – on the contrary.' On the other side, the corporate participants pursued a different path – faster development of a prototype based on cost-efficient technologies in addition to product design and engineering activities, in order to prove the design for the potential market.

This dual course resulted in parallel work, competition for critical resources, ineffective use of competences and delays of the clinical test.

Despite challenges related to different perceptions, in interviews both university and corporate participants seem to agree that the diversity in backgrounds and competences were primarily productive (it contained the seeds of the innovation), that the project partners basically had a common interest and that the emerging problems had been handled as challenges – not subversive conflicts.

Shifting the Scene of the Innovation Process

Changes in the top management of Coloplast were followed by a refocus of the innovation strategy towards the core of the business. The new focus is part of an overall streamlining of the organization and its activities to improve the (short-run) bottom line. Since the main purpose of the corporate venture was one of expanding the core by means of new technologies, the board decided to close it down at the end of 2010 and focus all Coloplast innovation (a team of about 200 people) solely on the core business. Some ongoing Incubator projects came to an end and other promising projects were spinned out into separate businesses, which was the case for the CAD Patch project.

This potential disruption of the innovation process required a new, and somewhat complicated, renegotiation of ownership between Coloplast and Aalborg University. By the end of 2009 the new company Acarix A/S (Ltd) was established under shared ownership with Peter as

CEO, Claus Bo as project manager and a third employee. The main part of the shares was owned by Coloplast and some by Aalborg University (in return for transfer of IPR). Shortly after, Coloplast offered and sold parts of their shares to the Acarix managers and some more symbolic parts to some of the university researchers involved.

Despite these challenges there was steady progress in the innovation process. Shifting from being part of a large organization to being on their own also put more stress on the small team, especially regarding the need for further funding in order to bring the product to the market.

Probing the Market

Christensen's (1997) statement 'A market that doesn't exist cannot be analysed' characterizes the situation often faced by innovators of radical innovation. Instead, early interaction with the market is suggested as a feasible way to understand, co-create and build the market. In the case of the CAD Patch, interaction with potential future users has been going on since its invention in an environment including a cardiologist, through tests of early prototypes in a hospital environment to more systematic investigations. During the collaborative project with Coloplast/Acarix the development of the business plan included interviews with one UK-based and nine Danish general practitioners (GPs) and several cardiologists. Based on this a first plan was made for positioning the product and segmenting the market. This was followed up by additional interviews with cardiologists and GPs in Denmark and Sweden and an international advisory board was established, also comprising GPs, cardiologists and a regulatory expert.

According to Peter and Claus Bo these market-learning activities have confirmed that the value proposition is strong and along with estimations of the potential market size this indicates a substantial potential for the CAD Patch.

The Acarix CAD Patch system consists of a CAD sensor unit and a disposable patch. The unit will carry a display for direct diagnostic reading and wireless transfer of data to a computer. The expected value propositions of the system include the following (Acarix, 2010):

- Ultra-fast method; the patient turnaround time is less than ten minutes
- Very competitive examination costs
- Adoptable in most clinical settings without interior changes
- Easy to use by all professional groups
- No patient risk during examination
- Sensitivity better than present non-invasive methods
- Disposable and hygienic patch
- Robust and portable device.

In addition to these market-learning and co-creation activities, market preparation also includes exposures to draw broader attention in terms of media news flashes and national broadcasts (reality programmes).[g]

Uncertainty Status

The value proposition is promising and with respect to market uncertainty there is at least one other potential player pursuing similar opportunities. Peter said: 'We know that a competing initiative has initiated a market investigation ... we have not identified other activities through our news and patent surveillance' (O'Connor *et al.*, 2008).

In term of technical uncertainties, the results are pending from a field test of the version 2 prototype on 450 patients, with expected improvements on some key performance factors due to improvements of the prototype's measurement method and the algorithms and measurement technology. The results are crucial for the pace of progress.

Regarding IPR, the situation for the Acarix series of patents is currently stable (according to Acarix).

Financial resources for further development and marketing have been achieved through the infusion of venture capital (€4.4 million) from industry-related international investors.

---

[g] Danish broadcasting channel DR2 runs a reality programme called *Mad or Genius* where inventors can pitch their ideas and get feedback from the host (it has some similarities to the BBC's *Dragons' Den*).

In addition Acarix has strengthened its competences by employing a chairman of the board with experience as senior vice president at a world leader in medical technology. In addition, the new industry-related investors may play an important role in the preparations for market launch and the establishment and acceleration of supply and delivery to the market.

Case Reflections

This chapter has outlined continuing case study research on the Acarix CAD Patch system. As mentioned, the patch system has not yet been introduced in the marketplace and thus is yet to be proven as a successful radical innovation. The patch system has, nonetheless, the potential for becoming a radical innovation and we will therefore end this chapter by comparing our case findings to more established findings in the literature on radical and discontinuous innovations.

If we perceive innovation as a process (Tidd and Bessant, 2009), it has been argued that this process – and elements within it – needs to be understood and managed differently if the interest is radical, discontinuous innovation rather than incremental, steady-state innovation (Bessant, 2008; O'Connor *et al.*, 2008; Bessant *et al.*, 2010;). This is in accordance with findings in the Acarix case.

If we evaluate the case from a *company perspective*, it started with Coloplast Incubation. This was a special venture unit aiming to do more than merely underpin steady-state innovation and, for that purpose, it was, among other things, based on a proactive, open innovation search agenda (Bessant, 2008). Coloplast Incubation (and preceding that, Nebula) may also be seen as an 'alternative decision-making pathway' which was structured and funded to 'have a "fuzzy" front end, which allows for building a potential portfolio of higher risk ideas and options' (Bessant *et al.*, 2010).

After Peter and Claus Bo, as Coloplast representatives, had identified an interesting invention and established relationships with competent researchers at Aalborg University, the CAD Patch system innovation process was started and developed in what might be termed a 'network for discontinuous innovation' (Birkinshaw *et al.*, 2007). Later in the innovation process it was shown that innovation practices need to be seen in light of overall strategic decisions at the company level. Coloplast's overall management decided to withdraw from activities within Nebula and corporate venturing, and Acarix emerged as a co-funded and co-owned spin-off company. In the context of this spin-off company the innovation progressed further, but as already stated it still needs to be finally established as a radical innovation, since claiming a case of radical innovation is doubtful when the invention has not yet hit the marketplace. However, despite many historical examples of failures and mistimed market launches, Sandberg (2008, p. 227) concluded from a multi-case study regarding marketing of radical innovations and how to act proactively towards customer:

> ...that although the market for a radical innovation develops along with its creation, it is not necessarily hidden from the firms developing it. On the contrary, these firms seem to be able to anticipate the opportunities in the market and develop radical innovation that fulfils the unarticulated needs of customers.

Only the future will show if the patch will catch on and fulfil the promises to our hearts.

References

Acarix (2010). Presentation material, received from CEO Peter Samuelsen July, 2010, used with permission.

Bessant, J. (2008). Dealing with Discontinuous Innovation Some European Experience. *International Journal of Technology Management*, 42 (1/2), 36–50.

Bessant, J. and von Stamm, B. (2007). *Twelve Search Strategies that Could Save Your Organisation.* Advanced Institute of Management Research (AIM), London.

Bessant, J., von Stamm, B., Moeslein, K. and Neyer, A.K. (2010). Backing outsiders: Selection strategies for discontinuous innovation. *R&D Management*, 40(4), 345–356.

Birkinshaw, J., Bessant, J., Delbridge, R. (2007). Finding, forming, and performing: Creating networks for discontinuous innovation. *California Management Review*, 49(3), 67–83.

Christensen, C.M. (1997). *The Innovator's Dilemma: When New Technologies Cause Great Firms to Fail*. Harvard Business School Press, Boston, MA.

Christensen, C.B.V. (2006). Challenges in Regards to Radical Innovation. Speech given at a DI Lab workshop, 28 March 2006.

Coloplast (2011). About Coloplast. Available at: http://www.coloplast.com/about/. [Accessed August 31 2011.]

Cooper, R.G. (1994). Perspective: Third-generation new product processes. *Journal of Product Innovation Management*, 11, 3–14.

Cooper, R.G. and Kleinschmidt, E.J. (1993). Stage-gate systems for new product success. *Marketing Management*, 1(4), 137–147.

Dock, W. and Zoneraic., S. (1967). A diastolic murmur arising in a stenosed coronary artery. *American Journal of Medicine*, 42(4), 617–619.

Enemærke, J. (2009). Internal Coloplast product development manual.

Leifer R., McDermott, C.M., O'Connor, G.C., Peters, L.S., Rice, M.P., Veryzer, R.W. and Rice, M. (2000). *Radical Innovation: How Mature Companies Can Outsmart Upstarts*. Harvard Business School Press, Boston, MA.

O'Connor, G.C., Leifer, R., Paulson, A.S. and Peters, L.S. (2008). *Grabbing Lightning – Building a Capability for Breakthrough Innovation*. Jossey-Bass, San Francisco, CA.

Samuelsen, P. (2011). Research Director of Coloplast Research and VP of Coloplast Incubation (September, 2011).

Sandberg, B. (2008). *Managing and Marketing Radical Innovations*. Routledge, London.

Schmidt, S.E. (2011) Detection of coronary artery disease with an electronic stethoscope. PhD Dissertation, Aalborg University Faculties of Medicine, Dept. of Health Science and Technology.

Semmlow, J.L., Akay, M. and Welkowitz, W. (1990). Noninvasive detection of coronary-artery disease using parametric spectral-analysis methods. *IEEE Engineering in Medicine and Biology Magazine*, 9(1), 33–36.

Semmlow, J.L. and Rahalkar, K. (2007). Acoustic detection of coronary artery disease. *Annual Review of Biomedical Engineering*, 9, 449–469.

Tidd, J. and Bessant, J. (2009). *Managing Innovation – Integrating Technological, Market and Organizational Change, 4th Edition*. Wiley, Chichester.

Chapter 17

Implementing Discontinuous Innovation within Philips Lighting

Dorothea Seebode
formerly Philips, Netherlands
Gerard Harkin
formerly Philips, Netherlands
John Bessant
University of Exeter Business School, UK

Introduction

Innovation management involves mostly steady-state maintenance of a stable position but occasionally also managing the radical, discontinuous shift to a new state. The long-standing challenge here is that capabilities for dealing with one are not the same as the other – the former is about maintenance whilst the latter is about entrepreneurial risk-taking and creation of new possibilities. How does a large established organization deal with this? The difficulty is striking a balance – maintaining the current business through steady-state improvements whilst also allowing some measure of entrepreneurial freedom to some people so that new possibilities can be generated. But how can the tensions between the two approaches be managed?

Perhaps the simplest response is some form of corporate venturing – to spin off, spin out, separate. In human terms it is about giving birth to children who will carry on the line. But another, more tricky approach seeks to engineer a change which retains the new spirit inside the old organization – posing the problem, how can you renew from within?

Implementing Discontinuous Innovation in a Large Organization: The Case of Philips Lighting

This was the challenge facing Philips Lighting in 2000. How could they move from a strong position in what was becoming a very mature market? The original business, founded over 100 years ago, had been about lighting but the limits to growth in what had become a commodity business were clear for all to see. The big question was where and how to move forward, and how to make a radical leap into the future. This wasn't just a matter of finding new ideas but getting acceptance for them, building a new vision of what the company could be – and then implementing it. In other words the challenge was nothing less than one of how to change the corporate mind.

Philips is a global corporation and an internationally recognized brand name, active in a variety of fields with a core emphasis now on healthcare, consumer lifestyle and lighting. Described in its company profile as a 'health and well-being' company, it had a 2007 turnover of €26,793 million and an EBITA of 7.7%.

Philips is one of a relatively small band of firms which have survived longer than a century – the original company was set up in 1891 by Anton and Gerard Philips as Philips Gloeilampenfabrieken N.V. – and the Eindhoven factory they built began producing light bulbs.[a] It has a proud history of innovation and has been responsible for launching several new-to-the-world product categories such as X-ray tubes in its early days, the Compact Cassette in the 1960s, the Compact Disc in the 1980s, and in the early 2000s, Ambilight TV. These successes are linked to Philips' deep understanding of innovation, enabled notably by significant R&D investments and strong traditions in design.

Since 2003, Philips has been engaged in a market-driven change programme to rejuvenate its brand and its approach to new product innovation with fast-moving consumer goods (FMCG) expertise on end-user insights. Eight years later and quite a few more end-user insights

---

[a] This case was originally prepared whilst the authors were part of the change team within Philips and it appears on the website accompanying John Bessant's textbook *Managing Innovation*: www.managing-innovation.com.

more significantly influenced the way Philips innovates, in line with the new brand promise of 'sense and simplicity'. Yet in 2000, new product innovation was still predominantly shaped by R&D, particularly in its lighting business. In that same year Philips, however, incurred a net loss of €3,206 million. Management was focused on dissolving the components business, returning the semiconductor business to profitability, simplifying the organization and making cost savings.

Philips' role in the global lighting industry had always been dominant. Philips Lighting was Philips' cash cow; it operated in a mature, low-growth oligopoly market in which finding new approaches to realize bottom line growth was the main challenge. End-user-driven innovation was a new approach to innovation, perhaps a truly radical one given the division's history. How was this new approach piloted?

Figure 1 gives an overview of this 'radical innovation journey' and in the following sections we will explore a number of themes including the makeup of the innovation team and its mode of operation, the value of key tools and links with the wider business. The chapter concludes with some reflections on the ways in which internal entrepreneurs can introduce radical change.

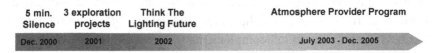

Fig. 1. Radical innovation journey.

Five minutes of silence

In December 2000, the manager of the Central Lighting Development Lab organized an innovation workshop for his group managers. He was responsible for the medium- and long-term innovation of the lamps business and his ambition was to increase the innovation effectiveness of his organization. The workshop's focus was on how to make this shift and it incorporated a creativity component. At the beginning of the two-day workshop the facilitator asked the following question to around 30 participants: 'You say your mission is to be a concept integrator; which types of concepts are you going to develop to safeguard the Lighting Future?'

Silence. For five long minutes, with a growing sense of discomfort, the participants remained quiet as the facilitator let the challenge sink in. People cleared their throats, shuffled chairs, papers, pens and pencils – anything to break the oppressive weight of the silence. Eventually, like a thunderstorm bursting from an impossibly humid night, the storm broke and a flood of talking followed. During the remainder of the workshop the participants struggled to understand what this silence meant and how to deal with it, with the key conclusion that growth would not come from small increments of change, 'doing what we do but better'. Instead they realised there was a need for a radical new vision.

Three exploratory projects in 2001

Following Albert Einstein's notion that 'insanity is doing the same things over and over again and expecting different results', senior management realized that something had to change as an outcome of the workshop. Consequently, in early 2001, the Chief Technology Officer of the lamps business initiated a set of complementary activities of an exploratory nature in order to catalyse learning opportunities and help shape a platform for a future vision. These activities were:

- A vision team in the Central Lighting Development Lab. This involved four employees with an equal male and female representation, two of whom were new to the development lab, while the other two were well-established and anchored informal leaders. The team's role was to bring outside inspiration into the development organization via lectures, workshops, visits and books. These activities resulted in the start of two out-of-the-box innovation projects in 2002, one of which led to the invention of Ambilight TV.

- An exploratory automotive project for car headlights. This involved piloting a combination of the dialogue decision process (DDP)[b] and a Philips Design innovation process based on socio-cultural insights.
- A Philips Lighting New Business Creation (NBC) group. This involved a team of four senior managers and one lateral thinker, whose role was to challenge mainstream business assumptions by asking simple questions. Established as a new organizational unit in a six-month period, the NBC group was set up to provide the environment for out-of-the-box business development. Once the unit was created, the main open question was how to fill the NBC idea pipeline.

The Think the Lighting Future project in 2002

Building on the experiences of these three exploratory projects and using other Philips knowledge on radical innovation, the Think the Lighting Future project (TTLF) was defined at the end of 2001. It was established in response to the CEO's ambition to identify a 10% top-line growth opportunity (approximately €500 million) which could be achieved in a five- to seven-year time frame. Senior management was instrumental in initiating the project.

The project had three tangible deliverables for the end of 2002:

- To clarify alternative scope definitions for Philips Lighting that could deliver 10% top-line growth in the longer term
- To define two to three new business creation projects
- To define a process for knowledge sharing and updating the NBC long-list.

---

[b] See Matheson (1997), *The Smart Organization*. The dialogue decision process suggests a dialogue between a preparation team, gathering relevant information and preparing decision scenarios, and the decision team, taking a high-quality, robust strategic decision with long-term feedback loops.

In addition there were several intangible aspirations for the project – for example, it was envisaged that it would:

- Provide a 'growing in' opportunity for the senior management team, thus creating commitment for additional scope
- Prepare for implementation (avoid the 'not invented here' syndrome) for critical mass of colleague
- Radiate, letting involved colleagues experience that the whole exercise is about doing different things ... and doing them differently
- Create the confidence to deal with a stretching vision.

The TTLF project was a 'presidential project' with core team participation from each Lighting business group, Philips Design and Philips Research, which was – next to its scope of ten years ahead – an innovation in itself. In addition, special attention was put on forming a diverse team to enable different views to be captured. Importantly this project provided opportunities for learning and improving the corporate innovation process – for example, the original three-step design process (information sharing, ideation, idea development and concept definition) was expanded by a fourth step (translation to action). Emphasis was also placed on creating broad ownership from the beginning, both in management via the DDP approach and in the executing functions via multi-functional workshops. Subsequently the dialogue process has been expanded to a 'trialogue' process between decision team, core team (or decision preparation team) and implementation team.

At the end of 2002, TTLF was concluded and was regarded as a successful exploration and visioning project. It led to the selection of a theme for new business: Atmosphere Provider, which was about 'empowering people to become their own light designers'.

It also led to three new business creation projects and delivered a list of ideas for new business creation. However, no additional turnover had yet been generated. The real work was about to start...

An unplanned, yet crucial incubation time: January to June 2003...

Due to internal restructuring, the first six months of 2003 turned out to be an incubation time for the new business theme, Atmosphere Provider. Formal progression of the project was on hold while other developments across the business took shape. For example, the NBC group's mission was redefined and it became the Solid-State Lighting business group. Consequently, the intended 'landing point' for Atmosphere Provider no longer existed. Eventually a new home was identified and Atmosphere Provider became the first Lighting-wide market-driven innovation theme in the global marketing organization.

These six months' incubation time proved later to have been an important 'sanity check' for the seriousness of the organization to engage in something radically different. Two members of the TTLF project continued to work on Atmosphere Provider, safeguarding the smooth transfer of the vision and both explicit and implicit knowledge about the theme and the cooperation spirit established during TTLF.

It was also during this period that Atmosphere Provider became more deeply rooted in a network of around ten colleagues at different levels and functions of the organization. In many conversations the 'quality' of the innovation challenge ahead was discussed (radical innovation, beyond incremental product improvements), the need for a different culture became explicit (see Fig. 2) and a shared intention and passion grew to make it happen.

PHILIPS

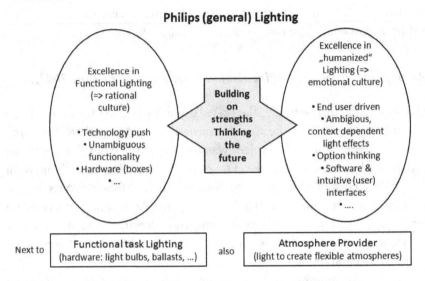

Fig. 2. The Atmosphere Provider innovation challenge.

Besides, the two former TTLF participants started to explore more deeply what 'end-user-driven' meant, identifying the scattered pockets of knowledge in Philips that were also exploring this new way of working and working on a comprehensive document to capture and structure all the Atmosphere Provider-relevant socio-cultural trend research in an absorbable format. For the first time in Philips Lighting, marketing knowledge was included in a roadmap of emerging, implicit, explicit and mature needs.

The Atmosphere Provider programme: July 2003 to December 2005

In July 2003 senior management launched the Atmosphere Provider programme. The programme lasted two and a half years and was given some explicit and several implicit deliverables.

Explicit:

- Bring Atmosphere Provider as a theme to life.

- Create a 'need-scape' for the new innovation area
- Envisage the boundaries/solution space of the innovation and growth opportunities
- Initiate the creation of a related patent portfolio.
- Prove the business potential by piloting the three new business creation projects.
  - Exploration towards new business proposition definition including initial product concepts
  - Prototyping and market testing
  - Business case development and transfer to mainstream business.

Implicit:

- Prepare for transfer and scaling up
- Initiate the building of an Atmosphere Provider network (with shared vision, creativity, cross-functional and cross-disciplinary perspectives, embracing the required new way of working, etc.)
- Pioneer end-user-driven innovation.

The programme was set up so that theme development and new business creation cross-fertilized each other; emerging insights from creating the new business were captured via foundation documents (mentioned earlier); general observations derived from the theme development were fed back into NBC projects.

The core of the programme was a team of four people: the overall programme manager who had led the TTLF project and three project managers, of whom one had been a TTLF core team member; the other two were new to Philips Lighting. Over time, a small support team became involved: a lighting designer, an experienced market researcher, a marketing specialist and several colleagues from Philips Design. The team was small and flexible; additional skills and capacity were brought in on an as-needed basis, which in turn required good communication skills from the project managers and commitment from senior management to ensure the needed resources were made available to the team when required.

One of the projects: Light Embedded in Furniture

Unlike today, in 2003 Philips Lighting had less structured processes in place for handling new business creation projects with significant complexity in terms of applications, technologies, business models, new alliances, etc. All Atmosphere Provider projects followed the phases described here. The duration of the phases differed depending on the degree of newness of the exploration area.

The project's two-and-a-half-year timeline was comprised of three core phases:

- Exploration to define the business proposition and product categories (12 months)
- Prototyping and market testing (9 months)
- Writing the business case, preparing for alliances and transferring the results to a business unit (9 months).

Phase 1: Exploration

Philips Lighting's mainstream culture – a culture steeped in successful product innovation – put emphasis on speed and throughput time, on functional lighting and new product definition.

- There were historical organizational beliefs that hampered exploration
- It wasn't apparent that different skills and tools were needed for exploration
- There was mounting pressure to complete the exploration as quickly as possible.

It was believed that it would take just a few weeks for the project team to define the proposition using traditional business tools and processes. Senior management, on the other hand, was more patient.

Exploration ended after 12 months with a new business proposition, seven product concept ideas across different product categories, ideas for service-based revenue streams and new business models for a newly emerging Philips Lighting business category. A comparison between exploration in steady-state[c] and radical innovation projects is shown in Table 1.

Table 1. Comparing steady-state and radical innovation in the exploration phase.

	Product innovation	**New business creation arising from radical innovation**
Key deliverables	Product proposition with target group and customer insight	New business proposition, ideas for product categories, service-based revenue streams, business model and a project vision embodied by the team
Duration of phase *	Approximately 2–3 months	Up to 9–12 months
Key skills	Generic project management skills and techniques for the idea and opportunity stages in an innovation process	As per steady-state but including: 1. Personal skills – intuition, natural timing, personal vision, reflection, awareness of the company's implicit beliefs, creating buy-in 2. Innovation skills – facilitation, ideation, workshop design

* Depends on many factors such as the level of environmental complexity, team size, organizational capability, management support, budget, etc.

Phase 2: Prototyping and market testing

This phase brought the vision and proposition to life with prototyped concepts showcased in a dedicated room at the Philips Lighting Application Centre in Eindhoven.

---

[c] There are different notions of innovation within existing product categories: incremental innovation, roadmap innovation, steady-state innovation, etc.

The prototypes formed an important bridge between the pioneers and mainstream business worlds. They helped people envisage the business potential and were a powerful communication tool for a range of target groups including Philips staff, furniture industry manufacturers, product development teams, market researchers and existing customers who wanted to see Philips Lighting's latest innovations.

The seven concepts were evaluated in market research. This led to prioritization, further end-user insight refinements and quantitative assessments.

Table 2 presents a comparison of steady-state and radical innovation in the prototyping and market-testing phase.

Table 2. Comparing steady-state and radical innovation in the prototyping and market-testing phase.

	Product innovation	New business creation arising from radical innovation
Key deliverables	Build a product prototype, conduct market testing, refine the product concept	Multiple hardware/software concepts shown in a context specific space. Qualitative and quantitative market testing. End-user insights. Inspire organizational momentum
Duration of phase*	Approximately 3–4 months	Up to 9 months
Key skills	Generic project management skills and techniques for a proposition stage in an innovation process	As per steady-state but including: 1. Personal skills – courage, stamina, patience, managing expectations, evangelizing, overcoming organizational resistance to the new vision 2. Innovation skills – prototyping a business theme rather than a single product, end-user insights

* Depends on many factors such as the level of environmental complexity, team size, organizational capability, management support, budget, etc.

Phase 3: Writing the business case, preparing for alliances and transferring the results to a business unit

By July 2005 the project was at a stage where a concrete business case could be written. In addition, the case was prepared for building strategic alliances with furniture companies. Successful meetings were held with industry leaders followed by a series of workshops. The project was then gradually transferred into the Solid-State Lighting business group.

As the project came to an end the team were visited by the then four board members of Philips Electronics, including CEO Gerard Kleisterlee. This was a strong sign of leadership and the hands-on approach by top management regarding growth and radical innovation. A smile and thumbs up from Gerard Kleisterlee was recognition that the team had successfully explored a new and exciting business opportunity.

Table 3 compares steady-state and radical innovation in the business case phase.

Table 3. Comparing steady-state and radical innovation in the business case phase.

	Product innovation	New business creation arising from radical innovation
Key deliverables	Approved business case with go-to-market plans	Approved business case. Furniture industry partners interested. Project transferred to correct business unit
*Duration of phase**	Approximately 2–3 months	Up to 9 months
Key skills	Generic project management skills and techniques for an investment stage in an innovation process	As per steady-state but including: 1. Personal skills – awareness of the mindset and cultural issues in relating to other industries 2. Innovation skills – being the proposition's guardian

* Depends on many factors such as the level of environmental complexity, team size, organizational capability, management support, budget, etc.

The end of the journey

By the end of 2005:

- In total > 1,800 people had been involved globally, cross-business group (BG) and beyond Philips Lighting
- Three foundation documents were published, > 1,000 copies distributed
- Patents: > 50 IDs submitted, > 25 patents filed, > 10 patents in pipeline.

Way of Working, Tools and Team

The previous section gave an overview of the events that marked the journey along its track. More detail as to how the journey was realized can be found in the following specifics regarding ways of working, some of the more important tools and dynamics around team-building. To grasp them more clearly, the beginning of the journey must be readdressed.

TTLF: The 'trialogue' process, creativity tools and visualization

Vital to orchestrating communication was the setup of TTLF as an extended dialogue ('trialogue') decision process around three key innovation dimensions:

- *People* – understanding and serving both end-users' explicit, current as well as their implicit, emerging needs.
- *Technology* – understanding and using current and emerging technology options to enable user-relevant functionality.
- *Business* – understanding current and emerging market characteristics and dynamics; applying appropriate, future-proof business models.

The major workload was carried by the core team of seven people, which was supported by a top management coaching team, whose role was to help translate the workshop results into the correct language and context for senior management. Since the project had a scope within Philips Lighting, but also beyond it, senior management acted as a steering committee and decision team; the CEO of Lighting took the role of project owner. This was essential since it gave the project the required weight and visibility.

Thirty-two colleagues were invited to two workshops. They came from different innovation backgrounds (marketing, business development and R&D) and from different Lighting businesses, Philips Design and Philips Research. Maximal possible global presence was established. Since TTLF was a highly visible presidential project, workshop participation was seen as an honour. The workshops served several tangible and intangible purposes, including:

- Enriching the core team work with existing corporate knowledge
- Generation of seeds for business ideas
- Preparing for later implementation
- Building a 'performing' team around a shared vision.

All workshop flows and all tools used during the workshops were specially designed such that the holistic outcomes became highly probable by simultaneously focusing equally on the different dimensions: *people* and their needs, *technology* enabling related new solution spaces and *business* (including generic competition, existing and emerging business models facilitating value creation).

The first workshop was about understanding the current business situation, looking at socio-cultural and technology trends, introducing emerging business models and potential generic competition. After the workshop, all information was documented in 'The Future Landscape' and made available to the steering committee and workshop participants, as preparation material for the ideation phase. This workshop played a very important role in terms of team building. In order to take participants 'out of the box', it used a variety of tools to bridge ideas in cross-functional groups and much of the workshop process involved building a shared vision and linkages across these groups.

In the second workshop around 140 business idea seeds were generated, of which 42 were further matured. The ideation teams were challenged to think from different geographical contexts and needs: Europe, North America, China and India. Ideation templates and specific creativity tools were developed (for example, building upon Edward de Bono's six thinking hats and lateral thinking methods (de Bono, 1985)).

Since any idea needed to incorporate all dimensions – people, technology and business – many 'rudimentary idea spots' were dismissed during the team process. This also increased the team spirit and mutual trust between the different disciplines and created an understanding for the complementarities of skills and competencies.

The third workshop was attended by senior management, which was a sign of their active interest and involvement in the project. Eleven possible scope extensions for the company were distilled from the initial 140+ ideas from the ideation session. Of the 11 options, senior management selected a theme called Atmosphere Provider as the company's scope extension to focus on in the coming years. The decision was in line with the contemporary Philips corporate discussion of healthcare, lifestyle and technology; in addition there was a feeling that it could deliver 10% top-line growth, it was consistent with many trends in the domain of business, people and technology, and other industries had previously transitioned from being component suppliers to higher-value products and services, the paint industry being one example. For the first time in its more than 100-year history, Philips Lighting had decided upon a fully people- and application-driven innovation theme, rather than the traditional technology-driven approach.

The fourth phase of the TTLF project was about creating a deeper understanding of the Atmosphere Provider challenge from many different angles. To support this, an Atmosphere Provider theme map reflecting the starting dimensions of people, technology and business was created. This theme map aided the selection process for the three new business creation projects that would form a basis of the Atmosphere Provider programme. Projects were selected so that they contained different newness levels to phase potential market entries. It was envisaged that a project with only one newness dimension would mature towards market readiness quicker than a project with multiple newness dimensions. Another consideration for the project definition was the complementarities between Atmosphere Provider parameters and new skills.

In this way three new business creation projects were carefully chosen on the basis of their potential to enrich the understanding of the Atmosphere Provider growth area, to build the right sorts of new capabilities and to identify new business models at Philips Lighting. The three projects were:

- *Flexible ambience in shops* – a new use of light in an existing application area. Since Philips Lighting had a prominent market share in the retail lighting business, this project would help shape the next evolution of that business.
- *Light embedded in furniture* – a new use of light in a new application area. This was new for Philips Lighting and it made sense for a variety of reasons: furniture is widely used for creating an atmosphere, alliances with furniture companies would be an important strategic consideration, embedded light could enable new business model opportunities, etc.
- *Light and fragrance* – a new use of light combined with a new sense (for a lighting company) in a new application area. This project was chosen due to the understanding that the perception of any atmosphere is based on multi-sensorial experiences.

Theme development: Atmosphere Provider foundation documents

Three foundation documents were published during the course of the Atmosphere Provider programme. Their purpose was to create a shared global understanding of this emerging growth opportunity and to provide the frameworks and communication tools for people from different functions, locations and hierarchical levels to have consistent conversations on the same topic, beyond their personal interpretation of an abstract notion such as Atmosphere Provider. Each document had a specific focus and was around 60–90 pages:

- *'Understand and Imagine Atmosphere'*, the first document, was people-centric. It decoded the meaning behind the word 'atmosphere', introduced a 'need-scape' framework for people's atmosphere needs and mapped these needs onto the market areas of home, workplace, commerce and outdoors with a view to identifying how willing people are to buy lighting solutions to fulfil their needs and how this willingness might change over ten years. This document also showed 21 cutting-edge examples of where light was being used as a form of Atmosphere Provider.

- *'Talk Atmosphere'*, the second document, was published in August 2004. While running the three projects it became evident that there was a language gap between the existing language for talking about lighting products and the anticipated language associated with Atmosphere Provider solutions. The new language with which to discuss the emotional and aesthetic qualities of light was uncovered by building on the projects' experiences and by involving different atmosphere creation experts such as light designers, interior designers, cognitive psychologists, etc. Besides this, suggestions were made about how to talk about these qualities with respect to atmosphere creation.

- *'Create and Build Atmosphere'*, the third document, was published in May 2005. It provided an insight into the different steps and process that people can take to enhance the atmosphere of their environments with light. Here the essence of the vision was formulated as 'Be enabled to be your own light designer'. Besides this it introduced an overview of the future functionality of lighting solutions for atmosphere creation and the impact this would have on technology roadmaps and intellectual property.

The creation of foundation documents represented a key mechanism for capturing and making explicit what had been shared, learnt and experienced – and also provided a way of communicating this to others. Writing the documents involved many different experts, mainly from within Philips. This approach brought in many perspectives and built commitment (another lever for facilitating change). Almost 2,000 booklets were distributed and went on to influence marketing strategies, sales training courses at the Lighting Academy, technology programmes and innovation roadmaps. Writing the documents also brought another important benefit – it forced the Atmosphere Provider core team of four to stay focused on the bigger picture of Atmosphere Provider as well as the new business creation projects. This provided a unique coherence because the shared overall vision was woven into the new business projects. This differs from some other change initiatives where the vision teams and new business teams are different groups of people.

Special attention was put on the graphical design and layout of the documents, since it needed to:

- Radiate the spirit of the Atmosphere Provider theme
- Provide a lot of deep knowledge in an easily absorbable way
- Inspire and enable the reader to start to contribute and act upon the vision.

Significantly, the original three documents are still in use by members of Philips Lighting, Philips Research and Philips Design.

Communication: Metaphors, concept demonstrators, visualizations

> You don't see something until you have the right metaphor to let you perceive it.
> – Thomas Kuhn (Kuhn, 1962)

It is worth exploring in more detail the challenge of creating a shared language in communicating and shaping the Atmosphere Provider ideas. Atmosphere Provider started off as very ambiguous with fairly unknown applications, processes, skills and tools – and, not surprisingly, the existing corporate mind did not understand what it was about. This led to early communication challenges – for example, when talking about progress and next steps with senior management they came up with unrealistic targets and timelines. This was a natural response –

essentially while monitoring and reviewing projects they were operating on an 'unconscious' level, shaped by the implicit – built over decades – knowledge of the corporate culture. Inevitably this led to some misunderstandings and tensions.

Metaphors

In order to make the difference between the two worlds explicit, the following truck and jungle metaphor (see Fig. 3), envisaging the difference between an 'operational excellence' way of working and a 'radical innovation' mindset, was introduced in one of the first senior management meetings of 2004.

This was a very important step to ensure confidence and keep space for further exploration. The metaphor resonated with senior management and they were open to the new insights that would come from exploring the Atmosphere Provider theme. This metaphor was also regularly used by different people to help bridge both worlds.

How to manage both cultures under one roof?

It's about **DISCOVERY**
It's about **ADAPTABILITY**
It's about **TRUST**

It's about **Efficiency Increase**
It's about **Optimization**
It's about **Control**

Fig. 3. The truck and jungle metaphor. The lorry on the road representing the well-known organisational routines and the jungle representing the chaos of the discontinuous innovation world.

Concept demonstrators

A new vision can evoke mixed reactions – some people's response when seeing the new prototypes was 'Where are the light bulbs?' – the 'known' business frame. So concept demonstrators and good timing also play a very important role in communication. At the steering committee meeting in early 2004, the demonstrator for the flexible ambience in shops projects was available for senior management to see, experience and play with – the 'seeing is believing' effect. The prototypes challenged a deeply entrenched Philips Lighting belief that they were in the business of making and selling light bulbs and other lighting-related hardware. From that day onwards the project team provided a short introductory talk before showing the Atmosphere Provider concepts, which managed expectations and helped people shift from a 'light-bulb mindset' towards something very new to the mainstream organization: putting the people in the centre of the story by talking about light effects and the impact of light effects on human wellbeing. This strengthened their understanding of the Atmosphere Provider theme and what the team was working on.

Soon, the demonstrator was also used by mainstream business to offer a special 'outlook into the future' for preferred customers. In the coming years hundreds of Philips colleagues and customers saw the demonstrators and this helped evangelize the Atmosphere Provider story and build commitment throughout many parts of the company.

Team: Diversity, management of expectations and consistency, coaching team

Since all change and innovation is ultimately carried forward by people, special attention was put on team building, inclusion of as much diversity as possible and open and trustful cooperation between different functions and hierarchical levels. Building momentum was a key requirement for spreading the vision and engaging a growing circle of players outside the core team. The 'ripple' model was crucial to building momentum and ensuring that the radical project started to become embedded within the mainstream of the business.

Diversity

The risk in a renewed effort for vision-building is that the new vision can easily become replication of the previous version. To avoid easy replication and to draw on explorations already going on elsewhere in the organization, efforts were made to recruit and maintain diversity across the growing teams involved in the process. As there were only very few members, it was even more important to ensure they differed in their perspective. In the selection was also an element of seeking out 'internal entrepreneurs' – people with the willingness to explore openly and take risks.

An important element in choosing candidates for the Atmosphere Provider team was their openness to learn and their pioneering attitude. Candidates were explicitly asked if they were able to cope with risks, what drove them in their lives and how important a 'quick and straight career path' was to them. It was made explicit from the very start that this was an out-of-the-box assignment.

As the projects gathered momentum, this diversity became a source of 'creative conflict'. For example, during the first Think the Lighting Future workshop it became clear that there was growing competition around which group represented the 'most creative' within the organization. This issue was explored openly in one of the plenary sessions. Fortunately the overall atmosphere during the workshop was so future-oriented and optimistic, that the group could grow beyond this dissonance and start to appreciate each other for the ways they complement each other. This was an important prerequisite for co-creating business idea seeds in the second workshop – it helped bring the groups out of their dominant design or technology orientation and generate concepts (business ideas) which built *across* their functional areas. The sequencing of the workshops with a four-week gap between them helped separate out early information sharing across these diverse groups and the later shared idea generation around new business possibilities.

Management of expectations and consistency

Facilitating the (highly experimental) TTLF project was accompanied by some challenges:

- *Managing expectations* – both the decision team and the workshop participants came from very diverse backgrounds, with varying personal and professional experiences and expectations. It was therefore very important to clearly explain what would be the tasks and what results could be expected. Working with metaphors helped, as did introducing visualizations and re-using them consistently throughout the whole process. It was also helpful that both the workshops and the board presentations radiated through their setup and execution that something different was going on.
- *Development and use of appropriate language* – the multidisciplinarity of the workshop team required a conscious choice of language. Additionally the board presentations radiated the newness of the approach through their conventional formats.
- *Encouraging and enabling reflection as the key to understanding, navigating, adjusting, communicating and managing expectations* – this also provided the starting point for the identification of appropriate metaphors.

During later stages it became important to maintain enough core capacity and understanding to provide the nucleus around which the project could grow – even during periods when corporate attention was diverted elsewhere. During the six-month incubation period between exploratory work (TTLF) and the Atmosphere Provider programme it was critical that two members of the TTLF project continued to work on Atmosphere Provider. These were the TTLF project manager who became the Atmosphere Provider programme manager and a core team member, who became responsible for one of the new business creation projects. These two safeguarded the smooth transfer of the vision and both visible and invisible knowledge about the theme and cooperation spirit established during the TTLF project. It was also during this period that the Atmosphere Provider theme became more deeply rooted in a network of around ten colleagues at different levels and functions of the organization. In many conversations the 'quality' of the innovation challenge ahead was discussed, and the need for a change in culture made apparent, from which a shared vision grew so that change could be implemented.

Coaching team

Another core theme was the challenge to appropriately communicate with senior management, thus maintaining their interest and support and to engage with them as partners rather than simply as sponsors. For example, in the early TTLF work conversations were structured around an underlying metaphor of the captain of a big tanker meeting the captain of a speed boat, both sharing responsibility for the company's future in an interdependent way with very different, yet complementary skills, resources and approaches. This shared responsibility was made explicit by signing the project start-up document at the beginning of the project.

   Steering committee meetings were about maintaining and nurturing the confidence into the future and providing a learning opportunity for senior management to understand the characteristics of the emerging radical innovation beyond incremental innovation and operational excellence. A key model of value was that of a 'coaching team' developed in TTLF and deployed again in Atmosphere Provider. In this capacity, the core project team met regularly with senior executives; initially this was about knowledge sharing, discussing progress and building trust. But experience in TTLF suggested that this group could also provide a valuable bridge to senior management elsewhere in Philips – for example, playing a 'translator' role, helping the Atmosphere Provider team to prepare for the senior management meetings and then to 'decode' these meetings afterwards. This was critical to manage expectations.

Later – when the Atmosphere Provider projects entered the phase of being transferred to a mainstream business – the coaching team role further developed to a 'godfather' role. 'Godfathers' were those managers who would most likely incorporate the projects into their business portfolio.

This approach had two advantages:

- The 'godfather' had the opportunity to become familiar with the new business for his organization
- The project manager was helped to understand how to prepare for a successful transfer.

Outcome

So was it worth it? How much changed as a result of the growing momentum behind radical change initiatives? Is innovation in the lighting division today significantly different from 2001 when the journey began? We can answer that in a number of ways.

Lighting remains one of the core strengths within Philips. The journey towards a new approach began back at the end of 2000 and has resulted in quite a shift in the business (Table 4). The envisioning project (TTLF) and Atmosphere Provider programme described here are successful examples of a variety of activities that were executed to rejuvenate the lighting business in the early 2000s. Currently, one of the strategic directions of Philips Lighting is scene-setting, a more concrete formulation of Atmosphere Provider.

Within Philips, the lighting division has once again strengthened its significance as one of the legs on which the future of the overall corporation stands (the others being consumer lifestyle and healthcare). Within Philips Lighting, there has been an expansion in its range of activities with the setting up of several new divisions to take advantage of opportunities. Within these divisions a wide range of new products are emerging. The seeds for current Philips flagship products such as Ambilight TV and Living Colors were developed in the course of the radical innovation journey described here.

Table 4. Comparing 2002 and 2009.

2002	2009
Lamps	Lamps
Luminaires	Professional luminaires and systems Consumer luminaires and systems
Lighting electronics	Lighting electronics and controls
Automotive and special lighting applications	Automotive and special lighting applications
	Solid-state lighting components and modules

Along the way considerable learning has taken place. The original pilot projects explored areas such as dynamic lighting in retailing, lighting embedded in furniture, links between lighting and other senses such as smell. Not all of these have moved into full-scale development, but the projects helped explore the space which lighting as atmosphere provider might create. These projects acted as seeds, providing further input to R&D, design, market research and beyond.

The process also provided valuable integrating mechanisms, drawing together different groups from across Philips – in fields such as technology development, R&D, design and marketing – and focusing their experience and interest on some core projects. These experimental and prototype ideas provided boundary objects which focused widely differing views and ideas and laid new pathways for future cooperation. In this sense there was an element of rewiring the corporate brain to work with new concepts – essentially the principle underlying Henderson and Clark's work on architectural innovation (1990).

Key Lessons for Innovation Management

Clearly, radical change not only involves the stages of formal projects and development programmes. Those explicit elements are surrounded by a complex, invisible architecture, composed of structures and processes designed to deal with the anxieties, aspirations, conflicts and other emotional elements which inevitably emerge during radical and risky change. What can be learned from exploring the contours of this invisible architecture during the innovation journey at Philips Lighting?

Think big! En-VISION the future

What emerged from the five-minute silence was an awareness of the lack of a compelling vision for radical alternatives to provide the growth the company needed. Creating, exploring and building such a vision then became the key task in the early projects which the Chief Technology Officer piloted and the CEO commissioned – essentially finding a target towards which a growing number of people could focus their innovation ideas and their creative energies.

Imagining the future and translating it into actionable opportunities is an explicit skill with a specific terminology. 'Big business' potential is captured by innovation themes that materialize in clusters of (cross-BG) product families – not in incremental product innovations.

Coaching team

Involving senior management in informal coaching sessions with the core teams of both the TTLF and Atmosphere Provider programmes was important, as was the creation of their 'godfather' roles when the new business creation projects matured to be transferred to mainstream organizations. The coaching team built a credible bridge to their colleagues in senior management, thus playing a crucial role in supporting the creation of a space for a high-risk activity within which ideas can incubate and be explored. They also helped to manage the senior management expectations, expand mental models and increase their degree of understanding of the characteristics of the chosen radical innovation path.

It can start with an incident, yet is a long journey

It is rare that people change their minds in a flash. Change is challenging and often seen as threatening, so bringing people along at a pace which allows them to let go of old (and reliable) ways of framing the world and take on a new vision needs to be seen as a learning process. Managing radical innovation as a phased journey – and using a map of the phases to guide the process – is critical.

The dialogue between intuition and facts

Intuition played an important role on the journey that followed the five-minute silence; especially throughout the TTLF and Atmosphere Provider programmes. In personal and group reflections an explicit dialogue was established that created the awareness that both intuition and facts are important compasses towards the right decisions. Regular team days were common for the TTLF and Atmosphere Provider core teams – giving the opportunity to reflect, validate with facts and then tune in to the current and next steps.

Building momentum means building community

The process of persuasion, of bringing others on board and building momentum, is not simply a matter of presenting a more compelling business case. It involves recognizing that there is a strong emotional dimension – people have commitments to the old models, may feel (justifiably) anxious about the uncertain new model, especially since by its nature it is tricky and uncertain. Letting go requires both a compelling vision towards which people can focus their emotional energies and some reasoned case for making the move. Early on in the process the information available about markets, technologies, competitors, etc., will be very limited and so the need for emotional support (energy around a vision, passion and enthusiasm for the new) has to be emphasized; as more is learned (via prototypes, test marketing, etc.) so the business case can take shape and reinforce the commitment to the new model.

It involves building and expanding a community of people who believe in the new idea and can then share it with others – essentially following an 'epidemic' model. In the early stages the core team requires a high degree of flexibility – the ability to explore, try out and let go of new concepts as they emerge. Gradually this will take shape – via a common language and vision – into a core concept which can be taken to the wider organization. But it is also important to ensure that – whilst the group needs a degree of autonomy early on in the process – there is provision for re-integrating that team back into the mainstream of the organization.

Working in integral projects first creates language tensions, and later enables quick decision-making, as all necessary perspectives are represented. Besides this they can provide the organizational elasticity for achieving results in risky and dynamic contexts.

The pioneer dilemma

If you talk about something new in the old language you lose its essence, if you describe the new with a new language, nobody understands what you want to say... The core group needs a common vision and language – the case shows the key role images and metaphors played in helping to define and shape the vision, especially in the early stages. As 'tangible' results are achieved, metaphors become useful to explain what the radical innovation team is doing – they become a strategic tool helping to create a dialogue between the different working styles, frame the demonstrators and manage expectations.

Boundary objects help engage others in shaping the future vision – and in bridging between their world and the new one. Making the vision real through physical prototypes provides experience and validation, since seeing and feeling is believing. At the same time capturing and articulating what is being learned and sharing – via the foundation documents – helps cement the new thinking in people's minds.

References

de Bono, E. (1985). *Six Thinking Hats*. Penguin, Harmondsworth.

Henderson, R. and K. Clark (1990). Architectural innovation: The reconfiguration of existing product technologies and the failure of established firms. *Administrative Science Quarterly,* 35, 9–30.

Kuhn, T. (1962). *The Structure of Scientific Revolutions*. Chicago University Press, Chicago.

Matheson, D. (1997). *The Smart Organization*. Harvard Business School Press, Boston.

Chapter 18

Fighting the Unknown – With Business Design

Manuel Götzendörfer
UnternehmerTUM, Germany

Introduction

Since the beginning of time, the success of innovations has been founded on knowledge advantages. Organisations can develop their edge in this area by acquiring new insights or cross-linking existing knowledge. In this context you can understand every innovation process as a learning process (Beckman and Barry, 2007). The goal of learning is ultimately to bridge knowledge gaps – and principles of design may have much to contribute to the process. This case study from the retail sector shows exactly how these principles can be applied, describing one example of an innovation project that put a business design approach into practice.

The Fear of Failure

Even today, fear of failure remains a key reason for many organisations not to capitalise fully on their innovative potential. Often, businesses prefer instead to opt for incremental change. This kind of fear is frequently caused by corporate cultures that make no allowance for conscious failure; many organisations simply do not plan for experimentation as a means of proceeding towards new horizons. Moreover, the problem appears all the more critical when one considers the fact that, in corporate practice as well as the sciences and politics, there is a broad consensus that in this age of global market mechanisms innovative ability counts as an essential factor for success as well as for survival (The Boston Consulting Group, Inc., 2010).

Against this background, it would appear interesting to examine the root causes of failure, as it is these that ultimately provoke feelings of fear. One major component of failure lies in a lack of knowledge. The question, therefore, is how to deal explicitly with knowledge shortfalls. For any innovation project, it is vital that every effort is made to tackle or fill any knowledge gaps in the early stages of work. And it is here that the working methods and principles of design offer a promising approach.

Business Design for Innovation

Based on knowledge issues within innovation projects, a business design approach was developed during a research project at UnternehmerTUM, the Centre for Innovation and Business Creation at the Technical University of Munich.

In a business and innovation context, the term 'design' signifies a generic approach to the resolution of a wide range of different problem types (Rand, 2000). This broader understanding of the term is becoming increasingly widespread in the sciences as well as in business practice, and its working methods are well suited to a range of applications. These include product and service design, process and business model design, or the design of entire organisations (Beckman and Barry, 2007).

In line with the concept of design outlined here, the business design approach centres on six principles (Fig. 1). These represent the fundamental mindset for this approach. Identified as the central elements of any innovation project, they can support a more conscious approach towards dealing with knowledge gaps by bridging them as early as possible in order to reduce risks. The six principles of business design can be applied in all three phases of the innovation process: search, select and implement.

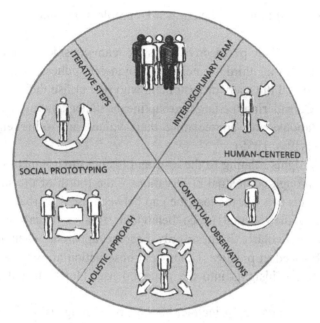

Fig. 1. The mindset of business design: Six design principles.

Design Principles as Fundamental Mindset

The business design approach is suitable for use by innovation teams from a range of different disciplines. With appropriate mentoring and the right experience, everybody on the project can become a business designer.

The first important factor is the interdisciplinary team. From the outset, this should include members from a wide range of areas across the organisation who bring with them a broad spectrum of qualifications.

This will enable the task at hand to be viewed from a wide range of different perspectives. Working in an interdisciplinary team is also a way of ensuring that influences and interests from a wide range of areas are taken into account as the task is resolved (Kanter, 1988).

Closely linked to this first design principle is the second, that of the holistic perspective. This encourages the project team to think in terms of systems but also to draw inspiration from other areas and industries to

Discontinuous Innovation

develop long-term approaches towards problem resolution (Papanek, 1984).

While the holistic perspective helps the team consider a wide variety of influences, the third principle, human-centredness, helps them examine in detail the users or customers who will utilise their solution in the future. Considering the target group means understanding their needs and expectations, and appreciating their values and other emotional aspects (Dreyfuss, 1955).

Many insights relating to the user and his/her environment can only be gained through contextual observations – the fourth of the six design principles. This sets out to close the gap between users' verbal or written accounts and their actual usage behaviour. It also reveals additional influences, particularly if these only become apparent when they are actually observed in practice. Contextual observation allows the team to gain elementary insights into the potential user (Johnson and Maston, 1998).

As the next design principle, social prototyping uses visualisation techniques to encourage creativity and communications within the project team. It also allows the project team to gain feedback from potential customers, users and experts early on in the development process (Schrage, 1993).

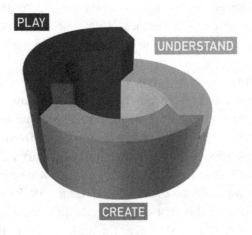

Fig. 2. Steps of an iterative approach.

Social prototyping also fosters the team to work on several solution options. These should be evaluated by social prototyping and reduced to their most promising elements. Once optimised through a series of iterations, the resulting options will offer the best possible end solution. The principle of iterative steps (Fig. 2) works by building up knowledge that can then be translated into visual ideas for solutions to generate swift feedback that will provide the foundation required for the next iteration (Dreyfuss, 1955).

Designing the Future of Retail Shopping: Multimedia Mobile Shopping Assistant

To show more clearly what the business design approach consists of and demonstrate what it can contribute to the way knowledge gaps are handled, this chapter details a case study. The innovation project outlined was a joint undertaking by UnternehmerTUM, Metro AG and Wanzl GmbH. Carried out as part of the Metro Future Store Initiative, the goal was to create a hybrid product combining product and service innovation.

The Future Store is an important component in the innovative strength of Metro. As a kind of innovation lab, it replicates real conditions in the type of self-service store ordinary customers use to do their daily shopping. The 'lab' has already produced a number of solutions around the issue of the Mobile Shopping Assistant, many of which rely heavily on the use of mobile telephones.

Given the rising customer demand for information and service, the project team was tasked with taking a broader view on the issue of the Shopping Assistant and set out to develop a range of concepts for a Multimedia Mobile Shopping Assistant (MMSA). This was to be done by generating a range of possible solutions that would combine ways of transporting purchases, storage options for the duration of the shopping trip, and information and service.

Convergence upon the unknowns

Working towards a holistic approach to process the task, the project team first of all set out to acquire a broad basic knowledge. On the basis of its analyses, it was able to build up a holistic picture of existing customer retail requirements. These were then clustered into specific search fields: standard shoppers, children, older shoppers, trolley, infotainment and entertainment. Next, the team developed a wide range of ideas as to where improvements might be made in each area. The different suggestions they came up with were then combined to produce new overall concepts. These concepts were translated into prototypes that the team then discussed with potential customers. After several iterations, a final concept for a solution emerged, which Metro and Wanzl followed up during the next stage of development.

In the following we describe how the innovation project applied each individual design principle to support the way it handled uncertainties.

Interdisciplinary team

The project team consisted of five students from different fields: aerospace engineering, technology and management-oriented business studies, information technology, business informatics, and comparative cultural sciences, Romance studies and psychology. This mixture of different disciplines was a major factor in enabling a wide range of perspectives to be introduced into the project team's work on the task. It also enabled them to adopt techniques from different areas, for example as they worked to generate ideas for solutions. The interdisciplinary nature of the team had a particularly positive effect on cross-linking knowledge from different fields, which in turn brought benefits in other respects such as the evaluation of possible solutions. Here, the team were able to address successfully a number of different uncertainties surrounding the solution options they had generated, including technical, business and social concerns.

Human-centredness

After carrying out an initial stakeholder analysis, the project team focused its efforts on the needs and expectations of potential Shopping Assistant users. In many innovation projects, considerable uncertainty surrounds the issue of users' needs and expectations, but in this instance broad-based research (see holistic perspective) enabled the project team to identify a series of different user groups: standard shoppers, children and the elderly.

For each of these groups, a specific set of needs was identified. Standard shoppers (i.e. middle-aged males and females), for example, value the ability to locate products easily, compare product qualities and ensure they have the right trolley. They also view the ergonomics of loading and unloading their shopping as being among the most important aspects of shopping.

Another significant stakeholder group the project team identified was children. Integrating, transporting and occupying them while shopping presented a particular challenge. However, once their needs are met, the shopping experience will become all the more satisfying for their parents.

The third important group the project team identified was the elderly, whose specific needs were also examined closely. Here, physical restrictions such as impaired vision, muscular weakness and deteriorating motor functions had to be dealt with.

By investigating prospective users in such great detail, the project team were able to accommodate their needs very well as they developed their solution concepts. Their work met with high levels of satisfaction among users, and at the same time the team was able to pre-empt the rejection of solutions that might be deemed unsuitable.

Contextual observations

In order to gain a genuine understanding of the needs and habits of Metro customers, the project team visited a wide range of retail outlets to observe shoppers in action. In doing so, they were able to gain a wealth of important insights. They found out, for example, that older shoppers tend to seek opportunities to take a break, as shopping and walking long distances inside the store can be very strenuous. They also noticed that children over a certain age like to get active, looking out for the products that are needed. Another interesting discovery was that some people structure their shopping lists according to the layout of the store. Observing how customers arrange the different products in their shopping carts provided further stimulating insights for the team.

As well as observing shoppers in different retail outlets, the innovation team took a close look at the shopping process as a whole. This begins when a particular grocery has been used up and is no longer available in the fridge at home, for example. A number of process steps then follow, from writing a shopping list and viewing special offers to loading purchases into the car after shopping and putting them away in the right place once the shopper has returned home.

The project team also used several development stages within the project to observe how prospective users of their Shopping Assistant handled different prototypes as they shopped in retail stores. Supported by surveys, findings from this phase of the project gave the team important early-stage feedback on the solutions they had generated so far. They also helped them identify where improvements might be made and gradually eliminate any uncertainties.

Holistic perspective

By taking a holistic approach to the task, the team were able to identify a number of unknowns. Many of these were highly relevant to the multifaceted topic of shopping and consequently had to be taken into consideration as the development process continued. The fact that they could be identified at all was an achievement of the holistic perspective, which enabled team members to generate knowledge in essential fields.

One example concerned the use of existing Shopping Assistants, trolleys and baskets. The project team examined these in detail and assessed the current situation in rival stores and other retail facilities such as DIY shops and textiles dealers. They also analysed retail trends in order to learn more about neuro-marketing or other physiological aspects. Additional factors such as monitor and radio technologies were the focus of the team's technology analyses.

In order to gain further new impulses, the project team looked further afield, turning their attention to other branches of industry. The leisure articles and consumer electronics industries, for example, offered plenty of inspiration. As described earlier, the team also analysed the entire purchasing, payment and logistics process and explored various financing concepts for the new Shopping Assistant. In addition, the holistic perspective was evident in the team's evaluation criteria for customer benefit, technical feasibility, timing and viability. These criteria were applied to decision-making throughout the project.

Social prototyping

As described above, social prototyping is a way of encouraging creativity and communication. Storytelling and visualisation techniques were among the methods most frequently used by the team on this project as a way of helping them generate plenty of ideas as work progressed. This resulted in a comprehensive collection of concepts. Project members also produced simple three-dimensional prototypes from materials such as card, foamboard and LEGO™. Constructing these models and producing 1:1 scale prototypes in wood generated additional suggestions for further alternatives.

The communication aspect of prototyping also played an important role in the project. From the early stages onwards, the team made strong use of visualisation techniques to achieve a consistent understanding within the project team. The team established a foundation for communication by working with sketches, drawings and prototypes from rough paper and LEGO™. They then used the models they had created to obtain early-stage feedback from potential customers and experts such as Metro AG employees. This enabled them to identify and address uncertainties arising from a range of different factors. Working with prototypes in this way often helps pinpoint areas where there is still a knowledge deficit.

Iterative approach

Throughout the project a whole series of iterative steps took place. Some of these, such as the workshop sessions with LEGO™, took just a few hours. Others lasted for several days. In the early stages of the project, these iterations were based on simple visualisations and prototypes made from card and foamboard. The feedback they generated then had to be interpreted and consolidated. This allowed the team to identify where improvements could be made and determine what their next steps would be.

After several evolutionary stages, the project team came closer and closer to finding a solution that combined and integrated the most important aspects they had identified. They then produced a life-sized prototype of their solution made from wood and plastic. This, along with some prototypical virtual services and a film about the entire purchase process, was used to demonstrate their solution. A series of rapid iterations enabled the team to recognise and fill any other remaining unknowns regarding customer acceptance and technical feasibility early on in the project. In this respect, the iterative approach sped up the overall process considerably.

A Revolutionary Concept for the MMSA

Being of various ages, genders and social backgrounds, Metro AG customers are a very diverse group – a fact which is reflected in their wide-ranging requirements of a Shopping Assistant. This represented a challenge for the project team, who responded by producing a modular concept. Their solution allows customers to configure their Shopping Assistant to suit their needs. While doing their shopping, customers select different modules (e.g. a fruits and vegetables module, a cooling module, drinks crates, etc.) from various points around the retail store and use them as required. As they place their chosen items in the trolley, a barcode scanner application (and later RFID (radio frequency identification)) records them ready for automatic payment. At the end of their shopping trip customers can then simply lift the modular containers (for which they have paid a deposit) and the purchases inside them directly into their cars ready to take home.

One feature that was much appreciated by older users is the Shopping Assistant's integrated seating option. This allowed elderly individuals to take a brief break when they needed one but also gave younger children a 'driver's seat' to sit in throughout their shopping trip. Alternatively, the integrated seat could be used to transport bulky items.

Another useful feature is the detachable, adjustable touch screen providing additional information and services for customers. Moreover, allowing customers to connect their own mobile phones to the screen (via Bluetooth for example) and use it as a calculator keeps investment costs for the Shopping Assistant down. One key aspect of the overall concept lies in strengthening customer loyalty by providing an all-round better service.

The solutions developed by this project team were transferred into Wanzl GmbH's innovation process and have now been developed to series standard. The final MMSA was a central feature of the company's trade show exhibition at the EuroShop 2011, where it was presented to the broader public in the retail sector.

The Fought Unknowns

Innovation projects often harbour considerable uncertainty regarding a product's desirability, technical feasibility and economic viability (Brown, 2009). This report on the MMSA project is just one example of how knowledge gaps of this kind can be managed or filled by applying the principles of business design. With suitable methods and tools to accompany the individual principles, project teams can rise successfully to the challenges of their innovation tasks. Clearly, business design can represent an important element in innovation management within organisations.

Corporate and innovation culture is an important factor in determining how knowledge gaps and the associated fears of failure (described in the introduction to this report) are handled. The business design approach, therefore, is closely linked to corporate and innovation culture and can only be implemented successfully if the project team has the space it needs to adopt an experimental approach. The management team commissioning the task must place a degree of trust in the method, as must any project team member who may still lack experience in this approach. Those involved in the project must have an open and curious mind that will shape the way they work and help them realise their successful innovations.

References

Beckman, S.L. and Barry, M. (2007). Innovation as a learning process: Embedding design thinking. *California Management Review*, 50(1), 25–56.

Brown, T. (2009). *Change by Design: How Design Thinking Transforms Organizations and Inspires Innovation*. Harper, New York.

Dreyfuss, H. (1955). *Designing for People*. Simon and Schuster, New York.

Johnson, B. and Maston, D. (1998). Understand what others don't. *Design Management Journal*, 9(4), 17–22.

Kanter, R.M. (1988). 'When a thousand flowers bloom: Structural, collective, and social conditions for innovation in organizations', in Staw, B.M. and Cummings, L.L. (eds). *Research in Organizational Behavior, 10th Edition*. JAI Press, Greenwich.

Papanek, V. (1984). *Design for the Real World, 2nd Edition*. Van Nostrand Reinhold Company, New York.

Rand, P. (1965). *Design and the Play Instinct*. Braziller, New York.

Rand, P. (2000). *A Designer's Art*. Yale University Press, New Haven, CT.

Schrage, M. (1993). The culture(s) of prototyping. *Design Management Journal*, 4(1), 55–65.

The Boston Consulting Group, Inc. (2010). *Innovation 2010: A Return to Prominence – and the Emergence of a New World Order*. Boston, MA.

Chapter 19

Center of Excellence: One Way to Implement Discontinuous Innovation

Peter Meier and Stefan Uhrlandt
Johnson & Johnson Medical, Germany

Introduction

Ethicon, Inc., a Johnson & Johnson company, sells absorbable and non-absorbable synthetic textiles, which are indicated for soft tissue repair (e.g. surgical hernia meshes) and used by abdominal, gynecologic, urologic, plastic and other surgeons to repair defects.

Medical device companies are facing similar challenges of shorter innovation cycles and fiercer global competition other industries do in today's rapidly changing world. Additionally, circumventing the anti-innovation bias of politicians and insurers in a publically regulated healthcare environment suffering from severe financial constraints (Torbica and Cappellaro, 2010) requires new approaches to innovation.

Given the high cost involved in developing and manufacturing high-tech medical devices in developed countries, technology leadership through innovation is one of the very few possibilities to maintain a competitive advantage.

The need to adapt to the changing economic environment, a focus on core competencies and capabilities and a shift to open innovation have led to the establishment of the Ethicon Mesh Technology Center (EMTC) outside of Hamburg, Germany.

Figure 1 shows the status of part of Ethicon Research & Development (R&D) before the EMTC was established. Two R&D groups on both sides of the Atlantic were developing surgical meshes.

Communication with customers, suppliers and internal departments took place in parallel via two different organizations. In addition, supporting functions such as medical and regulatory affairs were needed in both locations and different production sites were used. To leverage knowledge, improve the flow of communication and have all necessary functions in one location, Ethicon established the Mesh Technology Center with the vision 'To be recognized as a worldwide center of excellence for tissue reinforcement by our customers' (see Fig. 2). With R&D and New Product Introduction (NPI) being the main partners, the EMTC develops textile implants for the Ethicon franchises Mentor, Women's Health & Urology and Ethicon Products. Other key members of the EMTC team are representatives from Quality Assurance and Engineering, as well as Regulatory and Medical Affairs. In the future, further commercial functions such as marketing and sales may be integrated into the center's activities.

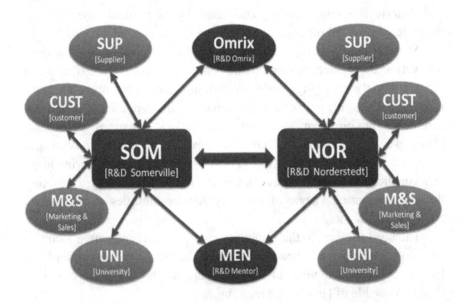

Fig. 1. Two R&D centers developing mesh implants (Ethicon until 2008).

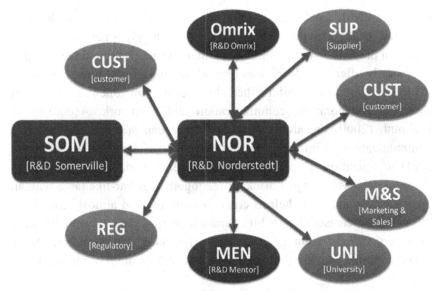

Fig. 2. R&D hub/integrated model of the EMTC.

According to the theory of international R&D organizations as described by Gassmann and von Zedtwitz, the EMTC is partly a R&D hub model and integrated R&D network with the core competence of developing textile implants. These integrated R&D networks can better exploit scale effects, reduce the amount of duplicate R&D and intensify cross-border technology transfer (Gassmann and von Zedtwitz, 1999).

The EMTC opened in May 2008 with an investment of €1.2 million and created 65 new jobs. Having all functions on board and being co-located with the European Surgical Institute (ESI), one of the biggest training centers for surgeons, provides the center with a substantial competitive advantage. In particular, the proximity of R&D and operations leads to a better handover of projects and consistent quality, which is essential in the production of surgical implants. Also, it is vital for successful discontinuous innovations to have direct contact and communication with all involved team members, which the EMTC offers. For example, an innovative umbilical hernia device project that dragged on for years without major progress was quickly developed and launched after it was transferred to the EMTC. Within a short time frame the center established a reputation for executing innovative hernia projects quickly and successfully. Physiomesh™, for example, was launched in 2010 by the EMTC team and is already a new standard for adhesion prevention hernia therapy in many hospitals around the world.

Shortly after the EMTC was opened the main parts of the remaining R&D building were refurbished to provide an open environment fostering collaboration, communication and teamwork. According to Freimuth (2000) the architecture of offices can substantially improve communication, team building and diffusion of knowledge within an R&D organization. Forum-like places were created, where people can meet for discussion or just drink coffee together. A bar-like table with an open kitchen and sofas helped create a more relaxed atmosphere, while glass doors increased the visibility and access to offices. This, in addition to a very diverse team of engineers, physicians, scientists and textile experts, helped increase the innovation and collaboration of the team.

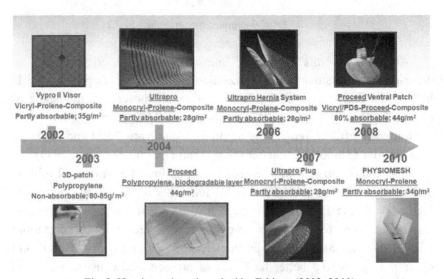

Fig. 3. Hernia products launched by Ethicon (2002–2010).

With this vast expertise and experience in mesh and textile technology and an open innovation approach (Chesbrough, 2003; Huston and Sakkab, 2006) of partnering with universities, Fraunhofer Institutes, customers and suppliers, Ethicon was able to launch a series of successful products, for instance those launched in the hernia market as detailed in Fig. 3. Products such as the first lightweight and large-pore mesh or partially absorbable synthetic meshes for better integration into the human tissue and less foreign body sensation were seen as transformational products by hernia surgeons helping patients to return to their pre-surgery lives and activities faster and with fewer complications. From our point of view a center-of-excellence approach as described, with a holistic view of innovation and a clear focus on its customers, is one of the best ways to make discontinuous product innovation a reality.

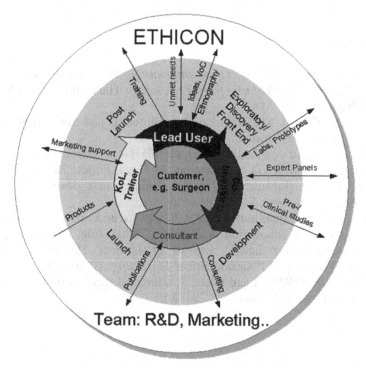

Fig. 4. Customer-centric life cycle approach.

A focus on customers and their unmet needs in all processes of the product life cycle (see Fig. 4), and an open-minded team as an integral part of global R&D, helped to increase the number of launched products to almost one every year. The lead user approach, as described by von Hippel (1986), is one of many innovation methods that helped to reach this goal. In our experience lead users can play a vital role in finding and diffusing surgical innovations.

The necessary continuous evolution of the EMTC was and will be achieved by improvements in teaming, people development and process optimization. The long-term goal of the EMTC is to become a future center of innovation for Ethicon in Europe, with the objective of 'restoration of bodies and lives'. We believe that the multitude of assets and processes in our center of excellence described here provides the means for more discontinuous innovations in the future.

References

Chesbrough, H.W. (2003). *Open Innovation: The New Imperative for Creating and Profiting from Technology*. Harvard Business School Press, Boston, MA.

Freimuth, J. (2000). Kommunikative Architektur und die Diffusion von Wissen. *Wissensmanagement*, 4, 41–45.

Gassmann, O. and von Zedtwitz, M. (1999). New concepts and trends in international R&D organization. *Research Policy*, 28, 231–250.

Huston, L. and Sakkab, N. (2006). Connect and develop. *Harvard Business Review*, 84, 58–66.

Torbica, A. and Cappellaro, G. (2010). Uptake and diffusion of medical technology innovation in Europe: What role for funding and procurement policies? *Journal of Medical Marketing: Device, Diagnostic and Pharmaceutical Marketing*, 10, 61–69.

von Hippel, E. (1986). Lead users: A source of novel product concepts. *Management Science*, 32, 791–805.

Chapter 20

Munich Airport: The Success Story of InfoGate

Monica Streck and Marcus Roßbach
Munich Airport, Germany

Introduction

In 2011, Munich Airport launched InfoGate, a new in-terminal information service designed for passengers and airport visitors. The service utilises cutting-edge technology such as video streams and radio-frequency identification (RFID) to provide users with personalised guidance and rapid orientation inside the airport's facilities. Originally developed for Munich Airport by in-house engineers, this highly innovative system is now being marketed around the world.

The Road to Innovation

Innovation management at Munich Airport follows the three classic steps: search for ideas, strategic idea selection and realisation. Idea selection draws on two main sources of input: first, an internal pool of ideas generated during day-to-day business, and second, open innovation workshops in which people from different departments discuss new and innovative ideas. The idea for InfoGate, the brainchild of Marc Lindike, head of IT Consulting at Munich Airport, was born in 2007 in one such workshop. At the time, the idea had two key propositions. The first was to create a 'time budget navigator' that would enable passengers to enjoy their stopovers even more at the airport. Because infrequent travellers tend to visit information desks more often than frequent flyers, the aim of the 'time budget navigator' was to help make a passenger's stay at the airport as convenient and agreeable as possible. This was to be accomplished by telling them how much time they have before their flight leaves and how long the distances are that they need to cover at the airport. This information would open up new possibilities for efficient and relaxed use of the passengers' dwell time. The second proposition was to introduce an innovative information service based on new means of communicating with passengers. These two propositions were combined and presented to a steering committee, which approved them in 2007. The idea had become a project (see Fig. 1).

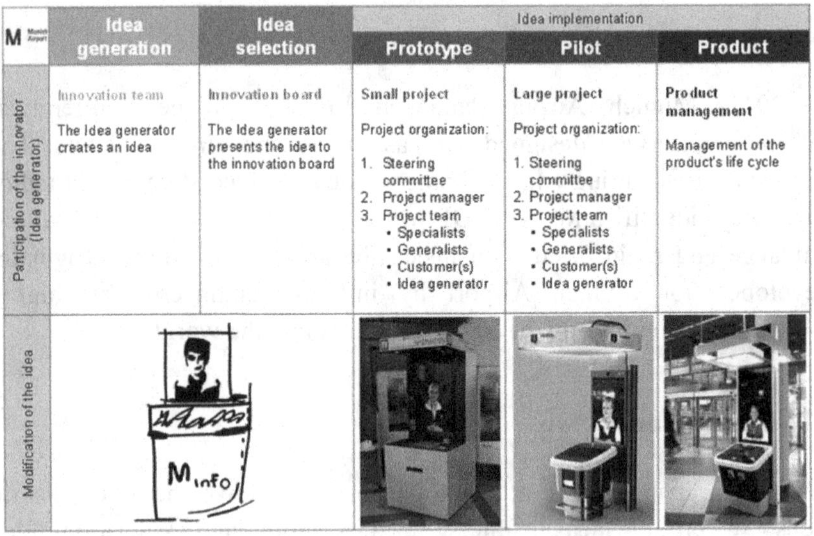

Fig. 1. The story of innovation.

The Road to Market

Introducing an idea to the market takes time. Many things need to be considered before an idea can mature into a product (or, in this instance, a service innovation). Because an idea is merely an initial indication of what a product might become, a decision had to be made on how to proceed with the development of the 'time budget navigator'. Setting up a project to prototype the idea meant allocating funding and the requisite budget was estimated at six figures (in euros). In March 2008, the prototyping project was launched under the leadership of Manfred Zötl, and the project name was changed from 'time budget navigator' to Human Interactive Personal Service, or HIPS for short. The project team chose a temporarily vacant hall as its test location, A/B West at Terminal 1, which had previously served as a passenger transfer area before Terminal 2 was built. The former terminal building was turned into an innovation centre. Through to September 2008 a group of five employees focused their efforts on building a test counter and on developing the IT infrastructure needed to operate it. They also filled the hall with a maze of provisional walls covered with life-sized photos of shop fronts to simulate the challenges faced by travellers of finding their way around during a typical stay at the airport. Test passengers were able to wander through the maze and use three counters to help find their way. A customer evaluation project was also started simultaneously to gather as much information as possible on the usability or lack thereof. In the summer of 2008, people from the local region were allowed to test the first counters. When it became evident that the prototyping project had gone well, the steering committee decided to take the next step towards market introduction. This meant incorporating missing information on the time needed by passengers to cover the walking distances to gates and on how they could find specific facilities (important for proof of the concept).

The successor project, known as Project i, was the most comprehensive of all. Running from 2009 to 2010, its objective was to finalise the pilot product and make it market-ready. This involved conducting a comprehensive analysis of customer needs as well as possible synergies with internal products and existing services. Employees were also trained in preparation for their new roles. The whole business case had to undergo several efficiency audits before the idea could be taken to market. In March 2011 the real road test began with the project's launch under the InfoGate brand.

The Road to Success

There were several reasons why the project promised to be successful. First, the 'idea generator' – the person who initially came up with the idea – was present during the entire development process and was therefore able to nurture his idea and advance its development at every stage along the way. Second, the whole development project was managed professionally. As a result, the idea was developed in an independent environment, an innovation laboratory, separated from daily business. Once all the technical requirements had been fulfilled and the system was operating, it was possible to build a real business case. Third, the project's success was due to the new service's ability to integrate with existing services at Munich Airport. Project i was not simply an add-on product but an integrated service platform within the wider portfolio. As a stand-alone product, it would not have been able to achieve the critical market fit as easily. And finally, communication was an important success factor.

This development process consisted not just of building prototypes for the customer validation tests, but also of continuous communication on the development of the product. Regular communication on the needs and requirements of external stakeholders helped to turn this project into a successful product innovation.

InfoGate proved a success within the first few days of operation. Not only did customer satisfaction rise thanks to the increased number of information points and better quality of information, but a team of just three employees was needed to respond to users' questions via video streams – the lowest number of personnel ever assigned to information point staffing in the company's history. Together, the boost in customer satisfaction and the cost-saving capacity of InfoGate confirmed the product's high commercialisation potential for a target group consisting of other airports and organisations in the so-called travel chain.

Appendix

The following is comprised of the questionnaires we used to conduct our interviews about discontinuous innovation and some aggregated results in diagrammatic form.

Questionnaire

	Respondent ID	
	Company	
	Name of respondent	
	Position Title	
	Location	
A. Learning about markets for Discontinuous Innovation	**A.1. Multiple market experiments**	We currently practice this in OUR COMPANY
	When we have a very new and different technology, we search for multiple applications and conduct several market experiments to discover promising markets.	This practice is important for DI in OUR COMPANY
	A.2. Market diagnostic tools	We currently practice this in OUR COMPANY
	To learn about unfamiliar markets, we rely on a set of unconventional market research tools to identify latent, yet unarticulated needs among different customer groups.	This practice is important for DI in OUR COMPANY
	A.3. Applying existing technologies in new markets	We currently practice this in OUR COMPANY
	We have a dedicated group of people (e.g. from marketing, sales, R&D) that explores new ways to apply our existing technology to new industries and new customers.	This practice is important for DI in OUR COMPANY
	A.4. Co-developing products with lead users	We currently practice this in OUR COMPANY
	We actively try to find those lead users who are actively innovating to solve problems present at the leading edge of a trend and seek to "co-evolve" new products and services together with them.	This practice is important for DI in OUR COMPANY
	A.5. Look beyond the customer to the consumer	We currently practice this in OUR COMPANY
	We make an effort to connect to our customers' consumers (end users) and obtain regular feedback on their demands, as we recognise that they drive what our customers need.	This practice is important for DI in OUR COMPANY
	A.6. Learning from outside industry boundaries	We currently practice this in OUR COMPANY
	We systematically seek out and learn from firms - within and in particular outside our industry - that are known to have well-functioning innovation practices in order to improve our own innovation system.	This practice is important for DI in OUR COMPANY
	A. Comment	
	A.P. How well do you think Our company performs in "learning about new markets for discontinuous innovations"?	
	A.I. How critical is it to develop further competencies in "learning about new markets for discontinuous innovation" for Our company in general?	

Fig. 1. Questionnaire.

423

B. Managing discontinuous idea generation	B.1. Idea hunters	We currently practice this in OUR COMPANY
	We have technical people with business development skills tasked with finding new sources of potential discontinuous ideas within our firm.	This practice is important for DI in OUR COMPANY
	B.2. Using themed projects to stimulate discontinuous idea generation of high strategic relevance	We currently practice this in OUR COMPANY
	In our organization, we try to stimulate discontinuous innovation by periodically commissioning teams to generate ideas around major platforms or themes that are strategically relevant to us.	This practice is important for DI in OUR COMPANY
	B.3. A central system to record and respond to ideas	We currently practice this in OUR COMPANY
	In our organisation, we have one company-wide centralised idea management system in place to which all employees can submit ideas for evaluation and receive quick feedback.	This practice is important for DI in OUR COMPANY
	B.4. Idea management team	We currently practice this in OUR COMPANY
	We have a team of people with responsibility for our idea management system.	This practice is important for DI in OUR COMPANY
	B.5. All ideas are welcome	We currently practice this in OUR COMPANY
	We encourage people to come forward with ideas, even if they have only a vague idea of the potential market applications for the idea.	This practice is important for DI in OUR COMPANY
	B. Comment	
	B.P. How well do you think Our company performs in "Managing discontinuous idea generation"?	
	B.I. How critical is it to develop further competencies in "Managing discontinuous idea generation" for Our company in general?	
C. The existence of an entrepreneurial environment	C.1. Heroes	We currently practice this in OUR COMPANY
	Successful innovators of breakthrough ideas are well-known and respected within the organization serving as inspiration for others.	This practice is important for DI in OUR COMPANY
	C.2. Entrepreneurial environment	We currently practice this in OUR COMPANY
	There is an atmosphere in our organisation which encourages everyone to take part in innovation.	This practice is important for DI in OUR COMPANY
	C.3 Risk-taking environment	We currently practice this in OUR COMPANY
	We have an environment where risk-taking is encouraged, e.g. to initiate discontinuous innovation projects and become entrepreneurs.	This practice is important for DI in OUR COMPANY
	C.4. Accepting failure in discontinuous innovation projects	We currently practice this in OUR COMPANY
	In our organisation failure is accepted in regard to discontinuous innovation projects and considered a natural part of the learning process.	This practice is important for DI in OUR COMPANY
	C.5. Career advancement through discontinuous innovation	We currently practice this in OUR COMPANY
	In our firm, participation in discontinuous innovation activities is seen as a broadening, career enhancing experience.	This practice is important for DI in OUR COMPANY
	C. Comment	
	C.P. How well do you think Our company performs in "The existence of an entrepreneurial environment"?	
	C.I. How critical is it to develop further competencies in "The existence of an entrepreneurial environment" for Our company in general?	

Fig. 1. Questionnaire (cont.).

D. Comment		
D.P. How well do you think Our company performs in "Culture support system for discontinuous innovation"?		
D.I. How critical is it to develop further competencies in "Culture support system for discontinuous innovation" for Our company in general?		
E.1 Seminars on discontinuous innovation		We currently practice this in OUR COMPANY
To assist in developing our corporate wide capabilities in discontinuous innovation, our employees and managers regularly get the opportunity to participate in seminars and courses on discontinuous innovation.		This practice is important for DI in OUR COMPANY
E.2 Coaching		We currently practice this in OUR COMPANY
In our organization, senior or top level managers coach discontinuous innovation teams.		This practice is important for DI in OUR COMPANY
E.3 Corporate innovation consultants		We currently practice this in OUR COMPANY
In our organization, we have individuals who have received special training in discontinuous innovation with the purpose of breeding "discontinuous innovation black-belts" who act as consultants on discontinuous innovation projects.		This practice is important for DI in OUR COMPANY
E.4 A dedicated support unit		We currently practice this in OUR COMPANY
Within the organization, we have an identified group of people charged with the responsibility of providing development support to discontinuous innovation company-wide.		This practice is important for DI in OUR COMPANY

E. Helping employees solve their problems with discontinuous innovation

Fig. 1. Questionnaire (cont.).

E. Comment		
E.P. How well do you think Our company performs in "Helping employees solve their problems with discontinuous innovation"?		
E.I. How critical is it to develop further competencies in "Helping employees solve their problems with discontinuous innovation" for Our company in general?		

F. Project management for discontinuous innovation		
	F.1 Developing the business model	We currently practice this in OUR COMPANY
	As we are developing discontinuous innovation opportunities, we are constantly asking ourselves what the eventual business model will be.	This practice is important for DI in OUR COMPANY
	F.2 Multidisciplinary and international diversity in discontinuous innovation teams	We currently practice this in OUR COMPANY
	When selecting our teams for discontinuous innovation projects, we aim to include members that are multidisciplinary (different functions) and when possible of different nationalities to achieve the greatest diversity.	This practice is important for DI in OUR COMPANY
	F.3 The skills of a discontinuous project manager	We currently practice this in OUR COMPANY
	We acknowledge that a project manager's required expertise for discontinuous innovation must be more about anticipating and monitoring uncertainties than about planning, controlling and delegating.	This practice is important for DI in OUR COMPANY
	F.4 Emergent strategy formulation as discontinuous innovation projects develop	We currently practice this in OUR COMPANY
	When we enter a new market with many uncertainties we allow our strategy to change, as we learn more about the market.	This practice is important for DI in OUR COMPANY
	F.5 Securing organizational support	We currently practice this in OUR COMPANY
	Our project managers are skilled at getting organizational buy-in for their projects.	This practice is important for DI in OUR COMPANY
	F.6 Fast track of projects	We currently practice this in OUR COMPANY
	In our organization a clear business case and project plan is not always required from the outset to get approval to pursue a potentially discontinuous opportunity further.	This practice is important for DI in OUR COMPANY

F. Comment		
F.P. How well do you think Our company performs in "Project management for discontinuous innovation"?		
F.I. How critical is it to develop further competencies in "Project management for discontinuous innovation" for Our company in general?		

Fig. 1. Questionnaire (cont.).

G. Network management system for discontinuous innovation	**G.1. Network brokers**	We currently practice this in OUR COMPANY
	In our organization, we have "network ambassadors" who can help discontinuous innovation teams connect with other people company-wide when new knowledge or insight is needed	This practice is important for DI in OUR COMPANY
	G.2. A company wide network system that gives access to locating experts on discontinuous innovation	We currently practice this in OUR COMPANY
	In our organization, teams engaged in discontinuous innovation projects can locate experts on various disciplines in discontinuous innovation when needed through accessing a database on our intranet.	This practice is important for DI in OUR COMPANY
	G.3. Expanding the resource network through knowledge sharing	We currently practice this in OUR COMPANY
	In our organization, we encourage discontinuous innovation teams to expand their resource network by tapping into the knowledge of any employee in our firm.	This practice is important for DI in OUR COMPANY
H. A flexible strategy for discontinuous innovation	**H.1 The significance placed on discontinuous innovation for the future of the organisation**	We currently practice this in OUR COMPANY
	Discontinuous innovation is clearly communicated throughout our organization as necessary for the long-term survival of our organization.	This practice is important for DI in OUR COMPANY
	H.2. Accepting that learning in discontinuous innovation projects takes time.	We currently practice this in OUR COMPANY
	Our senior managers understand that it takes times for discontinuous innovation projects to acquire the necessary learning experience before they can move forward.	This practice is important for DI in OUR COMPANY
	H.3. A continuous strategic commitment to the development of new business areas	We currently practice this in OUR COMPANY
	We remain committed to developing new business areas as a source of future growth - even in times when our main business is prospering.	This practice is important for DI in OUR COMPANY
	H.4. Strategic planning	We currently practice this in OUR COMPANY
	In our strategy process we engage in creative thinking about the future and we consider ways to take our business into new markets or new ways of competing.	This practice is important for DI in OUR COMPANY
	H.5. Top management readiness for the unexpected	We currently practice this in OUR COMPANY
	Our top managers are ready to accept promising ideas that challenge the firm to move beyond its current strategic focus even when these ideas are not in line with the current business strategy.	This practice is important for DI in OUR COMPANY
	H.6. Our future role in our industry value chain	We currently practice this in OUR COMPANY
	We remain open to re-consider our future position in our industry value chain and make shifts if we have to.	This practice is important for DI in OUR COMPANY
H. Comment		

Fig. 1. Questionnaire (cont.).

	I. Comment	
	I.P. How well do you think Our company performs in "Openness to external sources for discontinuous innovation"?	
	I.I. How critical is it to develop further competencies in "Openness to external sources for discontinuous innovation" for Our company in general?	
J. Transitioning discontinuous innovation projects to operations	**J1. Assessing transition readiness**	We currently practice this in OUR COMPANY
	When a discontinuous project is ready to stand on its own feet, we don't automatically assume that the project will be taken over by a operating business unit - but we carefully assess where it can get the best conditions for growth.	This practice is important for DI in OUR COMPANY
	J2. Forming a transition team	We currently practice this in OUR COMPANY
	When a discontinuous project is transferred to a receiving operating business unit, we form a 'transition team' consisting of personnel from the project team as well as people from the receiving operating unit to help a discontinuous innovation project cross the gap from development to operating status.	This practice is important for DI in OUR COMPANY
	J3. Managing leverage between new discontinuous venture and existing firm	We currently practice this in OUR COMPANY
	Our top managers oversee that new ventures develop independently but leverage optimally from the resources of the existing business.	This practice is important for DI in OUR COMPANY
	J4. Developing the culture of a start-up	We currently practice this in OUR COMPANY
	When a new internal venture is given its own home, it is provided with autonomy to allow it to develop a culture of a start-up.	This practice is important for DI in OUR COMPANY

Fig. 1. Questionnaire (cont.).

J. Comment		
	J.P. How well do you think Our company performs in "Transitioning discontinuous innovation projects to operations"?	
	J.I. How critical is it to develop further competencies in "Transitioning discontinuous innovation projects to operations" for Our company in general?	
K. Using alternative metrics for discontinuous innovation	**K.1 Flexible stage gate**	We currently practice this in OUR COMPANY
	When identifying a promising discontinuous innovation project, we develop it through a different and more flexible process than the traditional stage gate system.	This practice is important for DI in OUR COMPANY
	K.2 Measuring the success of discontinuous innovation by using a portfolio approach	We currently practice this in OUR COMPANY
	When we evaluate the success of discontinuous innovation in our organisation, we look at our ability to manage a portfolio of discontinuous innovation projects at various stages of development rather than on the success or failure of one single discontinuous project.	This practice is important for DI in OUR COMPANY
	K.3 Project evaluation by learning potential	We currently practice this in OUR COMPANY
	Instead of a preoccupation with profitability potential, we assess the promise of discontinuous projects by their potential to open up new territory and thereby provide opportunities for learning about technologies and markets.	This practice is important for DI in OUR COMPANY
	K.4 Staged funding	We currently practice this in OUR COMPANY
	Our funding process for projects is staged, based on their demonstrated progress.	This practice is important for DI in OUR COMPANY
	K.5 Longer time horizon for discontinuous innovation	We currently practice this in OUR COMPANY
	Discontinuous innovation projects are evaluated with a longer time horizon than other projects to allow time for them to mature and prove themselves.	This practice is important for DI in OUR COMPANY
K. Comment		
	K.P. How well do you think Our company performs in "Using alternative metrics for discontinuous innovation"?	
	K.I. How critical is it to develop further competencies in "Using alternative metrics for discontinuous innovation" for Our company in general?	
L. A venture capital system for discontinuous innovation	**L.1 Direct external investment in small start-ups**	We currently practice this in OUR COMPANY
	We have in our organisation an external venture capital program where we invest directly in promising start-up firms that operate at the edge of our own technologies.	This practice is important for DI in OUR COMPANY
	L.2 Investment in external venture capital funds	We currently practice this in OUR COMPANY
	We invest capital in external venture funds that specialize in managing a portfolio of firms that are related to our technological core competencies.	This practice is important for DI in OUR COMPANY
	L.3 Taking options in investments	We currently practice this in OUR COMPANY
	The team that manages the portfolio of internal and external investments exhibits an "options" mentality as it pertains to individual project selection.	This practice is important for DI in OUR COMPANY

Fig. 1. Questionnaire (cont.).

L. Comment		
L.P. How well do you think Our company performs in "A venture capital system for discontinuous innovation"?		
L.I. How critical is it to develop further competencies in "A venture capital system for discontinuous innovation" for Our company in general?		
M. Acquiring funding for discontinuous innovation	**M.1 A central place to seek funding for discontinuous innovation**	We currently practice this in OUR COMPANY
	We have a part of the organization to which an employee with a breakthrough idea can seek funding to take the project one step further.	This practice is important for DI in OUR COMPANY
	M.2 Using external sources to fund our projects through partnerships	We currently practice this in OUR COMPANY
	We are increasingly using external sources to fund our R&D projects within innovation through partnerships and alliances with other firms..	This practice is important for DI in OUR COMPANY
	M.3 Dedicated R&D budget for discontinuous innovation	We currently practice this in OUR COMPANY
	We have a corporate level fund in place dedicated to finance discontinuous innovation projects.	This practice is important for DI in OUR COMPANY
	M.4 Clear processes for accessing resources	We currently practice this in OUR COMPANY
	The process for accessing and leveraging corporate resources (funding, personnel, capital equipment, and other organizational resources) for discontinuous innovation	This practice is important for DI in OUR COMPANY
	M.5 Managerial budgets for small scale experiments	We currently practice this in OUR COMPANY
	In our organization, all managers have been allocated a small financial budget, which they can use for small scale experiments on discontinuous innovation projects.	This practice is important for DI in OUR COMPANY

Fig. 1. Questionnaire (cont.).

	M. Comment
	M.P. How well do you think Our company performs in "Acquiring funding for discontinuous innovation"?
	M.I. How critical is it to develop further competencies in "Acquiring funding for discontinuous innovation" for Our company in general?
Open-ended questions	1. What do you feel are the <u>3 biggest drivers</u> that contribute positively to discontinuous innovation in Our company? (please do illustrate with examples from your daily work/company in general)
	2. What do you feel are the <u>3 biggest hindrances</u> for discontinuous innovation in Our company? (please do illustrate with examples from your daily work/company in general)
	3. How do you see Our company can <u>overcome</u> these hindrances? (Any ideas are appreciated)
	4. Can you think of initiatives of other companies which you regard as best practitioners of discontinuous innovation that could be of interest for Our company? If so please list the name of the companies and briefly explain which initiatives they have implemented, and why you think these initiatives could be of benefit for Our company:

0 – Don't know
1 – I strongly disagree with this statement
2 – I disagree with this statement
3 – I neither agree nor disagree with this statement
4 – I agree with this statemen
5 – I strongly agree with this statement
6 -- missing value

Fig. 1. Questionnaire (cont.).

Dont't know	1 – I strongly disagree with this statement	2 – I disagree with this statement	3 – I neither agree nor disagree with this	4 – I agree with this statement	5 – I strongly agree with this statement

Fig. 2. Likert scale.

Discontinuous Innovation

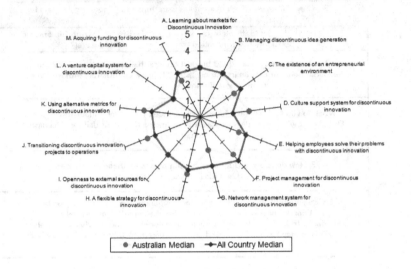

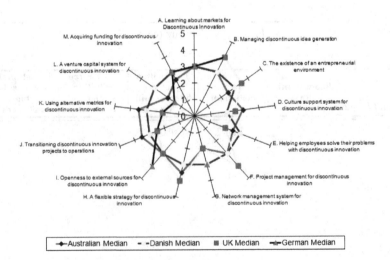

Fig. 3. Discontinuous innovation performance current practice.

Discontinuous Innovation Performance Importance

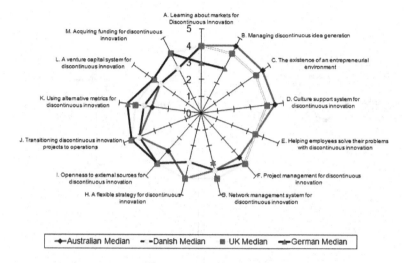

Discontinuous Innovation Performance Importance

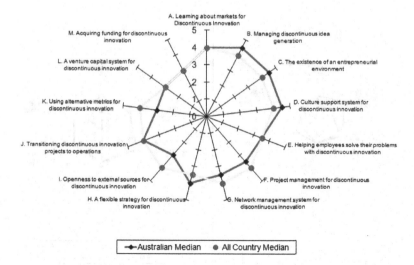

Fig. 4. Discontinuous innovation performance importance.

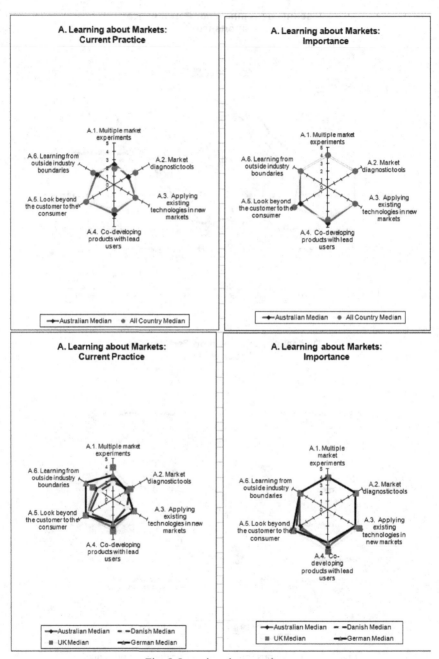

Fig. 5. Learning about markets.

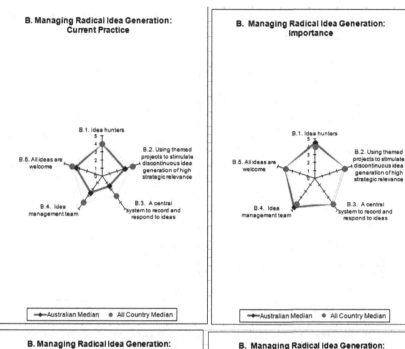

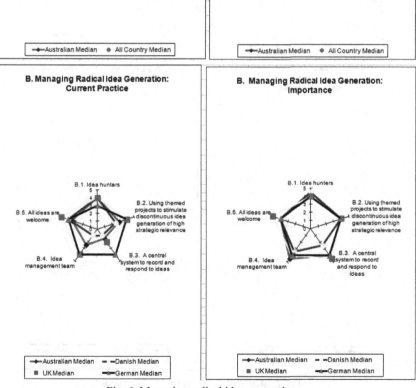

Fig. 6. Managing radical idea generation.

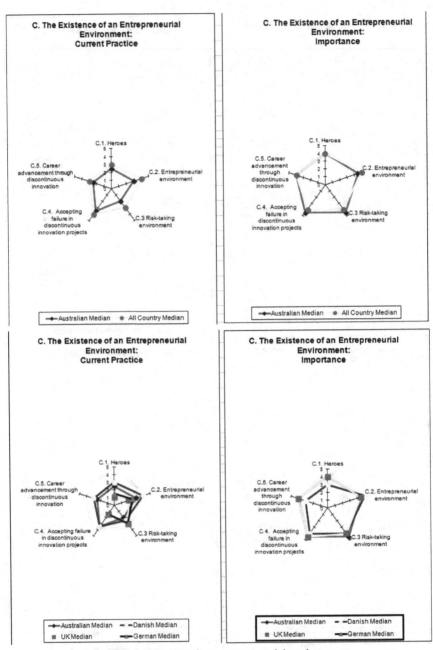

Fig. 7. The existence of an entrepreneurial environment.

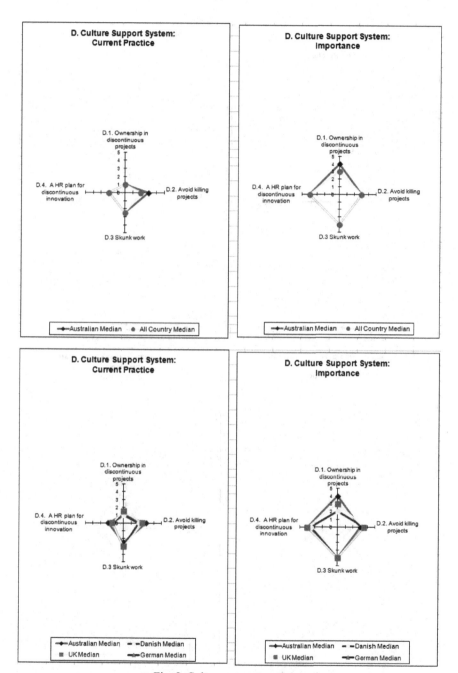

Fig. 8. Culture support system.

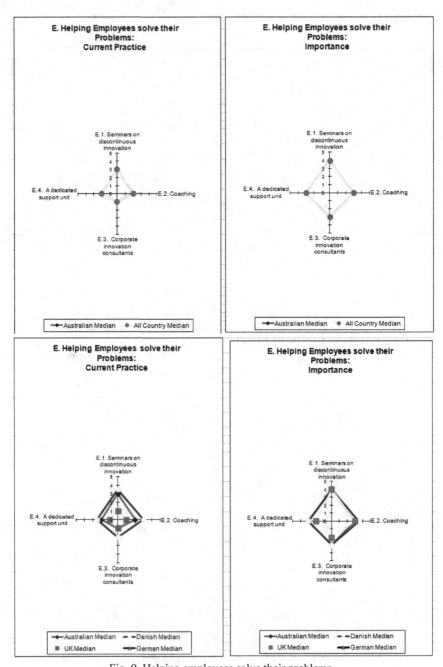

Fig. 9. Helping employees solve their problems.

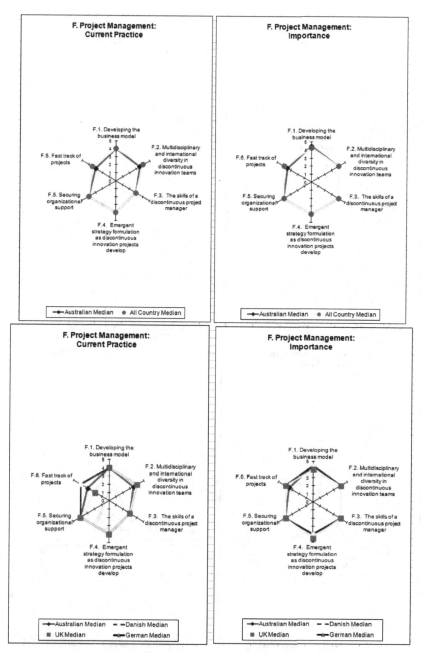

Fig. 10. Project management.

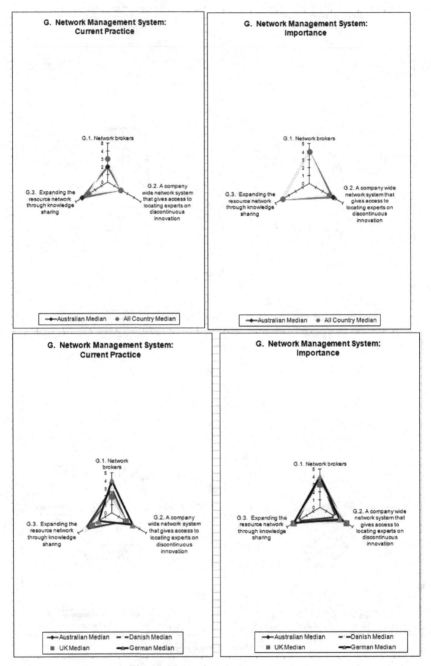

Fig. 11. Network management system.

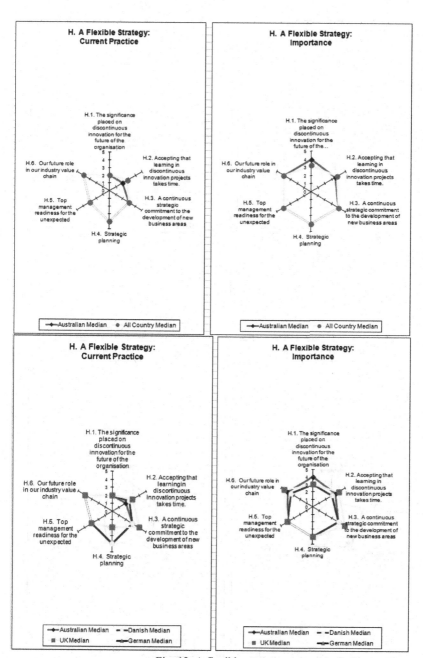

Fig. 12. A flexible strategy.

442 *Discontinuous Innovation*

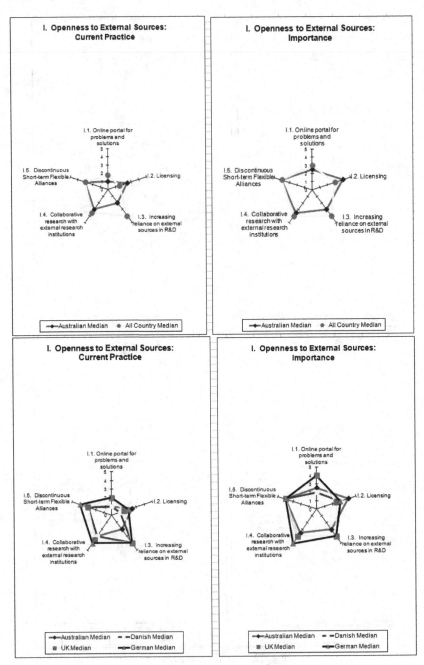

Fig. 13. Openness to external sources.

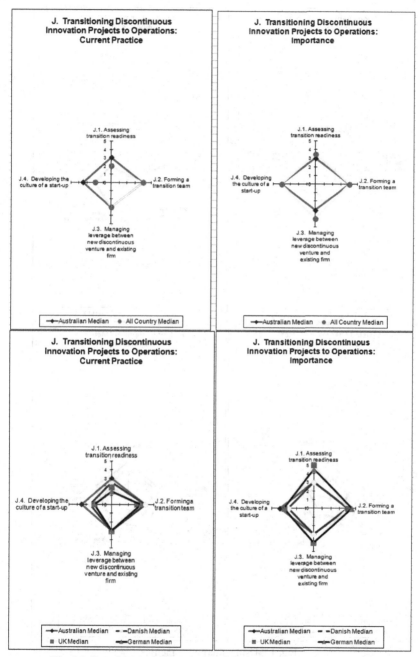

Fig. 14. Transitioning discontinuous innovation projects to operations.

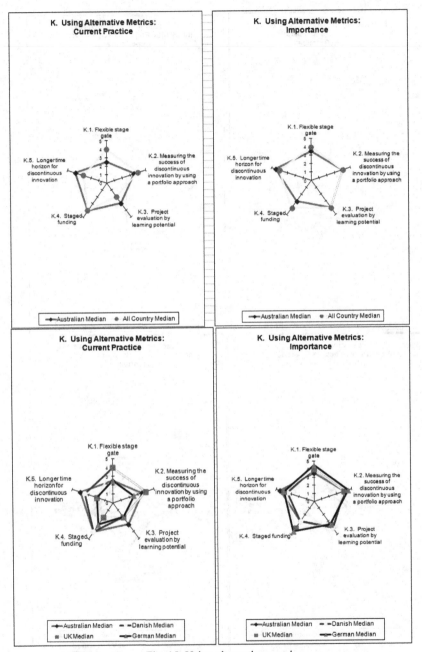

Fig. 15. Using alternative metrics.

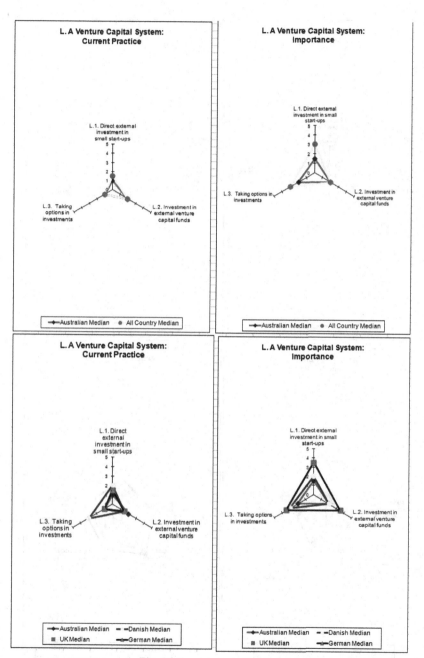

Fig. 16. A venture capital system.

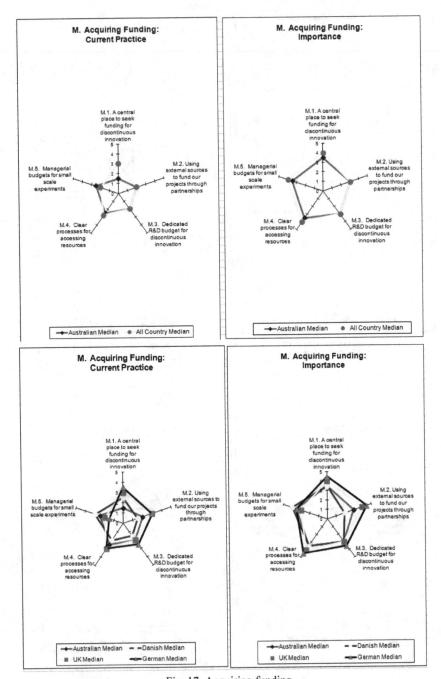

Fig. 17. Acquiring funding.